D1453070

The Peace and Violence of Judaism

The Peace and
Violence of Judaism

From the Bible to Modern Zionism

ROBERT EISEN

OXFORD
UNIVERSITY PRESS

2011

Library of Congress Cataloging-in-Publication Data
Eisen, Robert, 1960–
The peace and violence of Judaism : from the Bible to modern Zionism / Robert Eisen.
    p.   cm.
ISBN 978-0-19-975147-1
1. Peace—Religious aspects—Judaism. 2. Violence—Religious aspects—Judaism. 3. Bible. O.T.—
Criticism, interpretation, etc. 4. Rabbinical literature—History and criticism. 5. Jewish philosophy.
6. Philosophy, Medieval. 7. Cabala. 8. Zionism. I. Title.
BM538.P3E37   2011
296.3′827—dc22   2010043099

To my children: Adeena, Sarit, and Yoni
May the world you bequeath to your children be
more peaceful than the one you have inherited.

Preface

On the morning of September 11, 2001, I emerged from the subway in Foggy Bottom in Washington, D.C., as I did most mornings, to begin my workday at George Washington University. As I walked toward my office, I immediately noticed something odd. On a brilliantly sunny day, there was a dark cloud on the southern horizon. At first, I thought it was a rain cloud coming to spoil the beautiful weather, but the blue skies everywhere else belied that possibility. For a moment I thought that perhaps something terrible had happened, but I quickly rejected that speculation because I am sometimes prone to an overly active imagination. Yet, only minutes later I learned that something terrible had indeed happened. The cloud I was looking at was a massive plume of smoke from the fire that engulfed a portion of the Pentagon after it had been hit by one of the planes that terrorists had hijacked earlier that day.

Many lives were changed on 9/11, and mine was too. It was months before I fully absorbed the impact of what had happened, but even before the smoke had cleared from the Pentagon and the Twin Towers, I began to rethink what my role should be as an academic vis-à-vis the global community. This issue had not much concerned me up to that point in my life. I had been at GW for over a decade and was very much enjoying my career as an academic. I was a tenured professor, and I was in the process of finishing a second book in my area of specialty, medieval Jewish philosophy. I had wonderful students. I had a beautiful family and a house in the suburbs of one of America's most vibrant cities. Involvement in global issues was not really an interest of mine, and, in fact, there wasn't much room for it in my life anyway, given how busy I was. I also had a cynical streak. I avidly kept up with the news and knew full well that the world was a troubled place, but I was skeptical that anything I was going to say or do would help. So why not focus on the things that could be fixed? I was a good academic and a popular teacher. I was having an impact on young lives. Surely that was enough.

What happened on 9/11 convinced me that it wasn't, and that I could no longer remain aloof from broad global concerns. And, in fact, I was in a better position to do something about those concerns than most. After all, I was an expert in religion, perhaps the key factor not just in the 9/11 tragedy, but in the most divisive and dangerous conflicts in the world today. Moreover, while I was a specialist in Judaism, I was also an avid student of Islam. I knew some Arabic because many texts in medieval Jewish philosophy had been written in that language. I also taught a significant number of Muslim students. I therefore had the skills to grapple with two of the most troubled relationships in our world: the relationship between the Islamic world and the West and the relationship between Muslims and Jews.

My desire to become more active might not have gone very far had it not been for the friendship I had with Marc Gopin, a pioneer in the field of religion and conflict resolution both as an academic and an activist. Marc and I had been close friends for two decades. For years, Marc had gently urged me to come out of the ivory tower to work on global issues involving religious conflict, but I had steadfastly declined. Suddenly, what Marc had been saying for so many years began to make sense, and I therefore asked him to help me become involved in the work he was doing. Marc responded by opening any number of doors for me. Being in Washington certainly helped as well, given all of its political activity. Over the next several years, I became involved in a center Marc had established at his university: the Center for World Religions, Diplomacy, and Conflict Resolution. I participated in events at the United States Institute of Peace, a government agency that is one of the leading institutions in the world for promoting peace across the globe. I became active in the Common Word initiative, a worldwide movement promoting better relations between Muslims and Christians. I gave public lectures about religious conflict and the prospect for resolving those conflicts.

My academic interests were also affected by my involvement with interfaith dialogue and peace work. I increasingly focused my research on Jewish ethics, with a particular interest in issues connected with my work outside the university. The present book is the first major product of this research. It explores a basic and consistent ambiguity in Jewish ethics when it comes to issues of peace and violence. It demonstrates that in every major period in Jewish history, from the Bible to the modern period, one can find Jewish texts that seem to promote violence against non-Jews alongside texts that seem to promote a peaceful relationship with them. In many instances, even a single text can be read in both ways. My study also probes the reasons the texts are so ambiguous. I am interested not just in establishing the ambiguity of Jewish texts regarding peace and violence, but in understanding the interpretive procedures that make this ambiguity possible. Central to my interests here is how this ambiguity plays out in modern Zionism. This should come as no surprise. Zionism and the creation of the Jewish state in the modern period have thrust the issue of peace and violence into the forefront of Jewish ethics, and I, as an academic involved in interfaith dialogue and peace work, have spent much effort grappling with this issue as well. My analysis, while focused on Judaism, is by no means relevant to Judaism alone. All major religions are ambiguous regarding the issues of peace and violence.

The bulk of this study was completed during a sabbatical in 2007–8 during which I was supported by a generous grant from the United States Institute of Peace. As I mentioned earlier, USIP is one of the world's leading institutions in peacemaking, and I have been privileged to participate in its activities over the past several years and to have received its assistance in writing this book.

Earlier drafts of this study were read in their entirety by Kathy Beller, Stuart Cohen, Marc Gopin, Shaul Magid, Derek Penslar, David Smock, and Max Ticktin, and their valuable suggestions have much improved the final product. My father, Sydney Eisen, a retired academic, also read through and commented on an earlier draft. My father has always been one of the strongest supporters of my work but also one of my most challenging critics, and my scholarship has always benefited from that dual role he has played in my life. My mother, Doris Eisen, must be acknowledged for copy editing the entire final draft of this study. There is simply no one more skilled and thorough than she when it comes to this function. I received much help from others who read and commented on specific portions of earlier drafts: Marc Brettler, Bob Carroll, Aryeh Cohen, Ed Hostetter, Eran Kaplan, and Jeffery Rubenstein. I must also acknowledge Jon Levenson, who gave valuable advice and encouragement in the early stages of this project. Eli Holzer was very generous in providing me with a prepublication copy of his excellent study on militarism in religious Zionist thought, a study that is cited copiously in my chapter on Zionism. Finally, I offer thanks to Cynthia Read and all the folks at Oxford, with whom it has been a joy to work once again on this, my second major publication with them. Needless to say, whatever errors remain in this study after all the help I have received from others are entirely my own responsibility.

I have already mentioned Marc Gopin's contribution to my work—in particular, how he opened so many doors for me in the field of peace work. But there is more. I owe a great debt to Marc for teaching me an immense amount about religion and peacemaking through countless hours of personal conversation, by my witnessing on numerous occasions his remarkable skill in conducting interfaith dialogue, and by reading his writings. Most important of all, Marc has inspired me by the life he has lived, a life suffused with sensitivity to the suffering of others and a relentless desire to alleviate that suffering. I can only hope that what he has done for me will be paid back in some measure by the satisfaction he receives in seeing the fruits of his investment in these pages.

I mentioned earlier that for many years I resisted becoming involved in peace work because of a tendency toward cynicism that made me cast doubt on whether any efforts on my part to deal with global problems would do any good. My readers may be surprised to learn that my cynicism has not entirely disappeared. It is just that I have come to realize that I can find fulfillment in peace work even if I remain a skeptic about its outcome. Even if the world is not going to get better anytime soon, I believe that it is still incumbent on all of us to use our skills to improve the human condition. It may be that the efforts I exert will eventually have some impact. Or maybe they won't. I have also come to discover that even if nothing I do ever has an impact, peacemaking is a spiritual experience in its own right that brings deep meaning to one's life. Through this work, I have found fellowship with kindred spirits from distant places and foreign cultures whom I would never have met had I not been involved in this work. I have encountered remarkable individuals who have lived exemplary moral lives the likes of which I can admire but never fully emulate. Some of them are heroes who constantly risk their lives in order to make the world a better place. If the only result of the whole experience of peacemaking is to have allowed me to be in the presence of these people, it will have been worthwhile.

My cynicism has been restrained by yet one more factor. At the end of every day, I have the privilege of entering a place of refuge from the world's problems: my home. There, I am greeted by my wife, Naomi, the most wonderful life partner a person could ask for, and three beautiful and inspiring children: Adeena, Sarit, and Yoni. It is simply impossible for me to remain a cynic when I am around them, and I am convinced that if everyone in the world could experience the joy of a home like mine, the world would be a lot less troubled than it is. I dedicate this book to my children. I have helped bring them into a world that has the potential to give them much happiness but that will also challenge them with its sorrows. I can only hope that they experience all the joys that life has to offer, but that at the same time its sorrows will motivate them to use their gifts and talents to grapple with the world's troubles. In the meantime, they are a great blessing in my life.

Contents

1. Introduction, 3

2. The Bible, 15

3. Rabbinic Judaism, 65

4. Medieval Jewish Philosohy, 111

5. Kabbalah, 129

6. Modern Zionism, 141

7. Conclusions, 205

   Epilogue: Personal Reflections on Where We Go from Here, 217

   Bibliography, 239

   Index, 259

The Peace and Violence
of Judaism

I

Introduction

Few topics have received as much attention in recent years as religious violence. It has been examined from innumerable angles in every outlet of the popular and academic media. Books, newspaper editorials, television documentaries, and movies have steadily bombarded us with analyses of every aspect of this phenomenon. And no wonder. In the wake of 9/11, the Western world awoke to a new reality, one in which religious violence had taken center stage. The problem had been simmering under the surface for years, even decades, in regions and cultures throughout the world, but only after this momentous event did Westerners begin to realize that it involved them as well and that it had the capability of destroying everything they held dear. As a result, the problem of religious violence has become one of the most—if not *the* most—pressing issue of our time.

The present study is an attempt to contribute to the exploration of this phenomenon. It builds on the work of a number of pioneering scholars who have provided insight into religious violence by focusing on the ambiguity of religious traditions. Studies by such scholars as R. Scott Appleby and Marc Gopin have demonstrated that the major religions of the world have the capacity to inspire their adherents to adopt peaceful or violent behavior, and that the choice between these alternatives depends a great deal on how religious communities interpret their basic texts.[1] How those texts are read is in turn dependent on a complex interplay between religious traditions and outside forces in the political, social, and economic spheres. Appleby and Gopin are quite open about the type of religious ethic they prefer; they both express the hope that their work will provide peacemakers with the tools to structure dialogues between religious communities so that they will choose the path of peace, not violence. Much of what Appleby and Gopin have uncovered may seem obvious. Yet, the issues they have raised were little talked about before the publication of their work.

This study takes the insights of Appleby and Gopin a critical step further by exploring ambiguity on the issue of peace and violence in one religion in particular: Judaism. Although Appleby and Gopin have opened up new directions for research in religious ethics, their work has tended to be on the level of generality, as one would expect given its foundational nature. They provide numerous examples of how ambiguity is expressed in religious traditions but do not offer an in-depth analysis of any one of them. This type of analysis is, however, sorely needed. Each religion has its own history and dynamic, and one can therefore expect that each will embody its ambiguities on peace and violence in its own unique way. It is thus important that the work of Appleby and Gopin be brought to bear on individual religious traditions in a thoroughgoing manner, and that is precisely what I have attempted to do here. This type of exercise is not only of academic value; it should be of interest to peacemakers as well. Their success in encouraging religious communities to choose the peaceful alternative may depend on how well they understand the ambiguity of religious ethics in those communities.

The need for this kind of analysis becomes more urgent when one is aware of the prejudices that often creep into treatments of religious violence. Western writers who deal with this topic often define the problem and offer solutions to it that are appropriate for Christianity, but not other faiths. Thus, for instance, Western writers on religious violence are often unable to relate to Jewishness as an ethnic, historical, or cultural identity that is marginally connected to religion but is nonetheless a source of violence, because such a form of identity has few analogues in Christianity. For this reason, in their analyses of Zionism these writers miss a great deal. They tend to focus only on right-wing religious Zionism, but fail to recognize that no analysis of Zionism can be complete without coming to terms with Zionism in its left-wing, secular form. The mainstream of Zionism has always been in the latter camp, and its followers have been just as willing to

---

1 R. Scott Appleby, *The Ambivalence of the Sacred: Religion, Violence, and Reconciliation* (Lanham, Md.: Rowman & Littlefield, 2000); Marc Gopin, *Between Eden and Armageddon: The Future of Word Religions, Violence and Peacemaking* (New York: Oxford University Press, 2000); idem, *Holy War, Holy Peace: How Religion Can Bring Peace to the Middle East* (New York: Oxford University Press, 2002).

die for their cause as Zionists of a more religious stripe. Moreover, religious Zionism would not have become such a potent source of violence nowadays had it not been for the assistance it received from secular Zionists in earlier decades.[2]

For the purposes of my analysis, I have adopted a somewhat unusual format. I devote chapters to every major period in the history of Jewish thought and practice—biblical, rabbinic, medieval (including chapters devoted to medieval Jewish philosophy and Kabbalah), and modern—and in each chapter I offer two readings of texts relevant to peace and violence. One reading argues that the texts in the period under consideration promote violence toward non-Jews, while the alternative reading argues that they promote peace. It is important to point out that both readings value peace, even the one that argues that Judaism promotes violence. It is just that the latter viewpoint is skeptical that Judaism can guide people to peaceful behavior.

I deliberately describe the two viewpoints as positions that "promote" peace or violence because I am interested not just in Jewish sources that directly espouse one or the other, but also in sources that do so indirectly. For instance, the question of whether Judaism is violent or peaceful toward non-Jews is, of course, tied up with the question of how Judaism views non-Jews in general. Both readings in each chapter will therefore deal extensively with this concern before discussing the issues of peace and violence. Thus, a good portion of this study is devoted to the general question of tolerance even though it is not our ultimate concern.

In each chapter, I also examine the underlying reasons that account for the fact that the texts are ambiguous. That is, my intent is to show not simply that Jewish texts are ambiguous, but to explore *why* they are ambiguous. The focus here is therefore as much on the issue of interpretation in Jewish ethics as it is on Jewish ethics itself.

I have made every effort to ensure that neither of the two viewpoints presented in this study gets the upper hand. I alternate the order of viewpoints from chapter to chapter so that in some chapters the reading that sees Judaism as a violent religion comes first, while in others the reading that interprets Judaism as peaceful will begin the discussion. In this way, I do not allow one viewpoint to dictate the agenda of my study. At the end of each chapter, I also make sure to note difficulties with the second reading in the chapter so that this reading does not have the last word. Because the texts are ambiguous, there can

---

2 See, for instance, Mark Juergensmeyer, *Terror in the Mind of God: The Global Rise of Religious Violence* (Berkeley and Los Angeles: University of California Press, 2000), chapter 3; Oliver McTernan, *Violence in God's Name: Religion in an Age of Conflict* (Maryknoll, N.Y.: Orbis Books, 2003), chapter 4; Jessica Stern, *Terror in the Name of God: Why Religious Militants Kill* (New York: Ecco, 2004), chapter 4. This issue will be discussed in greater detail in chapter 6.

be no actual closure; the debate between the two viewpoints could continue beyond the confines of my treatment.

The topic that is of greatest contemporary significance in my study is, of course, modern Zionism. In truth, much of the inspiration for this project came from a desire to grapple with this phenomenon and the questions it raises. Therefore, the penultimate chapter of my study is devoted entirely to Zionism and should be viewed as in some respects a culmination of the chapters preceding it. It is for this reason that I have no separate chapter on modern Jewish thought. Zionism is so much at the center of modern Jewish speculations about violence toward non-Jews that I chose to focus on Zionism as the lens through which to view modern Jewish thinking on this issue.

It is remarkable that after 1800 years of stateless existence, Jews have regained sovereignty in their ancient homeland. For Jews, the creation of the state of Israel has been a great gift. However, this event has also brought with it moral challenges the likes of which Jews have not faced for centuries. Political power has entailed enormous responsibilities as Jews struggle to deal with Arabs living under their rule and on their borders who are hostile to the Jewish state. And the difficulties here have ramifications well beyond the Jewish sphere. The conflict between Israelis and Palestinians is at the center of the tensions between the Western and Islamic worlds, and it is no exaggeration to say that the well-being of our world in the long term may depend on its outcome.

The subject of Zionism is also the most complex of all the topics that I will be analyzing. In every chapter other than the one devoted to Zionism, the format I have just described was relatively easy to implement; however, with Zionism this was not the case, because two questions had to be dealt with that intertwined with the issues central to our study, and these questions invited responses that were no less ambiguous than the other matters with which we have had to grapple. The first was the degree to which Zionism has been violent. There is no question that Zionism has inspired Jews to take violent action against Palestinians and Arabs, but there is deep disagreement over the morality of such action. Some believe that Zionists have been violent only for defensive purposes, while others hold that their violent actions have been unprovoked and aggressive in the extreme, and there is every shade of opinion between the two positions. The second question involved the sources of Zionist violence. Regardless of whether the violence perpetrated by Zionists is defensive or aggressive in nature, it is not clear whether it has been inspired by Judaism, and if so to what degree. After all, other forces may have been responsible for violence in this instance—most notably, the influence of secular nationalism or fears of non-Jews spawned by modern anti-Semitism. Both factors played a significant role in the formation of Zionism. In my treatment of Zionism, therefore, I could not simply present two viewpoints, with one arguing that Judaism has promoted violence and the other arguing that it is peaceful; I had to deal with these other issues as well. Consequently, I have structured the discussion of Zionism as a more general debate between one position that provides a critique of Zionism and another that offers a defense of it, and that debate incorporates within it all the relevant issues. Yet, despite the complexity that Zionism brings to our discussion, here again the main point is to demonstrate ambiguity in Jewish ethics.

The two viewpoints I present in each chapter may appear to be artificial constructions, but they are not. They represent voices in my own head and heart that have been engaged in discussion for the past several years as I have wrestled with Jewish ethics. On one level, this study is thus quite personal. However, the viewpoints presented here are not so personal that others will be unable to relate to them. They have been constructed in large part with the help of insights of previous thinkers and scholars about texts that are often discussed in treatments of Jewish ethics. A good deal of what these viewpoints have to say is, therefore, dependent on opinions that are not my own. Much of what I have done is to bring them into dialogue.

A question that my format raises is whether the two viewpoints I present in each chapter are too polarized. Given the complexity of the subject-matter, is it not possible—or, better yet, likely—that the truth lies somewhere *between* the position that sees Judaism as violent and the one that views it as nonviolent? And if this is the case, why present such discrete positions? Why not simply provide one reading that carefully weighs the merits of each side on each point in an integrated discussion? Although it is true that the most judicious and nuanced positions often lie between the extremes I have presented, I believe the format I have adopted here has significant advantages. It highlights the nature of the moral difficulties with Jewish sources on peace and violence far more clearly than an integrated discussion would. Moreover, I view this study as a resource to inspire further discussion, and to this end, the presentation of two discrete viewpoints is advantageous because of the clarity it offers regarding the key issues.

Some may be disturbed by my approach here. Jewish readers who strongly identify with one of the two viewpoints may be unhappy that I have given support to the alternative position. As I described this project to Jewish relatives, friends, and colleagues, many wondered how I could possibly argue that Judaism promotes violence. A number of them pointed to the fact that much of the evolution of Judaism occurred during centuries when Jews did not have political power, let alone an army. Some also argued that even with the founding of the state of Israel, Jews have been remarkably restrained when it comes to violence. Others argued from the opposite perspective and pointed to the biblical imperatives to slaughter the Canaanites and Amalekites as evidence that Judaism was anything but peaceful. Some on this side of the debate also claimed that the actions of the state of Israel against Palestinians were evidence of just how violent Jews could be. All I can say in response to these reactions is that my readers should approach this study with an open mind and attempt to see the virtues of both perspectives. In some sense, my study is devoted to the very purpose of casting doubt on the one-sidedness of both sides in this debate.

There is yet another issue that may trouble my readers. If I am correct and Judaism is thoroughly ambiguous when it comes to the issues of peace and violence, can Jewish texts be of any utility in guiding Jews with respect to the exigencies of our age? How does one decide which path to follow? Are the peaceful and violent viewpoints equal? I do not have any easy answers to these questions. In my epilogue, I attempt to share some observations about how Jewish texts, despite their ambiguity, may still serve as valuable resources for Jews in sorting out ethical issues dealt with in this study. However, I would urge my readers not to be too focused on definitive answers. My epilogue will not necessarily solve all problems, and I do not want the ruminations in this chapter to take the emphasis away from the bulk of my study, which attempts to expose the fundamental ambiguities in Judaism on the issues of peace and violence. Honesty should be the highest value here, and if Jewish religious traditions are indeed ambiguous when it comes to peace and violence, the sooner Jews recognize this the better, even if it causes discomfort.

It may be that Judaism cannot provide clear guidance here. Perhaps its history is too long and its content too complex to give clear-cut answers with respect to the basic ethical problems that are the focus of this study. However, even if this is the case, it does not mean that Jews should throw up their hands and give up any effort to make sense of their religious traditions. It just means that they should accept that their decisions about what course of action to follow will involve a good deal of debate as they grapple with Jewish texts, and that it will be subject to constant reevaluation and review. As my readers will see, this point will be important in my epilogue, where I speculate on how we should act in light of ambiguity in our religious traditions.

These observations raise the question of where the divine voice is in all this and why it is so elusive. That is not a question I can answer in this study. It may be that God never intended to make things easy for us. I do not know. All I can do is exert my best effort to make sense of the texts that lie before me.

My method of analyzing Jewish texts combines academic scholarship and constructive religious ethics. As an academic, I have great confidence in scholarship as a means of enlightening us about the world in which we live. Its greatest virtue is its rigorous empiricism. To my mind, knowledge of any subject must begin with data that are discoverable through sense perception and that can be shared by all human beings, and academics have adopted this approach with great success in probing the subject of religion. My explorations of the various thought-worlds in Judaism will therefore be based on the insights provided by academic scholarship. Yet, if empiricism is the beginning of knowledge, it is not the whole of it, especially in a study such as this one. I am not merely interested in a historical inquiry into the history of Jewish ethics; I am also attempting to grapple with Judaism as a living tradition that can guide Jews in our troubled world. Hence, my study will have a constructive dimension as well.

I have benefited a great deal from the work of other academics who have written specifically on the subject of peace and violence in Judaism, and their work is cited throughout my study. However, I believe that this study goes beyond their work in a couple of important respects. First, there has been no comprehensive book-length study on peace and violence in Judaism of the kind that I have attempted here. There are scores of excellent journal articles and chapters in edited volumes on various aspects of this subject, but no one study has ever been written that deals with the entirety of the Jewish tradition on the issue. Moreover, the contributions to this subject of earlier scholars have tended to be fairly circumscribed. For instance, Jewish scholars often approach the question of peace and violence by focusing exclusively on the Jewish legal tradition regarding war. They generally do not deal with the related question of Jewish attitudes toward non-Jews, which is important for any evaluation of Jewish views on war and peace. They also do not consider the theological and philosophical traditions in Judaism, which are critical for analyzing this issue.

Of course, my determination to carry out such a project may be foolhardy. Perhaps no comprehensive study of peace and violence in Judaism has ever been attempted because it is too large a topic to tackle in one volume. I certainly recognize the daunting nature of the challenge here. However, I also believe that some insights into Jewish views on peace and violence can come to the fore only with a study of this sort. Often, one needs to see the sweep of ideas and practices in a tradition over an extended period of time in order to gain valuable insights into that tradition. Indeed, this approach runs the risk of missing things or making inaccurate judgments along the way given the enormous quantity of material involved. I have no doubt that my educated readers will identify deficiencies in my analyses. However, this is a risk I am willing to take, given the benefits that can be derived from getting the big picture in a broad study. I also welcome the criticism of those who feel that I have erred on specific points. The issues being dealt with here are extremely weighty, and I will be grateful to my colleagues for identifying weaknesses in my arguments so that I can incorporate their insights into my future work.

My study goes beyond previous scholars of Jewish ethics in one other respect. I have found that Jewish scholars who write on peace and violence often fall into the very same trap that I described earlier: unwillingness to confront the unpleasant elements in their religious tradition. Those who write about war, for instance, are apt to emphasize the restrictions that the legal tradition in Judaism has placed on waging war, but do not recognize the violent elements that inform that tradition. As I have already emphasized, my study attempts to improve upon such partial treatments of religious ethics by grappling head-on with Judaism's potential to inspire violence.

The present study should be of interest not just to Jews but to non-Jews as well. Christians and Muslims, in particular, may relate to many of the specific issues discussed in these pages. As religions that grew out of Judaism, Christianity and Islam contain ambiguities in their ethics very similar to those treated in this study. The observations I will be sharing may also resonate with adherents of other faiths as well. All the major religions nowadays are grappling with the problem of religious violence, and I would not be surprised if their respective adherents recognize elements in my discussion of Judaism that are familiar.

I also hope that my study will serve as inspiration for scholars of other religions to publish studies of ethics regarding their own faiths similar to the one I have produced here. The lack of balance in the treatment of religious ethics involving peace and violence is a problem by no means confined to Jews. Representatives of religious communities are often unwilling to critique their own traditions, to see the ugliness that resides in them alongside the beauty. They are often quick to criticize other religious traditions for their failings but exhibit an inability to recognize that their own traditions are part of the problem. At the same time, we find the converse phenomenon among critics of religion. Writers such as Sam Harris and Christopher Hitchens are so focused on the negative aspects of religions, so determined to vilify everything they represent, that they distort matters as much as their opponents do. The blinkered positions on both extremes is lethal in this time given that the well-being of our planet may very well depend on the willingness of people to adopt a balanced perspective on religion and to appreciate its capacities for inspiring both good and evil behavior.[3]

---

3 Sam Harris, *The End of Faith: Religion, Terror, and the Future of Reason* (New York: W. W. Norton, 2004); idem, *Letter to a Christian Nation* (New York: Knopf, 2006); Christopher Hitchens, *God Is Not Great: How Religion Poisons Everything* (New York: Twelve Hachette Book Group, 2007). As a person involved a great deal in Jewish-Muslim dialogue, I would particularly like to see a fellow Muslim scholar produce a thorough study on ambiguity in Islam regarding the ethics of peace and violence. One study that provides a good deal of insight into this issue is Khaled Abou El Fadl, *The Great Theft: Wrestling Islam from the Extremists* (New York: HarperSanFrancisco, 2005). However, it is slanted toward a peaceful reading of Islam.

I do not want to give the impression that my study is meant only for academics. I am interested in reaching practitioners of peacemaking as well. This group includes those who are involved in interfaith dialogue in their local communities, as well as professional peacemakers who spend their lives attempting to solve violent religious conflicts on the international level. In recent years, I myself have been active in interfaith dialogue and peacemaking efforts both on the local and the international levels, and much of the inspiration for this study has come from participating in those efforts. In this study, I am also interested in reaching laypeople who have an interest in the issues explored here. This group is as important as any other for grappling with the problem of religious violence. The problem is, after all, everyone's problem, and if it is to be addressed properly, the general public must be involved, not just academics and professional peacemakers.

With such a broad audience in mind, I have done my best to make my discussion accessible to a wide readership. I introduce each chapter with a good deal of background material. I have exerted every effort to explain concepts and terms that may not be known to those unfamiliar with Judaism. I realize that these addenda may test the patience of my academic colleagues and specialists in Judaism, but I would hope that they will understand why these are necessary. Some of my more esoteric observations are confined to my footnotes. My academic readers may therefore want to consult them for a more in-depth analysis than is presented in the body of the book.

One last issue that we need to deal with before moving on to our study is to define the terms "peace" and "violence" more precisely. Let us begin with the latter. There has been much discussion both inside and outside academia about what constitutes violence. For our purposes, the definition given by the World Health Organization is a good beginning. Violence is "the intentional use of physical force or power, threatened or actual, against oneself, another person, or against a group or community, that either results in or has the high likelihood of resulting in injury, death, psychological harm, maldevelopment, or deprivation."[4] This definition divides violence into three categories: self-inflicted, interpersonal, and collective. This study will be interested primarily in the third category. That is, we will be looking at how Jews as a people have envisioned their relationship with other peoples. We will not examine violence between Jews and other Jews or violence toward women or homosexuals. Nor will we be exploring violence that, according to the tradition, is perpetrated directly

---

4 *World Report on Violence and Health*, ed. Etienne G. Krug, Linda L. Dahlberg, James A. Mercy, Anthony B. Zwi, and Rafael Lozano (Geneva: World Health Organization, 2002), 5.

by God against human beings. However, we will occasionally refer to these forms of violence because in some instances they will be relevant to our discussion.

The WHO definition also describes what actions constitute violence. Primary among them are those that result in physical harm or death. When people commonly speak of violence, they generally have actions of this type in mind. Yet, included in the definition are other forms of injury, and most scholars agree that they too fall under the rubric of violence. Thus, mention is made in the definition of actions that result, or are likely to result, in "psychological damage." What this means is that the mere threat of violence and verbal abuse may be considered violence if they have a serious and deleterious psychological impact. Symbolic injury, such as the desecration of objects or places sacred to a particular religious group, may constitute violence for the same reason. Scholars also extend the definition of violence to what is often referred to as "structural violence," a category not clearly represented in the foregoing definition. This form of violence involves the systematic political, social, or economic exploitation and oppression of individuals or groups. This is perhaps the most subtle form of violence in that a group's physical and psychological well-being is gradually eroded over an extended period of time by a political, social, or economic system that discriminates against it.[5]

We must also consider the distinction between violence that is unprovoked or aggressive and that which is defensive in nature. Moral theorists—and the public at large—are generally quick to condemn the first type of violence, but

---

5 Johan Galtung, "Cultural Violence," *Journal of Peace Research* 27, no. 3 (1990): 291–305; Kathleen Mass Weigert, "Structural Violence," in *Encyclopedia of Violence, Peace, and Conflict*, ed. Lester Kurtz (San Diego: Academic Press, 1999), 3:431–36; Charles Selengut, *Sacred Fury: Understanding Religious Violence* (Walnut Creek, Calif.: Altamira Press, 2003), chapter 1; John J. Collins, "The Zeal of Phinehas: The Bible and the Legitimation of Violence," *Journal of Biblical Literature* 122, no. 1 (2000): 4; Elizabeth A. Castelli, "Feminists Responding to Violence: Theories, Vocabularies, and Strategies," in *Interventions: Activists and Academics Respond to Violence*, ed. Elizabeth A. Castelli and Janet R. Jacobsen (New York: Palgrave Macmillan, 2004), 3; Meredith Turshen, "Definitions and Injuries of Violence," in Castelli and Jakobsen, *Interventions*, 29–35; Hector Avalos, *Fighting Words: The Origins of Religious Violence* (Amherst, N.Y.: Prometheus Books, 2005), 19–20; Oliver Ramsbotham, Tom Woodhouse, and Hugh Miall, eds., *Contemporary Conflict Resolution: The Prevention, Management, and Transformation of Deadly Conflicts*, 2nd ed. (Cambridge: Polity Press, 2006), 9–11. Regina Schwartz argues that violence between groups also occurs in the very act of collective identity formation, whether it be in the sphere of nationality, religion, race, ethnicity, or gender. In fact, in Schwartz's opinion, imagining the separation and distinction of one's own group from other groups is the most frequent and fundamental form of violence that human beings commit. Violence is not just what we do to others; it is the very construction of the "other." See Regina Schwartz, *The Curse of Cain: The Violent Legacy of Monotheism* (Chicago: University of Chicago Press, 1997), 5. Schwartz's definition strikes me as too extreme. First, if collective identity formation is violence ipso facto, it would mean that the vast majority of people in the world perpetrate violence every day, since identity formation of this kind is ubiquitous. This definition of violence therefore becomes so diffuse that the notion of violence loses all meaning. Second, as we will argue at various points of our study, the construction of the other need not be for the purpose of doing harm to them.

very few oppose the second. However, it is sometimes very difficult to draw a distinction between the two. Defensive violence can be a cover for its aggressive counterpart. A group that acts violently toward another can claim that its actions are defensive on the basis of trumped-up or spurious accusations against the the other. In fact, we see this frequently in violent conflict between warring nations or ethnic groups. Thus, although in principle most people will approve of violence for the purposes of self-defense, the problem is figuring out when the argument for self-defense is honest and legitimate.[6]

The distinction between aggressive and defensive violence is especially important for our study because self-defense is a sacrosanct principle in Jewish ethics. Only on rare occasions do we find texts or thinkers in Judaism in support of pacifism in the strict sense—that is, the notion that violence is never justifiable even in self-defense. Biblical and rabbinic Judaism were quite clear that one is allowed to defend oneself when violently attacked even it means killing one's attacker.[7]

A definition of the term "peace" follows from everything we have said about violence: it is simply the converse of the latter. It is important to point out that according to this definition, peace does not mean simply the absence of war or the absence of actions causing physical injury between groups within a society. If that were the case, many countries with brutal dictatorships would be considered quite peaceful. Peace must also include the absence of structural violence, as well as the absence of actions by individuals or groups resulting in psychological damage.[8]

Our study will consider all these factors in our examination of Jewish views on peace and violence, but it will also assume that not all violent actions are equally harmful. Actions that result in physical injury or death—war is a prime example—will be viewed as worse forms of violence than those that are structural or psychological in nature, and therefore in this study we will focus primarily on the first kind of violence. This focus is appropriate because, as I mentioned earlier, most people associate violence primarily with actions that

---

6 Castelli, 3.

7 This issue will be discussed in chapter 3.

8 In recent years, the interdisciplinary field of human security has arisen from these premises. Its birth is based on the realization that the term "peace" is often synonymous with the absence of war and is therefore inadequate as a goal for human affairs. A society that is not at war may still experience rampant inequality, oppression, and suffering. Human security therefore strives to recommend policies that go well beyond ensuring the absence of war and that bring about human well-being in the broadest sense. I provide a Jewish perspective on this issue in "Human Security in Jewish Philosophy and Ethics," in *Globalization and Environmental Challenges: Reconceptualizing Security in the 21st Century*, ed. Hans Günter Brauch, Úrsula Oswald Spring, Czeslaw Mesjasz, John Grin, Paul Dunay, Navnita Chadha Behera, Béchir Chourou, Patricia Kameri-Mbote, and P. H. Liotta (Berlin: Springer-Verlag, 2008), 3:253–62.

cause physical injury or death. Moreover, in our day and age the greatest threat to our world is violence of this sort because it can be perpetrated on a massive scale owing to advances in technology. This form of violence is therefore more dangerous than structural and psychological violence. This does not mean that the latter forms of violence are of no interest to us. Over an extended period of time, structural violence can lead to violence of a more direct sort. These forms of violence will therefore be considered in our study as well.

2

The Bible

Our study must begin with the Hebrew Bible, the foundational text of Judaism. Yet, the importance of this text for our study is matched by the formidable challenges one encounters in analyzing it. The Bible is an anthology containing a wide variety of works in different literary genres, composed by authors who are mostly unidentifiable, and produced over a period of more than a thousand years beginning with the era of the nomadic origins of Jewish people c. 1500–1300 BCE and extending to the reign of Antiochus IV in the middle of the second century BCE. All genres of biblical literature are potentially valuable for ethical reflection, but because of its great heterogeneity, this corpus is filled with internal tensions, inconsistencies, and outright contradictions that make it difficult to formulate generalizations about any major theme, including those involving ethics.[1]

Until recently, biblical scholars generally ignored these problems and attempted to identify concepts or passages in the biblical text that functioned as foci for biblical ethics and allowed for the discernment of a unified and coherent body of ethical prescriptions. Christian scholars were particularly fond of this method on account of a desire to neatly organize the ethics of the Old Testament so that it could serve

1 I will be using the terms "Bible" and "Hebrew Bible" interchangeably in this chapter. Although the term "Bible" in Western scholarship refers to the Old and New Testaments, here it will refer only to the Old Testament unless otherwise indicated.

as a complement to the New Testament.[2] In recent years, there has been a reaction against this approach. Cyril Rodd represents an extreme expression of this reaction in contending that biblical ethics lacks any pattern or unity what-soever and that we must therefore be content with its fragmentary nature. Scholars who support Rodd's approach often note that in Western thinking, the very term "ethics" has to be understood against the background of the Western philosophical tradition that, since the period of ancient Greece, thought of ethics in systematic terms. Since the Bible does not provide systematic discussions regarding any philosophical topic, including ethics, it is questionable whether the term "ethics" is even appropriate here.[3]

Our approach will follow those scholars who attempt to strike a balance between the extremes. For instance, John Barton approaches biblical ethics from the premise that it is fragmentary, but he insists nonetheless that the Bible is "more than a jumble of isolated precepts with no underlying rationale." It contains "fundamental structures" of ethical thinking.[4] Jon Levenson similarly claims that, in spite of its anthological character, the Bible is a "coherent entity, not merely a concatenation of incompatibles," and that this coherence "enables us to regard the separate elements as parts of a total picture that may not in reality have been affirmed by the original authors."[5] We will therefore proceed on the assumption that generalizations about biblical ethics can be made, but only if they are worked out with due caution.[6]

Scholars of biblical ethics have examined the Bible from a variety of angles. One is focused on gaining insight into the ethical reflections of the Bible by exploring the social and historical contexts from which they emerge.[7] A second ignores historical and social context and examines biblical ethics from a literary

---

2 This issue is examined by Jon D. Levenson, *The Hebrew Bible, the Old Testament, and Historical Criticism: Jews and Christians in Biblical Studies* (Louisville: Westminster/John Knox Press, 1993), especially chapters 1, 3, and 6.

3 Cyril S. Rodd, *Glimpses of a Strange Land: Studies in Old Testament Ethics* (Edinburgh: T & T Clark, 2001), 1–4. The book of Job is perhaps the most philosophical book in the Bible, but it hardly qualifies as systematic philosophy.

4 John Barton, "The Basis of Ethics in the Hebrew Bible," *Semeia* 66 (1994): 12.

5 Jon D. Levenson, "The Universal Horizon of Biblical Particularism," in *Ethnicity and the Bible*, ed. Mark G. Brett (Leiden: E. J. Brill, 1996), 145–46.

6 Robert Wilson notes that scholars of ethics in the Hebrew Bible often favor one genre of biblical literature over another. Thus, for example, Bruce Birch focuses on narrative, while Walter Kaiser focuses on law. Brevard Childs focuses on the entire diversity of material in the Bible. See Robert R. Wilson, "Sources and Methods in the Study of Ancient Israelite Ethics," *Semeia* 66 (1994): 61–62. In this chapter, we will deal with all genres of biblical literature without giving priority to any single one, and therefore our approach is perhaps most similar to Childs's. However, Childs's canonical approach deemphasizes the importance of historical context in analyzing the Hebrew Bible, and my analysis will be very much interested in this issue.

7 This group can be further divided into two subgroups: those who explore social and historical context for the purpose of achieving a better understanding of the Bible, and those who, conversely, explore the Bible for the purpose of achieving a better understanding of its social and historical context.

standpoint, in which the focus is on how the text affects the reader through its artistry, ambiguities, and plays of meaning. A third method shows a similar lack of concern with social and historical context, but expends its efforts on mining the text for moral guidance and decision-making in today's world.[8] These approaches are not monolithic, and frequently scholars will combine them. In this study, the first and third will be of greatest interest to us. That is, we will be looking at the biblical text as a source of contemporary moral guidance, but we will do so by taking into account its social and historical context. As we noted in our introduction, this study attempts to strike a balance between academic scholarship and religious-moral reflection.

One more issue that should be mentioned here is that this chapter is unique in this study in being the only one that will depend a great deal on the scholarship of non-Jews. The Hebrew Bible is sacred to Jews and Christians alike, and it is one of the most influential works in the development of Western civilization in general. Therefore, non-Jewish academic scholars have taken as much interest in this text as Jews have. However, our analysis will be from a Jewish point of view, and we will therefore make use of non-Jewish scholarship only to the extent that it can help us construct a Jewish reading of the text.[9]

The Bible Promotes Violence

In recent years, the Bible has been subject to withering criticism. Authors such as Christopher Hitchens and Sam Harris have written best-sellers attacking both the Old and New Testaments for inspiring violence throughout the centuries. According to these authors, these texts have been held responsible for the endless wars waged by Christendom against heretics, Muslims, Jews, and fellow Christians in the medieval and early modern periods. Moreover, Hitchens and Harris believe that religious violence in the world today can be explained in large part by the legacy of the Jewish and Christian Bibles. Thus, Christian fundamentalists in the United States, an immensely powerful group, have inspired intolerant and violent American policies abroad. Jewish extremists in Israel have played a big part in fanning the flames of the Arab-Israeli conflict. Some hold the Bible responsible for Islamic extremism as well in that Islam is

---

8 This division is a modified version of a similar one presented by Douglas A. Knight, "Introduction: Ethics, Ancient Israel, and the Hebrew Bible," *Semeia* 66 (1994): 2–5.

9 We will not engage the tendentious Christian scholarship marred by Christian supersessionism and a negative attitude toward Judaism in general. This issue is dealt with throughout Joel S. Kaminsky's study of Israel's election, *Yet I Loved Jacob: Reclaiming the Biblical Concept of Election* (Nashville: Abingdon Press, 2007). Kaminsky expends a good deal of effort unveiling Christian biases regarding the biblical doctrine of election.

a direct outgrowth of biblical religion. In light of all of this, these critics contend, the world would have been better off without the Bible.[10] I would therefore like to begin the discussion in this chapter by offering a reading of the Bible from this viewpoint.

The Bible seems to start off on a universalistic note when we are told in the first chapter of Genesis that all human beings are created in the "image of God."[11] This phrase has invited an enormous amount of commentary, but at the very least it implies that human beings have an exalted status.[12] This argument is reinforced by comparing the use of this phrase in the Bible to its usage in ancient Near Eastern texts. In the latter, we find that kings are often described as being "in the image" of their patron gods.[13] By applying that phrase to all human beings, the biblical text is therefore making the statement that all people have royal status. The precise meaning of creation in God's image is a matter of dispute, but the most popular interpretation among scholars is that it refers to the notion that humans have dominion over the earth that God has created, a reading prompted by the fact that immediately after the text tells us that human beings are created in God's image, it reports that they are commanded to master the earth and subdue it.[14]

However, the universalism of the biblical text is short-lived. The next ten chapters of Genesis deal with the history of humanity before the advent of Abraham, and they tell us about God's repeated disappointment with the human beings he has created. His expectation was that they would be obedient to him, but they fail to live up to that hope. Shortly after creation, Adam and Eve disobey God's orders and are expelled from the Garden of Eden. Ten generations later, Noah's generation proves to be so wicked they have to be annihilated. And just before Abraham appears after yet another ten generations, human beings once again rebel against God in the Tower of Babel episode. By the end of the primeval history, there have thus been several cycles of human failure and divine punishment. At this point, it would seem that God adopts a new strategy to deal with his recalcitrant creatures. He chooses one individual, Abraham, and his line of descendants, and he forms a special relationship with

---

10 Harris, *The End of Faith*; and Hitchens, *God Is Not Great*.

11 Gen. 1:27.

12 An entire monograph has been written on this one phrase by Edward M. Curtis, entitled *The Image of God: Genesis 1:26–28 in a Century of Old Testament Research* (Stockholm: Almqvist and Wiksell, 1988).

13 Nahum M. Sarna, *The JPS Commentary on the Torah: Genesis* (Philadelphia: Jewish Publication Society of America, 1989), 12.

14 Gen. 1:27–28; James Barr, *Biblical Faith and Natural Theology* (Oxford: Clarendon Press, 1993),157–58. Scholars commonly note that Psalm 8 also talks about the exalted status of human beings in general without any reference to Israel. See Barr, 157–58, and Moshe Greenberg, "Mankind, Israel, and the Nations in the Hebraic Heritage," in *Studies in the Bible and Jewish Thought* (Philadelphia: Jewish Publication Society of America, 1995), 371.

them so that they will fulfill the expectations that up to this point humanity has dashed. From here on the biblical history is concerned almost exclusively with God's chosen: the three Patriarchs—Abraham, Isaac, and Jacob—and their progeny who become the Israelite people. The first chapters of Genesis are therefore nothing but a brief prologue to the rest of the biblical history, which is focused entirely on the special relationship between God and the Israelites.[15]

Some scholars have insisted that the choice of Abraham does not imply that God has forgotten about the rest of humanity. When God first summons Abraham in the opening verses of Genesis 12, he informs him that "all the families of the earth shall be blessed through you." Thus, all humanity will share in Abraham's blessing.[16] However, other scholars read the verse as saying that "all the families of the earth shall *bless themselves by you*" (my emphasis).[17] According to this latter translation, God is telling Abraham that non-Israelites will invoke Abraham in their blessings by saying something to the effect that "may you prosper like Abraham and his descendants." The passage therefore informs us that the nations of the world will share an aspiration to be blessed like Abraham but they may not actually receive that blessing.[18] This second reading is perhaps the more plausible one given that the rest of the biblical history is focused almost entirely on the Israelites.

What is troubling here is that God clearly privileges one people over all others. Moreover, the special status of Abraham and his descendants is not justified on any rational or empirical grounds. They do not seem to have earned their privileged status. God simply deems them chosen. When Abraham is contacted by God in Genesis 12 and informed that he and his descendants will be God's special people, no reason is given for his choice. Later on in the Torah, the seeming arbitrariness of God's selection comes out in a number of passages

---

15 John Strong claims that humanity as a whole ceases to be in God's image after the story of the Tower of Babel, and from Genesis 12 onward, this notion applies to Israel alone. See John T. Strong, "Israel as a Testimony to YHWH's Power: The Priests' Definition of Israel," in *Constituting the Community: Studies on the Polity of Ancient Israel in Honor of S. Dean McBride Jr.*, eds. John T. Strong and Steven S. Tuell (Winona Lake, Ind.: Eisenbrauns, 2005), 89–106.

16 Gen. 12:3; Sarna, 89; Moshe Greenberg, "A Problematic Heritage: The Attitude Toward the Gentile in Jewish Tradition—An Israeli Perspective," *Conservative Judaism* 48, no. 2 (1996): 25–26; Richard Elliot Friedman, *Commentary on the Torah* (San Francisco: HarperSanFrancisco, 2001), 49–51. The *nif'al* of *ve-nivrekhu* is read as a passive verb. Paul R. Williamson conducts a thorough discussion of Gen. 12:1–3 and translates Gen. 12:3 in a manner similar to that of Sarna and Greenberg. See Paul R. Williamson, *Abraham, Israel and the Nations* (Sheffield: Sheffield Academic Press, 2000), 220–34. A book-length discussion of the meaning of this important verse is provided by Keith Nigel Grüneberg, *Abraham, Blessing, and the Nations: A Philological and Exegetical Study of Genesis 12:3 in Its Narrative Context* (New York: Walter de Gruyter, 2003).

17 That is, the *nif'al* here of *ve-nivrekhu* should be taken as a reflexive verb, not a passive one.

18 Jo Bailey Wells, *God's Holy People: A Theme in Biblical Theology* (Sheffield: Sheffield Academic Press, 2000), 185–207; Kaminsky, *Yet I Loved Jacob*, 85; R. W. L. Moberly, *The Bible, Theology, and Faith: A Study of Abraham and Jesus* (Cambridge: Cambridge University Press, 2000), 123–25.

which state quite explicitly that God is the God of the Israelites not because they are more virtuous than other nations; rather, he is their God because of his inexplicable love for them, or because he must honor his original promises to the Patriarchs that he be loyal to their descendants.[19] In other texts, God's love for Israel is depicted in more intense terms in taking on a romantic guise. For instance, in the book of Hosea, God's love for Israel is likened to that between a husband and wife.[20] Certainly, the relationship between God and Israel is defined in part by a conditional element. Israel is expected to serve him by obeying his commandments and living pious lives. But the unconditional element remains the bedrock of that relationship; God never ceases to love the Israelites even if they fail to live up to their obligations and are punished.[21] The special relationship between God and Israel comes through in other ways. In some passages in the Torah, this relationship is described in language similar to that used in the ancient Near East to depict the relationship between a deity and a king whom the deity patronizes. Israel is thus viewed in royal terms.[22] In other places, Israel is seen as God's firstborn son. This biological metaphor implies once again that God will never disown the Israelites despite their sins.[23]

The most serious difficulty here from an ethical standpoint is that Israel's special status encourages a chauvinism that runs the risk of inspiring intolerance and violence against outsiders. Jeremy Cott, in an often-cited article devoted to this problem, believes that the idea of Israel's election is "the most pernicious notion inherited from the biblical tradition" and "the ultimate anti-humanistic idea." When one believes oneself to be elected, one "tends to want to do away with everyone who is not."[24] For Cott, the crux of the problem is that the notion of divine election is predicated on scarcity, that there is not enough blessing for all humanity to share. Divine blessing is reserved only for certain people, most notably the Israelites. It therefore creates competition for divine favor, which can in turn lead to violence. It is no accident that the Bible depicts the first murder as one that takes place between two brothers. Sibling rivalry comes about as a result of competition for fatherly love, and this conflict serves as a metaphor for what is to come later on in the biblical text. This psychological complex is eventually projected onto the relationship between Israel and other nations in that Israel must also compete to win the love of the heavenly father.[25]

19 Deut. 7:7–8; 9:4–7.

20 Hos. Is. 43:4, 54:8, 54:10, 63:7, 63:9; Jer. 2:2, 31:3; Mal. 1:2.

21 As noted in Jeremy Cott, "The Biblical Problem of Election," *Journal of Ecumenical Studies* 21, no. 2 (Spring 1984): 217.

22 Levenson, "The Universal Horizon," 153.

23 Ex. 4:22–23; Hos. 11; Jer. 31:18–20; Levenson, "The Universal Horizon," 154.

24 Cott, 202, 204.

25 Cott, 200–201.

Regina Schwartz develops Cott's ideas in *The Curse of Cain: The Violent Legacy of Monotheism*, a study considered by many to be a pioneering work on violence in the Bible. Schwartz argues that the formation of collective identity is always based on the principle of scarcity. A people predicates its sense of self on the possession of things that are viewed as being in short supply, such as land and wealth. Intangible items are also included in this equation; part of a people's identity is based on a sense of its own specialness and importance. Thus, identity itself is in short supply. It is this principle of scarcity that often spawns violence between nations, because they will compete for the limited resources, both material and psychological, that they believe define who they are. In the Bible, this tendency is refracted through the prism of monotheism.[26] The Israelites base their identity on their sense of chosenness and on the possession of their land, both of which have been conferred upon them by the one God. This God is not infinitely giving, but restricts his love to Israel. Schwartz, like Cott, also sees great significance in the sibling rivalries of Genesis—particularly Cain and Abel—which set the tone for the rest of the biblical history in that one sibling is rejected because God's love is a scarce resource, not to be shared by all. Most important, Schwartz contends that it is the principle of scarcity as embodied in monotheism that is responsible for Israelite violence against outsiders. Schwartz admits that there is another side to biblical monotheism in which God is depicted as infinitely giving, but she claims that it is the first depiction of God that unfortunately has held sway in Western culture and has been transformed and secularized in modern times into malevolent nationalism.[27]

In a recent study, Hector Avalos has adopted Schwartz's position and taken it further. Avalos contends that *all* religions are inherently prone to violence, not just monotheism, and that this tendency can again be explained by scarce resource theory. The key issue is that religion creates scarce resources on the

---

26 It is important to keep in mind that, according to many scholars, "monotheism" is not the precise term for describing the religious beliefs of ancient Israelites. In many instances, the term "monolatry" is more accurate. Monotheism assumes the existence of a single deity; the premise of monolatry is that there is one superior deity and that other, less powerful gods exist as well. A common view among biblical scholars is that ancient Israel initially supported monolatry and gradually adopted monotheism during the Babylonian exile. The beginning of this transition can be traced to the Josianic reform in the seventh century BCE, which implemented a highly centralized and intolerant monolatry. When Judahites were exiled a century later, they took up a belief in monotheism in order to cope with their misfortune. If there was only one God and he was the God of all nations, exile could be explained as emanating from this God and did not have to be attributed to a Babylonian deity. These issues are discussed in Robert P. Gordon, "Introducing the God of Israel," in *The God of Israel*, ed. Robert P. Gordon (Cambridge: Cambridge University Press, 2007), 3–8. This topic is also the subject of an essay in the same volume by Ronald E. Clements, "Monotheism and the God of Many Names," 47–59.

27 Regina Schwartz, *The Curse of Cain: The Violent Legacy of Monotheism* (Chicago: University of Chicago Press, 1997), xi, 9–10, 18–9, 20–21, 31, 33–34.

basis of metaphysical principles that are unverifiable, and thus conflicts over those resources can be settled only by violence, unlike conflicts over more tangible objects for which competing claims of ownership can often be verified. Avalos also broadens Schwartz's insights by arguing that religion creates scarce resources not just with respect to the formation of identity, but also in placing limits on which texts are considered holy, in defining which locations are deemed to be sacred space, and in restricting salvation only to certain individuals.[28]

The analyses of Cott, Schwartz, and Avalos present a number of difficulties. It is not clear that an economic model is the best paradigm to describe Israel's chosenness.[29] The explanation for the sibling rivalries in Genesis offered by Cott and Schwartz can be challenged as well. Much has been written on this issue, and neither Cott nor Schwartz engages other theories that may better explain this motif.[30] Avalos's point that religious conflicts can be settled only through violence because they are based on unverifiable principles can also be questioned. If religious conflicts are inspired by unverifiable principles, the same is true of conflicts having nothing to do with religion. For instance, conflicts created by competing nationalist mythologies are often based on principles no more verifiable empirically than those underlying conflicts involving religion.[31] Still, the basic problem raised by these three authors must be confronted: God

28 Avalos, *Fighting Words*; see especially 22, 29, 82–83, 103–10. On 17, Avalos claims that his book presents "a new theory of religious violence," but this statement seems exaggerated in light of the fact that so much of his theoretical framework is indebted to Regina Schwartz.

29 See Moberly's critique of Schwartz on sibling rivalries in R. W. L. Moberly, "Is Monotheism Bad for You? Some Reflections on God, the Bible, and Life in the Light of Regina Schwartz's *The Curse of Cain*," in *The God of Israel*, ed. Robert P. Gordon (Cambridge: Cambridge University Press, 2007), 106–11.

30 Frederick E. Greenspahn, *When Brothers Dwell Together: The Preeminence of Younger Siblings in the Hebrew Bible* (New York: Oxford University Press, 1994). Schwartz claims that God's choice of one brother over the other is "inexplicable," which supports her case that the Bible treats divine blessing as a scarce resource (82–83). Yet, we can understand these rivalries by looking at the historical context in which these stories were created and the need they fulfilled. The triumph of the younger brother in the sibling stories appears to have served an important function because it was a metaphor for Israel's desire to survive in a region dominated by older civilizations and large empires threatening it with destruction. God's choice of one brother over another in these stories is therefore not as "inexplicable" as Schwartz claims. We will be discussing this issue in the second reading of the biblical text, which will argue that the Bible does not promote violence.

31 I must also note here that Avalos's interpretations of the Bible are marred by a poor reading of sources, a one-sided selection of biblical passages, erroneous statements about Judaism in general, and unfair criticisms of fellow scholars. The following are some examples of these difficulties. (1) P. 128: Avalos proposes that the link between violence and the scarcity of sacred space is found in I Kings 14:25–26, when King Shishak raids the Temple of Solomon and takes away its treasures. Avalos admits that the motivation for Shishak's actions may have been monetary. Nonetheless, he still holds religion responsible since material goods had "accrued to that sacred space, which resulted in it becoming a target for violent action by opponents." This is spurious logic. There is no evidence from the text that Shishak took the treasures for any reason other than its monetary value; the fact that they were in the Temple is incidental. (2) Pp. 128–29: Avalos cites Amos 7:9, in which the prophet predicts that "the shrines of Isaac shall be laid to waste, and the sanctuaries of Israel reduced to ruins," as another example of violence caused by the scarcity of sacred space. But here the violence is only predicted in a prophecy, and Avalos himself claims that verbal violence is not violence unless it leads to actual physical violence (20).

singles out one nation as his chosen people, and intolerance and violence toward outsiders would seem to be a natural outgrowth of this idea.

In fact, this concern is borne out by the biblical text. God's love of Israel does indeed come at the expense of the well-being of others, most notably the Canaanites and Amalekites, who are treated with great cruelty on account of Israel's chosenness. The Canaanite conquest has received a great deal of attention from scholars of the Hebrew Bible not just because of the deeply troubling ethical questions it raises, but because of its importance in the overall scheme of the biblical history. From its very inception, Israel's election is combined with what one might call geographic election. God's summons to Abraham in Genesis 12 includes his promise that Abraham's descendants will dwell in the land of Canaan, a prophecy that is fulfilled several generations later. The fulfillment of that promise constitutes the underlying theme of the entire Torah and is crucial to the subsequent history of Israel in the rest of the Bible. Thus, as Cott notes, the conquest of the land is "the end-point of a distinct understanding of Israel's history, a story of promise and fulfillment."[32] Most important, dispossessing the Canaanites of their land means nothing less than wholesale slaughter. In several passages in the Bible, the Israelites are commanded to annihilate them—men, women, and children—upon entering the land, and to do so without mercy.[33] Particularly important here are the books of Deuteronomy and the Former Prophets—Joshua through II Kings—which, taken together, make up what scholars refer to as the Deuteronomic History. Scholars

---

(3) Pp. 137–44: Avalos focuses most of his critique of group privileging in the Bible on the Deuteronomic History and the command to annihilate the Canaanites contained in those texts. He fails to mention sources in the Deuteronomic History that are inconsistent with his viewpoint, such as its statements about the foreigner. (4) P. 168: Avalos argues against Susan Niditch's notion that there are peaceful countertraditions in the Bible. Yet, he focuses his critique solely on her brief exposition of II Kings 6:22–23 (Susan Niditch, *War in the Hebrew Bible: A Study in the Ethics of Violence* [New York: Oxford University Press, 1993], 136), while ignoring the discussion in the rest of Niditch's chapter on this topic. (Cf. as well Avalos's attack on Kaminsky's statement regarding Amalek on pp. 160–61, with Kaminsky's original statement.) (5) P. 148: Avalos states that salvation is a scarce resource in Judaism because "it can only be acquired through very specific means that are not available to outsiders." This is a one-sided judgment. Some Jewish sources restrict salvation to Jews, but some do not. For instance, a well-known rabbinic opinion claims that non-Jews have a share in the world to come just as Jews do. (6) In general, Avalos claims his critique is directed against "Judaism," but in fact it is directed against the Hebrew Bible, which is not synonymous with Judaism. Moreover, his discussion is not even really about the Hebrew Bible in that it is almost exclusively engaged with the Deuteronomic history, which represents only one stratum in the Bible.

32 Cott, 202–3. The centrality of land for the covenant is reinforced in Gen. 26:4, 28:4; Ex. 12:25, 33:1; Deut. 1:8; Josh. 1:6, 2:24. Regina Schwartz notes that the tie between Israel's chosenness and land is the most troubling legacy of monotheism. See Schwartz, *The Curse of Cain*, 39. W. D. Davies provides a broad-ranging essay on the significance of the land of Israel in Judaism from the Bible to modern Zionism in *The Territorial Dimension of Judaism: Jewish Constructs in Late Antiquity* (Berkeley: University of California Press, 1982). See especially pp. 6–28 for reflections on the land of Israel in the Bible.

33 Deut. 7:1–2, 20:16–17. See also Deut. 7:3–5, 20:16–18, 32:39; Josh. 6:21, 8:24–26, 10:28, 10:40, 11:11, 11:14, 11:20–21.

surmise that these books were all composed by the same school and therefore reflect a relatively unified and consistent viewpoint. It is in these texts that the violent implications of divine election are taken to their extreme.

The rationale of the Deuteronomists for the destruction of the Canaanites is no less disturbing than the destruction itself. God commands the annihilation of the Canaanites not only to fulfill his promise to the Patriarchs, but also to ensure that the Israelites will not be seduced by the idolatrous practices of the Canaanites and lust after their gods once they are settled in the land.[34] The Canaanites are therefore to be destroyed even though they have not really done anything wrong—at least not yet. For sure, the Deuteronomic History, along with other strata in the biblical text, expresses disgust with Canaanite religious practices—most notably child sacrifice—which implies moral justification for the destruction of the Canaanites, but the Deuteronomic authors never suggest that Canaanite religion be wiped out in all places.[35] Their religion is a problem only in the land of Israel, and that is because it is a temptation for God's chosen people.

Moreover, what emerges here is an unflattering picture of God, who commands the destruction of an entire population simply because he is insecure—even paranoid, one might argue. He cannot bear Israel's abandoning him for other deities, and he is willing to command genocide to preempt any possibility of that happening. When we come to the book of Joshua, we witness the terrifying results of God's insecurity when the war against the Canaanites is carried out.

Scholars have done a great deal of work to give us a better understanding of the imperative to annihilate the Canaanites.[36] That imperative is related to a larger phenomenon that appears in the biblical text: the institution of *herem*. This term is often translated as "ban," but James Barr's rendering of it as

---

34 Deut. 7:2–4, 20:16–18. See also Ex. 33:11–16. Lev. 18 takes a somewhat different approach toward the Canaanites than that found in the Deuteronomic History. In this chapter, the land "vomits out" the Canaanites because their sexual practices have defiled it. Yet, God warns that the Israelites and the foreigners among them will meet the same fate if they do not observe the commandments. Thus, here the Canaanites are being thrown out of the land because of their actual sins, not because they pose a temptation for Israelites. The Israelites are therefore in just as much danger of being removed from the land as the Canaanites are. One may infer from this observation that this chapter is less problematic from a moral standpoint than the passages in the Deuteronomic History because a demarcation is being drawn not between Israelites and non-Israelites, but between those who adhere to God's laws and those who do not. However, there is little consolation in this line of reasoning. God is still violent toward those who displease him; the line between those who invite God's censure and those who do not has simply been redrawn. Kaminsky presents an extensive comparison between the P source, which underlies Leviticus, and the D source, which underlies the Deuteronomic History, regarding the question of divine election. See Kaminsky, *Yet I Loved Jacob*, 95–105.

35 Deut. 4:19, 29:25, 32:8–9; Judg. 11:24. Jeffrey H. Tigay, *The JPS Commentary on the Torah: Deuteronomy* (Philadelphia: Jewish Publication Society of America, 1996), 470–71. See also Kaminsky, *Yet I Loved Jacob*, 101.

36 See, for instance, Philip D. Stern, *The Biblical* Herem: *A Window on Israel's Religious Experience* (Atlanta: Scholars Press, 1991). Susan Niditch provides an excellent survey of modern scholarship on war in the Hebrew Bible in *War in the Hebrew Bible*, 5–10.

"consecration to destruction" better captures its meaning. *Herem* was a special type of warfare in which the mechanics of war had a distinctly religious character. The killing of enemies and their animals was an act of consecration in that the victims were viewed as gifts to God in gratitude for victory. Killing was therefore akin to performing a ritual sacrifice of thanksgiving. Inanimate objects were also included in this ritual; gold and silver captured in battle were consecrated by being donated to God. Preparation for this type of war was also religious in character. The Israelites sought advice regarding the impending battle from the *urim ve-tumim*, an oracle attached to the breastplate of the high priest. The Israelites' faith in God was also necessary for a successful outcome. There is evidence that the Israelites were not the only people in the ancient Near East to engage in this type of warfare; other nations practiced it as well.[37]

Susan Niditch argues that there are in fact two versions of the *herem* in the biblical text that are often combined: "the ban as God's portion or sacrifice" and "the ban as God's justice." The ban as God's portion or sacrifice is what we have just described. It tried to win God's favor by offering human booty to God. The ban as God's justice, however, tried to gain divine favor by the expurgation of abomination and subversive enemies, and the latter included both outsiders and elements within the Israelite population itself. Although in the ban as God's portion the enemy was recognized as human and worthy of divine sacrifice, in the ban as God's justice the enemy was demonized and dehumanized as a monster, something unclean. According to Niditch, it was this second version of the ban that was most influential on the thinking of the Deuteronomic writers.[38]

Yet, however one understands the conceptual background of the Canaanite conquest, one must confront the moral problem that in the biblical text God commands genocide. Until recently, scholars either ignored this difficulty altogether or justified the genocide by arguing that the Canaanites deserved to be killed because of their wickedness.[39] In the former category are such

---

37 Barr, 207–9; Gerd Lüdemann, *The Unholy in Holy Scripture*, trans. John Bowden (Louisville: Westminster/John Knox Press, 1997), 39; John J. Collins, "The Zeal of Phinehas: The Bible and the Legitimation of Violence," *Journal of Biblical Literature* 122, no. 1 (2000): 4–10. Gerhard von Rad did pioneering work on the subject of *herem* in his classic work, *Holy War in Ancient Israel*, trans. and ed. Marva J. Dawn (Grand Rapids, Mich.: William B. Eerdmans, 1991). The term "holy war" has often been used by scholars to describe the nature of warfare in the Bible. It was first used by Friedrich Schwally in his study *Der heilige Krieg im alten Israel* (Leipzig: Deiterich, 1901). Yet, as Ben C. Ollenburger notes in his introduction to von Rad's book, the Bible never actually uses that term. Moreover, Ollenburger wonders about the usefulness of the term: "Whether or not the term is appropriate to the Old Testament, or to ancient Israel, depends largely on how the referent is conceived" (5–6). Ollenburger also notes that, according to Rudolf Smend, the appropriate term for warfare in the Bible is "Yahweh War" (23), a designation that is picked up by several Biblical scholars.

38 Niditch, *War in the Hebrew Bible*, 28–55.

39 Collins, 9–10; Barr, 212, 214; Lüdemann, 47–48.

scholars as H. H. Rowley, who, in his book-length study of the biblical doctrine of Israel's election, makes no mention whatsoever of the Canaanite
conquest.[40] The latter perspective is expressed by William Foxwell Albright,
who said that "it often seems necessary that a people of a markedly inferior
type should vanish before a people of superior potentialities."[41] George
Ernst Wright comes to a similar conclusion claiming that "the Canaanite
civilization and religion was one of the weakest, most decadent, and most
immoral cultures of the civilized world at the time."[42] Yet, no historical evidence supports these claims. There is evidence that the Canaanites practiced
child sacrifice, the parade example for Canaanite depravity in the biblical
text, but this surely would not justify genocide. Moreover, as Barr points out,
genocide would be a peculiar way to overcome the problem of child sacrifice,
seeing as it would involve killing the very children whose sacrifice was
deemed an abomination.[43]

Some relief from the moral problem of the Canaanite genocide may perhaps be found in the fact that a consensus has emerged among scholars that
the Canaanite conquest as described in the biblical text is more fiction than
fact, a conclusion supported by both textual and archeological evidence. We
find passages in the book of Joshua indicating that the Israelites did not
eliminate the Canaanites. Rahab's family survives, as do the Gibeonites and
other groups.[44] Archeological findings also raise questions about the historicity of the genocide in that no evidence has been found to support it.
Scholars are divided over the means by which the Israelites settled in the
land of Canaan. Some claim that it occurred by gradual infiltration into

---

40 Harold H. Rowley, *The Biblical Doctrine of Election* (London: Lutterworth, 1950). This observation is
made in Cott, 204.

41 William Foxwell Albright, *From the Stone Age to Christianity: Monotheism and the Historical Process* (New
York: Doubleday, 1957), 280–81, cited in Collins, 9–10.

42 G. E. Wright and R. H. Fuller, eds., *The Book of Acts of God: Christian Scholarship Interprets the Bible*
(London: Duckworth, 1960), 109, also cited in Collins, 9–10. Bradley Shavit Artson also implies that the Canaanites were deserving of punishment in *Love Peace and Pursue Peace: A Jewish Response to War and Nuclear Annihilation* (New York: United Synagogue of America, 1988), 119–21. See also Harry M. Orlinsky, "The Situational
Ethics of Violence in the Biblical Period," in *Violence and Defense in the Jewish Experience*, ed. Salo W. Baron and
George S. Wise (Philadelphia: Jewish Publication Society of America, 1977), 38–62. Orlinsky's discussion is
remarkable for its lack of concern for the ethical problems that the Canaanite genocide presents. See especially
pp. 45–47.

43 Barr, 217. Levenson has argued that child sacrifice was part of the early Israelite religious heritage itself,
an observation which calls into question whether a sharp a contrast can be drawn between Israelite morality and
Canaanite depravity. See Jon D. Levenson, *The Death and Resurrection of the Beloved Son: The Transformation of
Child Sacrifice in Judaism and Christianity* (New Haven: Yale University Press, 1993). Niditch offers evidence that
a number of scholars have great difficulty associating the institution of *herem* with the concept of sacrifice and
the realm of the sacred because of their discomfort with the idea that God would want human sacrifice. See
Niditch, *War in the Hebrew Bible*, 40–42.

44 Josh. 2, 9, 13:1–7, 16:10, 17:12–13.

the Canaanite population, while others claim that it came about through a peasant revolt.[45]

We must then ask why those who authored the story of the Canaanite conquest would create such a fiction. A majority of scholars think it served a political function. According to this theory, the Deuteronomic Hstory was produced in the seventh century BCE in the kingdom of Judah during the reign of King Josiah. This period was one of great insecurity and turmoil for the small kingdom because the Assyrian Empire had just destroyed the northern Israelite kingdom and was now threatening Judah as well. Moreover, Assyrian idolatrous practices were infiltrating Judah. Josiah responded to these challenges by strengthening his people's national identity through a series of reforms that centralized worship at the Temple in Jerusalem and banned the worship of other gods. The Deuteronomic historians supported these initiatives by composing a fictional account of the conquest of Canaan in which God commanded the slaughter of the Canaanite idol worshippers and prohibited the Israelites from adopting their practices, threatening them with grave punishment if they did. This narrative was designed to convince the Judahites that the war against idolatry was basic to their national self-understanding.[46]

Yet, if comfort may be found in the fact that the Canaanite genocide never happened, it does not really solve the moral difficulties of the story. The biblical text is still reprehensible for depicting genocide as a good thing; after all, it is commanded by God and carried out at his behest. As Barr argues, the key point is that even if the slaughter of the Canaanites is fictional, it is still "commended."[47]

Even more important, many believing Jews and Christians throughout the ages have believed, and still believe, that the Canaanite genocide *did* happen, and some of them have used this event as inspiration for violence against their enemies. In the Middle Ages, European Christians justified their battles against the Muslims by referring to war narratives in the Bible, including the Canaanite conquest. Centuries later, English Puritans found inspiration for their revolution against the monarchy in similar sources. In the same period, Cromwell identified his Irish Catholic enemies explicitly as Canaanites. Later on, Puritan colonists in New England spoke of their Native American enemies as Canaanites or Amalekites. Similar rhetoric persists down to the present. G. E. Wright reportedly reacted to those opposing the Vietnam War with the statement

---

45 See Lori Rowlett, *Joshua and the Rhetoric of Violence: A New Historicist Analysis* (Sheffield: Sheffield Academic Press, 1996); Kaminsky, *Yet I Loved Jacob*, 113–14; Rodd, 186. The first theory of Israelite settlement is supported by Albrecht Alt and Martin Noth; the second, by George E. Mendenhall and Norman K. Gottwald.

46 Rowlett, 12–13; Collins, 10–11; Kaminsky, *Yet I Loved Jacob*, 114.

47 Barr, 201–10. See also Cott, 202; Schwartz, The Curse of Cain, 61–62; Lüdemann, 44, all of whom agree with this assessment.

"Yahweh was no pacifist, nor am I." Right-wing religious Zionists have often justified violence against Palestinians by identifying them with Canaanites or Amalekites, a phenomenon we will discuss more extensively in a later chapter.[48]

The other call to genocide in the biblical text is that issued against the Amalekites. The Israelites upon leaving Egypt are attacked by them, and though the Israelites achieve victory with divine assistance, God declares perpetual war against Amalek until they are annihilated.[49] According to the biblical record, the Amalekites remained the enemies of the Israelites at least until the time of David. Even in post-exilic times, the specter of Amalek appears to persist in the person of Haman the Agagite, who is presumably descended from Agag, the Amalekite king whose death is described in I Samuel.[50] Joel Kaminsky, in his otherwise sympathetic study of the doctrine of Israel's election, believes that the imperative of genocide against the Amalekites presents moral problems even graver than those encountered in the case of the Canaanites. Israel was commanded to kill only those Canaanites who lived within the borders of Israel; with the Amalekites, though, borders were no barrier to the command to kill—the entire nation of Amalek was to be eliminated no matter where its people resided. Kaminsky concludes that sadly, the biblical attitude toward Amalek bears some resemblance to Nazi racial policies enacted against the Jews themselves centuries later.[51] Furthermore, we must note that the moral danger in the biblical text has been borne out in history. We saw earlier that throughout the centuries, it was not uncommon for Christians and Jews to view their enemies as Canaanites and Amalekites. To this we can add other examples in which the analogy with the Amalekites was preferred. Thus, for instance, William Gouge, the seventeenth-century English Calvinist used texts about Amalek to justify war against the Catholics. Cotton Mather drew on the image of Amalek in his diatribes against Native American Indians.[52] And

---

48 Roland Bainton, *Christian Attitudes towards War and Peace: A Historical Survey and Critical Re-evaluation* (Nashville: Abingdon Press, 1960), 148–49; Conrad Cherry, *God's New Israel: Interpretations of American Destiny* (Englewood Cliffs, N.J.: Prentice Hall, 1971), 11–12; Collins 13–14; Schwartz, *The Curse of Cain*, 122. Wright's statement is cited in Paul D. Hanson, "War and Peace in the Hebrew Bible," *Interpretation* 38 (1984): 341. Criticism of violence in the biblical text is sometimes expressed through an identification with the plight of the Canaanites. Robert Allen Warrior reacts to the biblical text in this manner. As an Osage Indian, he finds much common ground with the Canaanites in his article "Canaanites, Cowboys, and Indians: Deliverance, Conquest, and Liberation Theology Today," *Christianity and Crisis* 49 (1989): 261–66. This article has been repeatedly reprinted and is, according to Moberly, something of a modern classic (Moberly, "Is Monotheism Bad for You?," 97 n. 4). A position similar to that of Warrior is supported by Edward Said, a Palestinian author, who also reacts to Israeli violence against his people by identifying with the Canaanites. See Said, "Michael Walzer's *Exodus and Revolution*: A Canaanite Reading," *Grand Street* 5 (Winter 1986): 86–106.

49 Ex. 17:8–16; Deut. 25:17–19; I Sam. 15.

50 Esther 3:1; I Sam. 15.

51 Kaminsky, *Yet I Loved Jacob*, 115.

52 Bainton, 165–72; Kaminsky, *Yet I Loved Jacob*, 114.

Martin Luther and his student Johannes Brenz even identified Amalek with the Jews![53]

Our critique of biblical texts that encourage violence against outsiders would not be complete without making note of other war traditions in the Bible. These traditions are often not discussed by scholars of biblical ethics—perhaps because these traditions are frequently concerned with internal wars, most notably those between the northern Israelite kingdom and the southern kingdom of Judah, and therefore do not raise the same troubling questions as traditions that depict violence against outsiders. Furthermore, missing from such traditions is any genocidal drive of the kind we see with the Canaanites and Amalekites. Nonetheless, some of these alternative traditions are, in fact, about wars against other nations, and at times their brutality rivals that of the narratives involving the Canaanites and Amalekites.

Much insight on war traditions other than those involving the Canaanites and Amalekites can be found in the work of Susan Niditch, who has gone far beyond the well-trodden emphasis on the *herem* texts and has done pioneering work isolating and describing several strands of war traditions in the Bible. For instance, she identifies what she calls the bardic tradition, which appears in a number of biblical passages. This tradition glorifies war and heroic warriors. Here war is treated like a sport in which there are rules of fair play. For example, in these texts it is common to find the view that men should engage in battle who have similar experience and skill in warfare so as to ensure an equitable contest. Niditch believes that this tradition is an aristocratic one and may have its origin in the royal courts of Judah.[54] Another tradition, much more disturbing from an ethical standpoint, is what Niditch refers to as the ideology of expediency. This strand endorses naked aggression and conquest, often with God's blessing. It assumes that once a war is won, anything can be done to subjugate the enemy. War is treated here as a normal activity and reflects life in the ancient Near East.[55]

Cyril Rodd provides observations that help round out the cruel picture of war and its place in the Bible. Rodd notes that wars are everywhere in the biblical text and that only the book of Ruth and the Song of Songs are free from

---

53 Elliot Horowitz, "From the Generation of Moses to the Generation of the Messiah: The Jews Confront 'Amalek' and His Incarnations" (in Hebrew), *Zion* 65 (1999): 429.

54 Niditch, *War in the Hebrew Bible*, 90–105. Some of the passages Niditch examines are I Sam.17, which contains the story of David and Goliath, and II Sam. 2:12–16, which describes a battle between David and Saul's men.

55 Niditch, *War in the Hebrew Bible*, 123–32. Examples of this tradition are found in Judg. 18, where the Danites wage war against the Laishians; II Sam. 5:7–8, in which David treats the defeated Jebusites with great cruelty; and II Sam. 5:7–8, in which King Amaziah displays similar cruelty toward captives captured in his battle with Seir.

battles.[56] Most significant is that even in the Prophets, there is generally support for war.[57]

This last point needs to be expanded upon given that scholars and theologians, both Jewish and Christian, often view the Prophets as beacons for a universalistic and peace-loving ethic. Indeed, there are passages that can easily lead to this assessment, such as the moving eschatological visions in Isaiah 2 and Micah 4 that describe the nations of the world streaming to the Temple in Jerusalem to worship God and beating their instruments of war into gardening tools.[58] Yet, what these interpreters overlook is the eschatological passages in the Prophets that depict the end of days as a time when some of the nations of the world will be humiliated or destroyed. Second and Third Isaiah furnish the most vivid examples. In another instance, the messianic prophecy in Isaiah 49:23, the non-Israelites will serve the Israelites:

> Kings shall tend your children,
> Their queens shall serve you as nurses.
> They shall bow to you, face to the ground,
> And lick the dust of your feet.

Even worse are passages that predict violence against the gentile nations during the messianic era. In Isaiah 63:2–5, God is depicted as a blood-spattered warrior who wreaks vengeance on the nations that have not recognized him:

> Why is your clothing so red,
> Your garments like his who treads grapes?
> "I trod out a vintage alone;
> Of the peoples no man was with Me.
> I trod them down in My anger,
> Trampled them in My rage;
> Their life-blood bespattered My garments,
> And all my clothing was stained.
> For I had planned a day of vengeance,
> And My year of redemption arrived.
> Then I looked, but there was none to help;
> I stared, but there was none to aid—
> So My own arm wrought triumph,

---

56 Rodd, 185–86. Rodd notes that even the Song of Songs is not entirely bereft of associations with war because in some passages the female lover is described with military imagery.

57 Rodd, 190–91.

58 Is. 2:1–4; Mic. 4:1–5. See also Is. 19:16–25.

And My own rage was My aid.
I trampled peoples in My anger,
I made them drunk with My rage,
And I hurled their glory to the ground."

In light of these observations, some scholars have argued that in the Prophets the particularistic elements are no less prominent than the universalistic ones.[59] Other scholars have used the same observations to question whether there is any moral distinction between particularism and universalism that is so often discussed in biblical theology. The passages just cited suggest that the universalism of the biblical text seems no more benevolent than its particularism.[60] One could even argue that this universalism is even more pernicious than particularism. A particularism in which Israel focuses only on itself is perhaps less intolerant than a universalism dictating what the nations should do and believe.

A pair of sources in the biblical text that should also be mentioned are the passages in the books of Ezra and Nehemiah in which Ezra orders Jews who have just returned from the Babylonian exile to divorce their non-Jewish spouses.[61] These sources are frequently cited by critics of the Bible as examples of the perniciousness of the biblical doctrine of Israel's election. Here, the chosenness of Israel does not result in actual physical injury, but it may be argued that the forced breakup of marriages between Jews and non-Jews is not much better. This action could easily be classified as structural and psychological violence.[62] At the very least, one could argue that such strictures emanated from the very same chauvinism that lay at the root of Israel's violence against foreigners. Gerd Lüdemann notes the cruel irony that in later history Jews themselves would become victims of the very sorts of actions endorsed by Ezra and Nehemiah. In medieval Christendom Jews were forbidden to marry non-Jews. That policy would also be enacted in Nazi Germany.[63]

An issue generally not raised by ethicists who criticize biblical violence involves the role God plays in perpetrating violent action. The biblical text generally presumes that God is the source of all good and that the Israelites are therefore supposed to emulate his actions. A passage often quoted to support

59 Cott, 208; Mark G. Brett, "Nationalism and the Hebrew Bible," in The Bible in Ethics, ed. John W. Rogerson, Margaret Davies, and M. Daniel Caroll R. (Sheffield: Sheffield Academic Press, 1995), 151–57; Collins, 15–16; Kaminsky, Yet I Loved Jacob, 146–52.

60 Niditch, War in the Hebrew Bible, 134–36; Rodd, 196–97; Kaminsky, Yet I Loved Jacob, 144–45.

61 Ezra 9–10; Neh. 13.

62 See chapter 1.

63 Lüdemann, 74–75.

this idea is Leviticus 19:2, in which God commands the Israelites, "Be holy for I the Lord your God am holy." Many scholars regard the doctrine of imitation of God as central to biblical ethics, and many Jewish ethicists see it as central in Jewish ethics in general.[64] What concerns us here is the implications of this imperative in light of the fact that the biblical text describes God as a warrior. That depiction appears in a number of places. Perhaps the most frequently cited passage is Moses's description of God as a "man of war" in the Song at the Sea.[65] If the Israelites should imitate God, does it mean that they should take initiative and act violently toward God's enemies even in the absence of an explicit divine command? At issue here is the distinction between what scholars of ethics refer to as divine-command ethics and virtue ethics. Not only does God command the Israelites to commit specific acts of violence against foreigners, but his character is at times angry and violent, and given that the Israelites are supposed to imitate him, it would seem that they too would be expected—or at least permitted—to act violently against God's enemies when they see fit. Put another way, God does not determine human action just by issuing commands; he himself is a model for human actions, and presumably this includes violent ones as well.

One would not have much concern for this speculation were it not for the fact that there is indeed one well-known incident in the biblical text in which the logic of this surmise is played out. In Numbers 25, Phinehas slays Zimri and his foreign Midianite companion, Cozbi, as the two disappear into a tent with the apparent intention of consummating their relationship.[66] Phinehas is at no point commanded by God to take such action, but he is nonetheless

---

64 Martin Buber seems to have been the first modern Jewish thinker to focus on this theme in his essay "Imitation of God," in *Israel and the World: Essays in a Time of Crisis* (Syracuse: Syracuse University Press, 1997), 66–77. See also Baruch Levine, *The JPS Commentary on the Torah: Leviticus* (Philadelphia: Jewish Publication Society of America, 1989), 256. The centrality of *imitatio Dei* in Judaism in general is discussed in David S. Shapiro, "The Doctrine of the Image of God and *Imitatio Dei*," in *Contemporary Jewish Ethics*, ed. Menachem Kellner (New York: HPC Press, 1978), 127–51. Its importance in Jewish ethics is underscored by Louis E. Newman, *Past Imperatives: Studies in the History and Theory of Jewish Ethics* (Albany: State University of New York Press, 1998), 55–56. Non-Jewish scholars have been particularly interested in this issue. John Barton has written a great deal about it. See, for instance, Barton, "Understanding Old Testament Ethics," *Journal for the Study of the Old Testament* 9 (1978): 44–64; idem, "The Basis of Ethics"; Bruce C. Birch, "Moral Agency, Community, and the Character of God in the Hebrew Bible," *Semeia* 66 (1994): 31–33. Birch mentions several studies that further examine this concept: Paul D. Hanson, *The People Called God: The Growth of Community in the Bible* (San Francisco: Harper & Row, 1986); Bruce C. Birch, *Let Justice Roll Down: The Old Testament, Ethics, and the Christian Life* (Louisville: Westminster/John Knox Press, 1991); Walter C. Kaiser Jr., *Toward Old Testament Ethics* (Grand Rapids, Mich.: Academie Books, Zondervan, 1983).

65 Ex. 15:3. Other passages in which God is described as a warrior can be found in Deut. 32:41–42, Ps. 24, Is. 34:6. Rodd, 188–89, contends that the meaning of the frequent references to God as "Yahweh of hosts" and "Yahweh, God of hosts" also refer to Yahweh as a warrior because "hosts" (*tseva'ot*) refers to armies.

66 Num. 25:6–18.

rewarded by God with "a pact of priesthood for all time" because "he took impassioned action for his God."[67] This passage, it would seem, encourages human beings to take violent initiative on God's behalf when it is needed. And once again, this incident has had historical consequences in subsequent centuries. John Collins notes that in I Maccabees, Mattathias uses Phinehas's zeal as a model for his own violent actions against the Greeks. Phinehas also becomes a model for the zealots who fought against Rome in the first century CE and whom the rabbis blamed for the destruction of Jerusalem.[68] Yet, the rabbis themselves also emulated Phinehas. The Mishnah contains a ruling advocating that one should kill a Jewish man having sexual relations with a non-Jewish woman, and in the Gemara we are told that this ruling is modeled on Phinehas's actions. This ruling is unusual given that in all other instances, rabbinic law implements capital punishment only after due process, and even then only rarely.[69]

In sum, it can be argued that the Bible promotes violence. The key problem is God's covenantal relationship with the Israelites, which implies that the Israelites are superior to other nations. The moral difficulty with this idea comes out in full force in God's determination to annihilate the Canaanites and Amalekites. A central component of God's covenant with the Israelites is his promise that they will inherit the land of Israel, and therefore the Canaanites who reside there must be destroyed so that their idolatrous ways are not a snare to the Israelites. The lives of non-Israelites, it would seem, are of no consequence if they stand in the way of God's plan for the Israelites. The case of the Amalekites presents an even greater moral problem. In this instance, Israel's enemies are slated for destruction for all time. Other parts of the biblical text also seem to approve of violence and war against other nations. Even the books of the Prophets, which are normally seen as encouraging a peaceful ethic, contain texts in this category. Furthermore, there are a number of places in the Bible in which God himself is depicted as a warrior, and if the Israelites are expected to imitate God, then waging war is not only acceptable for achieving practical aims—it also becomes a means by which the Israelites can commune with God. It would seem, therefore, that in a number of respects the Bible encourages its adherents to act violently against outsiders. It is precisely that lesson that Christians gleaned from the biblical text in medieval and early modern Europe when they persecuted Jews and heretics and waged war against the Islamic Empire.

---

67 Num. 25:13.
68 Collins, 12–13.
69 Mishnah, *Sanhehdrin* 9:6, *Makkot* 1; Maimonides, *Mishneh Torah, Issurey Bi'ah* 12:4–5.

The Bible Promotes Peace

Let us now switch gears and look at the Bible from a different perspective. In this second reading, I will argue that the Bible is not the violent text that the first reading has made it out to be. The vast majority of non-Israelites are not the object of exclusion or scorn, much less genocide. Foreigners, both as individuals and as nations, have a complex and often positive relationship with the Israelites and their God.[70] Moreover, a close examination of the texts in the Bible that deal with the Canaanites and Amalekites will show that they are not nearly as troubling as the first reading suggests. I will also argue in this reading that in many respects, the Bible in fact promotes peace between Israelites and non-Israelites.

We will begin with the overall place of non-Israelites in the biblical narrative. According to the first reading, the Bible opens on a universalistic note with the notion that human beings are created in God's image, but it soon becomes clear that the real concern of the biblical narrative is the Patriarchs and their descendants, the Israelites, who become God's chosen people and remain the focus of the rest of the biblical history. Universalism therefore yields to particularism. However, another interpretation is possible that preserves the initial universalistic thrust of the biblical narrative. Beginnings of texts are always important in setting the tone for what follows. Thus, the very fact that the first chapter of the Bible places all human beings in an exalted relationship with God should be taken as normative for the biblical text as a whole, even after the narrative begins to focus on the Patriarchs and Israelites. The notion that human beings are created in the image of God is therefore the lens through which God's relationship to humanity must be viewed. A similar observation can be made with regard to Genesis 9:6, when we are told once again that human beings are created in God's image. In this instance, that idea is uttered in connection with a covenant God establishes with Noah promising that the world will never again be destroyed.[71] Here, too, it could be argued that the significance of this passage extends well beyond the immediate context. The covenant defines God's relationship to humanity as a whole. As Jon Levenson puts it, "Underlying this covenant is a theology that places all peoples in a relationship of grace and accountability with God," and therefore all later covenants with Abraham's descendants "have to be read against this background."[72]

---

70 Here I follow Kaminsky, who claims that those who criticize violence in the biblical text often confuse the "anti-elect" (Canaanites and Amalekites who are slated for destruction) with the "non-elect" (all other non-Israelites, who have a more positive relationship with the Israelites). See Kaminsky, *Yet I Loved Jacob*, 109.

71 Gen. 9:8–16.

72 Levenson, "The Universal Horizon," 147. A similar understanding of the primeval history is taken by Friedman, 3.

The exaltedness of humanity also seems to come out in the primeval history, the first chapters in Genesis before Abraham is chosen, in that the biblical narrative assumes an innate moral and religious sensibility in all human beings. Thus, for instance, God punishes Cain for Abel's murder and Noah's generation for its wickedness. The Bible therefore assumes that human beings have a natural capacity to discern right from wrong on their own, because otherwise divine punishment would be wholly unjust.[73] Therefore, one does not have to be in the line of Abraham or receive commandments from God to be held responsible for one's actions. The innate morality of human beings also comes across in the subsequent narratives regarding the Patriarchs. In Genesis 18 Abraham argues with God regarding the destruction of Sodom and Gomorrah.[74] When Abraham confronts God with the question, "Shall not the Judge of all the earth deal justly?," it would seem that Abraham is challenging God by referring to a standard of morality innate to him, not one revealed by God.[75] The same point seems to come out in other passages in Genesis both in the primeval history and in the Patriarchal narratives when we are informed that individuals unrelated to the line of Abraham possess *yir'at elohim* or *yir'at YHWH* (fear of God, or fear of the Lord), qualities that do not come from knowledge gained through divine revelation.[76] Some scholars, such as David Novak, have even gone so far as to argue that such passages are proof that embedded in the biblical text is a conception of natural law. A number of scholars have also located a theory of natural law in a much later stratum in the biblical text known as Wisdom literature, which includes such works as Proverbs, Job, and Ecclesiastes. In this body of literature, the Bible assumes an ethics that, it would seem, was commonly accepted across the ancient world, not one based on revealed law.[77] Whether the idea of natural law is appropriate

---

73 Novak, *Natural Law in Judaism* (Cambridge: Cambidge University Press, 1998) chapter 2. Novak is not technically in the field of biblical studies, and he approaches the Bible from the perspective of a traditional Jew (Novak, *Natural Law in Judaism*, 30). Nonetheless, I include his insights here because they are very relevant to this discussion. A similar position is taken by another scholar of Jewish ethics, Louis E. Newman. See his study *An Introduction to Jewish Ethics* (Upper Saddle River, N.J.: Pearson/Prentice-Hall, 2005), 40–41.

74 Gen. 18:22–33.

75 Gen. 18:25; John W. Rogerson, "Discourse Ethics and Biblical Ethics," in *The Bible in Ethics*, ed. John W. Rogerson, Margaret Davies, and M. Daniel Caroll R. (Sheffield: Sheffield Academic Press, 1995), 22; David Novak, *Natural Law in Judaism*, 39–47; Rodd, 54.

76 Levenson, "The Universal Horizon," 149; Greenberg, "Mankind, Israel and the Nations," 374. Moshe Greenberg also notes that God speaks directly to several individuals in the primeval history, and this reinforces the point that one does not have to be an Israelite to merit a special relationship with him. Adam, Cain, and Noah, for example, are all addressed by God. The biblical text reports that Enoch, too, is beloved by God. See Greenberg, "Mankind, Israel, and the Nations," 372.

77 John Barton, *Ethics and the Old Testament* (Harrisburg, Pa.: Trinity Press International, 1998), 65–68; idem, "The Basis of Ethics," 15–17; Rodd, 52–64.

here might be disputed.[78] Nonetheless, the first chapters of Genesis seem to assume that human beings have an innate moral capacity.

The effect of these observations is that the gap between the Israelites and the rest of humanity is not as significant as critics of the Bible often imagine. One does not have to be a member of God's chosen people to have a meaningful relationship with him. God expects that all people will adhere to basic principles of morality.

Nor does the choice of Abraham and his line necessarily imply that the status of humanity has been diminished in God's eyes. In fact, one can argue that Abraham is chosen because of God's *concern* for humanity. When God selects Abraham, it is not because he has no more interest in the rest of humanity. God's ultimate wish is that Abraham and his progeny will in some way or other provide the means for other nations of the world to share in his blessing so that they will someday be reunited with him. According to our first reading, God's summons to Abraham in Genesis 12:3 was exclusivist. When God informs Abraham that "all the families of the earth shall bless themselves by you," he is telling him that the nations will want the same sort of blessing that Abraham and his descendants receive, but they may not actually share in that blessing. However, one could also claim that the implication here is that in being able to appreciate God's blessing to Abraham and his descendants, non-Israelites will want to emulate them and draw close to God as well. Therefore, non-Israelites are not entirely cut off from God's beneficence. Furthermore, we should not dismiss the alternative translation mentioned in our first reading, in which God promises to Abraham that "all the families of the earth *shall be blessed through you*" (my emphasis). According to this rendering, Abraham in some fashion mediates blessings to the other nations, and therefore God continues to have a positive relationship with all humanity. A similar idea seems to come through in Exodus 19:6 when God informs the Israelites just before the revelation at Sinai that they are to become a "kingdom of priests and a holy nation." As Nahum Sarna points out, the notion of priesthood implies separation from the other nations, but also service to them. Across cultures, priests commonly take on that dual role.[79]

Scholars who support this understanding of God's relationship to the nations of the world in the biblical text have made a number of suggestions about how Israel will bring blessings to others. Nahum Sarna intimates that

---

78 For instance, Rodd, 59–64, rejects some of the sources Barton cites as proof of natural law in the biblical text.

79 Nahum M. Sarna, *Exploring Exodus: The Heritage of Biblical Israel* (New York: Schocken Books, 1987), 131; idem, *The JPS Commentary on the Torah: Exodus* (Philadelphia: Jewish Publication Society of America, 1991), 104; Friedman, 231–32.

Israel's mere presence among the nations will result in those nations' being blessed.[80] Paul Williamson suggests that the nations will receive blessings through Israel, but only if they are on good terms with Abraham and his descendants and do not disdain them.[81] Another possibility, suggested by Moshe Greenberg, is that if Israel obeys God's will, it will be rewarded with prosperity and peace, and the reports of God's rewards will spread to all the nations until they realize that he is indeed the one God. The nations will therefore be blessed by drawing close to God. Greenberg marshals a number of biblical sources to back up his reading that show the impact that God's actions have on non-Israelites, both as individuals and as nations. For instance, in Exodus the biblical text tells us that the plagues in Egypt and the parting of the Sea of Reeds (or the Red Sea) were meant to bring the Egyptians to a recognition of God.[82] Kaminsky entertains yet another approach to the whole matter by arguing that all nations will be blessed through Israel because Israel will serve in a mediating role between God and the nations. This interpretation is borne out by a careful reading of Genesis 18, in which Abraham functions in precisely that role when he pleads with God on behalf of Sodom and Gomorrah. In the course of that exchange, the text explicitly invokes the notion that all the nations will be blessed through Abraham.[83] What is most important for our concerns is that uniting these interpretations is the notion that God continues to care about the nations of the world and their well-being despite his unconditional love for Israel, and that Israel in some fashion helps them share in God's blessing.

We should also keep in mind that in the various narratives in Genesis involving sibling rivalries, the nonchosen person and his descendants are not

---

80 Sarna, *The JPS Commentary on the Torah: Genesis*, 89. According to Sarna, it is for this reason that in the opening verse of Genesis 12 Abraham's blessings proceed in three stages: "a blessing on Abram personally, a blessing (or curse) on those with whom he interacts, a blessing on the entire human race." Moberly notes that Umberto Cassutto and Benno Jacob entertained similar readings of this passage. See Moberly, *The Bible, Theology, and Faith*, 125.

81 Williamson, 220–34, especially 233. Williamson bases his interpretation on the following translation of Gen. 12:3: "Be a blessing, so that I may bless those blessing you and curse whoever despises you and so that through you all the families of the ground may experience blessing." In this translation the blessing that the nations receive is contingent upon their "blessing" Abraham and his descendants, which Williamson believes has to be understood in terms of the actions, not the words, of the nations toward the Israelites.

82 Greenberg, "A Problematic Heritage," 25–26, "Mankind, Israel, and the Nations," 376; Ex. 7:5, 7:17, 14:4. Greenberg points out that the events in Egypt also cause Jethro to recognize that God is sovereign (Ex. 18:11). They have the same effect on Rahab (Josh. 2:11). Greenberg refers as well to the example of Naaman the Aramean, who acknowledges God's sovereignty when he is cured of leprosy (II Kings 5:15). Israel's role in providing inspiration for the gentile nations to recognize God is also alluded to in a statement by King Solomon, who asks God to answer the prayers of gentiles so that they will know that he is God (I Kings 8:43). Greenberg also refers to Deut. 4:6, which predicts that the nations of the world will be impressed by the wisdom of Israel's laws, not just God's power.

83 Kaminsky, *Yet I Loved Jacob*, 82–83. Kaminsky, however, also notes the lack of clarity in Gen. 12:3 and supports the translation used in the first reading.

excluded from divine favor. Thus, for example, Ishmael and his progeny receive blessings despite the fact that Isaac is chosen.[84] The same goes for Esau and his descendants; they are blessed even though Jacob is chosen.[85] Admittedly, the nonchosen siblings receive divine favor only because they are descendants of Abraham, for whom blessing has been vouchsafed. Nonetheless, these observations show that the distinction between Israel and the other nations is not a sharp one.

One should also not exaggerate Israel's advantage in receiving God's unconditional love. It must not be forgotten that Israel will not experience well-being if it does not fulfill God's commandments. Passages later on in the Torah spell out in chilling detail the punishments Israel will receive if it does not obey his will. In fact, God twice threatens to annihilate the people of Israel, once after the sin of the golden calf and again after the sin involving the spies.[86] Moreover, in Deuteronomy we find legislation in which God commands the complete destruction of cities within Israel that have turned to idolatry.[87] Thus, even though God's unconditional love is reserved for Israel, Israel must be virtuous and expend considerable effort to get the full benefit of that love. As Levenson points out, the Bible assumes a duality in the conception of Israel's election. The specialness of Israel is "neither altogether self-sufficient, nor altogether instrumental." When Israel thinks its election is self-sufficient, it is reminded by God that its election brings accountability and that its people will be punished for their sins.[88] When Israel thinks its election is based on service to God and humanity, the Israelites are reminded that the covenant will never be rescinded whatever punishments God metes out to them.[89]

---

84 Gen. 21:13, 21:18.

85 Gen. 27:39–40. Frank Crüsemann, "Human Solidarity and Ethnic Identity: Israel's Self-Definition in the Genealogical System of Genesis," in *Ethnicity and the Bible*, ed. Mark G. Brett (Leiden: E. J. Brill, 1996), 65–68, 73–76; Kaminsky, *Yet I Loved Jacob*, 41. Elsewhere, Kaminsky points out that the category of the non-elect also has gradations within it, with some nations being more favored than others. Thus, for instance, in Deut. 23:3–8, the Moabites and Ammonites are treated differently from the Edomites and Egyptians. See Joel S. Kaminsky, "The Concept of Election and Second Isaiah: Recent Literature," *Biblical Theology Bulletin* 31 (2001): 138.

86 Ex. 32:14–15; Num. 14:11–20.

87 Deut. 13:13–18. Eliezer Schweid argues that these examples have the effect of leveling the difference between Israel and the Canaanite nations since the Israelites are threatened with destruction no less than the Canaanites. See Schweid, "The Annihilation of Amalek and Eradication of the Amorite" (in Hebrew), *Moznayim* 33 (1971): 201–9. However, Schweid overlooks the fact that God never threatens the Israelites with total annihilation. In both instances cited here, God promises Moses that he will rebuild the Israelite nation from his progeny. Still, the threat of killing all Israelites up to the last man is quite striking and points up the importance of Israel's virtues and deeds in being God's chosen people.

88 E.g., Amos 3:2, 9:7, to be discussed later.

89 Kaminsky also criticizes those scholars who understand the Prophets as supporting an exclusively instrumentalist view of Israel's election. These scholars are influenced by Christian supersessionism, according to which Israel's election is contingent on service; they failed in that service and have therefore forfeited their elected status. See Kaminsky, *Yet I Loved Jacob*, 152–53.

In the first reading, it was noted that the Prophets are commonly viewed as the most universalistic texts in the Bible but that this viewpoint is inaccurate. In these books, there is no lack of particularistic texts. Furthermore, when the Prophets describe the messianic period, they often depict it as an era during which the non-Israelite nations who have not recognized God will be humiliated or destroyed. Yet, even if we accept these observations, there is no denying that the books of the Prophets also contain universalistic texts that are among the most moving passages in all of religious literature. The most well-known passages describe the messianic period as an idyllic era in which the gentile nations will acknowledge God's sovereignty, humanity will be unified, and universal peace will reign. In effect, the messianic age recreates the original Eden and thus brings the biblical history full circle.[90] The most famous passage describing this state of affairs is in Isaiah 2:2–4 and repeated in Micah 4:1–3:

> 2 In the days to come,
> The Mount of the LORD's House
> Shall stand firm above the mountains
> And tower above the hills;
> And all nations shall gaze on it with joy.
> 3 And the many peoples shall go and say:
> "Come,
> Let us go up to the Mount of the LORD,
> To the House of the God of Jacob;
> That He may instruct us in His ways,
> And that we may walk in His paths."
> For instruction shall come forth from Zion,
> The word of the LORD from Jerusalem.
> 4 Thus, He will judge among the nations
> And arbitrate for the many peoples,
> And they shall beat their swords into plowshares
> And their spears into pruning hooks;
> Nation shall not take up

---

90 Greenberg, "Mankind, Israel, and the Nations," 388–90; Levenson, "The Universal Horizon," 164–65; Niditch, *War in the Hebrew Bible*, 134. Levenson claims that the state of affairs described in prophetic eschatology should be seen as a restoration of the situation in the primeval history in Genesis, not just Eden. That is true only in part. Surely, the wickedness of Noah's generation and the rebellion against God seen in the construction of the Tower of Babel are evidence that the recognition of God and universal peace do not characterize the entirety of the primeval history. Christian scholars, such as Harold H. Rowley and Walter Kaiser, tend to distort the meaning of the eschatological passages in the Prophets by claiming that they contain the idea that Israel's mission is to bring God's Word to the gentiles. The passages in question generally do not support this reading. For a discussion of this issue, see Kaminsky, *Yet I Loved Jacob*, 147.

>Sword against nation;
>They shall never again know war.

Even scholars who criticize the biblical doctrine of election are often stirred by this text. Thus, Jeremy Cott, who was cited earlier as a critic of the biblical doctrine of election, views this passage favorably. Cott notes that what is exalted here is God, not Israel (verses 2–3), and this has the effect of reducing the discrepancy between Israel's status and that of the gentile nations. Also, the nations do not merge with Israel; they maintain their separate identities. They visit the Temple but presumably return to their homelands. Weapons of war are converted into tools of agriculture only after the nations return to their homelands (verses 3–4), which means once again that the gentile nations are allowed to maintain their respective identities. Furthermore, peace comes from the "knowledge of God," not divine command. The nations come to God through internal compulsion, not from directives imposed on them.[91]

Another passage frequently cited to illustrate the universalism of the eschatological visions in the Prophets is Isaiah 19:16–25, a remarkable text in which the prophet predicts that in the end of days, Egypt and Assyria will worship God in their own lands and will receive God's blessing.

>In that day, there shall be a highway from Egypt to Assyria. The Assyrians shall join with the Egyptians and Egyptians with the Assyrians, and then the Egyptians together with the Assyrians shall serve [the LORD]. In that day, Israel shall be a third partner with Egypt and Assyria as a blessing on earth for the LORD of Hosts will bless them, saying, "Blessed be My people in Egypt, My handiwork Assyria, and My very own Israel."[92]

We must also take note of two intriguing passages in Amos frequently cited by scholars of the biblical text who see in it a universalistic message. In the first two chapters of this book, the prophet rails not only against Israel's neighboring nations who wage war on it; in an unusual move, he also criticizes those nations for waging war on each other! In particular, Amos condemns violence between Moab and Edom. This statement is all the more remarkable given that Edom is one of Israel's enemies. This passage therefore indicates that God is the God of all peoples, not just Israel.[93]

---

91 Cott, 207–8. Cyril Rodd, another scholar who often criticizes the biblical text for its violence and intolerance, is also impressed by this passage. See Rodd, 193–95.

92 See also Zech. 8:20–23.

93 Amos 2:1–3.

Later on in the book of Amos, the prophet makes another unusual statement in comparing the exodus of Israel from Egypt to saving acts which God
has performed for other nations:

> To Me, O Israelites, you are
> Just like Ethiopians—declares the LORD.
> True, I brought Israel up
> From the land of Egypt,
> But also the Philistines from Caphtor
> and the Arameans from Kir.[94]

Apparently, Israel is not unique in having been aided by God in its time of
need. Once again, God is the God of all nations, not just Israel.[95]

Other texts have also been cited by scholars and theologians to highlight the
universalism of the Prophets. In several passages, we find the notion that Israel
is expected to bring the gentile nations close to God by serving as witnesses to
his uniqueness and eternality.[96] Another text in the Prophets that is often cited
to support this idea is Isaiah's statement that Israel is to serve as "a light unto
the nations."[97] However, there is much disagreement regarding the meaning of
this phrase. It may refer to a faithful remnant of the Israelites who are meant to
inspire the Judean exiles to come home to Zion. Or it may allude to the idea that
the gentiles will be awed or dazzled by God's relationship with the Israelites. In
neither of these interpretations do the gentile nations necessarily come closer to
God with Israel's help.[98] Similar ambiguities plague many other passages in
Second and Third Isaiah in which God addresses the nations. It is not clear
whether in these passages God is calling on them to draw close to him or insisting that the nations acknowledge him only so that they will send the Jewish
exiles in their midst back home.[99] Yet, despite the ambiguity in these passages,
there are a number of texts in the Prophets that clearly reflect a benevolent and
peaceful ethic when it comes to Israel's relationship to the gentile nations.

94 Amos 9:7.

95 Kaminsky, *Yet I Loved Jacob*, 141. Kaminsky also cites John Collins and Walter Bruegemann, who
support a similar interpretation of these passages. Others, however, have objected to this interpretation. See
Harry M. Orlinsky, "Nationalism-Universalism and Internationalism in Ancient Israel," in *Essays in Biblical
Culture and Biblical Translation* (New York: Ktav, 1974), 85–87; Jon D. Levenson, "The Exodus in Biblical Theology:
A Rejoinder to John J. Collins," in *Jews, Christians, and the Theology of the Hebrew Scriptures*, ed. Alice Ogden Beilis
and Joel S. Kaminsky (Atlanta: Society of Biblical Literature, 2000), 272–73.

96 See, for example, Is. 43:10. Both Levenson and Kaminsky cite this passage as illustrative of this conception of Israel's role vis-à-vis the gentile nations. See Levenson, "The Universal Horizon," 155; Kaminsky, *Yet I
Loved Jacob*, 193.

97 Is. 49:2, 49:6, 51:4; Greenberg, "A Problematic Heritage," 26–27.

98 Orlinsky, "Nationalism-Universalism and Internationalism," 105; Kaminsky, *Yet I Loved Jacob*, 146–52.

99 Kaminsky, *Yet I Loved Jacob*, 142–43.

But is this really enough? Do the violent passages in the Prophets identified in the first reading not compromise this ethic? Why should we choose the
peaceful passages in the Prophets over the bellicose ones? Moreover, even
the passages in the Prophets that paint an idyllic and universalistic vision of the
end of days are still nationalistic and chauvinistic. In Isaiah 2 and Micah 4,
the Temple in Jerusalem is the center to which the nations come, and the wisdom they learn comes from the God of Israel.[100] A similar criticism can be
voiced against the eschatological vision in Isaiah 19:18–25. Here too a chauvinistic element is evident in the fact that the gentile nations are seen as worship-
ing the God of Israel.[101] Thus, peace in the messianic era does not necessarily
mean the absence of inequality between Israelites and the nations.[102]

We can respond to these concerns by looking at the historical context in
which the books of the Prophets were written. Classical prophecy thrived in the
period of 800–500 BCE, when the Israelites were threatened with annihilation
by the Assyrian and Babylonian Empires. The Assyrian Empire destroyed the
northern Israelite kingdom in 722 BCE, and the Babylonian Empire destroyed
the southern kingdom of Judah in 587 BCE and exiled its inhabitants to Babylon. In fact, the Israelites might have been nothing more than a footnote in the
history of the ancient Near East had it not been for the fact that the Persian
monarch Cyrus sent the Judahites back to their homeland in 538 BCE, after
defeating the Babylonians. The worldview of the classical prophets was largely
determined by the need to make sense of these events. We should therefore not

---

100 Orlinsky, "Nationalism-Universalism and Internationalism," 93–99.

101 See also Zech. 8:20–23, in which peace at the end of days assumes the subjugation of gentile nations.
Kaminsky gives a rebuttal to Christian scholars who see the servant songs in Second Isaiah as moving beyond the
notion that Israel's election is based on unconditional love to the idea that God's salvation is open to all and
Israel's mission is now to call the other nations to His service (Is. 42:1–4, 49:1–6, 50:4–11, 52:13–53:12). First, even
in these portions of Isaiah, God's love of Israel remains unconditional. If Israel's election were dependent only
on service, one would have a hard time explaining Second Isaiah's insistence that God restores Israel from exile
in spite of its failures and that it is still beloved by God (Is. 54:5–8). In fact, almost every book of the latter
Prophets ends on a note of hope for such restoration. Second, if the servant passages say that Israel brings blessings to the nations of the world, it is not by missionizing to them or converting them. Israel serves as mediator
of God's blessing while the nations remain non-elect. Finally, the primary role of the servant—whether this refers
to a group or an individual—does not concern the gentiles at all. Rather, his purpose is to reunite and reconstitute
the family of Israel. See Kaminsky, Yet I Loved Jacob, 153–57.

102 Rodd argues that the real meaning of shalom in the biblical text is not "peace," but "prosperity and wel-
fare." The term is sometimes contrasted with war, but rarely. It is most often used in describing a state of affairs
in which Israel's enemies have been subjugated. Therefore, there is no true parallel in the Bible to the modern
notion of a peaceable relationship based on mutual trust and respect between nations. Israel always strives to
defeat its enemies, and security comes through conquest. Rodd's observations are based on Johannes Pedersen's
analysis of the conception of shalom in the Bible. Niditch acknowledges that peace in the Bible often involves
Israel's dominance over other nations and their acceptance of Israel's worldview and their God, but she claims
that Pedersen's position is too extreme. The meaning of shalom is not confined to prosperity achieved through
domination. See Niditch, War in the Hebrew Bible, 134–36; Rodd, 196–97. Yet, in those cases in which peace does
imply Israel's subjugation of other nations, it is clear that structural violence becomes a messianic ideal.

be surprised or discomfited by the fact that the prophets envisioned God wreaking revenge on his enemies at the end of days or that the nations would come to pay their respects to the God of Israel at the Temple in Jerusalem. The prophets were grappling with the deep fears and insecurities that Israelites must have felt in their period, and it is understandable that they would hope for the defeat of their enemies or envision that those enemies would acknowledge the God of Israel. In addition, it is remarkable that, despite the distressing circumstances in which the prophetic texts were composed, we find passages in them that still paint a picture of the messianic era as one of peace between nations. We should therefore commend the prophets for being able to rise above the crises of their period and imagine a time in which there would be no more war.

Thus far, this second reading of the biblical text has dealt with non-Israelites in broad theological strokes. Yet, we can also show that a positive view of gentiles is evident in more specific instances of biblical narrative and law. In narrative portions of the Bible, individual gentiles are often cast as righteous people, such as Melchizedek, who greets Abraham after he frees Lot from his captors; Pharaoh's daughter, who saves Moses's life; Moses's father-in-law, Jethro, who celebrates the exodus from Egypt; and Rahab, who helps the Israelites conquer Jericho.[103] An entire biblical book is named after one such figure, Ruth the Moabite. The book of Jonah consistently depicts non-Israelites in a positive light.[104] Often, righteous gentiles are depicted as more pious than Israelites. Naaman, the Aramean general who acknowledges God's help in being cured of leprosy, is juxtaposed with Gehazi, Elisha's greedy and disobedient servant.[105] In Genesis, Abimelech appears to be more pious and God-fearing than Abraham.[106]

In several passages, one finds a remarkably positive attitude toward foreigners who have chosen to live among the Israelites while retaining their foreign identity.[107] The passages most often cited in this connection are found

---

103 Gen. 14:17–20; Ex. 2:5–10; Ex. 2:16–22, 18:1–12; Num. 10:29–32; Josh. 2; Judg. 1:16.

104 Greenberg, "Mankind, Israel, and the Nations," 372. Many scholars believe that the book of Jonah and Second and Third Isaiah were inclusive toward non-Jews as a direct response to the exclusiveness of the books of Ezra 9–10 and Nehemiah 13. See Daniel L. Smith-Christopher, "Between Ezra and Isaiah: Exclusion, Transformation, and Inclusion of the 'Foreigner' in Post-Exilic Biblical Theology," in *Ethnicity and the Bible*, ed. Mark G. Brett (Leiden: E. J. Brill, 1996), 118.

105 II Kings 5.

106 Gen. 20. These examples are cited in Levenson, "The Universal Horizon," 148; and Kaminsky, *Yet I Loved Jacob*, 124–26.

107 For the sake of simplicity, we will gloss over the fact that there are many terms in biblical Hebrew for foreigners, that each carries its own set of nuances, and that sometimes the same term can change from passage to passage. Christiana van Houten has made the case that one of the key terms, *ger*, evolved from earlier strata in Exodus to later strata in Leviticus and Deuteronomy, with the later texts being more accepting and inclusive of foreigners than the earlier ones. See Christiana Van Houten, *The Alien in Israelite Law* (Sheffield: Sheffield Academic Press, 1991); Kaminsky, *Yet I Loved Jacob*, 123–24.

in legal sections of the Torah. In Exodus 22:20, the Israelites are commanded not to oppress the foreigners in their midst, "for you were strangers in the land of Egypt." In Leviticus 19:33–34, the Israelites are told to "love" the foreigner. Deuteronomy provides legislation guarding the rights of the foreigner.[108] What is surprising is that these passages appear in places where one would least expect them. They are embedded in sources that are highly ethnocentric and intolerant. For instance, the passages in Deuteronomy that insist on kindness to the foreigner come from the very same school that authored the commands imploring the Israelites to slaughter the Canaanites.[109] A similarly receptive attitude toward foreigners living in Israel's midst can be found in the books of the Prophets, where one finds a number of passages in which foreigners become part of the Israelite community. Furthermore, there are instances of foreigners being invited to act as religious functionaries in Jerusalem.[110] The Prophets also echo the Torah in denouncing social wrongs against foreigners.[111]

If foreigners are so beloved, what explains the actions of Ezra alluded to earlier? Why did he force Jews to divorce their non-Jewish spouses after their return from exile in Babylon? Some scholars claim that the texts describing Ezra's actions are highly ambiguous and upon careful analysis are revealed to be less xenophobic than critics of the Bible have assumed. First, the texts may be referring to marriages with fellow Israelites who had stayed in the land of Israel and had adopted idolatrous practices. These texts may therefore have nothing to do with gentiles. Second, even if the marriages were with non-Jews, as many argue, Ezra's efforts to break them up were not necessarily due to hatred of non-Jews. Rather, the Jews were a beleaguered ethnic minority when they returned from exile, and Ezra's actions were an attempt to preserve their identity and culture. According to Daniel L. Smith-Christopher, to be troubled

---

108 Deut. 10:19, 24:17–22. The foreigner also takes part in the covenant ceremony before the death of Moses (Deut. 29:10) and is included in the septennial public recitation of the Torah (Deut. 31:12).

109 Collins, 9; Greenberg, "Mankind, Israel and the Nations," 377–79; Kaminsky, Yet I Loved Jacob, 122–23. The issue of intermarriage between Israelites and foreigners and the question of conversion is also discussed in Kaminsky, Yet I Loved Jacob, 126–28. Kaminsky notes that the Deuteronomists' attitude toward the enemy nations who live on Israel's borders is just as surprising as their attitude toward foreigners living among the Israelites. One would have expected the Deuteronomists to have a negative attitude toward Egyptians in light of the slavery in Egypt, but in Deuteronomy the Israelites are commanded to be kind to them because the Egyptians hosted them (Deut. 23:8–9). The Israelites are also commanded to respect the borders of Edom, Ammon, Moab, even though these nations were often their enemies (II Kings 3; Obad. 1; Ps. 83, 137). God assigned these nations their respective lands, and therefore Israel must respect their borders (Deut. 2:1–20). See Kaminsky, Yet I Loved Jacob, 123.

110 Is. 56:6–7, 66:23; Zech. 14:16–19; Greenberg, "Mankind, Israel, and the Nations," 379. Greenberg argues that the Isaiah passages are remarkable because they were written in the exilic period, when one might have expected the exiles to close ranks and exclude foreigners. Instead, they seem to have welcomed them.

111 Jer. 7:6; Ezek. 22:7; Zech. 7:10; Mal. 3:5; Greenberg, "Mankind, Israel, and the Nations," 378.

by the exclusivism of these texts is "to misunderstand profoundly the nature of group solidarity and survival of minorities."[112] Yet, even if the texts in question represent a strand in the Bible that is exclusivist, they do not negate the emphasis on inclusiveness in other portions of the Bible.

Mention may also be made once again of Wisdom literature. We saw earlier that scholars had detected a universalistic element in this genre in that it supports natural law. We can expand that observation for the purposes of this portion of our discussion by noting that, in fact, the whole thrust of this literature is universalistic and non-national in character. Entirely absent from these books is any reference to the motif of Israel's chosenness, the gift of the land of Israel to Abraham's descendants, or the covenant at Sinai. A good example of the universal character of the Bible's Wisdom literature is the book of Job, in which the main character is a non-Jew who is described as righteous and has a relationship with God.[113]

A key question that has yet to be addressed is what justifies Israel's chosen status. Why is God's relationship to Israel based on unconditional love? Even if it can be shown that Israel's special status does not preclude God's care for the gentile nations, the fact that there is an unconditional element in God's relationship with Israel still reflects a chauvinism that is deeply disturbing. No other nation is given this privilege.

A number of suggestions have been made by scholars to deal with this challenge. The best response, to my mind, draws from basic insights in the fields of the social sciences with which critics and defenders of the doctrine of Israel's election often seem unfamiliar. The privileging of one's own group is ubiquitous in world cultures throughout history. Almost all ethnic communities and nations form their collective identities by thinking of themselves as special in some way. This tendency is not only natural; many social scientists regard it as healthy because it confers meaning on the lives of the individuals who are members of the group.[114] In addition, religion often plays a vital role

112 Smith-Christopher, 123–26; Kaminsky, *Yet I Loved Jacob*, 129–33.

113 Kaminsky, *Yet I Loved Jacob*, 163–64.

114 The notion that ethnicity and nationalism fulfill vital psychological needs has roots in Freud and was later developed by Erik H. Erikson. Pioneering work from a social psychological perspective has been done on this issue by Henri Tajfel. Among his many studies, see, for instance, Henri Tajfel and John C. Turner, "The Social Identity Theory of Intergroup Behavior," in *The Psychology of Intergroup Relations*, ed. Stephen Worchel and William G. Austin (Chicago: Nelson Hall, 1986), 7–24. An overview of how social psychologists approach the question of social identity theory can be found in Dean G. Pruitt and Sung Hee Kim, *Social Conflict: Escalation, Stalemate, and Settlement*, 3rd ed. (New York: McGraw-Hill, 2004), 29–31. Another perspective is provided by Vamik Volkan, who has written pioneering studies on social identity theory from a psychoanalytic perspective. See, for instance, Vamik D. Volkan, *The Need to Have Enemies and Allies: From Clinical Practice to International Relationships* (Northvale, N.J.: Jason Aronson, 1988); idem, *Bloodlines: From Ethnic Pride to Ethnic Terrorism* (Boulder, Colo.: Westview Press, 1997). Social identity theory is also the subject of several essays in Richard D.

in shaping ethnic and national identity. As Max Weber once noted, "Behind all ethnic divisions, there stands quite naturally some idea of a 'chosen people.'"[115] Viewed from this perspective, Israel's sense of its own chosenness should be neither surprising nor disturbing.

Furthermore, a group's sense of chosenness need not preclude it from having universalistic attitudes. The reading we have offered of God's covenant with Abraham is a case in point. God forms a special relationship with Abraham and his descendants, but the other nations of the world benefit from that relationship by being blessed as well. Kaminsky argues that particularism and universalism in the Bible are not polar opposites in constant tension with each other; instead, one grows out of the other. He points out that many of the biblical texts that speak of inclusion of gentiles are the very same ones that emphasize Israel's election, an observation which shows the weakness of interpretations that assume a sharp distinction between universalism and particularism in the Bible. On the basis of these observations, Kaminsky suggests that the Bible sees universalism and particularism as conjoined and that Israel's particularism is, in fact, a source of its universalism. As Israel contemplated its chosen status in the biblical period, it also reflected on the implications of that status for the world around it. As Kaminsky puts it, "A deepening sense of Israel's own particularistic identity as God's elect gives rise to new thoughts about the wider implications of Israel's chosen status."[116]

Kaminsky and Levenson also argue that particularism in itself has positive benefits. We have been led to think otherwise because, as Levenson states, "the universalistic thrust of modern, democratic capitalist societies undermines all particularisms, especially those based on the claims of historical revelation."[117] The culprit here is the Enlightenment, which introduced a universalism that erases the distinctions between all human communities. We have now entered an age in which the universalistic claims of the Enlightenment are being criticized as imperialistic, and there is greater appreciation for particularism. Group identity is, in fact, a source of human vitality and should not be discarded. Jews therefore need not be apologetic about their religious tradition which speaks of their election.[118]

Ashmore, Lee Jussim, and David Wilder, eds., *Social Identity, Intergroup Conflict, and Conflict Reduction* (Oxford: Oxford University Press, 2001); Daniel Rothbart and Karina V. Korostelina, eds., *Identity, Morality, and Threat: Studies in Violent Conflict* (Lanham, Md.: Lexington Books, 2006).

115 Cited in Appleby, 60. See also Appleby's discussion of this issue, 58–63.

116 Kaminsky, *Yet I Loved Jacob*, 146–52. Brett also argues that in the Bible particularistic sources have universalistic elements in them and vice versa, but he stops short of trying to bring the two together as Kaminsky does. See Brett, 151–57.

117 Levenson, "The Universal Horizon," 145–46.

118 Kaminsky, *Yet I Loved Jacob*, 9.

Some have argued that concepts of ethnic and national identity should not be applied to ancient Israel because to do so imposes modern categories on a people that lived in an era very different from our own.[119] If this is the case, then the foregoing arguments lose much of their strength. However, a number of studies have demonstrated that the application of these concepts to ancient Israel is not at all improper, and that it is meaningful to speak about ethnicity and nationalism in ancient Israel.[120] Moreover, there is evidence that Israel was by no means the only nation in the ancient Near East that believed it had a special status. A sense of chosenness was common among other peoples belonging to that world.[121]

Yet, just because we have shown that the ancient Israelites should not be criticized for seeing themselves as chosen, it does not follow that the violence which results from that sense of chosenness is moral. We still have to deal with God's commands to annihilate the Canaanites and Amalekites, commands that are a direct outgrowth of Israel's election.

A number of strategies can be used to confront this challenge. We will begin with the Canaanites. A large number of interpretations have been provided by scholars to mitigate the violence of the Canaanite conquest, and we cannot possibly discuss them all. We will therefore avail ourselves of only those interpretations that seem most plausible.

One approach is to argue that the biblical narratives describing the Canaanite conquest treat war as God's prerogative, not Israel's. Millard Lind was the initiator of this reading, and it has been taken up by other scholars, including Susan Niditch. Lind argues that whenever holy war is waged in the biblical text, it does not spring from human initiative. It is God who wages war, and it is he who is responsible for ensuring that Israel achieves victory. The Bible therefore does not endorse holy war as a normal human activity, but only as an activity practiced in exceptional circumstances when God explicitly permits or commands it. Because

---

119 Levenson, "The Universal Horizon," 160; Crüsemann, 69. Levenson seems to draw a distinction between "particularism," which can be applied to ancient Israel, as we have just noted, and ethnic and national identity, which cannot.

120 Brett, "Nationalism and the Hebrew Bible"; E. Theodore Mullen Jr., *Narrative History and Ethnic Boundaries: The Deuteronomic Historian and the Creation of Israelite National Identity* (Atlanta: Scholars Press, 1993); Kenton L. Sparks, *Ethnicity and Identity in Ancient Israel: Prolegomena to the Study of Ethnic Sentiments and Their Expression in the Hebrew Bible* (Winona Lake, Ind.: Eisenbrauns, 1998); Steven Grosby, *Biblical Ideas of Nationality Ancient and Modern* (Winona Lake, Ind.: Eisenbrauns, 2002). Sparks discusses the difficulties in addressing the issue of ethnicity in ancient Israel but at no point questions whether ethnicity is an appropriate category for analyzing society there. His major concern is whether the Israelites were, in fact, a defined ethnic group, given research showing that they emerged out of a mixture of Canaanite and Israelite culture. See Sparks, 1–6.

121 Frank Moore Cross, *Canaanite Myth and Hebrew Epic* (Cambridge, Mass.: Harvard University Press, 1973), 105.

this concept of war insists on minimal human involvement in war, it represents, in effect, an ideology of nonviolence.[122]

The passages in the Bible most frequently cited as evidence for this view of
warfare come from the narrative in the Torah describing the exodus from
Egypt. Just before the splitting of the Sea of Reeds, Moses tells the Israelites,
"The Lord will battle for you: you hold your peace!"[123] After the Israelites cross
the Sea, Moses exults:

> The Lord is the Warrior—
> The Lord is His name!
> Pharaoh's chariots and his army
> He cast into the Sea;
> And the pick of His officers
> Are drowned in the Sea of Reeds.[124]

In this passage, God receives all the credit for the defeat of the Egyptians.

A similar perspective on war can be found in the book of Joshua. In contrast
with the exodus example, Israel in this instance fields an army and physically
fights the enemy. Yet, we are also told on several occasions that it is really God's
miraculous intervention that brings victory. In Joshua 24:12, God promises
victory because he will send the "hornet" to fight for Israel against the Canaanites. We are also told that Israel achieves victory over the Canaanites because
God hardens the hearts of the enemy.[125] The Israelites conquer Jericho because
God causes its walls to come tumbling down.[126] In Gibeon God makes the sun
stand still so that Joshua and his army can defeat the enemy before nightfall
sets in.[127]

Patricia McDonald provides a detailed analysis of the book of Joshua along
these lines. She argues that a proper understanding of the narrative regarding

---

122 Millard C. Lind, *Yahweh Is a Warrior: The Theology of Warfare in Ancient Israel* (Scottsdale, Pa.: Herald
Press, 1980); Niditch, *War in the Hebrew Bible*, 143–49. Niditch views this conception of war as being part of a
larger ideology of nonparticipation found in various places in the biblical text. We will be taking up Niditch's
observations on this ideology shortly.

123 Ex. 14:14.

124 Ex. 15:3–4.

125 Josh. 11:20.

126 Josh. 6:20.

127 Josh. 10:12–13. Other biblical sources reflect this ideology of warfare: II Chron. 2, which deals with a war
waged by Jehoshaphat against Moab and Ammon; Is. 36–37, which describes Hezekiah's defense of Jerusalem
against Assyria; and the Gog and Magog prophecies in Ez. 38–39, Zech. 14, and Joel 4. These examples are noted
in Shalom Carmy, "The Origin of Nations and the Shadow of Violence: Theological Perspectives on Canaan and
Amalek," in *War and Peace in the Jewish Tradition*, ed. Lawrence Schiffman and Joel B. Wolowelsky (New York:
Yeshiva University Press, 2007), 184–85. Lois Barrett, *The Way God Fights: War and Peace in the Old Testament*
(Scottsdale, Pa.: Herald Press, 1987), argues from a confessional Christian perspective that the ideology discussed
here is characteristic of biblical attitudes toward warfare in general. See especially 22, 71–72.

the Canaanite conquest requires that one look at the book of Joshua as a whole and not focus solely on its violence. A careful reading of Joshua shows that the point of the book is to demonstrate that Israel can take none of the credit for inhabiting the land of Canaan and that it is a gift from God to his people. Military activity is sanctioned only when God says so, and for this reason all victories are depicted as God's doing, not Israel's. The book of Joshua therefore does not advocate or glorify military activity for its own sake. The point of the book is to teach that Israel's faith in God is responsible for victory, not military might. If one learns from the book to engage in military activity, it is, according to McDonald, "a distortion of its message." A similar lesson comes across in the text's depiction of Joshua the person. Joshua is a military leader but does not seek military glory. What is emphasized is his fidelity to God. Thus, upon his death, he is described as a "servant of the Lord" (Josh. 24:29).[128]

A second approach to explaining the violence of the Canaanite conquest is to place the episode in its historical context. We used this strategy in attempting to come to terms with the depictions of violence in the messianic period in the books of the Prophets, and here we can do the same. First of all, there is good evidence that the Israelites were not any worse or better morally than other nations in the ancient Near East when it came to warfare. Violence and the sacred went hand in hand in polytheistic cultures in the ancient Near East, long before the advent of Israelite monotheism.[129] It should therefore occasion no surprise that the Deuteronomic historians should construct the story of the Canaanite conquest in which war is viewed in a positive light.[130]

128 Patricia M. McDonald, *God and Violence: Biblical Resources for Living in a Small World* (Scottsdale, Pa.: Herald Press, 2004), 115–42. A similar discussion is found in Artson, 108–15. Artson's study is more openly theological in orientation than McDonald's and should therefore be seen as a work representative of modern Jewish thought as opposed to a work of historical scholarship. Nonetheless, Artson relies a good deal on scholarly sources.

129 Collins, 3–4; Manfred Weippert did pioneering work in this area by showing that none of the ritual and ideological elements of von Rad's theory of war in ancient Israel was unique to Israel. See Weippert, "'Heiliger Krieg' in Israel und Assyrien: Kritische Anmerkungen zu Gerhard von Rads Konzept des 'Heiligen Krieges im alten Israel,'" *Zeitschrift für die alttestamentliche Wissenschaft* 84 (1972): 490–92.

130 Moshe Greenberg presents another argument invoking historical context. He claims that the conquest of Canaan did not offend the sense of justice of the biblical authors because of the historical setting in which they lived. Their depiction of the Canaanite conquest was based on three premises: the eradication of enemies was acceptable in the ancient Near East, the success and survival of Israel depended on the exclusive worship of God, and a relatively small and young nation would likely be seduced by idolatrous culture because it was living in a sea of paganism. Greenberg expands on the last point by noting that biblical authors were concerned about the violence of Canaanite culture, as exemplified by the practice of child sacrifice, and the Canaanites' sexual immorality. The conquest of Canaan was thus "the brutal embodiment, coarse and brutal as those times were, of a praiseworthy concern lest biblical religion and morality be undermined by pagan enticements." See Greenberg, "A Problematic Heritage," 30. See also idem, "Mankind, Israel, and the Nations," 383; idem, *Election and Power* (in Hebrew) (Haifa: Ha-Kibbutz Ha-Me'uhad, 1985), 19.

But even more important, we have to consider Israel's specific situation in the ancient Near East during the period in which the Deuteronomists composed this story. Niditch reminds us that the Deuteronomic History was composed in Judah in the seventh century BCE. This period was part of an epoch in which the Israelites experienced great turmoil and insecurity as they attempted to cope with the presence of large empires on their borders that threatened to conquer them, an observation we have made earlier in our discussion of violence in the Prophets. During the seventh century BCE, Judah was confronted with the Assyrian Empire, which had destroyed the northern Israelite kingdom and was about to wage war on it. The Assyrian Empire was also a cultural threat to Judah because its idolatrous practices were infiltrating Judah. When King Josiah came to power, he attempted to repel the Assyrians both physically and religiously by shoring up Israelite identity, and he therefore attempted to root out the Assyrian-inspired idolatry from his kingdom. The Deuteronomic historians composed the biblical narrative about the Canaanite conquest to support Josiah's reforms by projecting the war against idolatry onto a distant past and making that struggle foundational to Israel's national identity. We can therefore explain the account of the Canaanite conquest in much the same way that we accounted for the violent passages in the Prophets: it was a response to deep-seated fears and anxieties that permeated Israelite society at a certain point of its history.[131]

Niditch uses this information to account for the larger war ideology that underlies the narrative about the Canaanite conquest, "the ban as God's justice" noted earlier. Niditch also uses a similar historical approach to explain other war ideologies in the biblical text. For instance, she explains the war ideology of "tricksterism" by referring to the same insecurities that motivated the Deuteronomic historians to compose the narratives about the Canaanite conquest. In the biblical sources that reflect this ideology are tales of military victory achieved by deception. Examples of such stories are the rape of Dinah, Samson and the Timnites, Jael and the murder of the Canaanite general Sisera, and Ehud and Eglon.[132] Niditch argues that the ideology of tricksterism reflects once again an Israelite society insecure because of its lack of power and the threat of aggression from outsiders. Narratives reflecting this ideology were designed to teach the Israelites that being "pragmatic, self-sufficient, and street-smart" was the best way to deal with their subjugation. She notes that in many other cultures deception is one of the ways marginal peoples imagine

---

131 Niditch, *War in the Hebrew Bible*, 74–77; Louis Stulman, "Encroachment in Deuteronomy: An Analysis of the Social World of the D Code," *Journal of Biblical Literature* 109 (1990): 613–32.

132 Gen. 34; Judg. 3:12–30, 4–5, 14–15.

themselves improving their lot at the expense of the more powerful.[133] Moreover, Niditch surmises, the stories reflecting the ideology of tricksterism probably had a multigenerational audience in ancient Israel. Such stories "would have special appeal to Israelite societies as a whole during periods of external political, economic, and cultural subjugation, which accounts for virtually the whole of Israel's history."[134] Thus, according to Niditch, Israel was insecure not just in the seventh century BCE, but throughout the period in which the biblical history was recorded, and an understanding of Israel's war ideologies requires that we take this broad historical context into account.

Niditch makes similar claims regarding another war ideology in the Bible, which she calls the ideology of nonparticipation. In this ideology, one finds a range of outrightly negative attitudes to war ranging from circumspection to opposition. That there should be such an ideology in the biblical text is significant in itself, and we shall discuss it shortly. For the purposes of the present discussion, what is most important is Niditch's observations regarding the historical context which produced this ideology. Niditch claims that the ideology of nonparticipation also reflects the mentality of an Israelite society constantly confronting threats from the outside and unsure about its ability to defend itself. These trepidations resulted in the Israelites' adopting a viewpoint that cast war in a negative light, since war was more likely to hurt than help them.

These observations also enrich our understanding of the first approach to the Canaanite conquest discussed earlier. We saw that according to Lind and other scholars, the violence of the biblical narratives describing the Canaanite conquest was mitigated by the fact that Israel does not fight for itself—rather, God fights for the Israelites. According to Niditch, this way of thinking is, in fact, one of several expressions of the ideology of nonparticipation. Reservations about war are expressed in the fact that all the responsibilities of war are foisted on God, not human beings. Niditch also surmises that this expression of the ideology of nonparticipation is woven into the Deuteronomic History and the story of the Canaanite conquest alongside other ideologies such as the ban as God's justice. Thus, we now understand the historical context out of which the view arose that God fights Israel's wars. As with other expressions of the ideology of nonparticipation, here too the insecurity of Israel's situation is the background against which this view was formed.[135]

---

133 Niditch has explored this connection in her study *Underdogs and Tricksters: A Prelude to Folklore* (San Francisco: Harper & Row, 1987), 44–50.

134 Niditch, *War in the Hebrew Bible*, 106–22.

135 Niditch, *War in the Hebrew Bible*, 134–49. Thomas Römer provides another interpretation of how the "God as warrior" motif emerged out of the historical context of the seventh century BCE. He argues that this idea was specifically a reaction to pressure from the Assyrians to recognize their kings as gods. This is why the

Mark Brett goes in a direction similar to Niditch's overall approach in invoking Israel's insecurities to explain the Bible's nationalistic tendencies. Brett cites Liah Greenfeld, who claims that nationalism is almost always connected with a people's struggle for dignity. Brett goes on to argue that Greenfeld's insight can be used to support the claim that nationalism can be found in the Bible. In the biblical text, the Israelites constructed a national identity as they struggled to maintain their dignity in the face of outside threats throughout the entire biblical history. As Brett puts it, the story of Israel can be read as "a series of counter-assertions of dignity: the exodus solidarity half-created by Egypt; the united monarchy half-created by the Philistines; the Deuteronomic constitution half-created by Assyria; the imagined empire of Second Isaiah half-created by Babylon. The construction of nationalism was simply one feature of this long, culturally-mediated conversation about what it means to be a community before God."[136] Peter Machinist makes similar claims in attempting to explain the notion that according to the biblical narrative, Israel's origins lie outside Canaan. Machinist notes that many cultures have mythologies that place their origins outside the land in which they live, as a way of establishing their distinctive ethnic identity; Vergil's *Aeneid* comes to mind here. The Bible does the same by depicting Abraham as an outsider to Canaan and by having his descendants take possession of the land through conquest after a lengthy exile. Machinist goes on to argue that this mythology is found in multiple strata in the Bible because of Israel's constant need to affirm its identity. But what is most important for our concerns is that, according to Machinist, this need was felt most strongly during the period of the eighth to the sixth century BCE, when the Israelites were threatened by Assyria and then exiled by Babylon. Machinist therefore brings the question of the Israelites' insecurity to bear on their entire self-definition.[137]

Relevant here as well are remarks made by Joel Kaminsky, who cites Israel's perennial sense of insecurity to explain the pattern, running throughout Genesis, of a sibling rivalry in which the younger brother consistently trumps the older. According to Kaminsky, it is hard to escape the conclusion that there is a historical element underlying these narratives. The prominence of the motif of

---

Deuteronomic History is so strident in declaring that only God is king, imbuing God with the same warlike qualities as those possessed by the Assyrian kings, and claiming that only God makes war. See Römer, *Dieu obscur: Le sexe, le cruauté et la violence dans l'Ancien Testament* (Geneva: Labor et Fides, 1996). Lüdemann discusses Römer's views on pp. 49–51.

136 Brett, 161–62.

137 Peter Machinist, "The Biblical View of Emergent Israel and Its Contexts," in *The Other in Jewish Thought and History*, ed. Laurence J. Silberstein and Robert L. Cohn (New York: New York University Press, 1994), 35–60.

subverting primogeniture must surely be driven by "Israel's perception of herself in relation to her older, venerable, and more dominant neighbors, Egypt and Mesopotamia." The authors of these stories were attempting to come to terms with "Israel's sense of her late-born status" by seeing it as "evidence of her worthiness to become God's chosen people." This is why the Genesis narratives always have the younger son subverting the position of the older one.[138]

What emerges from all this is that the Bible's monotheism-chosenness complex, its concept of Israel's national identity, and its depictions of violence against the Canaanites were all connected, in that they were a means by which ancient Israel coped with an environment that was hostile to it through a good portion of its history. These ideas were meant to give the Israelites a strong sense of solidarity by cementing a feeling of religious and national identity.[139] Viewed from this perspective, the Canaanite conquest appears far less morally problematic than a plain reading of the biblical text would suggest. It was a historical fiction produced by authors who lived among a people who were constantly threatened by neighboring nations bent on their destruction, and who had to come to terms with their own vulnerabilities. If the narratives composed by these authors about the conquest of the Canaanites seem inhuman, the motives that produced those stories were utterly human.[140]

Let us also keep in mind the perspectives of social scientists mentioned earlier that provide insight into the common mechanisms by which groups form ethnic and national identity. Many social psychologists have noted that not only does the construction of ethnic and national identity create a distinction between insiders and outsiders, but this distinction can easily lead to hostility toward the latter. That hostility, of course, will be exacerbated when the outsiders constitute a real physical threat to the group. Under these circumstances, ethnic and national groups will demonize the enemy.[141] This process is evident in the literature of the Deuteronomic historians, and, yet, interestingly enough, these writers demonized not the Assyrians, who were their real enemies, but rather the Canaanites, a largely fictional group from the distant past.

138 Kaminsky, Yet I Loved Jacob, 76–77. This same idea has been suggested by others. See Everett Fox, "Stalking the Younger Brother: Some Models for Understanding a Biblical Motif," Journal of the Study of the Old Testament (1980): 60. Fox entertains a number of other explanations for the motif of sibling rivalry and concludes that it may have been perceived in different ways throughout the history of Israel.

139 The rudiments of these insights are also expressed in Cott, 224–25.

140 Moberly draws an ethical lesson from the fictional nature of the Joshua narratives. He argues that if the Joshua narratives are not historical, as most people now claim, and were a product of Josianic reform, they should be read "metaphorically" as a paradigm for what it meant to live faithfully and unfaithfully in ancient Israel. Moberly adds that this type of interpretation resonates with that of early Christian interpreters, who also spiritualized the Canaanite narrative by reading it allegorically. See Moberly, "Is Monotheism Bad for You?," 103.

141 See sources cited in n. 114.

A third strategy that can be used to mitigate the violence of the narrative about the Canaanite conquest is to point to other portions of the biblical text which in some way or other soften the impact of that narrative. What makes this approach different from the first two is that the focus here is on portions of the biblical text that have nothing to do with the narratives about the Canaanite conquest and that form a counterweight to it. For instance, a number of scholars note that some strata in the Bible view the Canaanites in far more positive terms than is the case in the Deuteronomic History. A good deal of attention has been paid to the book of Genesis for this purpose. Thus, for instance, in Genesis 23 and 38, the Patriarchal families interact peacefully with the Canaanites. In Genesis 34, Jacob criticizes Simeon and Levi for the massacre of the inhabitants of Shechem. The attitude of the biblical text toward the Canaanites is therefore more complex than is apparent from focusing on the Deuteronomic History alone.[142]

Relevant here as well is the strand in the Bible Niditch calls the ideology of nonparticipation, which is critical of war in general. We saw that this ideology is sometimes expressed in texts which place all responsibilities for war on God. Another source connected to this tradition was mentioned in our discussion of Israel's election: the first chapter of Amos. Here the prophet objects not only when Israel's neighbors wage war on it, but also when they wage war on each other. In this passage, the prophet also criticizes Israel and its neighbors alike for their excessive cruelty in war.[143] The most prominent example of the ideology of nonparticipation, according to Niditch, is the sustained critique of war that runs through I and II Chronicles. These books are comprised of late traditions "groping toward peace." They retell the biblical history in a way that often mutes its violence. Most notable is the rewriting of the stories of King David in I Chronicles that plays down his qualities as a warrior and his violent activities as described in II Samuel.[144]

Patricia McDonald also argues that strata in the biblical text that have a negative view of war counterbalance its more violent narratives. She points out that the Bible is "a rich and varied place for imagining other and better ways of being that range from mere avoidance of violence against one's neighbor to cultivating an attitude of compassionate service to others." The book of Genesis, for instance, provides a perspective on violence very different from that found in the Deuteronomic History. In Genesis, the Patriarchs are depicted as

---

142 Robert L. Cohn, "Before Israel: The Canaanite as Other in Biblical Tradition," in *The Other in Jewish Thought and History: Constructions of Jewish Culture and Identity*, ed. Laurence J. Silberstein and Robert L. Cohn (New York: New York University Press, 1994), 74–90; Kaminsky, *Yet I Loved Jacob*, 113.

143 See p. 40 in this volume.

144 Niditch, *War in the Hebrew Bible*, 132–33, 139–44, 149.

essentially nonviolent individuals.[145] Moreover, throughout Genesis, God shows favor to those who are mild-mannered. The quiet Isaac is the chosen child of Abraham, not his brother Ishmael, who will be a "wild ass of a man." In the next generation, the tent-dwelling Jacob is chosen over his brother, Esau, the hunter. Simeon and Levi are cursed by Jacob for their violence against the city of Shechem. Joseph rises to prominence despite the violence perpetrated against him by his brothers.[146] McDonald also claims that when violence does occur in the biblical text, it is never presented in positive terms. At no point is violence portrayed in a manner "intended to appeal to readers."[147]

We must now say a word about the Amalekites, whom God also instructs the Israelites to annihilate. Scholars have examined this issue much less than the destruction of the Canaanites, which is no surprise. The war against the Amalekites does not have nearly the prominence in the biblical history that the conquest of the Canaanites does, either textually or conceptually. The Canaanite conquest is also tied in with the original Abrahamic covenant. Moreover, my sense is that scholars of biblical ethics shy away from discussing the Amalekites because, as noted in our first reading, the war against them presents moral difficulties that are in some ways worse than those raised by the war against the Canaanites. God commands the Amalekites to be killed wherever they are and for all time, while the command against the Canaanites applies only to those living within the borders of the promised land and at a specific point in the biblical history. This observation perhaps explains why Jewish Bible scholars who attempt to take the sting out of the command to kill the Amalekites almost always refer to sources in the rabbinic tradition that try to address the moral difficulties of this imperative.[148] The biblical text itself seems unredeemable.

However, Diana Lipton offers an intriguing analysis that confronts the issue of the Amalekites from a scholarly perspective, and she does so without reference to the rabbis. There are two accounts of Israel's confrontation with the Amalekites in the Torah, one in Exodus and a second in Deuteronomy,[149] and Lipton argues that the account in Deuteronomy represents an attempt to rewrite the earlier one in Exodus. Lipton notes that the passage in Deuteronomy tells us that the crime of Amalek was in attacking a people that were hungry and weary after having just left Egypt, and no such reason is given for the attack

145 The exception is Abraham waging war in Gen. 14, but in all fairness he does this to free his nephew Lot from captivity.

146 Gen. 16:12, 25:27; McDonald, 59–72.

147 McDonald, 18, 22, 27. See Rodd, 197–204, for a discussion and critique of other attempts not considered here to read the biblical narratives regarding the Canaanite conquest in a positive light.

148 We will look at these sources in the next chapter.

149 Ex. 17:8–16; Deut. 25:17–19.

in Exodus. Lipton surmises from this observation that the Deuteronomic authors rewrote the earlier Amalek episode to criticize social injustices against the weak and sick in their own society. That is, Amalek becomes a metaphor for the predators in the Israelite aristocracy who abused the disadvantaged. Such criticism would fit with the general tendency of the authors of Deuteronomy to criticize Israelite society by projecting its sins onto the gentile nations. For instance, the sin of idolatry in Judahite society is censured in Deuteronomy by projecting it onto the Canaanites, who are condemned for that sin. In the case under discussion here, the sin of ill-treatment of the underprivileged is projected onto the Amalekites. Such criticism also fits with Deuteronomy's focus on the poor, widows, and orphans—the weakest members of society.[150] In effect, Lipton's reading uses a strategy similar to the second approach that we used to explain the Canaanite conquest: looking to historical context to explain the violence of the Deuteronomic History and interpreting the latter as a political allegory meant to grapple with that context.[151]

Lipton's analysis does not entirely solve the moral problems raised by the war against the Amalekites. After all, according to her analysis, the original story in Exodus still stands. Moreover, the imperative to slaughter the Amalekites reappears again in I Samuel 15 when Saul is ordered by God to go to war on them. Still, Lipton's insights into the Deuteronomy passage are significant. The initial violent story in Exodus may have been recast by the Deuteronomic historians to impart a message that was in some respects diametrically opposite its original intent. Instead of teaching about violence, the story of the Amalekites became a lesson in compassion for the underprivileged.

Those who view the Bible as a text that promotes violence still hold what would seem to be a trump card. The fact is that in subsequent history the biblical texts dealing with the Canaanites and Amalekites have been used as inspiration for violence, as noted in our first reading. Whatever sophisticated explanations one may give to soften the violence of the Bible, it remains a text that has encouraged bloodshed.

We can answer this challenge with a number of responses. First, critics of violence in the Bible almost never acknowledge that biblical religion has also

---

150 Deut. 15:7–8, 16:9–12. Diana Lipton, "Remembering Amalek: A Positive Biblical Model for Dealing with Negative Scriptural Types," in *Reading Texts, Seeking Wisdom: Scripture and Theology*, ed. David F. Ford and Graham Stanton (Grand Rapids, Mich.: William B. Eerdmans, 2004), 139–53.

151 Jeffrey Tigay hints at another strategy to deal with the Amalek episode. The command to annihilate Amalek may have emanated from a fear among the biblical authors that the Amalekites were plotting to annihilate Israel. This surmise is based on Ps. 83:4–9, which refers to Amalek as part of a group of nations who say regarding the Israelites, "Let us wipe them out as a nation; Israel's name will be mentioned no more." Thus, according to this reading, the imperative to destroy Amalek would be a purely defensive measure. See Tigay, *The JPS Commentary on the Torah: Deuteronomy*, 236.

inspired a considerable number of peace movements throughout the centuries.[152] Thus, although these critics frequently point to the Crusades as an example of the Bible's pernicious influence, they do not mention the fact that prominent religious clerics who read the same Bible led peace movements in an attempt to stop the Crusades.[153] This oversight may be due in part to the fact that throughout history, peace movements have not been nearly as successful as movements that have perpetrated violence on a mass scale, and therefore relatively little has been written about them. Once violence gets going, it is often impossible to stop until it has done a great deal of damage. Wars have always been a primary mover of world events, and therefore violence has shaped world history in a way that peace movements have not. We can add in defense of biblical religion that it has inspired numerous liberationist revolutions that the critic of the Bible should admire. The story of the exodus, for example, has spawned such movements for centuries, including that of the Puritans, who came to the New World seeking a new life, and those of modern-day African Americans, Latin Americans, and black South Africans, all of whom have used the story of the exodus as a paradigm for achieving freedom from oppression.[154] A balanced assessment of the historical impact of the Bible must therefore take into account the more benevolent influences of the Bible.

In assessing the effects of the Bible in history, we also have to consider the influence that it has had in ordinary people's lives throughout the centuries, an issue that its critics have failed to raise. Were the everyday lives of Jews and Christians enriched or made worse by this text? Did the acts of goodness and kindness that biblical religion spawned in people's day-to-day existence outweigh the acts of cruelty and brutality it inspired? These questions are difficult to answer given the lack of information we have on these matters and that standards for measuring the amount of good or evil produced by biblical religion in people's private lives is impossible to determine. But at the very least these questions cast doubt on the assessment of some critics that civilization would have been better off without the Bible.

One more issue that needs to be addressed is the question of God as a model for human action. In our first reading, we argued that the Bible often depicts God as acting violently and that if one puts this portrayal together with

---

152 Here I am referring to the Bible as inclusive of the New Testament because the critics whose charges are being answered here are directing their criticism against both the Old and New Testaments.

153 Ronald G. Musto, *The Catholic Peace Tradition* (Maryknoll, N.Y.: Orbis Books, 1986). The Crusades are discussed on pp. 76–96.

154 Schwartz, *The Curse of Cain*, 152–54.

the biblical imperative to imitate God's actions, the Bible seems to be giving the Israelites license to take violent action against their enemies even when not explicitly commanded to do so. This concern seems to be borne out by the story of Phinehas, who, out of zeal for the Lord, kills Zimri and his Midianite companion and is amply rewarded.

One response we can give to this concern is that, according to a number of scholars, when the biblical text invokes the notion that human beings should imitate God, the text generally refers to his benevolent actions—those emanating from his mercy, justice, and compassion—and not his tyrannical ones. Thus, in Deuteronomy the injunction that Israel is supposed to act justly and love the orphan, widow, and foreigner is based on the idea that God himself does these things.[155] As noted earlier, Leviticus 19:2 contains the command to the Israelites to be holy because God himself is holy.[156] We also saw in an earlier discussion that, according to Lind's hypothesis, when holy war is waged by the Israelites in the biblical text, it is effectively God who initiates war and achieves victory, not Israel. Once again, implicit in this observation is that God's violent actions should not be imitated. Only God has the right to declare war, not human beings. Thus, ironically the violent portrayals of God encourage the reader of the Bible to eschew violence, not to embrace it. The tale of Phinehas, therefore, should be seen as an exceptional case.

We may look to other biblical sources to provide a theological rationale for the imperative that only God's benevolent actions should be imitated. A number of biblical passages emphasize that only God is truly powerful, not humans; that humans must recognize their limitations; and that they should therefore put their faith in God. An example is a passage in Psalm 33:

> Kings are not delivered by large force; warriors are not saved by great strength; horses are a false hope for deliverance; for all their great power they provide no escape. Truly, the eye of the LORD is on those who fear Him, who wait for His faithful care to save them from death, to sustain them in famine. We set our hope on the LORD, He is our help and shield; in Him our hearts rejoice, for in His holy name we trust. May we enjoy, O LORD, Your faithful care, as we have put our hope in You.[157]

---

155 Deut. 10:17–19.

156 Barton, "The Basis of Ethics," 17–20. Eryl W. Davies takes a similar position in an analysis of the biblical injunction to "walk in God's ways": Davies, "Walking in God's Ways: The Concept of *Imitatio Dei* in the Old Testament," in *True Wisdom*, ed. Edward Ball (Sheffield: Sheffield Academic Press, 1999), 99–115. See Deut 8:6, 10:12, 11:22, 26:17, 28:9, and Davies' interpretation of these passages (113).

157 Ps. 33:16–22. See also Jer. 17:5–7; Ps. 20:8, 44:1–7.

We can infer from this passage and other similar statements in the Bible that human beings should not attempt to imitate God's violent attributes because they have to maintain their humility. The adoption of those attributes may tempt people to see themselves as the source of their own power and thereby compromise their recognition of God's sovereignty and their faith in him as the ultimate source of deliverance.[158] Thus, once again, God's violent behavior is expected ironically to breed the opposite in human beings.[159]

A completely different approach to this whole issue is to argue that the Bible does not encourage human beings to look to God's violent actions as a model for behavior, even implicitly, because the imperative to imitate God is not central to biblical ethics at all. Rodd has been particularly adamant in arguing that the imitation of God is not important in the ethics of the Bible. According to him, very few passages in the biblical text speak about the imitation of God, and thus claims about the importance of this idea in biblical ethics are overstated. Ethics in the Bible is generally dictated by divine command, not by looking to God's actions as a model for behavior.[160] We may also add here that it is generally non-Jewish scholars who have shown the greatest interest in the imitation of God as a theme in biblical ethics, an interest that may reflect a Christian bias. The imitation of Christ is central to Christian ethics, and it would seem that non-Jewish scholars therefore have attempted to highlight the

---

158 David S. Shapiro, "The Jewish Attitude towards Peace and War," in *Studies in Jewish Thought* (New York: Yeshiva University Press, 1975), 1:320–23.

159 A prominent source often cited as evidence that human beings should not aspire to be like God is Gen. 3:22, in which God expresses discomfort that human beings have come to resemble him in some fashion by eating from the Tree of Knowledge of Good and Evil, and they must therefore be expelled from Eden lest they eat from the Tree of Life. In a passage frequently cited by Christian scholars and theologians, the prophet Zechariah claims that even God prefers not to exercise power: "Not by might, nor by power, but by My spirit—said the Lord of Hosts" (Zech. 4:6).

160 Rodd, 65–76. Rodd also questions whether those who support the notion that the Israelites should imitate God have properly understood Lev. 19:2, which they frequently cite as a source for this idea. According to Lev. 19:2, one is supposed to be holy as God is, but that does not necessarily mean that holiness for God and holiness for humans are the same. Rodd also argues that in some instances, the Bible may be speaking more about mirroring God's actions than actual imitation. Imitation means doing as God does. Mirroring means no more than that "the actions of the worshiper are similar to those attributed to God" (72). One wonders, however, whether the distinction Rodd is making here is a little too fine. It is not clear to me how mirroring is different from imitation. Rodd also offers another reason that the imitation of God is not central in biblical ethics, besides its focus on divine commandments: a conviction running through the Bible that God is "other" than humans, and therefore imitating him is not really possible (76). This argument is not terribly convincing. Certainly, God is different from human beings, but Rodd has made a sweeping judgment about a complex issue, the sort of judgment he himself frequently decries in the works of scholars on biblical ethics. The Bible is filled with anthropomorphisms and frequently assumes a similarity between God and human beings. John Barton has recently responded to Rodd's arguments in his "Imitation of God in the Old Testament," in *The God of Israel*, ed. Robert P. Gordon (Cambridge: Cambridge University Press, 2007), 35–46.

notion of imitating God in the Hebrew Bible more than it deserves. In truth, the imitation of God never served the role in the Hebrew Bible or in Judaism in general that it did in Christianity.[161]

Our second reading of the Bible thus yields an interpretation that differs markedly from that provided by the first. According to this second reading, the Bible has a mostly positive view of non-Israelites. The value of all human beings is established in the first chapter of Genesis, when we are told that humans are created in God's image, and that view of humankind is assumed throughout the rest of the biblical text. When Abraham and his line are chosen, the gentile nations are not forgotten by God, nor are they regarded as inferior; Israel's purpose is to serve in some sort of mediating role so that the nations receive God's blessings as well. This notion is more fully developed in passages in the books of the Prophets, which depict the messianic era as a period in which all nations will be at peace with each other and will be united in their recognition of God. If one is still troubled by the unconditional element that lies at the foundation of God's relationship with Israel, one has to keep in mind that almost all ethnic and national communities regard themselves as having a special status, and religion is often used to bolster that belief. Moreover, particularism need not preclude universalism. It may even enrich it.

Our biggest challenge was to deal with the biblical narratives involving the Canaanite conquest. Yet, with a careful examination, we discovered that these texts were not as problematic as they seemed. First, they emphasize that it is God's initiative to wage war, and therefore, ironically, they teach us that human beings should not engage in such activity of their own volition. Their focus appears to be on the value of faith; the Israelites inherit the land because of their trust in God. Second, these texts have to be viewed in historical context in order to appreciate that they are less an expression of naked aggression than a reflection of the deep insecurities felt by an Israelite people threatened by their enemies during a specific period in their history. Finally, there are other texts in the Bible that counterbalance the violence of the Canaanite conquest, either by depicting the Canaanites in a positive manner or by casting doubt on the value of war in general.

---

161 This may also explain another problem with the way in which Lev. 19:2 has been interpreted. Among non-Jewish scholars, the imitation of God's holiness is often assumed to refer to God's ethical attributes. The context of the chapter, however, would suggest otherwise: the issue of holiness is connected to concerns regarding purity that is ritualistic in nature. See Levine, 256–57; Baruch J. Schwartz, "Commentary on Leviticus," in *The Jewish Study Bible*, ed. Adele Berlin and Marc Zvi Brettler (New York: Oxford University Press, 1999), 252–53. Once again the position of non-Jewish scholars may reflect a Christian bias toward seeing Jesus as the model for ethics.

Conclusions

Just because we have allowed our second reading to have the last word here does not mean that it is necessarily correct. A number of arguments in this reading can be called into question by those who support the first reading. For example, one can challenge Kaminsky's claim that in the biblical text universalism grows out of particularism. Kaminsky does not sufficiently clarify what the precise relationship is between the two concepts, and, in general, attempts to find a compromise between extremes will tend to favor one side, whether the one making the compromise likes it or not. One can argue that, according to Kaminsky's reasoning, the particularist voice dominates the universalistic one in that universalism is understood through particularism, which is still the bedrock of the relationship between God and Israel. We are therefore left with the original ethical problem of trying to justify Israel's special status from a moral standpoint.

One can also question the arguments in the second reading regarding the Canaanite conquest. It was argued that the destruction of the Canaanites is not as troubling as it seemed because it is God who wages war, not Israel, and the point of the story is to inculcate faith in God as the one who brings victory. A number of objections can be raised against this approach. Niditch admits that according to this interpretation, Israel still does the killing, even if God takes the lead. Moreover, the notion that God wages war on Israel's behalf is dangerous: if God is portrayed as doing all the killing, human beings can absolve themselves of guilt for their own violence.[162] One also has to wonder about an argument which states that the violence in the biblical text is acceptable because it was not for its own sake but was meant to teach the reader about faith in God. The problem is that violence is often not for its own sake; it is frequently perpetrated with other goals in mind. Religious fanatics who have killed people throughout the ages have always argued that their actions served a higher purpose; our own era is filled with people making just this claim. We do not tend to view violence as acceptable simply because it is rationalized by this type of reasoning.

---

162 Niditch, *War in the Hebrew Bible*, 148. Avalos argues that this approach is also flawed because there are other instances in the biblical text in which it is clear that Israel does the fighting on its own, and he cites the episode with the Amalekites as an example. However, Avalos overlooks the fact that in Exodus, the war against the Amalekites succeeds only because Moses raises his hands to God during battle. It is not entirely clear what this gesture accomplishes, but it would seem that here too God has some role in helping Israel win (Sarna, *The JPS Commentary on the Torah: Exodus*, 95; Jeffrey H. Tigay, "Commentary on Deuteronomy," in *The Jewish Study Bible*, ed. Adele Berlin and Marc Zvi Brettler (New York: Oxford University Press, 1999), 142). Another objection that Avalos raises is that from a moral standpoint violence by proxy is not necessarily better than violence committed directly. I am not sure I agree with Avalos here. Much depends on what is meant by "proxy," and Avalos does not explain. See Avalos, 164–66.

The second reading also attempted to deal with the Canaanite genocide by going outside the narratives involving the conquest and pointing to other portions of the biblical text that contain more peaceful attitudes toward the Canaanites, such as the book of Genesis. A variation on this approach was to refer to other parts of the Bible that have nothing to do with the Canaanites at all but seem to express reservations about war in general. The problem with this approach is that while one can be comforted by other texts in the Bible that give a message very different from the one found in the narratives describing the Canaanite conquest, they do not really rid us of its moral problems. The depiction of genocide must still trouble us. Rodd also questions whether the strand in the biblical text critiquing war is as prominent as some would like to believe. Rodd's criticisms are directed at Niditch in particular, who had claimed that one can identify an ideology of nonparticipation in the biblical text in a number of places that speak out against war. Rodd is not convinced that such an ideology is a significant strand in the biblical text.[163]

Yet, the debate between the two readings could be endless. Supporters of the second reading can challenge these rebuttals as well, inviting further rebuttals from those in favor of the first reading. It would seem that the Bible is genuinely ambiguous on the moral questions central to our study, and any attempt to find a definitive interpretation will prove illusory.

This ambiguity stems from a number of factors. Many of the differences between our two readings had to do with simple ambiguities in semantic meaning at every level of the biblical text. First, there were ambiguities about the meaning of individual phrases or verses. Genesis 12:3 resulted in different interpretations in our two readings because the text itself was unclear. Sometimes the ambiguities occurred in much larger units of the biblical text: chapters, narratives, or even entire books. The two readings, for instance, presented very different understandings of the message of the primeval history in Genesis regarding God's relationship to non-Israelites. More central to our

---

163 Rodd, 191–93. The book of Genesis may also not be as helpful as the second reading claimed. Certainly, the Canaanites are portrayed there in a more positive light than in the Deuteronomic History, but more as individuals than as a nation or a series of nations. Therefore, Genesis does not provide much help in overcoming the moral difficulties of the violence directed against the Canaanites in other strata of the biblical text. Moreover, the book of Genesis provides information that may explain from a canonical perspective why there is no inconsistency between the way the Canaanites appear in that text and the way they are depicted in the Deuteronomic History. When God forms a covenant with Abraham in Gen. 15 and promises that his descendants will inherit the land of Canaan, he tells Abraham that his descendants will have to wait four generations before taking possession of the land because "the sin of the Amorites is not yet complete" (Gen. 15:16). Assuming that the Amorites and the Canaanites are referred to interchangeably in the biblical text, we are being told that at present the Canaanites are not sufficiently deserving of punishment to be dispossessed of their land. There is thus a good reason the Canaanites in Genesis appear to be less malevolent than they do in the Deuteronomic History. They are not the same Canaanites who later become sinful and therefore deserving of punishment.

concerns were ambiguities surrounding the narrative describing the conquest of the Canaanites in the book of Joshua. The first reading seemed to make an excellent case that this text, in commending genocide, was irredeemably violent. However, the second reading presented a number of arguments that cast doubt on this assertion. There were also ambiguities in the largest textual unit of all: the Bible itself as viewed from a canonical perspective. Here the unit of analysis was not a section or book of the Bible written by an individual author or school that could be read in different ways; rather, it was the entire Bible. Thus, for instance, we saw one perspective on the issue of Israel's election and its relationship to the outside world in the more exclusivist Deuteronomic History, and quite a different perspective on those issues in the more inclusivist texts of the Bible known as Wisdom literature. The ambiguity here was due to the fact that these components were written by different authors living hundreds of years apart and in widely different circumstances.

Another source of disagreement between the two readings was ambiguity regarding the question of what weight to give a particular passage or portion of the biblical text. For example, our two readings had markedly different views on the significance of the notion that human beings are created in the image of God. In the first reading, it was argued that the idea that human beings were created in the image of God was not a factor in the Bible after the primeval history. Rather, this notion was pushed into the background as the covenant between God and Israel took center stage, and there it remained for the rest of the biblical history. In the second reading, it was argued that this conception was central to the entire worldview of the Bible because it came at the beginning of the biblical history and therefore set the tone for it.[164]

Some scholars, especially in recent years, have questioned whether one can *ever* argue that any one passage in the Bible has more significance than another. The Bible is a heterogeneous mixture of many different types of material written over a vast period of time and under a wide variety of circumstances, and therefore no individual text can be identified as more normative for biblical ethics than another. Rodd has been particularly vocal in arguing for this viewpoint. We must certainly be indebted to these scholars who have made us aware of the problem of arbitrarily assigning too much importance to individual texts in the Bible. These judgments often tell us more about the person offering them than about the Bible itself. However, the importance of a particular

---

164 Kaminsky has a similar complaint about the weight given by Christian scholars to Is. 19:18–25, mentioned earlier. Christian scholars have often treated this passage as emblematic of Isaiah's theology and prophetic theology as a whole because of its pronounced universalism. However, there is no indication that this text is any more important than any other passage in Isaiah when it comes to relations between Israel and the nations. See Kaminsky, *Yet I Loved Jacob*, 151.

passage can sometimes be determined from evidence both within and outside of the Bible. Thus, for instance, there is reason to believe that Genesis 12:1–3 is a pivotal text within the framework of Genesis and the biblical history as a whole.[165] The problem is that there can also be disagreements about what standards to use to determine the importance of a particular passage. In the first reading, it was assumed that the universalistic implications of the notion that all human beings are created in the image of God is of little consequence once the biblical text focuses on Abraham because that concept is never mentioned again in the Bible, and the rest of the biblical history is concerned with Abraham's descendants. The second reading made the argument that this notion was normative for the biblical text as a whole because beginnings are generally important in texts in general. Therefore, in some instances, judgments can be made about the relative importance of a given biblical passage, but even those are subject to dispute because of disagreements over the standards one may use to make such judgments.

Another significant source of disagreement between the two readings revolved around ambiguities regarding the use of historical context to make sense of the biblical text. The first reading assumed that one had to judge the text as is, without invoking historical context. If the Bible depicted violence in any sort of positive way, it had to be judged as morally reprehensible. The second reading relied a good deal on historical context to explain violent passages in the Bible on the grounds that if one understands the historical circumstances under which these passages were composed, the moral difficulties in them are largely alleviated. Thus, in the second reading, the argument was made that the narratives about the Canaanite conquest and the violent eschatological passages in the Prophets were composed in a time of great insecurity and turmoil in ancient Israel, and these texts therefore should not be censured. They were less the product of a desire to glorify violence than a legitimate expression of the fear and vulnerability the Israelites felt as they struggled to cope with outside threats.

The differences between the two readings can thus be largely explained by three sources of ambiguity in the Bible: ambiguity in the semantic meaning of the biblical text, from the smallest to the largest units; ambiguity in the relative weight given to particular phrases, passages, or concepts within the overall scheme of the Bible; and ambiguity regarding the use of historical context to explain violent passages.

---

165 Wells, 185–207. Wells is openly indebted to Brevard Childs's canonical criticism, which invites an analysis of the biblical text that weighs the relative significance of one passage against another. Because canonical criticism analyzes the Bible as a unified canon, judgments about its meaning must grapple with the importance given to specific passages within that canon.

3

Rabbinic Judaism

Rabbinic Judaism emerged in Palestine in the first two centuries of the Common Era, a period of great turmoil in Jewish history. The Roman Empire had recently taken control of the Judean kingdom, and between the years 66 and 135 the Jews waged two rebellions against Roman rule, both of which were crushed. The first occurred in 66–73 and resulted in the destruction of the second Temple, a major catastrophe for Jews. The second revolt took place in 132–35 and was led by the military commander Simeon bar Kokhba.[1] During this period, the rabbis were just one of many groups competing for leadership of the Jewish community. They were religious scholars known primarily for their expertise in biblical interpretation, which relied on a combination of ancient oral traditions and creative exegesis. Yet, it was the rabbis who emerged victorious from among the groups vying for authority by providing an effective program for the reconstruction of Judaism in a time of devastation. Almost all the other groups disappeared, while the rabbinic version of Judaism became standard for all Jews. The process by which rabbinic Judaism became ascendant, however, was a lengthy one. It took several hundred years for the rabbis to

---

1 A third revolt was waged in 115–17 by the Egyptian Jewish community, which was also under Roman domination, and it was also crushed. However, this revolt is not relevant to our concerns here.

achieve full dominance over the Jewish communities in Palestine and the Diaspora.[2]

The rabbinic program consisted of an innovative understanding of Judaism that allowed Jews to cope with the destruction of the Temple and the loss of Jewish sovereignty. The rabbis convinced their fellow Jews that catastrophe had befallen them because of their sins, but that they could repair their relationship with God by continuing to observe the divine commandments in the Bible. Some commandments, of course, could not be practiced anymore, most notably the sacrifices that had been performed in the Temple, but the rabbis insisted that the remaining commandments could function as a body of law that would allow Jews once again to find favor with God. Several generations of rabbis worked diligently to organize, systematize, and elaborate upon the commandments with the help of oral traditions and creative methods of interpretation, and the system of law they eventually created encompassed all aspects of civil and religious life. The rabbis believed that if this system of laws was properly observed, God would eventually reward the Jews by sending a messiah who would reestablish Jewish sovereignty in their homeland and rebuild the Temple.

Key to the rabbinic enterprise was the theological justification the rabbis gave to the oral traditions upon which they relied for their interpretation of the Bible. According to rabbinic belief, God had given an entire oral Torah to Moses on Mount Sinai that was meant to supplement the written Torah and that had been subsequently handed down by word of mouth from generation to generation. The authority of the rabbis was therefore rooted in this second Torah.

The literature produced by the rabbis was both vast and complex. The most important work was the Babylonian Talmud redacted c. 525, though editing activity on this text continued at least a century past that date. It, in turn, was comprised of two works. The first was the Mishnah, which was produced c. 200 in Palestine and recorded discussions of the rabbis regarding all matters

---

2 Summaries of events and developments in Jewish religious ideas and practices in the second Temple period can be found in Lawrence H. Schiffman, *From Text to Tradition: A History of Second Temple and Rabbinic Judaism* (Hoboken, N.J.: Ktav, 1991); Shaye J. D. Cohen, *From the Maccabees to the Mishnah*, 2nd ed. (Louisville: Westminster/John Knox Press, 2006); Martin S. Jaffee, *Early Judaism: Religious Worlds of the First Judaic Millennium*, 2nd ed. (Bethesda, Md.: University Press of Maryland, 2006); Steven T. Katz, ed., *The Cambridge History of Judaism*, vol. 4, *The Late Roman–Rabbinic Period* (Cambridge: Cambridge University Press, 2006). Unfortunately, the importance of the early rabbis in the formation of Judaism is still not sufficiently appreciated in some circles. Some scholars still reflect a Christian bias, according to which viable Judaism ended with the canonization of the Hebrew Bible. They therefore overlook the rabbinic tradition and its centrality in Judaism. The influence of Protestant Christianity has been particularly problematic in this regard, having been guided since its inception by Luther's notion of *sola scriptura*, the idea that the biblical text alone is the source of divine guidance. For example, in his study, *Fighting Words*, Hector Avalos has a chapter entitled "Judaism and the Hebrew Bible" that discusses Judaism and the Bible interchangeably without any cognizance that they are by no means synonymous.

of Jewish law. The second was the Gemara, which was produced in Babylon and contained the discussions of the rabbis regarding the Mishnah recorded during the three centuries after the redaction of the latter text.[3] The Babylonian Talmud ranks second only to the Bible in importance among the sacred texts of Judaism. In standard editions, it fills some twenty volumes. In addition to the Talmud, the rabbis produced several works of Midrash. These were commentaries on various books of the Bible arranged according to the order of verses in the biblical text, unlike the Talmud, which was ordered according topic.

Rabbinic literature is also commonly divided into two genres. Halakhah refers to literature that is concerned with matters of Jewish law. Aggadah refers to literature that deals with issues other than law: homiletic expositions, stories about the rabbis, interpretations of biblical narratives, and discussions of theology. These genres are found in varying proportions in rabbinic texts. Thus, for instance, the Babylonian Talmud is mostly focused on Halakhah, but at least a third of it is Aggadah.[4]

Given the variety of modern academic approaches to rabbinic Judaism, it is important to say something about the methodology used here. I will examine the rabbinic tradition in accordance with the approach taken by scholars of Jewish ethics, such as Reuven Kimelman, Avi Sagi, and David Novak, to name a few. These scholars tend to look at the rabbinic tradition as a coherent and cohesive phenomenon from the first century onward. They focus on commonalities and continuities among rabbis in different places and periods rather than on their differences. They do not entirely ignore the historical context, which may have affected and shaped the views of individual rabbis. However, it is regarded as background to understanding the ongoing discussion of ethical issues in which the rabbis were engaged throughout the centuries. A consequence of this approach is that it does not draw sharp lines of distinction between early rabbinic Judaism, on the one hand, and its medieval interpreters, on the other hand. I will be doing the same in this chapter. My analysis will be framed primarily by sources in early rabbinic Judaism, but I will also adduce medieval rabbinic material that is closely tied to those sources, particularly in

---

3 A second Talmud was produced in Palestine that was redacted c. 425. It consists of the Mishnah and a different Gemara based on the discussions of Palestinian sages. The Palestinian Talmud, however, never achieved the stature that the Babylonian Talmud did. All references to the Talmud in this chapter will therefore be to the Babylonian Talmud unless otherwise specified.

4 Surveys of rabbinic thought and literature can be found in Shmuel Safrai, ed., *The Literature of the Sages* (Philadelphia: Fortress Press, 1987); Ephraim E. Urbach, *The Sages: Their Concepts and Beliefs*, trans. Israel Abrahams (Cambridge, Mass.: Harvard University Press, 1987); H. L. Strack and G. Stemberger, *Introduction to Talmud and Midrash*, trans. Markus Bockmuehl (Edinburgh: T & T Clark, 1991); Jaffee, *Early Judaism*; Charlotte Elisheva Fonrobert and Martin S. Jaffee, eds., *The Cambridge Companion to the Talmud and Rabbinic Literature* (Cambridge: Cambridge University Press, 2007).

the realm of Halakhah. I will not delve into medieval Jewish philosophy or Kabbalah, even though these schools also draw a great deal from early rabbinic Judaism. Separate chapters will be devoted to these phenomena.

This methodology is open to criticism. One can question whether there is enough commonality among rabbis living in widely different historical contexts to speak of a unified rabbinic tradition. The debate over this question has been particularly intense among scholars of early rabbinic Judaism, who focus on the first seven or eight centuries of the Common Era, the period during which the foundational texts of the rabbis were composed. The question here is whether one can speak of a unified rabbinic tradition even within this time period. Rabbinic works composed in this era are anthologies composed by editors whose identities are unknown to us, and each text typically contains enormous numbers of rabbinic sayings. The anonymous editors of these texts were often content to collect multiple rabbinic opinions on a given matter of Jewish thought or practice without making any attempt to determine which view was correct. Therefore, it is very difficult to come up with an unequivocal rabbinic attitude on any one issue in rabbinic law or theology.[5] The problem is compounded if we include medieval rabbinic interpreters in the equation, given that their viewpoints were shaped in periods and places far different from those of the earlier rabbis.

Yet, despite these problems, the methodology of these scholars has merit. To my mind, those who emphasize only the fragmentary nature of rabbinic Judaism go too far in seeing no unity whatsoever in this dimension of Judaism. Even if early rabbinic texts provide a wide range of opinions on a given issue and are composed in different contexts, they deal with similar issues in theology and law, and they are in dialogue with one another with respect to those issues. Moreover, in the Middle Ages and the modern period the rabbis certainly viewed themselves as the inheritors of a unified tradition. A figure such as Maimonides, despite living in a place and time very different from the early rabbis, saw himself as belonging to and as an interpreter of a cohesive body of texts, particularly in the area of Jewish law. His views on war, for instance,

---

5 This problem is exacerbated by the fact that the sayings of the rabbis were recorded long after they were spoken, sometimes hundreds of years later, and in historical contexts completely different from that in which the statements were originally made. It is therefore not clear whether a particular saying is to be understood as the view of the rabbi in whose name it has been reported or represents the view of the editor of the anthology, who lived long after that rabbi and may have attributed the saying to him. It therefore seems impossible to accurately trace the history of early rabbinic ideas. Virtually all scholars of early rabbinic Judaism address the problems discussed here, including those cited in this study. See, for example, Isaiah M. Gafni, *Land, Center and Diaspora* (Sheffield: Sheffield Academic Press, 1997), 14–16; Robert Goldenberg, *The Nations That Knew Thee Not: Ancient Jewish Attitudes toward Other Religions* (New York: New York University Press, 1998), pp. 81–83.

which will be examined later in this chapter, are based explicitly on early rabbinic texts dealing with this issue, and they cannot be understood in the absence of familiarity with those texts.

But perhaps the most important reason we will adopt the methodology of such scholars as Kimelman, Sagi, and Novak is that they are interested in rabbinic Judaism not just as a historical phenomenon, but as a source of normative guidance. It is for this reason that they tend to emphasize continuities in rabbinic thinking. Because our study has a constructive dimension to it as well, their method is appropriate for our purposes. Still, caution is in order so as not to imagine too much unity in the rabbinic tradition and to believe mistakenly that all rabbis from the first century on are of one mind on all issues. Thus, I will refer to opinions of "the rabbis" with the understanding that there is a cohesive tradition here, but I will also assume that one may speak only of tendencies in their thinking, not views universally held by all rabbis in all periods and places up to the end of the Middle Ages.

Rabbinic Judaism Promotes Peace

Most commentators in the field of Jewish ethics believe that rabbinic Judaism has a strong commitment to a peaceful ethic—much more so than the Bible. Ehud Luz's illuminating study of power and morality in modern Zionism provides an excellent example of this reading of rabbinic Judaism. As background to his treatment of Zionism, Luz discusses biblical and rabbinic views on violence, and although he sees ambivalence toward violence and warfare in the Bible itself, he claims that "there is an even greater ambivalence toward military power in rabbinic literature." Talmudic law, he claims, is "not pacifistic," but "it tends to impose severe limitations on the use of force." The rabbis, instead of glorifying military heroism, exalt piety, devotion to God, and Torah study. We thus see in the rabbis a "tendency to sublimate or transform the martial ethos of the Bible."[6] In many instances, Jewish scholars are not as explicit

---

6 Ehud Luz, *Wrestling with an Angel: Power, Morality, and Jewish Identity*, trans. Michael Swirsky (New Haven: Yale University Press, 2003), 21–24. See also Michael S. Berger, "Taming the Beast: Rabbinic Pacification of Second-Century Jewish Nationalism," in *Belief and Bloodshed: Religion and Violence across Time and Tradition*, ed. James K. Wellman Jr. (Lanham, Md.: Rowman & Littlefield Publishers, 2007), 47–62. Perhaps the most comprehensive analysis of rabbinic Judaism from this standpoint is Artson, *Love Peace and Pursue Peace*. The notion that the rabbis accentuated the peaceful dimension of Judaism permeates Artson's study. As noted in the previous chapter, Artson's book is primarily theological in its orientation and should therefore be seen as a work representative of modern Judaism as opposed to a work of historical scholarship (see p. 49 n. 128, this volume). However, Artson bases much of his thinking on a scholarly analysis of sources, and it is therefore appropriate for him to be cited here.

as Luz. The presumption that the rabbis adopted a nonviolent orientation is simply taken for granted.[7]

This view of the rabbinic tradition seems to have a long history. In the late nineteenth and early twentieth centuries, early Zionist thinkers debated the significance of rabbinic nonviolence as they grappled with the question of Jewish identity in light of the possibility of Jews regaining sovereignty in their ancient homeland. Ahad Ha-Am (1856–1927), for instance, glorified rabbinic passivity because, in his opinion, it saved Judaism from destruction. By opting to focus on piety and study, as symbolized by the rabbinic retreat to Yavneh after the destruction of the second Temple, and by eschewing further confrontation with Rome that would have certainly resulted in Jewish defeat, the rabbis preserved Judaism for centuries to come. For Ahad Ha-Am, the rabbis provided proof that the strength of Judaism was in the realm of spirit, not in the realm of military power, and modern Zionism should adopt a similar emphasis in formulating its own ethos. An opposing understanding of the rabbinic tradition was given by such thinkers as Micha Joseph Berdichevsky (1865–1921) and Yosef Hayim Brenner (1881–1921), who vociferously criticized the rabbis for their passivity. According to them, the model for modern Zionism should be the Bible, which glorified military strength and power as exemplified by warriors such as Joshua and King David.[8] What is significant for our purposes is that despite their differences, the viewpoints on both sides of the debate assumed that the rabbinic tradition was nonviolent. The only question was whether that disposition should serve as a model for the construction of a modern Jewish identity.[9]

Our first reading in this chapter will therefore begin with the position that rabbinic Judaism promotes peace. But before we argue in favor of this viewpoint, let us look at rabbinic attitudes toward non-Jews in general. A peaceful understanding of rabbinic Judaism would certainly be bolstered if it could be shown that the rabbis had positive views of non-Jews, and, in fact, a number of scholars support this reading by citing sources to that

---

7 Examples of this tendency will be adduced below.

8 Anita Shapira, *Land and Power: The Zionist Resort to Force, 1881–1948*, trans. William Templer (New York: Oxford University Press, 1992), 21–23; Luz, *Wrestling with an Angel*, 42–44, 54–55.

9 Why modern Jewish thinkers and scholars developed this view of the rabbis is an interesting question in its own right but would require separate treatment. This understanding of the rabbis is likely related to the common apologetic tendencies of nineteenth century Jews, who were fighting for emancipation and painted a positive picture of Judaism to prove that it was at least as ethically sophisticated as Christianity, if not more so. This approach has roots in Moses Mendelssohn, an eighteenth-century figure considered by many to be the first great modern Jewish thinker, and is found in fully developed form in such prominent late nineteenth-century figures as Mortiz Lazarus and Hermann Cohen.

effect.[10] In the Mishnah we are told that God created the human race from a single individual so that no person could say, "My father is greater than yours."[11] This dictum implies equality between Jew and non-Jew in that they are both descended from a common ancestor. The Gemara informs us in several places that a non-Jew who occupies himself with the study of Torah is equivalent to a high priest.[12] In the Tosefta, R. Joshua is quoted as saying that righteous non-Jews have a share in the world to come.[13]

Positive statements about non-Jews in rabbinic literature often focus on specific traits or characteristics that the gentile nations possess. Thus, for instance, several sources claim that God gave wisdom and understanding to all nations. In some sources, the rabbis praise individual nations or non-Jews for their wisdom.[14] Sometimes it is the ethical behavior of non-Jews that receives commendation. In several passages a non-Jew, Dama bar Netina, is presented as a model for such behavior.[15] In some instances, rabbinic praise is directed to non-Jews in biblical narratives. The rabbis often depict figures such as Job, Jethro, and Rahab as righteous gentiles.[16]

An important innovation in rabbinic law also reflects a positive attitude toward non-Jews. According to rabbinic tradition, God gave non-Jews seven commandments as a basic code for governing religious and ethical behavior.[17] Opinions differ as to when these laws were given, but the rabbis generally believe that they originated in the time of Adam or Noah.[18] They are referred to as the "seven laws of the sons of Noah" because Noah is the common ancestor of all humanity after the world was destroyed in the flood.

---

10 These include Greenberg, "Mankind, Israel, and the Nations"; David Novak, *The Election of Israel: The Idea of the Chosen People* (Cambridge: Cambridge University Press, 1995); idem, *Natural Law in Judaism*; idem, *Covenantal Rights: A Study in Jewish Political Theory* (Princeton: Princeton University Press, 2000); Anthony J. Saldarini and Joseph Kanofsky, "Religious Dimensions of the Human Condition in Judaism," in *The Human Condition: A Volume in the Comparative Religious Ideas Project*, ed. Robert C. Neville (Albany: State University of New York Press, 2001), 101–32.

11 Mishnah (henceforth M.), *Sanhedrin* 4:5.

12 Babylonian Talmud (henceforth B.T.) *Sanhedrin* 59a, *Bava Kamma* 38a, *'Avodah Zarah* 3a.

13 Tosefta (henceforth T.) *Sanhedrin* 13:2. Tosefta is a collection of rabbinic discussions dating from the period of the Mishnah and closely paralleling the Mishnah in content, but it is of lesser authority.

14 B.T. *Megillah* 16a; Sacha Stern, *Jewish Identity in Early Rabbinic Writings* (Leiden: E. J. Brill, 1994), 209–10.

15 B.T. *'Avodah Zarah* 23b–24a, *Kiddushin* 31a; Jerusalem Talmud (henceforth J.T.) *Pe'ah* 1:1, *Kiddushin* 1:7; Goldenberg, *The Nations That Knew Thee Not*, 83–84.

16 *Genesis Rabbah* 57:4; *Mekhilta de-Rabi Yishma'el, 'Amalek* 1; B.T. *Megillah* 14b.

17 The Noahide code is analyzed in a number of books and articles. Among the most important are Aaron Lichtenstein, *The Seven Laws of Noah* (New York: Rabbi Jacob Joseph School Press, 1981); David Novak, *The Image of the Non-Jew in Judaism* (Lewiston: Edwin Mellen Press, 1983); Suzanne Last Stone, "Sinaitic and Noahide Law: Legal Pluralism in Jewish Law," *Cardozo Law Review* 12 (1990–91): 1157–1214; Nahum Rakover, *Law and the Noahide: Law as a Universal Value* (Jerusalem: Library of Jewish Law, 1998).

18 The earliest reference to this tradition is T. *'Avodah Zarah* 8:4. The central discussion of these laws in the Talmud is found in *Sanhedrin* 56a–60b.

There is some disagreement regarding the content of these commandments. A common list contains prohibitions against idolatry, blasphemy, forbidden sexual relations, murder, theft, and tearing off a limb from a live animal
and eating it, and a positive command to establish courts of law to enforce
these regulations.[19] Some rabbis include prohibitions against eating blood
from a live animal, practicing magic and related occult arts, cross-breeding,
and the cross-grafting of trees.[20] In one talmudic source, a tradition is cited
which claims that there are thirty such commandments but their content is not
specified.[21] Seven, however, appears to have become the normative number for
the rabbis. It should also be added that, according to several rabbis, each of the
seven laws is merely a rubric for many more regulations. Each one is accompanied by a substantial body of rabbinic legislation when applied to Jews, and one
can therefore presume that the same legislation applies to non-Jews as well.[22]

The Noahide laws are often understood by contemporary Jewish ethicists
as an ethical advance over the biblical worldview because they represent the
notion that non-Jews are no different from Jews in having the capacity to be
religious and moral beings, establish a relationship with God, and achieve
reward in the afterlife. Although in the Bible there are numerous instances in
which God has a relationship with non-Jews both as nations and as individuals,
those relationships are nowhere placed on the kind of systematic footing that
we find in the rabbinic conception of the Noahide laws. The Noahide code
therefore strengthens the universalistic elements in Judaism that are rooted in
the Bible.[23]

Some go as far as claiming that the Noahide code is a Jewish version of
natural law. As we saw in the previous chapter, David Novak argued for the
existence of natural law in the Bible, and he does the same for rabbinic Judaism. According to this viewpoint, the rabbis believed that the seven laws could
be discovered through rational reflection and without the aid of revelation, and
indeed some rabbinic sources seem to support that idea.[24] This approach is

---

19 Ibid.

20 B.T. *Sanhedrin* 56a–57a.

21 B.T. *Hullin* 92a.

22 This is argued in the present day by Lichtenstein.

23 All the scholarly studies of the Noahide code listed in n. 17 support this interpretation either explicitly
or implicitly. See also Jon Levenson, "The Universal Horizon," 148, whose view on the Noahide code is in line
with these interpreters as well.

24 Novak argues for this position in a number of his works; see especially *Natural Law in Judaism*, chapter
6. A similar view is held by Rakover; see especially chapter 3. This view was first suggested at the end of the eighteenth century by Moses Mendelssohn and was later adopted by Jewish thinkers in the nineteenth-century
Reform movement. See Newman, *An Introduction to Jewish Ethics*, 118–22. Sources often cited to support the
notion that the rabbis believe in natural law are B.T. *Yoma* 67b and *Sifra, Aharey Mot* 9:10.

helpful in solving an obvious conundrum: how is it that a non-Jew may come to know these laws if he or she has not been privy to the tradition of the Noahide code? That these laws are discoverable through reason answers that question.[25]

Some commentators have also argued that the Noahide laws provide a proper balance between universalism and particularism in Jewish ethics. An emphasis on universalism in any system of thought can become tyrannical because it may become uncompromising in assuming that there is one truth for all human beings, and therefore it can easily lead to intolerance and violence against those who are unwilling to adopt that truth. However, an emphasis on particularism also runs the risk of intolerance and violence against outsiders because it encourages isolationism in focusing only on the interests of one's own group.[26] The Noahide code represents an intriguing compromise between the two extremes in that non-Jews are expected to keep some of the most basic of Jewish norms but not others. God cares enough about non-Jews to give them laws regulating the fundamentals of moral and religious conduct, but he does not envision a world in which everyone must adopt Judaism. This compromise, in fact, has a strikingly modern and progressive ring to it. Over the past half century, world leaders, ethicists, and religious thinkers have struggled to define a minimal set of rights that all nations must uphold. The Universal Declaration of Human Rights, issued in 1948, is the best-known of these attempts. At the same time, the framers of such rights generally acknowledge that communities should be allowed to live in accordance with the values dictated by their respective cultures. Thus, on the one hand, one wants to avoid insisting on an absolute morality, but, on the other hand, one wants to avoid total moral relativism, which can be harmful in allowing every culture or individual to decide what is morally correct. The challenge in coming up with a code of universal rights is to find a compromise between the two positions. The details of the compromise are far from settled, but the important point for our purposes is that the rabbinic conception of the Noahide code could serve as a model for balancing these extremes.[27]

A positive attitude toward non-Jews also comes through in a number of rabbinic statements and laws about how Jews should interact with them. In one

25 The question of whether Judaism as a whole supports natural law has been a matter of debate. For a survey and analysis of the positions on this issue, see Newman, *Past Imperatives*, chapter 6.

26 Daniel Boyarin makes similar observations in *A Radical Jew: Paul and the Politics of Identity* (Berkeley: University of California Press, 1994), 232–36.

27 Jonathan Sacks argues this point in *The Dignity of Difference: How to Avoid a Clash of Civilizations*, 2nd ed. (London: Continuum, 2003), viii, 20–21.

rabbinic passage, Abaye says that a person should always strive to be on peaceful terms with others, including non-Jews, so as to be beloved by God and fellow human beings.[28] Another rabbinic source tells us that R. Yohanan ben Zakkai always made a point of greeting other people before being greeted, including non-Jews.[29] Most important is a series of special decrees referred to in the Mishnah, which were instituted by the rabbis "on account of the paths of peace" (mipney darkey shalom), and were meant to create a more peaceful world. Some of these involve non-Jews. Thus, Jews must give charity to non-Jews in order to foster better relations with them. They must also visit their sick and bury their dead for the same purpose.[30]

Yet, no one familiar with the rabbinic tradition can deny that it also contains numerous negative statements about non-Jews, and any honest discussion of rabbinic views on non-Jews must come to terms with these sources. Sacha Stern notes that the rabbis often treat Jews and non-Jews as "radically different entities," with Jews being superior to non-Jews.[31] Some sources attest to the notion that Jews are beloved by God while non-Jews are not.[32] In another source, the rabbis inform us that one Jew is more beloved by God than all the nations of the world combined.[33] In the standard morning liturgy composed by the rabbis, a Jew is required to recite a blessing every morning thanking God "who has not made me a non-Jew."[34]

The difference between Jews and non-Jews is frequently attributed to a distinction in their religious and moral natures.[35] Non-Jews are assumed to be inherently wicked, and they therefore have tendencies to worship idols, commit murder, steal, lie, and violate basic sexual norms, including proscriptions against homosexuality and bestiality.[36] Several sources express the belief that non-Jews are unable to perform the divine commandments that were given to

---

28   B.T. Berakhot 17a.

29   B.T. Berakhot 17a.

30   M. Gittin 5:8–9; B.T. Gittin 61a, 62a, 'Avodah Zarah 6b; M. 'Avodah Zarah 1:1.

31   Stern, Jewish Identity, 2–3. Gary Porton makes a similar judgment about rabbinic attitudes in the Mishnah and Tosefta. See Gary G. Porton, Goyim: Gentiles and Israelites in Mishnah-Tosefta (Atlanta: Scholars Press, 1988), especially chapter 8.

32   Stern, Jewish Identity, 2–3. Thus, in Esther Rabbah 7:13, we are told that "the nations are 'strangers' before the Almighty; Israel is close to Him, [and is] His 'sons.'"

33   Sifre Deuteronomy 97.

34   T. Berakhot 7:18.

35   Stern, Jewish Identity, 22–31. See also Raphael Loewe, "Potentialities and Limitations of Universalism in the Halakhah," in Studies in Rationalism, Judaism and Universalism: In Memory of Leon Roth, ed. Raphael Loewe (London: Routledge and K. Paul, 1966), 131; Goldenberg, The Nations That Knew Thee Not, 83.

36   With respect to idol worship, see J.T. Berakhot 8:6; murder, see M. Shabbat 2:5; theft, see B.T. Sukkot 30a, Bava Batra 45a; lying, see B.T. Bekhorot 13b; sexual promiscuity, see T. Ketubot 1:6, B.T. Ketubot 13b.

Israel.[37] Another rabbinic source goes in a similar direction by claiming that in the messianic period non-Jews will abandon idol worship and attempt to convert to Judaism but will soon relapse and take up their old ways again.[38] Yet another rabbinic source explains that non-Jews are unable to keep the commandments because even when they do good deeds, it is only to gain prestige.[39]

The difference between Jews and non-Jews is often couched in the contrast between purity and impurity.[40] Thus, for instance, we read in one midrashic source that the nations are from "the seed of impurity," while Israel is from "the seed of truth and holiness."[41] As part of the *havdalah* ceremony, instituted by the rabbis to mark the conclusion of the Sabbath, one recites a blessing that celebrates the distinction God has made "between holiness and the profane," one manifestation of which is the division "between Israel and the nations."[42] Some rabbinic sources go as far as comparing non-Jews to animals, likening them to dogs, bears, horses, and donkeys. The last association is particularly common.[43]

Some scholars have argued that the low regard that the rabbis had toward non-Jews resulted in a worldview that was solipsistic.[44] As Stern puts it, in rabbinic thought the nations "are excluded from the experience of Israel and are totally insignificant to it."[45] In some sense, the very existence of non-Jews is called into question in that they do not figure into the rabbinic worldview.[46] A verse in Isaiah 40:17 declaring that "all the nations are like nothing before Him" is frequently quoted by the rabbis as evidence that non-Jews are nothing, not just in God's eyes but in an absolute sense.[47]

Prejudice against non-Jews also expresses itself in the realm of rabbinic law. In their legislation, the rabbis sometimes attempted to keep Jews separate

---

37 Stern, *Jewish Identity*, 200–202. This idea comes out in a famous midrash in which the Torah is offered to various nations but is rejected because each nation is unable to keep a specific commandment. The Edomites cannot accept the commandment prohibiting murder, Ammon and Moab are unwilling to keep the commandment banning adultery, and Ishmael is unable to adhere to the interdiction against theft. Only Israel accepts the Torah without reservations. See *Mekhilta de-Rabi Yishma'el, Ba-Hodesh* 5; *Sifre Deuteronomy* 343; B.T. *'Avodah Zarah* 2b.

38 B.T. *'Avodah Zarah* 2a–3b.

39 B.T. *Bava Batra* 10b.

40 Stern, *Jewish Identity*, 31–33.

41 *Tanhuma, Naso* 7.

42 B.T. *Pesahim* 103b.

43 Stern, *Jewish Identity*, 33–39.

44 Stern, *Jewish Identity*, 200–223; Goldenberg, *The Nations That Knew Thee Not*, 84–85, 106.

45 Stern, *Jewish Identity*, 200.

46 Stern, *Jewish Identity*, 216.

47 *Leviticus Rabbah* 27:7.

from non-Jews.[48] In some sources in rabbinic law, non-Jews are treated more harshly than Jews. In mishnaic law, we are told that a Jew whose ox gores the ox of a non-Jew is never culpable for damages, even though in some instances, if the injured ox was owned by a Jew, he would be. Conversely, if the ox of a non-Jew gores the ox of a Jew, the non-Jew is always culpable for full damages, even though in some instances, if the owner of the goring ox was a Jew, the owner would pay only half the damages.[49] In the Tosefta we learn of even more disturbing regulations: a Jew who kills or steals from a gentile is not culpable.[50]

However, a number of considerations help soften the harshness of these sources. First, when it comes to rabbinic laws that discriminate against non-Jews, a careful examination reveals that the issues are more complex than a cursory reading of these laws would suggest. In a study of these laws, Steven Fraade notes that the early rabbis seem to have been uncomfortable with their legislation.[51] Thus, for instance, the Tosefta, which states that a Jew is not culpable for robbing a gentile, goes on to state in another passage that a Jew who robs a gentile must return the object. It also informs us that a Jew robbing a gentile is worse than a Jew robbing another Jew because of the principle of *hillul ha-shem*, desecration of the divine name.[52] The Tosefta, therefore, appears to mitigate its discriminatory stance regarding non-Jews, at least when it comes to the issue of theft.[53] Fraade demonstrates that in other passages similar tensions are evident.[54] Fraade then goes on to argue that such inconsistencies can be

48 Stern, *Jewish Identity*, 139–98. This effort is frequently connected with a concern for ensuring that Jews avoid any association with idol worship. In early rabbinic Judaism, idol worship became a metaphor for non-Jewishness in general. Therefore, by dissociating from idol worship, the rabbis dissociate themselves from non-Jewish culture in general. It is not that idol worship is seen as attractive to the rabbis. The concern is to avoid assisting non-Jews in idol worship or deriving any benefit from it even inadvertently or indirectly. See Stern, *Jewish Identity*, 156–57; Goldenberg, *The Nations That Knew Thee Not*, 83–98; Mireille Hadas-Lebel, *Jerusalem against Rome*, trans. Robyn Fréchet (Leuven: Peeters, 2006), 311–23.

49 M. *Bava Kamma* 4:3.

50 T. *'Avodah Zarah* 8:4–5.

51 Steven D. Fraade, "Navigating the Anomalous: Non-Jews at the Intersection of Early Rabbinic Law and Narrative," in *The Other in Jewish Thought and History*, eds. Laurence J. Silberstein and Robert L. Cohn (New York: New York University Press, 1994), 145–65.

52 T. *Bava Kamma* 10:15. According to the principle of *hillul ha-shem*, a Jew must strive to avoid all activity that would bring opprobrium upon the Torah and its divine giver, and robbing a gentile would constitute such an activity. This principle is the inverse of *kiddush ha-shem*, sanctification of the divine name, which requires that a Jew serve as an exemplar of moral decency and kindness in all of his or her actions because such behavior reflects positively on the Torah and its divine giver. See B.T. *Yoma* 86a, *Hullin* 94b.

53 Rabbinic discomfort with the discriminatory legislation under discussion here can also be found in an aggadic passage in *Sifre Deuteronomy* 344. Here a story is told that the Roman government sent two officers to disguise themselves as converts to study Jewish law. After doing so, the officers concluded that the Torah was praiseworthy but that the rule that a Jew could rob a gentile with impunity was not. Still, the officers decided not to report this particular law to the government. In another version of the story in J.T. *Bava Kamma* 4:3, Rabban Gamliel reacts to the observation of the officers by instituting a prohibition against robbing gentiles.

54 Fraade, 150–52, 153.

explained by the fact that the rabbis were caught between countervailing tendencies that were not always compatible with each other. On the one hand, gentiles had no juridical status within Jewish law because they did not accept its terms. On the other hand, Jews were required to bring non-Jews to a recognition of God's goodness by serving as models for exemplary religious and moral behavior. Fraade appears to be arguing that while rabbinic legislation in the Mishnah and Tosefta is discriminatory when it comes to non-Jews, this phenomenon has to do less with prejudice than with legitimate confusion over the place of non-Jews in rabbinic law.[55]

We must also note that by the time we get to the Middle Ages, much of the discriminatory legislation in early rabbinic Judaism was gradually restricted or eliminated entirely. The fascinating process by which this occurred in Jewish communities living in Christian Europe is described in a classic study by Jacob Katz.[56] This process is too complex to be reviewed here in full. Let us just note the remarkable figure of R. Menahem ha-Meiri, to whom Katz and others have devoted a great deal of attention.[57] Meiri, a fourteenth-century rabbi in southern France, was a bold innovator on the issue of legislation regarding non-Jews. Meiri claimed that the discriminatory laws of the early rabbis applied only to idolaters in ancient times, whose culture was immoral and violent. It did not apply to non-Jews who had created a civilized society based on what he considered to be the fundamental principles of religion. Nations in this latter category were called "nations bound by the ways of religion" (ummot ha-gdurot be-darkey ha-datot). For Meiri, Christian society was in this category, and therefore none of the rabbinic legislation discriminating against non-Jews applied to them. Meiri in no way believed that Christianity was on a par with Judaism, and he continued to regard it as a flawed and inferior religion. Nonetheless, his position was remarkably daring and enlightened in the context of the Middle Ages in showing appreciation and respect for Christians and the society they had created.[58]

---

55 Fraade, 157–58.

56 Jacob Katz, Exclusiveness and Tolerance: Studies in Jewish-Gentile Relations in Medieval and Modern Times (New York: Behrman House, 1961), especially chapters 3–5, 10.

57 Gerald J. Blidstein, "Menahem Meiri's Attitude toward Gentiles: Apologetics or Worldview?" in Binah: Jewish Intellectual History in the Middle Ages, ed. Joseph Dan (Westport, Conn.: Praeger, 1994), 3:119–33; Moshe Halbertal, Between Torah and Wisdom: Rabbi Menachem ha-Meiri and the Maimonidean Halakhists in Provence (in Hebrew) (Jerusalem: Magnes Press, 2000), especially 80–109; David Berger, "Jews, Gentiles, and the Modern Egalitarian Ethos: Some Tentative Thoughts," in Formulating Responses in an Egalitarian Age, ed. Marc D. Stern (Lanham, Md.: Rowman & Littlefield, 2005), 93–101.

58 Stern believes that developments in Halakhah in the medieval period are critical for correcting the negative views of the early rabbis regarding non-Jews (Jewish Identity, 5). Stern's remarks are significant in light of the fact that his book sees early rabbinic Judaism as mostly hostile to non-Jews.

Yet, the rabbinic sources that are most negative about non-Jews are not in the realm of law. We have already recounted a litany of homiletic rabbinic statements that depict non-Jews as wicked and impure and that compare them to animals. But here too the harshness of the sources can be blunted by taking a number of considerations into account. First, as Stern has noted, the rabbis often vilify their fellow Jews in terms similar to those used in their criticisms of non-Jews. Much has been written on early rabbinic attitudes toward 'amey ha-arets, "the common people," or ordinary Jews. The Babylonian rabbis had particularly negative things to say about this sector of the Jewish community. Some sources hurl scathing criticisms at the 'amey ha-arets for their lack of learning and piety. Some go as far as excluding them from the people of Israel. At times, they are compared to donkeys, just as non-Jews are. Yet, in other sources, the rabbis' views of the 'amey ha-arets are quite positive. In these passages, the 'amey ha-arets are very much part of Israel and are praised for their righteousness. The rabbis therefore displayed the same inconsistencies regarding 'amey ha-arets as they did with non-Jews.[59] These observations place the harsh rabbinic rhetoric regarding non-Jews in a broader perspective by demonstrating that such statements reflect the difficulty that some rabbis had with anyone who was outside their circles—including fellow Jews. Therefore, the issue here is not how the rabbis dealt with non-Jews, but how they dealt with non-rabbis. One may still criticize the rabbis for their reprehensible statements about non-Jews and 'amey ha-arets alike, but the problem was not necessarily non-Jewishness per se.

We also gain valuable perspective on the negative statements of the early rabbis regarding non-Jews by noting that these statements find a parallel among other groups in their place and time. Rabbinic prejudices against non-Jews were similar to prejudices expressed by Greeks toward oriental peoples, and by

---

59 Stern, *Jewish Identity*, 114–20. Stern cites the scholarship of Lee Levine, which explains the inconsistency here as due to historical development: negative sources about the 'amey ha-arets are from the earlier tannaitic period, while the favorable sources are from the later amoraic period. Eventually, Levine argues, the whole category faded into insignificance in the Middle Ages. Stern prefers another theory. Rabbinic attitudes toward other Jews are characterized by what he terms "centripetal experience." For the rabbis, the whole notion of "Israel" refers primarily to the rabbinic class, with the common people being peripheral. This viewpoint does not mean that the rabbis were sectarians in the way the Qumran sect was, for instance; but they did differentiate between themselves and the rest of Israel that did not adhere strictly to their agenda (Stern, *Jewish Identity*, 132–38). William Scott Green goes in a similar direction in his study, "Otherness Within: Toward a Theory of Difference in Rabbinic Judaism," in *To See Ourselves as Others See Us: Christians, Jews, and "Others" in Late Antiquity*, ed. Jacob Neusner and Ernst S. Frerichs (Chico, Calif.: Scholars Press, 1985). Green claims that rabbinic identity is predicated primarily on the notion of a "textual community" in which being literate in certain texts defines identity, and that it is for this reason that the rabbis have such difficulty with the 'amey ha-arets. Because the latter do not have knowledge of rabbinic texts, they cannot be a part of the rabbinic community. However, as Jews, they are not entirely excluded from the rabbinic community either.

non-Jews against Jews.[60] This observation does not make the rabbis any better, from an ethical standpoint, than their non-Jewish neighbors, but it does not make them any worse either.

This last observation raises the basic question of the historical context in which the rabbis formulated their views, and, as in our discussion of the Bible, this factor is extremely helpful in explaining the negative portrayals of non-Jews. In the first two centuries, Jews suffered terribly from the brutality of Roman rule, and this was undoubtedly a major cause of the rebellions against Rome. From Jewish and Roman sources, we also learn that the destruction caused by these rebellions was quite devastating, particularly that which occurred in the wake of the Bar Kokhba revolt. A number of rabbinic sources describe, sometimes in mythical terms, the depth of Jewish suffering in the wake of this rebellion.[61] Women and children were slain in great numbers, great rabbis were summarily executed, and rivers of blood flowed so deep that horses waded in them up to their nostrils.[62] Dio Cassius, the Roman historian who documents the events of this period, seems to confirm that the devastation was great, though without the mythical flourishes. He refers to 580,000 Jewish deaths on the battlefield but notes that many more Jews died of famine, sickness, and fire. The entire region of Judea experienced such destruction that it became depopulated as Jews fled to the Galilee or Babylon.[63] It was in these circumstances that rabbinic Judaism emerged.

Is it any wonder, then, that the rabbis had such terrible things to say about non-Jews—that they saw them as inherently immoral and depraved? The same circumstances help explain why some rabbinic sources speak in such grandiose terms about Israel's inherent superiority. Not only did this perception follow from a sense of revulsion at the conduct of their non-Jewish enemies, but as Stern puts it, it was "an escapist fantasy" to deal with the harsh reality of the servitude to Rome. If they could not beat the Romans on the military front, they could at least be comforted by their ascendancy in the realm of spirit.[64]

We must also keep in mind that the indignities Jews suffered at the hands of the Romans were not a new experience. With the exception of the Hasmonean state, which lasted less than a century, Jews had been subjugated to foreign peoples for hundreds of years, including the Assyrians, Babylonians,

---

60 Stern, *Jewish Identity*, 5.

61 Richard G. Marks, *The Image of Bar Kokhba in Traditional Jewish Literature: False Messiah and National Hero* (University Park, Pa.: Pennsylvania State University Press, 1994), 8; Hadas-Lebel, 179–93, 398–409.

62 Hadas-Lebel, 190–91; B.T. *Berakhot* 61b, *Gittin* 57a, *Sanhedrin* 14a, *'Avodah Zarah* 18a; *Lamentations Rabbah* 2:5.

63 Hadas-Lebel, 398–99.

64 Stern, *Jewish Identity*, 44.

Persians, and Greeks. Any anger that the rabbis felt toward non-Jews was no doubt compounded by an increasingly bitter cache of Jewish historical memory. As Robert Goldenberg puts it, rabbinic hostility toward gentiles was fed by "endless subjection to foreign conquerors and the frustrated national ambitions of the Jews themselves."[65]

In light of all these observations, it is perfectly understandable that rabbinic sources would contain negative statements about non-Jews. Furthermore, we can invoke once again the insights of social psychology to better understand these statements. We noted in the last chapter that in recent decades social psychologists have begun to believe that it is natural for human beings to identify with their ethnic and national groups, and that such identification often leads to negative views toward outsiders. We also noted that according to the same psychologists, ethnic and national groups that have experienced extensive persecution are far more likely to adopt hostile views of outsiders than those that have not.[66] Given the history of Jewish subjugation to outsiders both before and during the rabbinic period, it should therefore come as no surprise that rabbinic Judaism would speak badly about non-Jews.

In light of these observations, the many positive statements about non-Jews in rabbinic sources summarized earlier are all the more impressive.[67] It would seem that a good number of rabbis were able to rise above the animosity stirred by non-Jewish violence against Jews and look at non-Jews in positive terms. The same can be said about many medieval rabbis. If Jews suffered terribly at the hands of the Romans, things did not improve much in the medieval period. We need not summarize the litany of persecutions that Jews experienced, particularly in Christian Europe; they are well-known and well documented. Yet, here too, Jews were able to express positive opinions about non-Jews. R. Menahem ha-Meiri, whom we discussed earlier, is an excellent case in point. Meiri had firsthand experience with Christian persecutions against Jews in Provence, where he lived. He was an eyewitness to the expulsion

---

65 Goldenberg, *The Nations That Knew Thee Not*, 90.

66 See this volume, pp. 44-5, 53.

67 Some scholars note that the Talmud contains a number of remarkably positive statements about the morality and culture of the Persians, and they conclude from this observation that the venomous statements about non-Jews in early rabbinic sources are directed primarily at the Romans, not at all non-Jews. That the Babylonian rabbis would have a positive view of their Persian neighbors makes sense given that Jews were relatively well treated by them over several centuries. See David Novak, "Gentiles in Rabbinic Thought," in *The Cambridge History of Judaism*, vol. 4, *The Late Roman–Rabbinic Period*, ed. Steven T. Katz (Cambridge: Cambridge University Press), 654–65. Stern's study also notes the positive remarks about Persians in the Talmud (Stern, *Jewish Identity*, 6–7 n. 33, 226–27 n. 175). However, Stern mentions this issue only in passing and does not go as far as Novak does. In truth, only a relatively small number of rabbinic sources speak about the Persians at all, and thus caution is in order here.

of Jews from France in 1306. His writings also contain several statements expressing bitterness over the Jewish condition in exile. And yet, despite all this, Meiri crafted a highly original doctrine which saw Christians as Noahides and ruled that none of the discriminatory rabbinic legislation against non-Jews applied to them.[68]

If one is dissatisfied with this defense of rabbinic Judaism, what is most important for our concerns is that whatever dislike the rabbis felt toward non-Jews, that antipathy did not seem to translate into a violent ethic. On the contrary, a case can be made that rabbinic Judaism was mostly nonviolent, even with respect to their hated Roman enemies. Thus, if the rabbis did not always like non-Jews, this did not mean that they wanted to go to war against them. In light of the suffering that the rabbis experienced at the hands of their non-Jewish overlords, their restraint with respect to violence is quite commendable.

That the rabbis adopted a peaceful ethic is reflected in a number of rabbinic sources dealing with the Romans. As noted earlier, the Jews rebelled against Roman rule twice within a seventy-year period, and there is evidence that some rabbis endorsed the violence. R. Akiva, one of the most prominent and beloved rabbinic figures, appears to have supported the Bar Kokhba revolt and believed that Bar Kokhba himself was the messiah. However, there are also indications that some rabbis were unhappy with Akiva on this matter. Moreover, once the rebellion was put down, most rabbis seem to have come to the conclusion that war against Rome was futile and destructive and that living in peace was preferable to political independence. This position is evident in the negative depiction of the figure of Bar Kokhba in rabbinic texts. As Richard Marks has shown, early rabbinic opinion was divided over whether he was a messianic impostor or a failed military hero, but in both depictions he was criticized for his arrogance and self-aggrandizement.[69]

An acquiescent attitude toward Rome can also be found in sources describing the surrender of Jerusalem after the first rebellion in 66–73. A famous story in a number of rabbinic sources reports that in the midst of the rebellion, R. Yohanan ben Zakkai, a leading rabbinic figure in Jerusalem at the time, wished to surrender to the Romans but was unable to because the Zealots, a faction determined to fight at all costs, threatened anyone taking such a position. R. Yohanan was able to arrange for a surrender only through subterfuge; he was smuggled out of Jerusalem in a coffin and negotiated with the Roman

---

68 Katz, *Exclusiveness and Tolerance*, 128.

69 Marks, *The Image of Bar Kokhba*, chapter 1. Differences of rabbinic opinion on Bar Kokhba are found in a number of sources, most notably J.T. *Ta'anit* 4:8; *Lamentations Rabbah* 2:4.

general Vespasian.[70] While this story may have some basis in fact, it is found in texts redacted long after the first revolt, and thus it is likely that it reflects the stance of the rabbis toward Rome that became consolidated after the Bar Kokhba revolt.[71]

The nonviolent ethic of the rabbis vis-à-vis Rome is also reflected in rabbinic sources that draw a contrast between the peaceful ways of Israel and the warring ways of Rome. Thus the following dictum is reported in the name of R. Hiyya: "[Moses] said to them [i.e., Israel]: 'If you see that he [i.e., Esau] seeks war against you, do not resist but hide from him until his world has passed.'"[72] The rabbis commonly identified Rome with Edom, the nations that descended from Esau, and thus, when Moses is described in this source as warning Israel not to respond to Esau's provocations, one can assume that the lesson concerns the Jews and their response to Roman aggression.[73]

The nonviolent attitude of the rabbis regarding Roman rule seems to have developed into a more general embrace of nonviolence. Rabbinic passivity would become a key ingredient in a theology designed to make sense of the catastrophe the Jewish people had experienced in the first century and to give Jews guidance about how to cope with their subjugation to the gentile nations as the Middle Ages unfolded. Although this nonviolent theology is never systematically worked out by the rabbis, its outlines are fairly clear. First, the rabbis believed that the second Temple was destroyed and the Jews forced into exile because of their sins. This notion was eventually encapsulated in the phrase *mipney hata'einu,* "because of our sins," which appears in the festival liturgy. Second, the only way Jews could repair their relationship with God was through repentance, which was equated with the strict observance of Halakhah. Third,

---

70 B.T. *Gittin* 55b–56b; *Lamentations Rabbah* 1:5:30; *Avot de-Rabi Natan,* version A, 4; *Avot de-Rabi Natan,* version B, 6.

71 Michael Berger makes this point in "Taming the Beast," 50, 59 n. 13, 15.

72 *Deuteronomy Rabbah* 1:19.

73 In other midrashic passages, similar symbolism is used to make the same point. Thus, in *Genesis Rabbah* 98:5, Jacob chides Simeon and Levi for their violence against the Shechemites (Gen. 49:5) by telling them that the implements of war belong only to Esau, not to them. A similar message is communicated in *Mekhilta de-Rabi Yishma'el, Be-Shalah* 2, which comments on Ex. 14:10. According to the biblical verse, the Israelites cry out to God while being pursued by the Egyptian army, and the rabbis comment on the Israelites' action by drawing a contrast between the Edomites, who pride themselves in the sword when dealing with enemies, and the Israelites, who pride themselves on prayer. Once again, the reference to the Edomites is almost certainly an allusion to Rome. The association between Esau, Edom, and Rome is dealt with in a classic article by Gerson D. Cohen, "Esau as Symbol in Early Medieval Thought," in *Studies in the Variety of Rabbinic Cultures* (Philadelphia: Jewish Publication Society of America, 1991), 243–69. See also Stern, *Jewish Identity,* 18–21; Elliot Horowitz, *Reckless Rites: Purim and the Legacy of Jewish Violence* (Princeton: Princeton University Press, 2006), 112–13, 114–16, 125–28; Hadas-Lebel, 498–511. Some rabbinic sources also associate Rome with Amalek, the nation that descended from Esau's grandson and that, as we have seen, was deemed the eternal enemy of the Jewish people.

if the Jews fulfilled this condition, God would send the messiah, punish the nations that had oppressed Israel, and lead the Jews back to their homeland to regain sovereignty and rebuild the Temple. Finally, in the meantime, patience was needed; Jews should focus their efforts on repairing their relationship with God through the observance of his laws and not to dwell on messianic specula-tions that might lead to more self-destructive violence.[74]

Each of these premises deserves elaboration. According to most scholars, the early rabbis were unanimous in the belief that the destruction of the Tem-ple and the exile were punishment for sin, though there was disagreement on which sin or sins were responsible for the tragedies.[75] In settling on this expla-nation, the rabbis were clearly drawing from biblical sources. The Torah con-tains lengthy passages warning the Israelites that if they do not obey God's commandments, they will be punished, and that punishment often includes exile.[76] The prophet Jeremiah famously develops this line of thinking when he reacts to the onslaught of the Babylonians by urging his fellow Jews to submit to them and accept exile because they are being punished for their sins.[77] The book of Lamentations, written in the wake of the destruction of the first Temple, also repeatedly invokes the idea that Israel has been punished for its sins. What made biblical sources about the first exile so meaningful to the rabbis was that the rabbis appear to have conflated the images of Babylon and Rome, on the premise that history is cyclical. Both Babylon and Rome were Edom, the ancient enemies of the Jewish people descended from Esau.

---

74 The general outline of this theology is described in Luz, *Wrestling with an Angel*, 25–26.

75 Robert Goldenberg, "The Destruction of the Temple: Its Meaning and Consequences," in *The Cam-bridge History of Judaism*, vol. 4, *The Late Roman–Rabbinic Period*, ed. Steven T. Katz (Cambridge: Cambridge University Press, 2006), 199; Gafni, 21, 24–27; Berger, "Taming the Beast," 52–54; Hadas-Lebel, 132–44, 152–57. An example of a rabbinic source that attempts to identify the sin responsible for the destruction of the Temple is B.T. *Yoma* 9a, which claims that "groundless hatred" was its cause. Another relevant source here is a well-known rabbinic aggadah in B.T. *Gittin* 55b–57a, which attributes the destruction of the Temple to a series of events be-ginning with a certain individual who holds a party and throws out a guest who was invited by mistake. Golden-berg plays down the significance of the first source, claiming: "The answer that 'groundless hatred' is the moral equivalent of idolatry or fornication seems no more than homiletical moralizing" (Goldenberg, *The Nations That Knew Thee Not*, 197 n. 17). I must respectfully disagree. Goldenberg does not appreciate the stringency of rabbinic ethics when it comes to interpersonal behavior. Hadas-Lebel voices an opinion regarding the second source similar to Goldenberg's: "The inconsequential nature of the cause for a war demonstrated in the anecdote only served to underline the inevitability of a long-premeditated punishment" (Hadas-Lebel, 155). Here too I disagree. The action of throwing someone out of a party is clearly emblematic of a deeper moral decay in Jewish society as whole and is reflected in the fact that in the source, we are told that the rabbis who attended the party did nothing to stop the insult.

76 E.g., Lev. 26, Deut. 28.

77 Jer. 5:19, 9:15. A number of rabbinic sources specifically cite Jeremiah to support the notion that one should not actively seek the destruction of one's enemies. See the sources adduced in Reuven Kimelman, "Non-Violence in the Talmud," *Judaism* 17 (1968): 321–22.

The rabbis therefore understood the descriptions of the first exile as applying directly to their own situation.[78]

What is important for our purposes is that the doctrine of *mipney hata'einu* effectively pacified Jewish anger and its potential for violence by deflecting it away from the Romans. According to the rabbis, the real culprit responsible for the destruction was the evil impulse within the Jewish heart. If the Jews had been obedient to God, there would have been no destruction. Furthermore, the rabbis insisted that the only way for Jews to reverse their predicament was through repentance and piety. Thus, the cause of the destruction and its remedy had little to do with their relationship with the Romans and everything to do with their relationship with God. In effect, the rabbis took the whole matter out of the physical realm and transferred it to the realm of spirit.

A second rabbinic strategy for keeping Jewish violence at bay is evident in the rabbis' messianic doctrine. As several scholars have pointed out, when the rabbis depict the redemption of the Jewish people at the end of days, the task of defeating and punishing its enemies is generally assigned to God. Violence therefore comes through divine, not human, agency.[79] This idea receives particular emphasis in several rabbinic passages in which R. Yohanan is quoted as saying that all redemptions up to his time had been failures because they had come through human initiative. The same stance toward eschatological violence is evident in the liturgy composed by the rabbis. In these texts, messianic salvation is referred to repeatedly as coming from divine initiative.[80]

The emphasis on divine agency in the messianic era is another idea that may have been inspired by biblical sources. In the last chapter, we saw that when Israel went to war in the biblical text, frequently the text emphasized that it was God who fought on Israel's behalf. The same held true for passages depicting the defeat of Israel's enemies in the messianic era. Here too, it was God who waged war. We also saw that some scholars focus on this observation as proof of the Bible's peaceful orientation, since war is initiated by God, not

78 Cohen, "Esau," 246–47. Cohen theorizes that Edom became the symbol for Rome because Obad. 1 and Lam. 4:21–22 focus on Edom as the archenemy of the Jewish people. Hadas-Lebel notes that the parallel between the first and second destruction is found in pre-rabbinic literature of the first century in such texts as *II Baruch* and the *Apocalypse of Abraham* (118–20). That association is picked up by the rabbis in several passages suggesting that Rome is the inheritor of the legacy of Babylon as Israel's enemy (466–68).

79 Davies, *The Territorial Dimension of Judaism*; Boyarin, *A Radical Jew*, 258; Berger, "Taming the Beast," 54–55.

80 David Kraemer, *Responses to Suffering in Classical Rabbinic Literature* (New York: Oxford University Press, 1995), 215–18; Berger, "Taming the Beast," 56. This motif in early rabbinic literature is analyzed in Adiel Shremer, "Midrash and History: The Power of God and the Hope of Redemption in the World of the Tannaim in the Shadow of the Roman Empire" (in Hebrew), *Zion* 72 (2007): 5–36. The same motif as it appears in medieval sources is discussed in Israel J. Yuval, "Vengeance and Damnation: From Jewish Martyrdom to Blood Accusations" (in Hebrew), *Zion* 58 (1993): 36–45.

human beings. The same argument can be made regarding rabbinic eschato-logical texts as well.[81]

We noted in the last chapter that one could take issue with this approach by arguing that in many instances in the Bible, most notably the narratives describing the conquest of Canaan, Israel still did the killing even if God initi-ated the violence. Moreover, the notion of God waging war on behalf of Israel was morally problematic because it allowed human beings to absolve them-selves of guilt for their own violent deeds. However, neither of these criticisms is applicable to rabbinic texts because the rabbis generally do not envision Israel playing any role in the defeat of its enemies when the messianic period comes; God, it would seem, always acts alone in these texts in bringing down Israel's foes. Moreover, the vanquishing of Israel's enemies in the mes-sianic era according to rabbinic texts differs markedly from the Canaanite con-quest—and, for that matter, the destruction of the Amalekites—in that there is no suggestion by the rabbis that in the end of days Israel's enemies must be entirely wiped out. The goal here is not genocide, but to judge the Jews' adver-saries for their ill-treatment of them and to allow the Jews to get back their sovereignty.

The final element in the theology we are analyzing also reflects a commit-ment to nonviolence on the part of the rabbis. In urging Jews to be patient in accepting their subjugation and to focus on repairing their relationship with God through obedience to His laws, the rabbis were trying to guide their fellow Jews away from messianic speculations and the violence they might engender. This strategy is evident in the Mishnah, which focuses almost entirely on Jew-ish law—including those regulating rituals in the Temple. More than one com-mentator has marveled at how this text is almost completely detached from the catastrophe that the Jewish people had just experienced. Most important for our present purposes, it contains little discussion of the messianic doctrine.[82]

We also find numerous statements in rabbinic texts addressing the prob-lem of messianic speculation directly by opposing any attempt to predict the time of the coming of the messiah. For instance, in the Talmud, R. Jonathan

---

81 One question not addressed by rabbinic sources is why the non-Jewish nations should be punished in the messianic period if the exile is due to Israel's sins. The medieval exegete Rashi attempts to answer this ques-tion by arguing that the nations afflicted the Jews beyond what was required as punishment for their sins, and the nations must therefore be punished in turn (cited in Katz, *Exclusiveness and Tolerance*, 17).

82 Jacob Neusner, *Messiah in Context: Israel's History and Destiny in Formative Judaism* (Philadelphia: For-tress Press, 1984), 74–78; Hadas-Lebel, 490–92; Lawrence H. Schiffman, "Messianism and Apocalypticism in Rabbinic Texts," in *The Cambridge History of Judaism*, vol. 4, *The Late Roman–Rabbinic Period*, ed. Steven T. Katz (Cambridge: Cambridge University Press, 2006), 1062–64. Mishnaic references to the messianic era can be found in M. *Sotah* 9:15, though there is some speculation that this section is a later addition. Passages in M. *Sanhedrin* 10:1 and M. *Tamid* 7:4 also refer to the messianic period but without providing much detail.

ben Eleazar curses those who "calculate the end."[83] Rabbinic texts also speak out against messianic activism. For instance, in rabbinic sources one finds a tradition describing three oaths: two that God forced upon the Jewish people, and one that he forced upon the gentile nations. God made Israel swear not to rebel against the nations of the world, nor to go *en masse* to the land of Israel. He made the gentile nations swear not to persecute the Jews beyond what the latter deserved as punishment for their sins. This tradition seems to have been designed to convince Jews that they should accept their subjugation and not attempt to bring the messiah by force.[84] Opposition to messianic activism, albeit in more subtle form, also seems to be the intent of a charming statement attributed to R. Yohanan ben Zakkai: "If there is a seedling in your hand and you are informed, 'King Messiah has arrived,' first go plant the seedling, afterwards go forth to greet him."[85] A number of rabbinic sources also describe a period of great destruction that will precede the coming of the messiah, prompting several rabbis to say, "Let him [i.e., the messiah] come and let me not see him."[86] One wonders if these descriptions were meant to discourage messianic activism as well.

The patience the rabbis preached in anticipation of the redemption also explains a number of sources in which they attempted to accommodate themselves to Roman rule.[87] Thus, in some rabbinic passages the view is expressed that Rome holds power because it is the will of God.[88] In other passages the emperor is likened to God himself on the presumption that it was God who had allowed him to rule.[89] In the same spirit, the rabbis mandate that a Jew must make a blessing upon seeing a non-Jewish monarch.[90] In some places, the rabbis even express admiration for Rome and its technological achievements.[91]

83 B.T. *Sanhedrin* 97b. See also *Pesahim* 54b. This issue is discussed in Nahum N. Glatzer, "The Attitude toward Rome in Third-Century Judaism," in *Essays in Jewish Thought* (University, Ala.: University of Alabama Press, 1978), 5; Hadas-Lebel, 492–96.

84 B.T. *Ketubot* 110b–111a. A variation of this passage is found in *Song of Songs Rabbah* 2:7, where reference is made to four vows. This source also makes explicit mention of the Bar Kokhba revolt as a failed attempt at redemption. For a discussion of these oaths and the tradition of medieval commentary on them, see Aviezer Ravitzky, "Appendix: The Impact of the Three Oaths in Jewish History," in *Messianism, Zionism, and Jewish Religious Radicalism*, trans. Michael Swirsky and Jonathan Chipman (Chicago: University of Chicago Press, 1996), 211–34.

85 *Avot de-Rabi Natan*, version B, 31.

86 B.T. *Pesahim* 118a, *Sanhedrin* 98b.

87 This theme is discussed in Glatzer, "The Attitude towards Rome," 2; Hadas-Lebel, 265–95;

88 *Mekhilta de-Rabi Yishma'el, Pisha* 13; B.T. *'Avodah Zarah* 18a.

89 *Genesis Rabbah* 94:9.

90 B.T. *Berakhot* 58a.

91 B.T. *Shabbat* 33b.

The rabbinic imperative to wait patiently for redemption would become a staple of later medieval Judaism. For instance, Judah Halevi, the eleventh-century Spanish Jewish poet and philosopher, argues that the very weakness and humiliation that the Jewish people had experienced are a sign of their chosenness. Halevi bases his position on the observation that all three monotheistic faiths value humility, and yet, from his perspective, only the Jews truly embody that virtue, on account of their being in exile. The Maharal, a sixteenth-century rabbi in Prague, also finds virtue in Jewish weakness by claiming that Jewish powerlessness is maintained by God in order to keep Jews separate from non-Jews.[92]

While we have demonstrated that the rabbis embraced peace, we have focused mostly on sources reacting to the failure of the two rebellions against Rome. Our argument can be strengthened by looking at rabbinic sources that deal with violence and war in more general terms. While one cannot easily separate statements by the rabbis about these topics from the background of the tragedies that Jews experienced in the first centuries, we do find sources indicating that the rabbis endorsed nonviolence as a far-reaching value applicable beyond their own immediate circumstances.

There are any number of rabbinic sources that reflect a negative view of violence and war in general. Many of them are, in fact, more explicit than any such statement in the Bible.[93] In rabbinic texts, war is often conceived as the product of primordial human sin and wickedness. This idea is reflected in a number of passages that trace the origins of war back to figures in the early biblical history, such as Cain, Tubal-Cain, or the four kings who waged war against the five kings in the time of Abraham.[94] In a number of passages, the rabbis give a concrete application of their antipathy to violence by urging their readers to greet violence with nonviolence.[95] Thus a statement reported in the name of R. Abbahu: "A man should always strive to be of the persecuted rather than of the persecutors because there is none among the birds more persecuted than doves and pigeons, and yet Scripture made them [alone among birds] eligible for the altar [i.e., sacrifice]."[96] In another passage, the rabbis

---

92 David Biale, *Power and Powerlessness in Jewish History* (New York: Schocken Books, 1986), 37; Luz, *Wrestling with an Angel*, 35.

93 General treatments of this issue can be found in Nahum N. Glatzer, "The Concept of Peace in Classical Judaism," in *Essays in Jewish Thought* (University, Ala.: University of Alabama Press, 1978), 36–47; Kimelman, "Non-Violence in the Talmud."

94 Gen. 4, 14, 20; *Tanhuma, Lekh Lekha* 7; Aviezer Ravitzky, "Peace: Historical Versus Utopian Models in Jewish Thought," in *History and Faith: Studies in Jewish Philosophy* (Amsterdam: J. C. Gieben, 1996), 29.

95 Kimelman, "Non-Violence in the Talmud," 330–34.

96 B.T. *Bava Kamma* 93a.

declare: "Who is the hero of heroes? One who transmutes foe into friend."[97] Often, the nonviolent ethic of the rabbis is expressed in statements about the value of peace. For instance, the rabbis inform us that "Great is peace for all blessings are contained in it. . . . Great is peace for God's name is peace."[98] Another passage extols in moving terms the work of the peacemaker, claiming that no harm should come to such an individual, for if one is forbidden to use a sword to build an altar that brings peace, one should certainly be forbidden to use a sword against a human being who performs the same function.[99] Many of the major prayers in the liturgy fashioned by the rabbis end with a prayer for peace, including grace after meals, the 'amidah, the priestly blessing, and the kaddish. A number of volumes in the Talmud conclude with a dictum by R. Hanina bar Hama, who praises the students of Torah because they bring peace to the world.[100]

Rabbinic opposition to war is often couched in negative statements about its implements. Thus, the rabbis interpret the biblical commandment that an altar for sacrifices not be built with stones cut with metal (Ex. 20:22) as a symbolic rejection of the implements of war.[101] We have another source that says the carrying of weapons on the Sabbath is forbidden because they are a disgrace to those who bear them.[102] According to another passage, one is forbidden to carry weapons into a house of study, the premise being that Torah study and violence are incompatible.[103]

A number of passages go as far as to connect peaceful behavior with the principle of imitating God.[104] The difficulty with this idea is that God's actions in the Bible are often violent. A number of commentators address this problem by noting that when the rabbis explicitly invoke the principle of imitating God, mention is made only of his benevolent attributes, not his violent ones, and it is therefore only those actions that they have in mind when they speak

---

97 Avot de-Rabi Natan, version A, 23.

98 Numbers Rabbah 11:7.

99 Mekhilta de-Rabi Yishma'el, Ba-Hodesh 11.

100 Glatzer, "The Concept of Peace," 42; Ravitzky, "Peace," 23–25. The volumes of the Talmud that end with a prayer for peace are Berakhot, Yevamot, Nazir, Tamid, and Keritot. Glatzer notes (43) that the importance of peace in rabbinic Judaism is reflected in several collections of sayings on peace that appear in various places in rabbinic literature: for example, Sifre Numbers 42, Leviticus Rabbah 9:9, Numbers Rabbah 11:16–20, Deuteronomy Rabbah 5:12ff., Perek ha-Shalom (a late compilation printed as chapter 10 of the minor tractate Derekh Erets Zuta).

101 M. Middot 4:3.

102 B.T. Shabbat 63a.

103 B.T. Sanhedrin 82a.

104 B.T. Shabbat 133b; Tanhuma 10; Shapiro, "The Jewish Attitude," 1:332; Kimelman, "Non-Violence in the Talmud," 316–21.

of imitating God.[105] As seen in the previous chapter, a number of scholars make similar observations about the concept of imitating God expressed in the Bible.

Recently, a number of scholars have written about a psychological shift in rabbinic thought regarding the notion of manhood, a shift that is an important ingredient in the rabbis' peaceful ethic. The rabbis tend to exalt those virtues which in many cultures are associated with the feminine, such as modesty, humility, meekness, and compassion. At the same time, the rabbis completely redefine the typically male virtues of physical power, bravery, and militarism, in terms that denude them of their violent meaning.[106] Thus, the rabbis often refer to themselves as "warriors," but not in the literal sense; instead, they are warriors of Torah, fighting each other in intellectual combat to give the best interpretation of God's laws. A source just cited reflects this idea: "Who is the hero of heroes? One who transmutes foe into friend."[107] Similarly in Mishnah *Avot*, we read: "Who is mighty? He who subdues his passions."[108] In Isaiah 28:6, reference is made to one "who repels attacks at the gate," and according to one rabbinic passage, the text is alluding to "those who thrust and parry in the war of the Torah."[109] Along the same lines, we find numerous rabbinic sources in which the great warriors of the biblical tradition, such as Joshua and David, are depicted as pious rabbinic scholars.[110] This transmutation is particularly striking with David, whose character as a warrior is extensively developed in the biblical text. On some occasions, David is depicted by the rabbis not only as a Torah scholar, but as someone distinctly uninterested in war.[111] The rabbis sometimes recognize the fact that David did wage war, but they are just as quick to condemn his brutality.[112]

These last observations lead us to another collection of rabbinic sources that reflect a peaceful ethic by reinterpreting narratives about wars of the past

105 For, e.g., Emanuel Rackman, "Violence and the Value of Life: The Halakhic View," in *Violence and Defense in the Jewish Experience*, ed. Salo W. Baron and George S. Wise (Philadelphia: Jewish Publication Society of America, 1977), 127.

106 Daniel Boyarin has written most extensively on this issue in *Unheroic Conduct: The Rise of Heterosexuality and the Invention of the Jewish Man* (Berkeley: University of California Press, 1997), 1–186. This issue is also dealt with by scholars predating Boyarin. See the discussion in Artson, chapter 5. See also brief references to this notion in Shapiro, *The Jewish Attitude*, 1:322–24; Glatzer, "The Concept of Peace," 37–38; Luz, *Wrestling with an Angel*, 23. The tendency to transmute war imagery has been noted in other religions. See, for instance, Appleby's remarks regarding Christianity in *The Ambivalence of the Sacred*, 11.

107 *Avot de-R. Natan*, version A, 23.

108 M. *Avot* 4:1.

109 B.T. *Megillah* 15b.

110 B.T. *Berakhot* 4a, *Megillah* 3a, *Temurah* 16a.

111 B.T. *Berakhot* 4a.

112 J.T. *Rosh ha-Shanah* 1:1.

described in the biblical text.[113] For instance, in one passage the rabbis attempt to make sense of God's statement to Abraham in Genesis 15:1, "Fear not Abraham, I shall shield you and your reward shall be very great." What, the rabbis ask, was the source of Abraham's fear in this verse? Several suggestions are made, but what is of interest to us is an opinion that claims that Abraham was afraid that he may have killed someone innocent while waging war to free his nephew Lot from captivity.[114] In this passage, Abraham is depicted as an individual with deep concerns about the moral consequences of using violence.[115] A source frequently cited in support of a peaceful rabbinic ethic is a talmudic passage that explains why the *hallel* service, which is recited on Jewish festivals in praise of God, is shortened on the last six days of Passover. The explanation given is that when the Egyptian army was destroyed at the Sea of Reeds, the angels expressed the desire to sing songs of praise to God for saving Israel, but God rebuffed them, saying: "My creatures are drowning in the sea, and you sing songs of praise?"[116]

An attempt to come to terms with the moral difficulties inherent in the Canaanite conquest is contained in a number of striking sources that focus on Moses's initiative in seeking peace with Sihon, an Amorite king whose territory the Israelites had to traverse en route to entering the land of Canaan.[117] In the biblical text, Moses receives no explicit command from God to pursue peace in this instance, prompting a number of rabbis to offer an explanation for Moses's actions. According to some sources, God commanded Moses to go to war with Sihon, but he refused to do so because he did not want to kill the innocent with the guilty, and he therefore approached Sihon with the hope of making peace. In one of these sources, God was so impressed by Moses's actions that he made Moses's initiative the rule for all subsequent confrontations with the Canaanite nations. Joshua was therefore instructed by God to offer the Canaanites three choices before waging war on them: surrender, depart the land of Canaan, or fight. We are then told that the Gibeonites made peace, the Girgashites left and

---

113 Glatzer discusses some of these sources in "The Concept of Peace," 37–38.

114 *Genesis Rabbah* 44:4. A similar interpretation is found in *Genesis Rabbah* 76:2, which attempts to explain why in Gen. 32:8 we are told that Jacob "was greatly afraid and distressed" before his reunion with Esau after years of separation. The rabbis tell us that he was "afraid" lest he kill and "distressed" lest he himself be killed if there was a violent confrontation between him and his brother.

115 See Yitzchak Blau, "Biblical Narratives and the Status of Enemy Civilians in Wartime," *Tradition* 39, no. 4 (2006): 14–15, for an analysis of later medieval commentators on this midrash and its implications for a nonviolent Jewish ethic. This midrash is also cited and discussed for the same purpose in Uriel Simon, *Seek Peace and Pursue It: The Bible in Light of Topical Issues, Topical Issues in Light of the Bible* (in Hebrew) (Tel Aviv: Yediot Ahronot, 2002), 273.

116 B.T. *Megillah* 10b.

117 Num. 21:21.

were rewarded by being given another land, while the rest of the nations chose to fight and were annihilated.[118] This fanciful retelling of the biblical narrative seems to reflect an attempt on the part of the rabbis to soften the brutality of the Canaanite conquest.

The rabbis also grappled with the moral challenges inherent in the commandment to destroy Amalek. A rabbinic source frequently cited by modern Jewish ethicists and commentators who address this issue is a passage concerning God's command to King Saul in I Samuel 15 to wage war against the Amalekites and annihilate them and their livestock:

> When the Holy One, blessed be He, said to Saul "Now go, attack Amalek" (I Sam. 15:5), he said: "If on account of one person, the Torah said: Perform the ceremony of the heifer whose neck is broken,[119] how much more [should consideration be given] to all these persons! And if human beings sinned, what [crime] has the cattle committed? And if adults have sinned, what have the little ones done?" A divine voice came forth and said, "do not overdo goodness" (Ecc. 7:16).[120]

In this passage, the rabbis create a dialogue that depicts Saul protesting God's command. Some argue that this passage reflects the rabbis' discomfort with the imperative to destroy Amalek, with Saul functioning as their mouthpiece in challenging God about the morality of this commandment.[121]

The same discomfort with the commandment to annihilate Amalek in early rabbinic Judaism seems to have carried over into medieval and modern Judaism, as Avi Sagi has demonstrated in an exhaustive study of Jewish attitudes toward Amalek from the rabbinic period onward. Sagi's basic line of argumentation is that Jewish sources consistently convey unease with the commandment to destroy Amalek by attempting to give a rational explanation for this imperative.[122] The talmudic source just cited is a case in point. In the medieval period, Sagi cites Abravanel, a sixteenth-century exegete, who explains

---

118 *Numbers Rabbah* 19:27; *Tanhuma Tsav* 3; *Deuteronomy Rabbah* 13–14.

119 This reference alludes to a ceremony in Deut. 21:1–9, which is performed when a murder victim is found in a field outside the jurisdiction of any city and it is not known who the assailant was. The elders of the city closest to the location where the victim is found perform the ceremony. The rabbinic passage under consideration here interprets the ritual as a reflection of the concern that must be shown when an innocent human life has been taken.

120 B.T. *Yoma* 22b.

121 Simon, 274–75; Avi Sagi, "The Punishment of Amalek in Jewish Tradition: Coping with the Moral Problem," *Harvard Theological Review* 87, no. 3 (1994): 328–29.

122 Sagi, "The Punishment of Amalek."

the decree against Amalek by arguing that Amalek transgressed against the norms of just war and therefore had to be punished. After all, Amalek had no cause for going to war because no territory was at stake. They also fought the war unfairly by not allowing the Israelites to prepare for battle and by attacking the weakest among them. The commandment to blot out Amalek was therefore born of the severity of their crime and meant to teach resistance to evil in all forms.[123] Sagi also adduces the views of Nahmanides, a thirteenth-century commentator, who argues that the Amalekites were punished severely because they were trying to rebel against God himself. Other nations trembled when they heard about God's miracles in liberating the Israelites from Egypt, but Amalek did not and attacked the Israelites without hesitation.[124] According to another set of medieval sources cited by Sagi, the commandment to annihilate Amalek is justified using a symbolic approach. According to this line of inter-pretation, Amalek represents evil of one sort or another, whether it be meta-physical evil in general, the evil of abusing physical power, or the evil inclination within us. Thus, the commandment to destroy Amalek is, in effect, referring to one of these evils. This approach disengages the whole episode from concrete history and elevates it to a spiritual plane.[125]

Sagi believes that these sources tell us something important about the relationship in Judaism between morality and religion in general. The very fact that Jewish thinkers from the rabbinic period onward consistently saw the need to justify the commandment to annihilate Amalek demonstrates that Judaism assumes morality to be autonomous from religion and that even God's decrees must conform to the parameters set by morality. As Sagi puts it, "Jewish tradi-tion acknowledges the autonomy of morality and assumes that divine com-mands abide by moral considerations."[126]

We have yet to look at how the rabbis dealt with war in Jewish law, and it is to that subject that we now turn. The rabbis did not give extensive treat-ment to the laws of war because most rabbinic texts were redacted when Jews no longer had political sovereignty or an army. Nonetheless, their discussions of this topic seem to reveal the same nonviolent ethic that we have seen up to now.

---

123 Sagi, "The Punishment of Amalek," 325–26; Abravanel, *Commentary on the Torah* on Deut. 25:17.

124 Sagi, "The Punishment of Amalek," 326–27; Nahmanides, *Commentary on the Torah* on Ex. 17:16.

125 Sagi, "The Punishment of Amalek," 330–36. Sagi also applies this approach to sources in Jewish law, and these will be discussed later.

126 Sagi, "The Punishment of Amalek," 324. Gerald Cromer provides an analysis of the Jewish views on Amalek that overlaps with that of Sagi in a number respects in "Amalek as Other, Other as Amalek: Interpreting a Violent Biblical Narrative," *Qualitative Sociology* 24, no. 2 (2001): 191–202. Horowitz, *Reckless Rites*, chapter 5, provides a thorough historical treatment of Amalek in Jewish thought, literature, and poetry throughout the ages.

Halakhic sources divide wars into two categories: those that are obligatory and those that are discretionary.[127] In the category of obligatory wars are those commanded by God. In early rabbinic literature only two examples of this type of war are mentioned: the war against the seven Canaanite nations and the war against the Amalekites.[128] Later medieval authorities would include in this category wars waged in self-defense.[129] Discretionary wars, according to the Talmud, are meant to expand the borders of Israel "as King David did."[130] The great medieval authority Maimonides adds that the goal of this expansion was "to increase the greatness and prestige" of the Israelite king or of Israel as a whole.[131] This second type of war requires that certain stipulations be fulfilled. They must be initiated by a king; they must be approved by the Sanhedrin, the highest rabbinic court in Temple times; and the king must consult the *urim ve-tumim*, an oracle attached to the breastplate of the high priest.[132]

What is significant in these formulations is that the rabbis implicitly deny any justification for Jews to initiate war in the post-biblical period—with the exception of wars waged in self-defense.[133] With respect to obligatory wars, consensus emerges among the rabbis that the Canaanites are no longer an identifiable group because Sennacherib, the ancient Assyrian conqueror, "commingled the nations."[134] The rabbis are referring here to the practice of conquerors in the ancient world transferring and mixing entire populations in order to destroy defeated nations and ensure that subject peoples would not rebel. Because the Canaanites were victims of this practice, and were no longer in existence, there obviously could be no commandment to wage war against them. A similar consensus regarding the Amalekites is harder to find. Yet, a good many medieval rabbis take the position explicitly or implicitly that the

---

127 General discussions of rabbinic views on war can be found in Shapiro, "The Jewish Attitude," 1:340–43; Everett E. Gendler, "War and the Jewish Tradition," in *Contemporary Jewish Ethics*, ed. Menachem Kellner (New York: HPC Press, 1988), 197–200; Reuven Kimelman, "The Ethics of National Power: Government and War from the Sources of Judaism," in *Authority, Power, and Leadership in the Jewish Polity*, ed. Daniel Elazar (Lanham, Md.: University Press of America, 1991), 247–94; Elliot N. Dorff, *To Do the Right and the Good: A Jewish Approach to Modern Social Ethics* (Philadelphia: Jewish Publication Society of America, 2002), 165–71.

128 B.T. *Sotah* 44b; Maimonides, *Mishneh Torah* (henceforth, M.T.) *Melakhim* 5:1.

129 This right is implicit in the Talmud's ruling that Israelite towns may defend themselves in some instances on the Sabbath (B.T. *'Eruvin* 45a). It becomes a more general law in Maimonides in M.T. *Melakhim* 5:1.

130 B.T. *Sotah* 44b.

131 Maimonides, M.T. *Melakhim* 5:1. Maimonides' language is not clear about whether this type of war is meant to increase the greatness and prestige of the king or of Israel. I have therefore given both possibilities here.

132 B.T. *Berakhot* 3b, *Sanhedrin* 2a, 16a, 20a. The *urim ve-tumim* are described in Ex. 28:30, Lev. 8:6–8, and Num. 27:21.

133 This position is found in Avi Ravitzky, "Prohibited War in Jewish Tradition," in *The Ethics of War and Peace: Religious and Secular Perspectives*, ed. Terry Nardin (Princeton: Princeton University Press, 1996), 119; Artson, 105–6, 117–18; Luz, *Wrestling with an Angel*, 22.

134 M. *Yadayim*; B.T. *Berakhot* 28a; Maimonides, M.T. *Melakhim* 6:1.

commandment to engage in war against the Amalekites is no longer operative, either because the Amalekites had ceased to exist or because the battle against them has been postponed to the messianic era.[135] It was also noted earlier that a strain of rabbinic thought interpreted the commandment to destroy Amalek in symbolic terms by equating it with evil of one sort or another and that this approach had the effect of taking the commandment out of the physical realm and transferring it to the realm of spirit. Here too the imperative to wage actual war is effectively nullified. Discretionary wars, it would seem, are also inoperative, according to the rabbis. They require the collaboration of a Jewish king, the Sanhedrin, and the *urim ve-tumim*, and all three institutions were defunct by the fifth century.[136]

Rabbinic reservations about war are also evident in laws regulating the conduct of Jewish armies once war has already been waged—what ethical theorists often refer to as *jus in bello*. A great deal of attention has been given to a stipulation of Maimonides regarding Jewish conduct in the obligatory wars against the Canaanites and Amalekites. According to Maimonides, Jewish armies were always required to offer terms of peace to the enemy before going to war, including those nations.[137] Now one might be able to find biblical and rabbinic justification for the ruling that one offers such terms to the Canaanites. A text in Deuteronomy is somewhat ambiguous regarding this issue and could be read in accordance with Maimonides' ruling.[138] A much clearer source for this imperative can be found in an early rabbinic passage that we have

---

135 The first claim is supported in R. Joseph Babad, *Minhat Hinukh* (New York: Pardes, n.d.), mitsvah no. 604, and the second by R. Moses of Coucy *Sefer Mitsvot Gadol* (Venice, 1522), negative mitsvah no. 226, and *Hagahot Maymoniyyot* on M.T. *Melakhim*, chapter 5, letter *alef*. See also Artson, 129; Kimelman "The Ethics of National Power," 266; Eugene Korn, "Moralization in Jewish Law: Genocide, Divine Commands, and Rabbinic Reasoning," *Edah Journal* 5, no. 2 (2006): 6; Horowitz, *Reckless Rites*, 133–34.

136 Artson, chapter 8. Artson, 176–85, also discusses the rabbinic interpretation of the exemptions from army service in Deut. 20:5–10, in particular the exemption allowing those who are "afraid" of war not to serve (Deut. 20:8). According to R. Jose, this exemption applies to discretionary wars and includes anyone who has committed even the most minute sin and therefore should be "afraid" of going to war seeing as he may not receive divine protection from harm (B.T. *Sotah* 44b). Artson surmises that since practically every individual commits such sins, R. Jose's stipulation effectively means that no army can ever be assembled to wage discretionary war. R. Jose therefore seems to treat discretionary war as an idealized mitsvah much like that regarding the rebellious son (B.T. *Sanhedrin* 71a). A similar argument is made in Donniel Hartman, "The Morality of War," *S'vara* 2, no. 1 (1990): 20–24.

137 M.T. *Melakhim* 6:1.

138 This point is often overlooked by modern commentators. In Deut. 20:10–14, the Israelites are commanded to offer terms of peace to their enemy, and if they do not accept those terms, war is to be waged and all the male inhabitants put to the sword. In the verses immediately following these stipulations (Deut. 20:15–16), the text tells us, "Thus shall you do with all the towns that lie very far from you," but the text specifies that when it comes to the inhabitants of those towns belonging to Canaanites, "you shall not let a soul remain alive." It is not clear whether the qualification regarding the Canaanites includes offering terms of peace.

already seen claiming Joshua was required to seek peace with the Canaanite nations.[139] However, no biblical or early rabbinic sources require that the same gesture be made to the Amalekites. Avi Sagi concludes that Maimonides' ruling here is very bold and is clearly inspired by the principles of compassion, mercy, and peace that he endorses elsewhere in his writings. And here too Sagi feels that we have proof that in Judaism, morality trumps religion when the two are in conflict.[140] Eugene Korn takes a similar position and argues that what is significant about Maimonides' ruling is that it implies that the Canaanites and Amalekites are evil only because of their deeds, not because they are inherently evil.[141]

Other rulings by medieval rabbinic authorities regarding conduct during war reflect the imperative that Jews have compassion for their enemies. In the biblical text, we are told that the Israelites are forbidden to destroy fruit trees outside a city under siege,[142] and a possible reason is that cutting down the trees deprives the enemy of its food supply. In fact, this injunction inspired a number of medieval rabbis to rule that one is prohibited from cutting off any basic necessities from the enemy, such as water or food.[143] Another directive that instructs Jews to be compassionate in wartime is a ruling found in a number of early rabbinic and medieval sources specifying that when attacking a city, Jews are required to leave one direction open to allow civilians to flee. Nahmanides says that this ruling is meant to teach soldiers "to act compassionately with our enemies even during wartime."[144] According to some authorities, one is not permitted to wage war if it is anticipated that more than one-sixth of the enemy population will be killed.[145]

139 See also the extensive discussion in *Lehem Mishneh* on M.T. *Melakhim* 6:1, which deals with this issue.

140 Sagi, "The Punishment of Amalek," 341–45.

141 Korn, 7–11. An interpretation of Maimonides similar to those of Sagi and Korn is offered by Artson, 131–32.

142 Deut. 20:19.

143 For example, M.T. *Melakhim* 6:7–10.

144 This idea is first found in *Sifre Numbers, Matot* 157, and is made into law by Maimonides in M.T. *Melakhim* 6:7. In his addenda to Maimonides' *Sefer ha-Mitsvot*, mitsvah no. 5, Nahmanides complains that Maimonides omits this law in his list of 613 commandments. For a discussion of this issue, see Kimelman, "The Ethics of National Power," 275, and Blau, 17–18. Blau notes that for most authorities this requirement applies only to discretionary war.

145 This ruling is based on a talmudic statement by Samuel, a third-century Babylonian authority, who claims that a government is not liable for punishment if it kills fewer than "one out of six" during wartime. It is not clear whether the "one out of six" refers to Jewish casualties or those of the enemy. Later commentators would be divided on this question, with some claiming that it refers to the latter. For details, see Gendler, 202–3; Ravitzky, "Prohibited War," 119; Reuven Kimelman, "Judaism, War, and Weapons of Mass Destruction," in *Ethics and Weapons of Mass Destruction*, ed. Sohail Hashmi (West Nyack, N.Y.: Cambridge University Press, 2004), 365. See also Artson, chapter 7, which draws together much the same material cited here regarding *jus in bello*.

One has to acknowledge that the rabbis were not pacifists in the strict sense. The most extreme pacifists reject all violence, and that is a position that the rabbis do not support. As we have just seen, they permit the waging of war in self-defense. In fact, the right of self-defense is so sacrosanct a principle in rabbinic Judaism that it applies to individuals and nations alike, whether they be Jews or non-Jews. One is always permitted to defend oneself against violence. Still, rabbinic Judaism is broadly nonviolent because the rabbis make every attempt to minimize violence beyond that needed to ward off harm.[146]

An important aspect of rabbinic Judaism that allows the rabbis to develop their peaceful ethic is their methodology in interpreting the biblical text. What has emerged in the course of our discussion is that the rabbis were bold and daring interpreters willing to impart innovative meanings to the biblical text in order to support their views. We have seen numerous examples in which biblical narrative and law were supplemented, stretched, or completely reread by the rabbis. This interpretive method assumes a highly exalted view of human beings, who function as partners with God in the development of the Torah's ideas and laws. The rabbis operated on the premise that God handed the Torah to human beings and gave them the authority to determine its meaning. A great deal has been written about this aspect of rabbinic Judaism, and it is a large topic that cannot preoccupy us here.[147] What is important for our concerns is that the rabbinic method of interpretation is a key factor in allowing rabbinic Judaism to advance beyond the ethics of the Bible in so many respects.

In sum, there is ample evidence that early and medieval rabbinic Judaism adopted a peaceful ethic and that this ethic was more pronounced than that which we find in the Bible. The rabbinic view of non-Jews is mixed. Certainly, rabbinic literature contains numerous sources that express a positive attitude toward them, but there are many sources that express a negative attitude as well. However, a number of considerations help explain the negative sources, most important the historical context in which the rabbis lived. Moreover, when it comes to the issue of violence, the picture seems clearer. In the wake

146 Maurice Lamm, "After the War: Another Look at Pacifism and Selective Conscientious Objection," in *Contemporary Jewish Ethics*, ed. Menachem Kellner (New York: HPC Press, 1988), 221–38; Rackman, 114–15, 124–26; Gendler, 208–9; Yehudah Mirsky, "The Political Morality of Pacifism and Nonviolence: One Jewish View," in *War and Its Discontents: Pacifism and Quietism in the Abrahamic Traditions*, ed. J. Patout Burns (Washington, D.C.: Georgetown University Press, 1996), 47–66; Dorff, *To Do the Right*, 161.

147 Numerous studies have been written by scholars and theologians in the Conservative and modern Orthodox movements emphasizing the boldness of rabbinic interpretation. Representative examples include Eliezer Berkovits, *Not in Heaven: The Nature and Function of Halakha* (New York: Ktav, 1983); Louis Jacobs, *A Tree of Life: Diversity, Flexibility, and Creativity in Jewish Law* (New York: Oxford University Press, 1984); Joel Roth, *The Halakhic Process: A Systematic Analysis* (New York: Jewish Theological Seminary of America, 1986); Elliot N. Dorff, *The Unfolding Tradition: Jewish Law after Sinai* (New York: Aviv Press, 2005).

of two failed rebellions against Rome, the early rabbis reject violence as a means of dealing with their enemies. According to the rabbis, these events came about because of the sins of the Jewish people, and the rabbis thus instruct their followers to repair their relationship with God by leading pious lives and waiting patiently for the coming of the messiah. Only in the messianic era will Israel's enemies be defeated, but even then the rabbis do not envision violence as a Jewish initiative; it is God who will wage war against the nations that have oppressed Israel. The nonviolent ethic of the rabbis, however, is not just a response to Roman rule; it is embraced as a basic religious value that is expressed in any number of ways. Rabbinic literature contains numerous statements in praise of peace and critical of war. The rabbis rethink the entire meaning of manhood in extolling such virtues as humility and compassion and in transposing military activities into nonviolent practices, such as the study of Torah. The rabbis significantly soften the violence in the Bible through innovative rereadings of its narratives describing war. According to rabbinic law, wars are no longer permissible except those waged in self-defense. In their legislation regarding the conduct of Jewish armies during war, the rabbis set forth a number of conditions that attempt to minimize violence against civilians. What makes rabbinic creativity possible is their belief in the power of human beings to reread the Bible, a power that allows them to reshape its ethics in new and innovative directions.

Rabbinic Judaism Promotes Violence

As in our discussion of the Bible, rabbinic Judaism invites another reading because of its many ambiguities. Let us begin by looking at rabbinic attitudes toward non-Jews. In our first reading, we saw that rabbinic views on this issue were mixed; some were positive, while others were negative. However, some of the rabbinic texts that seem to espouse a positive view of non-Jews can be read in a very different way.[148] For instance, in the first reading, a number of early rabbinic sources were adduced expressing favorable opinions about non-Jewish figures in the Bible, such as Job, Jethro, and Rahab. Yet, Sacha Stern points out that in some sources the rabbis also tell us that a number of these individuals

---

148 The presentation of this second reading of rabbinic attitudes to non-Jews is greatly indebted to Sacha Stern. Stern's study is focused on Jewish identity in early rabbinic writings, but in the course of dealing with this issue, he provides an exhaustive analysis of rabbinic attitudes toward non-Jews and reveals that they were mostly negative. Nor is Stern alone in this assessment. See Loewe, 115–50; Goldenberg, *The Nations That Knew Thee Not*, 83–85; Elliot R. Wolfson, *Venturing Beyond: Law and Morality in Kabbalistic Mysticism* (New York: Oxford University Press, 2006), 31–41.

eventually converted to Judaism. From this observation, Stern concludes that "to be non-Jewish and righteous is so inherently contradictory that the only viable option, for these exceptional individuals, is to convert."[149] Rabbinic sources about these biblical figures, therefore, do not necessarily reflect a universalistic embrace of non-Jews.

This is not to deny that some rabbinic sources are unequivocal in speaking positively about non-Jews. It is just that the preponderance of rabbinic opinion regarding non-Jews is arguably more negative than positive. Marc Hirshman draws that very conclusion with respect to early rabbinic Judaism. Hirshman demonstrates that the school of R. Ishmael in the second and third centuries had a strong universalistic bent. It believed that the Torah was intended for all people, it welcomed converts, and it also encouraged non-Jews who did not convert to study Torah and observe its precepts. Hirshman claims that this way of thinking reflected the atmosphere in Palestine in the first centuries, where the lines between religions were not firm. We have, for instance, the phenomenon of the "Godfearers" or *Theosebeis*, which scholars have discussed extensively. These were non-Jews who were connected to the Jewish community but did not formally convert. However, in the final analysis Hirshman admits that universalism was not the norm for the early rabbis and that the rabbinic tradition eventually adopted a more isolationist approach.[150]

It can also be argued that significant ambiguities can be found in rabbinic sources dealing with the Noahide code. In our first reading, this code was touted as a leading example of rabbinic inclusivism, and that is the way it is most often understood by modern Jewish ethicists. However, Stern provides insights proving that another interpretation is just as plausible. This code appears to denigrate non-Jews in giving them only seven commandments to observe, in comparison to the 613 commandments given to Jews.[151] This understanding of the Noahide code seems to be reflected in a midrashic source telling us that non-Jews were not given the 613 commandments because they have trouble observing even the seven they received.[152] Other sources inform us that non-Jews are so incapable of obeying the seven commandments that God exempted them from observing these laws, and for this reason non-Jews who

---

149 Stern, *Jewish Identity*, 30.

150 Marc Hirshman, *Torah for All the World's Peoples* (in Hebrew) (Ha-Kibbutz ha-Me'uhad, 1999). An English-language summary of Hirshman's findings can be found in Hirshman, "Rabbinic Universalism in the Second and Third Centuries," *Harvard Theological Review* 93, no. 2 (2000): 101–15.

151 Stern, *Jewish Identity*, 204–6.

152 *Genesis Rabbah* 24:5.

adhere to them receive no reward.[153] In some rabbinic passages, non-Jews are forbidden to observe commandments not included in this code even if they want to. For instance, according to rabbinic law, non-Jews are not permitted to observe the Sabbath.[154] And even though the first reading cited a rabbinic opinion declaring that a non-Jew who studies Torah is equivalent to a high priest, it must also be noted that according to one passage that reports this tradition, the dictum refers only to the study of the Noahide laws. A non-Jew who studies other parts of Torah is punished by death.[155] In other rabbinic passages, we find opinions that reinforce this view by stating that the study of Torah is dangerous or even lethal for non-Jews. It is as if their nature is so inimical to Torah that for them, studying it is like imbibing a poison.[156] In these sources, the Noahide code therefore represents as much a barrier between Jews and non-Jews as it does a basis for commonality.

The inclusivism of the Noahide code is also called into question by the fact that the few laws that are imposed on non-Jews represent what is, in effect, a Jewish form of religion and morality. It is not that the rabbis had any real hope of enforcing this code; they did not have the political power to do so. Nonetheless, this code assumes that non-Jews may have a relationship with God only through laws defined by Jewish tradition. Moreover, attempts to circumvent this problem by equating the Noahide code with natural law are not necessarily convincing. Most rabbinic sources generally view the Noahide code as a series of commandments dictated by God, not as norms that reason can discover on its own.[157]

In light of these observations, the Noahide may represent an ethical step backward from the Bible. In the biblical text, non-Jews are generally not governed by divine law. The first chapters of Genesis make clear that God expects all human beings to be moral in some basic sense, but no moral norms are given to them with the exception of the prohibition against murder.[158] When it comes to matters of belief, the Bible provides no prescriptions whatsoever. Certainly, God commands the Israelites to slaughter the Canaanites because they are idol worshippers, but the problem with Canaanite religion is that it constitutes a

---

153 *Sifre Deuteronomy* 343; B.T. *Bava Kama* 38a, '*Avodah Zarah* 2b–3a. The fact that non-Jews are not rewarded is based on the rabbinic assumption, found in a number of sources, that the reward for performing an action commanded by God is greater than that obtained when one does it on one's own initiative.

154 Stern, *Jewish Identity*, 206–14; B.T. *Sanhedrin* 58b.

155 B.T. *Sanhedrin* 59a.

156 *Exodus Rabbah* 5:9, 33:7; *Leviticus Rabbah* 1:11.

157 Stone, 1167–70, 1180–84. See also Newman, *Past Imperatives*, chapter 6; idem, *An Introduction to Jewish Ethics*, 122–23.

158 Gen. 9:5–6.

temptation to the Israelites who may abandon God because of it, not that the Canaanites must believe in the one God. Also, there is no suggestion in the Bible that the Israelites must enforce monotheism outside the land of Israel. By contrast, it would seem that the rabbis are not so tolerant. The Noahide code requires non-Jews to adhere to a series of specific religious and moral norms, and if the rabbinic legislation appended to these laws is taken into account, it is a substantial body of law. Most striking are the religious norms: idolatry and blasphemy are now forbidden for all non-Jews, whether they live in the land of Israel or not. We might not have trouble accepting the Noahide laws that address the norms of basic morality. Most of them, such as the prohibition against murder and theft, are norms that have been adhered to by most societies throughout history. However, the imposition on non-Jews of commandments that dictate religious beliefs and practices is more difficult to accept. Scholars and theologians who support an inclusive understanding of the Noahide code tend to overlook this problem and think of the code only as a set of moral prescriptions.[159]

The potential for the Noahide code to be a source of intolerance comes out quite strongly in Maimonides' medieval code of Jewish law. According to Maimonides, non-Jews living under Jewish rule must keep the Noahide code, and if they do not, they are to be put to death. Moreover, non-Jews are required to recognize that this code was given by God and commanded as part of the revelation at Sinai. Failure to recognize these truths results in the non-Jew's losing privileges as a resident alien and righteous gentile, and such an individual is not entitled to receive reward in the world to come.[160] Maimonides also rules that when Jews go to war, one of the conditions for peace that they must present to their enemies is the acceptance of the Noahide code; if they refuse this condition, war is to be waged.[161]

All in all, rabbinic views of the Noahide code seem to confirm the assessment of some scholars that the rabbis were solipsists.[162] The whole world is understood and judged by the rabbis through their frame of reference.

In the first reading, we argued that although early rabbinic Judaism contained discriminatory legislation regarding non-Jews, there was countervailing

159 For example, Stone's analysis of the Noahide laws tends to assume that they are moral norms, and almost no attention is given to the religious precepts.

160 M.T. *Melakhim* 8:10–11. Since the time of Mendelssohn, a great deal of discussion and controversy has surrounded Maimonides' views on the Noahide, with much attention given to M.T. *Melakhim* 8:11. See Stone, 1167–70, who discusses this issue and cites the relevant scholarship. A more detailed discussion of this passage can be found in the following chapter.

161 M.T. *Melakhim* 6:1.

162 See p. 75, this volume.

legislation that insisted on a more positive relationship with them. For example, the rabbinic concept of *mipney darkey shalom*, "on account of the paths of peace," mandates that Jews foster good relations with non-Jews through such activities as supporting their poor, visiting their sick, and burying their dead. Moreover, throughout the Middle Ages the rabbis phased out much of the discriminatory legislation. Yet, here again there is a great deal of ambiguity. A number of scholars believe that the concept of *mipney darkey shalom* mandates kind treatment of non-Jews only for pragmatic reasons: the rabbis were simply trying to avoid arousing the hostility of non-Jews who might do them harm.[163] The rabbis' primary concern, therefore, may have been self-preservation. A similar explanation may account for changes in rabbinic legislation regarding non-Jews in the medieval period. A point that is often overlooked in Jacob Katz's great work on this issue is his belief that the phasing out of discriminatory legislation toward non-Jews in this period emanated again from pragmatic considerations, not from an attempt to find a place for the non-Jew in the Jewish worldview.[164] The one major exception is Meiri. His new way of thinking regarding Christians and Christianity represents a significant advance over earlier views. It has to be pointed out, however, that Meiri is something of an anomaly in that few medieval rabbis were willing to be as tolerant of Christians and their religion as he was.[165]

To sum up our second reading thus far, rabbinic attitudes toward non-Jews may not be as equally mixed as the first reading claimed. These attitudes may, in fact, be more negative than positive.

On the subject of rabbinic views of violence toward non-Jews, here too we find much ambiguity. The first reading depicted the rabbis as figures who fashioned a peaceful understanding of Judaism in the wake of the failed rebellions against Rome. Yet, it can be argued that the rabbis did not, in fact, renounce violence at all. Let us look once again at the theology that the rabbis fashioned in response to the failed rebellions. The first reading claimed that rabbinic eschatology attempted to quell Jewish violence by postponing redemption to a distant future era and by encouraging Jews to focus in the meantime on living pious lives. However, one can question whether the rabbis really rejected violence here. After all, an important feature of rabbinic eschatology is that war will eventually be waged against Israel's oppressors, and revenge will be taken

---

163 Stern, *Jewish Identity*, 146. On this point, Stern expresses agreement with Porton, who comes to a similar conclusion. See Porton,231–32. The same view is held by Goldenberg, *The Nations That Knew Thee Not*, 85, 104.

164 Katz, *Exclusiveness and Tolerance*, 63.

165 Similar sentiments are expressed in Loewe, 144.

on them. The rabbis therefore embrace violence but postpone it to a messianic era in which the Jews will be dominant. Of course, as we saw in our first reading, the rabbis believed that the war in the end of days would be waged by God, not by the Jewish people. However, it is possible that the rabbis took this position only because of their state of powerlessness, not because of any desire to renounce human-initiated violence. With no prospect of the Jews' regaining independence through military means any time soon, the rabbis may have put forward the notion that God would wage war against their enemies because in their situation they could not imagine otherwise. One can also add here that a number of prominent medieval rabbis did not feel that Jews had to wait for God's help. In an analysis of twelfth-century Jewish thinkers, H. H. Ben-Sasson demonstrates that major Jewish figures, such as Maimonides and Abraham ibn Ezra, were defiant about the Jewish exile and expressed the view that if Jews had the power, they would go to war against their oppressors.[166]

Elliot Horowitz has argued that medieval Jewish anger against non-Jews also had historical consequences. Horowitz claims that, throughout the Middle Ages, Jews expressed outrage at their subjugation to Christians in the form of ridicule, insults, and, on some occasions, even violence. Frequently, it was the Purim holiday that inspired this behavior because it celebrated the story of the book of Esther, in which Jews in Persia in the sixth century BCE triumphed over a wicked advisor to the monarch bent on their destruction and wreaked revenge on their foes by killing them in large numbers. This story emboldened Jews throughout the centuries to confront their Christian overlords. However, I concur with a number of scholars who believe that Horowitz has overreached somewhat. For instance, Hillel Halkin has pointed out that Horowitz musters only three concrete instances in which Jews initiated violence against non-Jews from late antiquity onward. All the other instances Horowitz discusses involve Jewish ridicule of Christians and Christianity, but no actual violence.[167] Still, one can argue that the propensity for violence was kept alive in rabbinic Judaism, even if it was not acted upon.

Moreover, we can invoke a point similar to one raised in the last chapter concerning the messianic doctrine in the biblical text. Regardless of how the rabbis envision the means by which the Jews will achieve redemption, the rabbinic understanding of the messianic period is a triumphalist one. There is

166 H. H. Ben-Sasson, "The Uniqueness of the Jews According to Twelfth-Century Figures" (in Hebrew), *Perakim* 2 (1971): 145–218. The major exception with respect to this attitude is Judah Halevi, who sees Jewish suffering as emblematic of Jewish chosenness, as noted earlier (see p. 87, this volume). Ben-Sasson analyzes Halevi's position as well but claims that the alternative view was far more popular.

167 See Halkin's review in *Commentary* 121, no. 6 (2006): 65–69.

much disagreement in rabbinic sources on what gentiles will do in the period of the messiah.[168] In some sources, they will convert to Judaism.[169] In other sources, they will not convert because God will no longer be receptive to their becoming Jews. In still others, they will attempt to convert and fail because of their inability to be fully obedient to God's commandments.[170] But according to all these viewpoints, the world that emerges in the messianic period is definitely one in which the Jewish people are ascendant.

One can also question whether the doctrine of *mipney hata'einu* represents a renunciation of violence. Certainly, the rabbis directed the blame for the destruction of the Temple against themselves, not the Romans. However, this concept celebrates violence by endorsing the destruction that the Romans brought on the Jews as an expression of God's will. As we saw in our first reading, Jewish and Roman sources attest to the fact that this destruction was quite devastating, particularly that which occurred in the wake of the Bar Kokhba revolt, and according to the doctrine of *mipney hata'einu*, all this violence was justified because God, with the help of the Romans, was punishing the Jews for their sins. Of course, this idea is as old as the Bible itself. The prophet Jeremiah thought of the Babylonians as God's messengers in inflicting harm on the Israelites, and he urged them to submit to God's judgment.[171] The rabbis seem to have accepted this way of thinking without reservation.

In our first reading, we spoke about a psychological shift in the rabbinic conceptions of manhood, a shift in which gentle virtues were exalted and militaristic ones were transmuted into acts of piety, such as the study of Torah. Here as well another interpretation is possible. Indeed, the rabbis commonly equated debates over matters of Torah with warlike imagery, and they viewed themselves as soldiers battling for the true interpretation of God's word. Yet, a study by Jeffrey Rubenstein sheds a whole new light on the rabbinic use of military motifs.[172] Rubenstein argues that the culture of debate in the Babylonian rabbinic academies that redacted the Talmud (450–600) was quite fierce—even brutal. It was characterized by outbursts of anger, abusive language, insults, and malicious behavior. Rubenstein surmises that this style of argumentation can be explained by the highly structured and hierarchical nature of the rabbinic academies. One advanced in the hierarchy only

168 Goldenberg, *The Nations That Knew Thee Not*, 91–93.

169 B.T. *Berakhot* 57b.

170 B.T. *'Avodah Zarah* 2a–3b.

171 Jer. 27.

172 Jeffrey L. Rubenstein, *The Culture of the Babylonian Talmud* (Baltimore: Johns Hopkins Press, 2005), 54–66.

by showing one's ferocity in debate and by thoroughly thrashing one's opponent.[173] Rubenstein also demonstrates that the same combative style of debate
continued in the medieval period.[174] Thus, one should not necessarily assume
that by using warlike imagery to describe debates in the rabbinic academy, the
rabbis had substituted militarism with a benevolent ethic. Rubenstein's analysis
indicates that military violence was simply replaced by another kind of violence, violence of a psychological nature. Certainly, the latter type of violence
did not involve actual bloodletting, but according to our definition of violence
in the introductory chapter, it was violence nonetheless.[175]

Let us also look again at rabbinic laws of war. In our first reading, we argued
that the nonviolent ethic of the rabbis is evident in the fact that, according to
these laws, no wars may be waged in the post-biblical period except in self-
defense. Here again another interpretation is possible. Perhaps the rabbis could
not conceive of waging war in most instances because for them it was not an
option. Without political independence and an army, the rabbis could not speak
of war in any practical sense. They therefore did not renounce war as a legitimate activity. And, in fact, they had no difficulty with the genocidal wars conducted against the Canaanites and Amalekites in biblical times that were deemed
obligatory wars. Therefore, rabbinic laws on war can be understood as reflecting
the stark reality of Jewish powerlessness, rather than as an ethic of peace.[176]

Other elements in rabbinic laws on war can be adduced to support this
assessment. In our first reading, the claim was made that the call to violence
inherent in the command to destroy Amalek was not a problem because,
according to many medieval rabbis, Amalek had ceased to be an identifiable
group, and therefore the command was no longer in effect. Yet, it is well-known
among scholars of rabbinic Judaism that the image of Amalek was highly malleable in the imagination of the rabbis and that they commonly identified
their adversaries with this ancient enemy, whoever they might be. In the first

---

173 Rubenstein, pp. 62–63. Rubenstein cites the work of Walter Ong to explain this phenomenon. Oral
cultures, like that of the rabbis, tend to be combative because disagreements are face to face, as opposed to literary cultures, in which those engaged in debate relate to each other through the written word. This explains why
Palestinian rabbis were much less prone to combative behavior. Their culture was based more on writing than
that of the Babylonian rabbis, a feature characteristic of the Greco-Roman world in general.

174 Rubenstein, 147–51.

175 We have to admit, however, the Rubenstein arguments do not necessarily apply to Palestinian rabbinic
culture. His analysis concerns the rabbis of the Babylonian academies.

176 Artson briefly entertains this possibility but dismisses it as irrelevant because one should judge the
sources on the basis of their contents, not the intentions that shaped them (106). But Artson undercuts his reasoning here in the ensuing discussion, where he argues that one should judge the biblical narratives involving
the conquest of Canaanites by their intended meaning—which, according to Artson, is to teach the Israelites
about faith in God, not violence (108–15).

centuries, Amalek was the Roman Empire, while in the medieval period, Amalek was Christian Europe.[177] This tendency has continued in the modern period. Many Jews identified the Nazis as Amalek, and in modern day Israel, some right-wing religious Israelis have done the same with the Palestinians. Certainly, up until recent times, the consequences of this phenomenon have been limited because the rabbis had no power to act on their hatred of Amalek. However, as Horowitz has argued, Jews were surprisingly forthright in the medieval period in openly ridiculing and insulting Christians and Christianity. Much more serious and troubling is that in the modern period, Jews have regained political power, and the propensity of right-wing Israeli settlers to identify the Palestinians with Amalekites has sometimes had deadly consequences.[178] The commandment to exterminate the Amalekites was therefore preserved by the rabbis, and for that reason it remains a potential source of violence.[179]

Let us also look again at the talmudic passage in Yoma 22b, which was cited as evidence that the rabbis were morally conflicted about the imperative to destroy Amalek:

> When the Holy One, blessed be He, said to Saul "Now go, attack
> Amalek" (I Sam. 15:5), he said: "If on account of one person, the
> Torah said: Perform the ceremony of the heifer whose neck is broken,
> how much more [should consideration be given] to all these persons!
> And if human beings sinned, what [crime] has the cattle committed?
> And if adults have sinned, what have the little ones done?" A divine
> voice came forth and said, "do not overdo goodness" (Ecc. 7:16).

As noted in the first reading, some claim that the rabbis' discomfort with the command to annihilate Amalek comes through in Saul's challenge to God. However, this passage is really not so clear-cut. One can point to God's rejection of Saul as evidence that the rabbis were, in fact, quite comfortable with the directive to destroy Amalek. God urges Saul to accept the divine decree and, quoting from Ecclesiastes, tells him not to "overdo goodness." This passage can therefore be read as an example of divine command morality. God's directives determine right and wrong just because they are his commands.[180]

---

177 This issue is analyzed in Cohen, "Esau."

178 Horowitz, *Reckless Rites*, 1, 3–4. We will analyze this issue in greater detail in a later chapter.

179 Boyarin, *A Radical Jew*, 248, claims that the "literalism" of rabbinic hermeneutics did not allow the rabbis to apply the commandment to slaughter the seven Canaanite nations to other groups. Boyarin, however, overlooks the case of Amalek and its treatment in rabbinic Judaism, which provides an excellent illustration of that very phenomenon.

180 This refutes Avi Sagi and Daniel Statman, who claim that there is no divine-command morality in Judaism in "Divine Command Morality and the Jewish Tradition," *Journal of Religious Ethics* 23 (1995): 49–68.

We can also question Avi Sagi's moral defense of the rabbinic tradition regarding Amalek. Sagi argues that the very fact that Jewish thinkers throughout the ages attempted to justify the commandment to destroy Amalek is evidence that in Judaism morality is separate from and takes priority over religion. The problem with this approach is that it is based on the assumption that any reasoning justifying the war against Amalek is by definition moral. One can challenge this claim by arguing that even people whose actions are clearly immoral often use reasons to justify their actions. A justification for an action is therefore not enough. Standards have to be established to determine which justifications are moral and which are not.

Sagi's examples illustrate the difficulty with his position. Abravanel claims that the Amalekites received the punishment they did because they had no justification to go to war and because they attacked the weakest of the Israelites. According to Sagi, this is an example of a Jewish thinker who gives moral considerations independent status and places them above religion in attempting to justify the ongoing war against Amalek. Yet, one can question how truly moral Abravanel's position is if it has no trouble accepting the decree against Amalekites which dictates that they should all be annihilated—men, women, and children—and specifies that the decree is for all subsequent generations who had nothing to do with the initial war. Sagi has focused on the fact that Abravanel gives reasons for his position but has not examined whether those reasons stand up to moral scrutiny. One can also question whether Abravanel's justifications for annihilating Amalek are independent of religion, as Sagi claims. Abravanel's criticism of Amalek for lacking mercy more likely emanates from his own Jewish value system than from an independent moral position. This surmise fits well with the fact that Abravanel is well-known as a conservative when it comes to the use of philosophy in religious matters. Also problematic is Sagi's claim that Nahmanides' view of Amalek is justified by moral considerations independent of religion. According to Nahmanides, Amalek was punished as harshly as it was because other nations feared God after hearing about the exodus from Egypt, while Amalek did not. It is difficult to see how Nahmanides' reasoning here is guided by a morality independent of religion if he believes that the decree against Amalek is motivated by their lacking fear of the Israelite God![181]

---

181 Doubts can also be raised regarding Sagi's argument that the symbolic approach circumvents the moral difficulties with the commandment to annihilate Amalek. Sagi argued that this approach, which sees Amalek as the embodiment of evil and Israel as the embodiment of good, disengages the commandment "from the concrete, historical dimensions of the event, as well as from the literal perception of Amalek's punishment in the biblical text" (p. 330). Yet, no evidence is presented to sustain this reading. Just because a commandment has been interpreted in a symbolic vein does not mean that it automatically loses its literal meaning. The literal and the symbolic meanings can coexist.

We must also take a closer look at the category of discretionary wars in rabbinic law. As noted in our first reading, this category includes wars fought by the kings of Israel in order to expand the territory of the ancient Jewish state. Maimonides adds that these wars were meant to increase the power and prestige of the king or of Israel. According to rabbinic law, the king could initiate a war of this kind only with the approval of the Sanhedrin and the high priest's oracle. Here, too, it was argued that the rabbis adopted a nonviolent stance because, according to their stipulations, discretionary wars could no longer be fought in rabbinic times owing to the absence of a Jewish king and a Sanhedrin. Yet, once again, one can question whether the rabbis believed that this category of war was no longer operative because of moral considerations or because they were unable to think otherwise in light of their powerlessness. Furthermore, the wars in the biblical period included in this category were wars of conquest and would be judged reprehensible by any contemporary standards of just war, not to mention some medieval ones. Nonetheless, the rabbis raise no moral objections to these wars.

We must also delve more deeply into rabbinic sources dealing with *jus in bello*, laws concerned with the conduct of a Jewish army when war has already been waged. In our first reading, we noted that modern Jewish ethicists often express admiration for Maimonides' view that both the Canaanite nations and the Amalekites had to be offered terms of peace before war was waged against them, even though no stipulation of this kind is mentioned in the biblical text. According to these ethicists, Maimonides' rereading of the Bible can be attributed to moral considerations. Yet, what these ethicists overlook is that, according to Maimonides, the terms of peace offered to the Canaanites and Amalekites include the demands that these nations accept the Noahide laws and submit to servitude. Moreover, if these terms are not accepted, the original biblical injunction against them is applied: the entire enemy population must be annihilated—men, women, and children.[182] Maimonides therefore gives us something of a mixed message here.

The moral difficulties with Maimonides' position are further illuminated by Elliot Horowitz. Horowitz argues that for Maimonides the commandment to annihilate Amalek is still in effect in his own period and that Amalek is still in existence somewhere in Christian Europe. Maimonides also emphasizes the imperative to hate Amalek as much as possible in his writings and is far more strident on this point than were the rabbis who actually lived in Christian countries.[183]

182 M.T. *Melakhim* 6:1–4.
183 Horowitz, *Reckless Rites*, 129–34.

It should also be mentioned here that, according to Maimonides, laws regulating conduct in discretionary wars are similar to those applicable in obligatory wars, and the former raise the same moral problems as the latter. In
discretionary wars, Jews are again required to offer the enemy the choice of
observing the Noahide laws and living in servitude as conditions for avoiding
war. If they do not accept these conditions, war is then waged, and if the Jews
are victorious, they are mandated to kill all the males and force the women and
children into servitude.[184]

To sum up our second reading, we have argued that many of the rabbinic
sources cited in the first reading as proof of a positive attitude toward non-Jews
can be interpreted as expressing antipathy toward them. On balance, rabbinic
views on non-Jews may have therefore been more negative than positive. We
have also shown that another reading is possible for rabbinic sources that deal
with the issue of violence. One can argue that expressions of anger against
non-Jews and the desire to do violence to them are alive and well in rabbinic
texts; it is just that the rabbis recognized that they could not act to satisfy those
feelings. The rabbis therefore spoke about war as something that either
belonged in the distant past or had to be postponed to the distant future. Thus,
the rabbis continued to affirm the justice of the obligatory genocidal wars
against the Canaanites and the Amalekites in biblical times, and they had no
difficulty with the notion that discretionary wars were waged in ancient Israel
for the purpose of conquest. The vendetta against Amalek was also kept alive in
rabbinic and medieval Judaism by the ever-shifting target to which it was attached. As for the future messianic era, war would be waged once again when
God would wreak vengeance on the gentile nations and make Israel dominant
among the nations. Therefore, the rabbis did not renounce violence; they
merely recognized that in the long period of exile it had to be restrained. None
of this is to deny that there are sources in rabbinic texts that support peace. In
fact, on balance, it is fair to say that the early and medieval rabbinic tradition
has more sources that speak about the value of peace than those espousing
violence. However, a violent dimension in rabbinic Judaism is evident in some

---

184 Gerald J. Blidstein gives a deft and detailed analysis of Maimonides' legal rulings on war in *Political
Concepts in Maimonidean Halakhah*, 2nd ed. (in Hebrew) (Ramat Gan: Bar Ilan University Press, 2001). Blidstein
shows that, according to Maimonides, one is not permitted to wage discretionary war for the purpose of forcing
a population to adopt the seven Noahide laws, but once territory is captured, one is required to coerce the enemy
to obey those laws (230–45). Blidstein also makes a comparison between Maimonides' views on war and Islamic
views of *jihad* and demonstrates that Maimonides was likely influenced by elements of the latter doctrine
(253–63). However, as Robert Goldenberg notes, Jews, unlike Christians or Muslims, never advocated war in
defense of their ancestral religion or as proof of its superiority. This is true even in the biblical period. See Goldenberg, *The Nations That Knew Thee Not*, 102f.

of its core doctrines and in its prescriptions regarding war, and it has often been glossed over by Jewish scholars and ethicists.

Conclusions

The discussion need not end here. Those supporting the first reading can certainly find fault with the second. For instance, according to the second reading, the fact that the rabbis formulated laws of war based on events in the biblical period indicates that they saw war as a legitimate activity. In response, one can claim that this understanding of the rabbis is off the mark because the rabbis could never claim that the wars waged in the Bible were morally reprehensible. The Bible, after all, was God's revelation, and the only way the rabbis could voice their objections to violence in the Bible was through reinterpretation. That is why they claimed that wars were legitimate during the biblical period but could no longer be practiced. Furthermore, one can find any number of instances in which the rabbis dealt with morally problematic elements of the biblical tradition in a similar way.[185] Therefore, it is quite possible that rabbinic laws of war do indeed reflect a peaceful ethic.

Moreover, even if one admits that the rabbis continued to endorse war as a legitimate activity, they should be commended for what they did, not for what they failed to do. Within the context of the Jewish tradition, the rabbis took a significant moral step beyond the earlier biblical tradition by relegating war to the distant past or distant future and by denying that it was an option in their own period. Similar arguments can be made with respect to Maimonides. Certainly, Maimonides' rulings on war contain harsh elements, but let us emphasize his achievements in making bold moral advances beyond the Bible and the early rabbis. Maimonides' notion that the Israelites had to offer peace to the Amalekites and Canaanites before waging war should be viewed as a remarkable example of how morally problematic texts can be overturned through reinterpretation.[186]

185 See, for instance, the rabbinic discussion of the case of the rebellious son in B.T. *Sanhedrin* 71a, which is often cited as an example of the rabbis' use of interpretation to circumvent a morally problematic law. The characterization of rabbinic legislation offered here is argued most cogently by David Weiss Halivni, "Can a Religious Law Be Immoral?" in *Perspectives on Jews and Judaism: Essays in Honor of Wolfe Kelman*, ed. Arthur A. Chiel (New York: Rabbinic Assembly, 1978), 165–70.

186 There is material in Maimonides' philosophical work on Amalek that we have not examined here. It is explored in Josef Stern, "Maimonides on Amalek, Self-Corrective Mechanisms, and the War against Idolatry," in *Judaism and Modernity: The Religious Philosophy of David Hartman*, ed. Jonathan W. Malino (Hampshire: Ashgate, 2006), 359–92. We will look at this material and Stern's interpretation of it in the next chapter.

What, then, are the underlying reasons for the ambiguities in rabbinic Judaism? First, as we discovered in the discussion of the Bible, there were many instances in which texts or ideas were ambiguous because much depended on how one understood the intentions of the authors. While such intentions are always hard to discern, the challenge is particularly difficult with rabbinic texts, which are known for their terse and elliptical style. In these texts, the ambiguity was usually focused not on individual words or phrases, as was the case in the discussion of the Bible, but on passages or a series of passages with a connected theme. Thus, for example, the midrash about Saul's challenge to God regarding the killing of the Amalekites was an instance of a single passage that was interpreted very differently in these two readings. The Noahide code and the laws regarding war were instances in which a whole series of texts was involved.

Another source of ambiguity similar to that encountered in the previous chapter was the question of historical context and its role in interpreting religious ethics. In the first reading, historical context was used on several occasions to mitigate the harshness of rabbinic views on non-Jews and violence. These views had to be understood against the background of centuries of foreign domination and persecution. In our second reading, the assumption was that historical context was of no consequence. One had to judge the rabbis by using contemporary ethical standards. If rabbinic texts made disparaging statements about non-Jews or spoke positively about violence, they had to be regarded as morally problematic.

We also encountered a source of ambiguity not seen in the previous chapter. A major issue was how one judges the rabbis as interpreters of earlier traditions. In our first reading, the rabbis were commended as interpreters who read new meaning into the biblical text and in doing so made significant ethical advances beyond it. In our second reading, the claim was made that the rabbis did not go far enough, and that whatever violence was contained in their literature should be subject to criticism. The source of ambiguity here was again tied to the issue of context, but this time the focus was not historical context, but the context of the Jewish textual tradition. In the first reading, that context was taken into account in judging rabbinic texts, while in the second reading the texts were evaluated by what they said and on their own merits.

4

Medieval Jewish Philosophy

In this chapter and the next, we will explore two schools of thought that developed in the medieval period: philosophy and Kabbalah. These schools based their thinking on the Bible and rabbinic Judaism but drew much of their inspiration from ideas outside the Jewish sphere. Philosophy was particularly dependent on non-Jewish thought systems. In neither of these schools do we find a wealth of information on peace and violence. Nonetheless, they had a good deal to say about non-Jews and were influential in shaping Jewish attitudes on that issue not just during the Middle Ages, but in the modern period as well.

We will begin by examining medieval Jewish philosophy, which flourished between the tenth and the sixteenth centuries.[1] It encompassed a wide variety of thinkers, but the one feature that united them was the belief that the rational human mind had access to truths in all areas of knowledge, from natural science to theology. Moreover, they believed that all matters of religion—doctrines, practices, and sacred texts—should be interpreted in accordance with those rationally

1 Surveys of medieval Jewish philosophy include Isaac Husik, *A History of Medieval Jewish Philosophy* (Philadelphia: Jewish Publication Society of America, 1958); Julius Guttmann, *Philosophies of Judaism*, trans. David Silverman (New York: Schocken Books, 1973), pt. 2; Colette Sirat, *A History of Jewish Philosophy in the Middle Ages* (Cambridge: Cambridge University Press, 1986); Daniel H. Frank and Oliver Leaman, eds., *A History of Jewish Philosophy* (London and New York: Routledge, 1997), pt. 2; and idem, eds., *The Cambridge Companion to Medieval Jewish Philosophy* (Cambridge: Cambridge University Press, 2003).

determined truths. Medieval Jewish philosophers also depended a great deal on ancient Greek philosophy, particularly the philosophies of Plato and Aristotle. A parallel phenomenon existed in the other two Abrahamic faiths: Christianity and Islam also witnessed the development of rational schools of thought with roots in Greek philosophy.

The Islamic philosophers played a pivotal role in introducing Greek philosophy to thinkers in the other two faiths. They were the first to appreciate the importance and profundity of Greek philosophical texts, and the leading figures among them—most notably Alfarabi, Avicenna, and Averroes—composed a series of commentaries on these texts along with original treatises that were highly influential on Jewish and Christian philosophers. Medieval Jewish and Christian philosophy was therefore shaped in large part by Greek philosophy as understood by Islamic thinkers.

Medieval Jewish philosophy had its formal beginning with Saadiah Gaon in the tenth century. However, it was Maimonides who in the twelfth century lent it an authority it had not had previously. Moreover, Maimonides' creative synthesis of Judaism and Aristotelian thought in his major philosophical treatise, *The Guide of the Perplexed*, would have a lasting impact for centuries to come. Even today, Jewish philosophers find inspiration in Maimonides' thought.

Medieval Jewish philosophy would also spawn a great deal of controversy, particularly in the two centuries after Maimonides' death in 1204. Jews were divided over whether a rational understanding of Judaism was possible or even desirable. Even within the philosophical camp there were deep divisions over the extent to which rationalism could be used to interpret religion. On one end of the spectrum were philosophers who believed that rational speculation on religious matters was fine so long as it did not challenge Judaism's basic beliefs. These thinkers were therefore conservative in their interpretations of Judaism. On the other end were philosophers who were far more willing to adopt philosophical positions that were at odds with traditional Jewish doctrines and who therefore expressed views that were at times quite radical.[2] For instance, a number of philosophers in this latter camp believed that God could not be a personal being. Their view, which was based on Aristotle's philosophy, was that God kept nature functioning according to predictable laws and therefore could

---

2 The controversy in medieval Judaism over the study of philosophy is discussed by Joseph Sarachek, *Faith and Reason: The Conflict over the Rationalism of Maimonides* (Williamsport: Bayard Press, 1935); Daniel J. Silver, *Maimonidean Criticism and Maimonidean Controversy, 1180–1240* (Leiden: E. J. Brill, 1965); Bernard Septimus, *Hispano-Jewish Culture in Transition: The Career and Controversies of Ramah* (Cambridge, Mass.: Harvard University Press, 1982); Idit Dobbs-Weinstein, "The Maimonidean Controversy," in Frank and Leaman, *A History of Jewish Philosophy*, 331–49.

not change his will, speak to human beings, or intervene in nature to perform miracles. A number of medieval Jewish philosophers believed that Maimonides himself supported this radical brand of philosophy but concealed his true views in hints and clues in his writings so that only the elite philosophers could discern what he believed. This reading of Maimonides is also supported by a significant number of modern academic scholars.[3]

Most academic scholars tend to believe that medieval Jewish philosophy expressed highly positive views regarding non-Jews. In fact, it is often held up as the beacon of universalism in premodern Judaism. This tendency goes back to the early nineteenth century, when Jewish Studies began to take root in European universities. During this period Jews were gaining citizenship in European countries for the first time and trying to find acceptance among non-Jews in the social, cultural, and intellectual spheres. One challenge they faced was fighting the Christian stereotype that Judaism was a primitive and unenlightened religion. Jewish academics were drawn to medieval Jewish philosophy because it seemed to prove that assumption wrong by demonstrating that medieval Jewish philosophers were just as appreciative of Greek philosophy as medieval Christian philosophers were.

There was another reason modern Jewish intellectuals took an interest in medieval Jewish philosophy. They drew inspiration from the entire enterprise of medieval philosophy as manifested in the three Abrahamic religions because it presumed that all human beings possessed a rational faculty and therefore had access to ultimate truth. A good argument was valid no matter what religious community it originated in. That is why Maimonides could openly draw inspiration from the views of a Muslim philosopher, such as Alfarabi, while a Christian philosopher, such as Thomas Aquinas, could make use of insights put forth by Maimonides. In short, medieval philosophy seemed to provide a model for exactly what Jews had been striving for: the equality of all human beings, including Jews.

In recent decades, the popularity of medieval Jewish philosophy in academic circles has waned significantly as the apologetic motives inspiring its study have lost their relevance. In today's world, ethnicity has become more a source of pride than of shame. Jews no longer need medieval Jewish philosophy

---

3 A vast literature could be cited on this issue since it relates to every aspect of Maimonides' thought. I will just note that representatives of the conservative reading of Maimonides include such scholars as Isadore Twersky in his *Introduction to the Code of Maimonides* (Mishneh Torah) (New Haven: Yale University Press, 1980); Marvin Fox, *Interpreting Maimonides* (Chicago: University of Chicago Press, 1990). The radical reading is championed in the many works of Leo Strauss, including *Philosophy and Law*, trans. Fred Baumann (Philadelphia: Jewish Publication Society of America, 1987); idem, "The Literary Character of the *Guide of the Perplexed*," in *Persecution and the Art of Writing* (Glencoe, Ill.: Free Press, 1952), 38–94.

to prove their worth in the eyes of non-Jews. In addition, the existence of the state of Israel has played an important role in strengthening modern Jewish identity. Medieval Jewish philosophy therefore does not have the centrality in Jewish Studies it once had. Yet, it still remains a subject to which many are drawn, and some Jewish intellectuals continue to find inspiration in its universalistic premises. After all, universalism is still appealing to many Jews even if they no longer feel the need to fight for acceptance.

Our discussion will focus mostly on Maimonides because he is the towering figure in medieval Jewish philosophy. We have already discussed Maimonides at some length in the previous chapter because he was also one of Judaism's greatest halakhic authorities and was therefore an important representative of medieval rabbinic Judaism. Our discussion in this chapter will focus primarily on Maimonides the philosopher. We will therefore concentrate on his major philosophical work, *The Guide of the Perplexed*, whereas in the last chapter we looked mostly at his legal compilation, *The Mishneh Torah*. However, we will also look at passages in the *Mishneh Torah* that have implications for Maimonides' philosophical thought, because the philosophical and halakhic dimensions of Maimonides' thought cannot be entirely separated.

Medieval Philosophy Promotes Peace

Given that academic scholars have emphasized the universalism of medieval Jewish philosophy, our first reading will defend this position and will also argue that this universalism implies support of a peaceful ethic. We will begin by delineating the universalistic premises that underlie Maimonides' philosophy. According to Menachem Kellner, Maimonides subscribes to a "non-essentialist" viewpoint when it comes to the distinction between Jews and non-Jews.[4] Maimonides believes that all human beings can achieve closeness to God by perfecting their intellects. Intellectual perfection involves the mastery of rational wisdom about the world and God—or, in medieval philosophical parlance, "physics" and "metaphysics"—and for Maimonides the content of these two areas of knowledge is defined primarily by Aristotelian philosophy. The greater an individual's intellectual perfection, the more God will protect him from harm, and the greater his chances are of being rewarded with immortality in

---

4 Menachem Kellner, *Maimonides on Judaism and the Jewish People* (Albany: State University of New York Press, 1991), chapter 1. Much of my interpretation of Maimonides in this first reading is indebted to Kellner's study. I should also note that for the time being, I will sidestep the question of whether Maimonides' philosophy is conservative or radical.

the afterlife. Those who cultivate the highest levels of intellectual perfection can become prophets. Jews have an advantage over non-Jews in reaching intellectual perfection because of the Torah, which, through its doctrines and practices, inculcates lessons in physics and metaphysics. Most important are truths in the latter area, which include proofs for the existence of God and an understanding of his nature, to the extent that this is possible for the rational human mind. This description of the Torah's truths may sound strange to modern ears given that the Torah seems to provide little information about Aristotelian physics and metaphysics, but Maimonides believes that lessons in these areas of knowledge are contained in the Torah and can be discerned in it when one knows how to unlock its esoteric meaning. However, the most important point for our purposes is that what separates Jews from non-Jews for Maimonides is only that Jews have the Torah which provides them with a shortcut to achieve intellectual perfection and closeness to God. There is no essential distinction between the Jew and the non-Jew. Hence the notion that Maimonides takes a nonessentialist position with respect to the distinction between them. Thus, if the non-Jew wants to achieve closeness to God, that person can cultivate his intellect and receive the very same rewards a Jew will. The non-Jew may not have the advantage of the Torah, which makes this process easier. Nonetheless, nothing stops the non-Jew from experiencing providence, prophecy, and immortality.[5]

One can better appreciate Maimonides' universalism by contrasting his nonessentialist position with the other major viewpoint in medieval Judaism regarding the difference between Jews and non-Jews. This position, which Kellner terms the "essentialist" position, is that there is a fundamental distinction between Jew and non-Jew and that God has graced the Jew with a soul superior to that of the non-Jew. Non-Jews, therefore, can never come as close to God as Jews can, no matter how hard they try. This view, which echoes a concept we have already encountered in rabbinic texts, is developed in the medieval period by Judah Halevi, an eleventh-century Spanish figure, and is later adopted by most Kabbalists. We will have occasion to discuss this view in more detail in the next chapter. What is most important for us at this point is to understand the contrast between essential and nonessential conceptions regarding the

---

5 Kellner, chapter 1. See also Ya'akov Levinger, "Human Perfection among the Gentiles According to Maimonides" (in Hebrew), in *Hagut 2: Bein Yisra'el La-'Amim* (Jerusalem: Ministry of Education and Culture, 1978), 27–35. Levinger's article focuses primarily on the issue of prophecy. Levinger notes that Maimonides is the first medieval Jewish philosopher to believe that non-Jews can experience prophecy (35). See also Lawrence J. Kaplan, "Maimonides on the Singularity of the Jewish People," *Da'at* 15 (1985): 5–27 (English section). Kaplan's analysis discusses how Maimonides balances universalism with particularism by differentiating between a universal Abrahamic community, which receives its truth through reason, and the Jewish community, which receives the same truths through revelation.

difference between Jews and non-Jews, to appreciate the universalistic orientation of the nonessentialist position, and to recognize that Maimonides firmly
upholds this latter viewpoint.[6]

Maimonides' nonessentialist position explains why he openly expressed
deep admiration for non-Jewish philosophers. In correspondence with Samuel
ibn Tibbon, his most famous student, he gives the highest praise to Alfarabi,
Ibn Bajja, and Averroes—all Muslim philosophers.[7] In the *Guide*, Maimonides
refers to Aristotle as "the chief of the philosophers" and claims that he achieved
the greatest level of human perfection available to human beings short of
becoming a prophet.[8] No Jewish philosopher ever receives this kind of commendation from Maimonides.[9]

Some scholars also argue that Maimonides supported natural law, the
notion that all human beings have the natural capacity to discern right from
wrong.[10] A full treatment of this issue is beyond the scope of our discussion
here. However, one can certainly appreciate on a general level why Maimonides
could support such a view given his universalistic orientation.

Maimonides' universalism also comes through in his treatment of Christianity and Islam in the final section of the *Mishneh Torah*.[11] Essentially, Maimonides' position is that Christianity and Islam serve a critical role in God's
plan by preparing the world for the messianic period, in which non-Jews will
recognize the truth of Judaism. Because Christianity and Islam are Judaism's
offspring, adherents of these faiths will come to the messianic period with a
good deal of knowledge about Judaism, and therefore they will easily accept its
premises when it becomes clear to them that it represents the highest truth. It
is a matter of dispute whether Maimonides believed that non-Jews would

6 Kellner, 1–5. Kellner gives credit to Jacob Katz for his distinction between essentialist and nonessentialist positions. See Jacob Katz, *Tradition and Crisis: Jewish Society at the End of the Middle Ages* (New York: Schocken
Books, 1971), 26. Avi Sagi provides a discussion of Jewish views of non-Jews that revolves around distinctions
similar to those made by Kellner in *Judaism: Between Religion and Morality* (in Hebrew) (Tel Aviv: Hakibbutz
Hameuchad, 1998), chapter 8.

7 *Iggerot ha-Rambam*, ed. and trans. into Hebrew by Ya'akov Shilat (Jerusalem: Ma'aliyot Press, 1995),
2:553. Maimonides' views on Muslim thinkers are discussed in George Hourani, "Maimonides and Islam," in
Studies in Islamic and Judaic Traditions, ed. William M. Brinner and Stephen D. Ricks (Atlanta: Scholars Press,
1986), 161–63.

8 Maimonides, *The Guide of the Perplexed*, trans. Shlomo Pines (Chicago: University of Chicago Press,
1963), I:5, p. 28.

9 A thorough analysis of the influences of non-Jewish thinkers on Maimonides' *Guide* is found in Shlomo
Pines's classic essay, "Translator's Introduction," in *The Guide of the Perplexed*, lvii–cxxxiii. See also the supple-
mentary observations of Alfred Ivry, "Islamic and Greek Influences on Maimonides' Philosophy," in *Maimonides
and Philosophy*, ed. Shlomo Pines and Yirmiyahu Yovel (Dordrecht: Martinus Nijhoff, 1986), 139–56.

10 Steven S. Schwarzschild, "Do Noachites Have to Believe in Revelation?" *Jewish Quarterly Review*, n.s. 53
(1962): 50–52; Novak, *Natural Law in Judaism*, 92–121.

11 M.T. *Melakhim* 11:4, censored out of most printed editions of the *Mishneh Torah*.

actually convert to Judaism in the messianic era or adopt a universal religion in which they would worship the God of Israel while remaining non-Jews.[12] Yet, regardless of one's position on this issue, Maimonides seems to express a positive attitude toward Christianity and Islam in that they serve a crucial role in bringing about the world's redemption.

Let us now look at Maimonides' philosophical views on peace and violence. We discussed material relating to war in the *Mishneh Torah* in the previous chapter, and we saw that Maimonides' views on this issue were somewhat ambiguous. In some respects, he endorsed war, but he also seemed to allow a moral element to influence his treatment of this issue by ruling that Jewish armies had to offer terms of peace to their enemies in all instances, including the Canaanites and Amalekites. We can further highlight this moral strand by referring to an article by Josef Stern, who provides a provocative examination of Maimonides' views on the Amalekites. Stern explores the material in the *Mishneh Torah* that we have already examined, but he also offers insights based on passages in the *Guide* that give his analysis a philosophical focus. Stern argues that Maimonides saw an esoteric philosophical meaning in the commandment to annihilate Amalek. He believed that Amalek symbolically represented idolatry and the denial of the unity of God, and the war against Amalek was therefore representative of an intellectual war that must be waged against these erroneous concepts at all times. Stern speculates that the object of Maimonides' concern here may have been Christianity, which he believed was guilty of upholding faulty concepts of this kind because of its belief in the Incarnation and the Trinity. What is most important for our purposes is that according to this analysis, the war against Amalek is focused on the eradication of incorrect philosophical conceptions and is therefore not concerned with physical violence. Stern also argues that in various passages Maimonides framed his interpretation of the commandment to destroy Amalek in a manner designed to preempt violence by Jews against Christians. As we have already noted, Christians were commonly identified with Amalek in medieval Judaism, and therefore Maimonides wanted to discourage acts of violence against them.[13]

We can also draw on Maimonides' political philosophy as it emerges in the *Guide* to demonstrate that he supported nonviolence. A central conception in

---

12 The view that non-Jews will convert to Judaism is argued in Kellner, chapter 5. The view that non-Jews will adopt a universal religion is argued in Blidstein, *Political Concepts in Maimonidean Halakhah*, 245–53.

13 Stern, "Maimonides on Amalek," 359–92. Stern's arguments, however, are complex, and some issues remain unclear. Most important, it is not certain from Stern's analysis how Maimonides viewed Amalek's original attack against the Israelites as reported in the Torah. Does his allegorical understanding of the war against Amalek supplant the historicity of the story, or does it just give the story an added layer of meaning?

this area of Maimonides' thought is the notion that society must be constructed in a way that allows those who are intellectually gifted to pursue intellectual perfection, and this pursuit requires a peaceful society free from strife and violence.[14] While Maimonides focused primarily on peaceful relationships between individuals and classes *within* a given society, his position would seem to have implications for relationships *between* societies as well. It is hard to imagine that Maimonides would have a positive view of war, seeing as it would be just as disruptive to those pursuing intellectual perfection as violence within a society.

This surmise is supported by the concept of the messianic period that is spelled out in several of Maimonides' works. Maimonides envisions the messianic era as one of peace because the world will be filled with "the knowledge of God," which for Maimonides means intellectual perfection, and violence and war are inimical to achieving that perfection. Thus, when Maimonides describes the ideal society, it is one from which war is completely absent.[15] The nonviolent character of this society comes through in one passage in particular:

> The sages and the prophets did not long for the days of the Messiah
> that Israel might exercise dominion over the world, nor rule over the
> Gentiles, nor be exalted by the nations, nor eat and drink and rejoice,
> but that they be free to devote themselves to the Torah and its
> wisdom, with no one to oppress or disturb them.[16]

Here Maimonides tells us that in the messianic era Jews will be so focused on achieving intellectual perfection that even the exercise of power over non-Jews will be of little interest to them compared with their intellectual pursuits.

While Maimonides was certainly the most significant Jewish philosopher in the medieval period, we should not ignore other medieval Jewish philosophers who reflected on the issues discussed here. A number of them betray an openness to non-Jewish wisdom and assume a common humanity shared by Jew and non-Jew, as Maimonides did. This viewpoint can be found among Jewish philosophers well before Maimonides. Saadiah Gaon, who lived in tenth-century Iraq and was the first important Jewish philosopher, was clearly open to non-Jewish religious thought, as evidenced by the fact that he was heavily influenced by Mu'tazilite theology, the most popular school of Islamic

14 *Guide* III:27, pp. 510–12; Howard Kreisel, *Maimonides' Political Thought: Studies in Ethics, Law, and the Human Ideal* (Albany: State University of New York Press, 1999), chapter 6.

15 M.T. *Melakhim* 12:5; Ravitzky, "Peace," 33–34.

16 M.T. *Melakhim* 12:4.

theology in his period.[17] Abraham ibn Ezra, the renowned twelfth-century Spanish Bible commentator, was interested in philosophy and drew most of his ideas from Neoplatonism, a branch of philosophy that had its roots in Plato.[18]

A positive attitude toward non-Jews is particularly evident among a number of Jewish philosophers who lived in the two centuries after Maimonides and were influenced by him. In the previous chapter we discussed R. Menahem ha-Meiri, a thirteenth-century figure in Provence who espoused remarkably tolerant views of non-Jews. It is no accident that Meiri was an avid follower of Maimonides' philosophy. In Meiri's thinking, the universalistic principles underlying Maimonides' thought were exposed and expanded well beyond their original application.[19] Another example is Jacob Anatoli, a thirteenth-century figure who spent time in the court of King Frederick II of Italy. In his major work, *Malmad ha-Talmidim*, Anatoli shares insights about philosophical matters gleaned from conversations with a Christian colleague, Michael Scot, who was also in Frederick's court, and seems to have been quite familiar with Maimonides' *Guide of the Perplexed*. Anatoli tells us in the introduction to his work that his Jewish readers should not be concerned that he sought counsel from a non-Jew regarding philosophical matters because ideas should be judged by their validity, not by the person with whom they originate.[20] Here we have an excellent articulation of the nonessentialist position of Maimonides. An outstanding example of a Jewish philosopher with a universalistic bent is Judah Romano, a fourteenth-century Italian figure. Romano believed that in order to properly interpret the Bible, one had to experience prophecy, and this required that one study philosophical texts, which would inspire the mind to see truths latent in the Bible. The result was a form of biblical interpretation that was very associative and creative. What is most significant for our purposes is that Romano believed that philosophical truths were universal, and he therefore had no qualms about reading the works of Christian philosophers to achieve prophetic inspiration. He speaks glowingly about the writings of such figures as Thomas Aquinas, whom he read to experience this level of inspiration.[21]

17 Much has been written on the influence of Islamic theology on Saadiah's thought. A recent treatment of this issue is Sarah Stroumsa, "Saadya and the Jewish *kalam*," in Frank and Leaman, *The Cambridge Companion to Medieval Jewish Philosophy*, 71–90.

18 A summary of Ibn Ezra's philosophy and the Neoplatonic influences on it can be found in Sirat, 104–12.

19 Halbertal, *Between Torah and Wisdom*, chapter 3.

20 Jacob Anatoli, *Malmad ha-Talmidim* (Lyck: M'kize Nirdamim, 1866), introduction, 177b; Martin L. Gordon, "The Philosophical Rationalism of Jacob Anatoli" (Ph.D. diss., Yeshiva University, 1974), 225.

21 Giuseppe Sermoneta, "Prophecy in the Writings of R. Yehudah Romano," in *Studies in Medieval Jewish History and Literature*, vol. 2, ed. Isadore Twersky (Cambridge, Mass.: Harvard University Press, 1984), 337–74.

Mention should also be made here of the medieval Jewish philosophers who used Maimonides' writings to construct a radical brand of philosophy according to which God was an impersonal being. Thinkers who supported this approach included Samuel ibn Tibbon, Isaac Albalag, Moses Narboni, and Joseph ibn Kaspi, and, as mentioned earlier, many medieval Jewish philosophers and modern academic scholars attribute this approach to Maimonides himself. This branch of philosophy was informed by universalistic premises as well. Philosophers in this camp believed that institutional religions were designed by the prophets primarily for controlling the masses, who were incapable of understanding the subtleties of philosophy and who required the myths of religion in order to live ethical and peaceful lives. The notion of a commanding God who rewards and punishes individuals for their deeds was particularly important in this scheme because it encouraged people to conform to the directives of the prophet. Yet, ultimate truth was to be found in philosophy, which demonstrated that God was an impersonal being who was unable to reward and punish in the manner described by traditional religion. The radical philosophers also believed that philosophical truths should be made available only to the elite who had the intellectual capability to understand them and handle their implications, and that such truths had to be carefully concealed from the masses. While one may be put off by the elitism of this way of thinking, what is significant for our discussion is that it assumed that there was one universal philosophy that was valid for all places and times and that did not favor any one religion in particular.[22]

Medieval Jewish philosophers other than Maimonides also believed in the desirability of peace. For instance, some Jewish philosophers in the Maimonidean school seemed to uphold a nonviolent reading of the wars described in the biblical text by interpreting them as referring to the struggle between the different faculties of the soul.[23] This approach resembles Maimonides' interpretation of Amalek, according to Stern.[24] In a number of medieval Jewish philosophers, the notion of peace between nations as an ultimate ideal comes through in depictions of the messianic era, as it does in Maimonides. Abravanel adopts Maimonides' basic conception of the messianic period in this regard.[25] We can also cite Abraham bar Hiyya, a philosopher predating

22 There is no one study that deals with all these thinkers as a group. Information on the individuals mentioned here can be found in Sirat. For Samuel ibn Tibbon, see 217–22; for Albalag, see 238–43; for Narboni, see 332–41; for Kaspi, see 332–30.

23 Anatoli, 22b, 31b, 85b; Moshe ibn Tibbon, *Perush 'al Shir ha-Shirim* (Lyck: M'kize Nirdamim, 1874), 14b; Ravitzky, "Peace," 31.

24 This type of symbolic or allegorical interpretation of the Bible was quite common in medieval Jewish philosophy in general.

25 Ravitzky, "Peace," 41.

Maimonides, who believes that the messianic period will be one in which God will bring about a miraculous change in human nature that will cause all people to adhere to the principle of loving one's fellow human being as one loves oneself.[26] According to this notion, the hallmark of the messianic era is the fraternity of all human beings, Jews and non-Jews alike.

Medieval Jewish Philosophy Promotes Violence

It is rare to find academic analyses that criticize medieval Jewish philosophy for intolerance, and I know of no analyses that accuse it of promoting violence against non-Jews. Nonetheless, an attempt will be made here to present a critique of medieval Jewish philosophy on both counts.

We can begin by looking once again at the premises underlying Maimonides' philosophy, which, according to our first reading, promoted tolerance. One can argue that Maimonides did not really get rid of intolerance but, rather, redrew the boundaries between ingroup and outgroup. Instead of expressing anger toward non-Jews, Maimonides directs his ire at those who do not seek intellectual perfection. According to Maimonides, the notion that Adam was created in God's image means that his perfect intellect resembled that of his Creator. However, after Adam's expulsion from the Garden of Eden, this was no longer the case; human beings now had to exert great effort to achieve intellectual perfection.[27] Those who did not were no better than animals, and intellectually perfected individuals should stay as far away from them as possible.[28] Intolerance toward non-Jews has therefore been replaced by intolerance toward those who have not achieved intellectual perfection. Moreover, achieving intellectual perfection is not just a matter of will. Some people, by their very nature, are incapable of it no matter how hard they try.[29] Thus, if Maimonides rejects an essentialist viewpoint when it comes to the distinction between Jews and non-Jews, he seems to subscribe to that very viewpoint when

26 Abraham bar Hiyya, *Hegyon ha-Nefesh ha-'Atsuvah*, ed. Geoffrey Wigoder (Jerusalem: Mosad Bialik, 1971), sec. 4; Ravitzky, "Peace," 35.

27 *Guide* I:1; Hannah Kasher, "'Beloved Is Man Who Is Created in the Image [of God]'; Conditional Humanism (According to Maimonides) vs. Unintentional Humanism (According to Leibowitz)" (in Hebrew), *Da'at* 41 (1998): 21.

28 *Guide* I:7, p. 33; I:36, p. 172; III:51, pp. 618–19; Kasher, 22.

29 *Guide* I:34, p. 73; Kasher, 22. Maimonides also believes that many people cannot experience prophecy because of natural limitations. Besides needing a strong intellect, the prophet must also have a strong imaginative faculty, and because this faculty is a disposition of the body, its strength is determined at birth (*Guide* II:36, p. 372). Thus, people born with a weak imaginative faculty can never become prophets no matter how much they develop their intellects.

dealing with the distinction between those who achieve intellectual perfection and those who are unable to.

It can also be argued that if one looks carefully at what Maimonides is say-ing, the old biases against non-Jews have not entirely disappeared. It is cer-tainly true that from a theoretical standpoint nothing stops the non-Jew from achieving intellectual perfection because Jews and non-Jews are born with the same type of intellect. Yet, as we mentioned in our first reading, Jews have an advantage over non-Jews because they possess the Torah, which provides them with easy access to the knowledge they need to achieve intellectual perfection. For this reason, even scholars who emphasize Maimonides' tolerance of non-Jews admit that, according to his thinking, it would be extremely unlikely for non-Jews to experience prophecy because that faculty is possible only for those at the extreme limit of intellectual perfection.[30] Thus, for Maimonides, Jews and non-Jews are equal only in a theoretical sense; in practice, Jews remain superior to non-Jews. While Maimonides did not believe that there was abso-lute congruence between non-Jews and those who were intellectually deficient, he believed that there was significant overlap between the two groups.

On the basis of similar observations, Hannah Kasher concludes that in some respects Maimonides' views are more problematic than Judah Halevi's from a moral standpoint. Indeed, Halevi believed that Jews were superior to non-Jews on the basis of essential differences between the Jewish and non-Jewish soul. However, Halevi also believed that all human beings were a step above animals in possessing a rational faculty. He never equated people who were ignorant of philosophical wisdom with animals, as Maimonides did. It was just that in Halevi's thinking, Jews had a special type of soul that elevated them above the rest of humanity.[31]

We can also find support for Maimonides' belief in the superiority of Jews and Judaism in a passage in the *Mishneh Torah* that has garnered a great deal of attention:

---

30 Kellner concedes that Maimonides "was convinced that Jews, as a national group, were in every way superior to other national groups" (81). See also Kellner, 121 n. 11; Levinger, 34. Levinger also cites a passage from Maimonides' commentary on the Mishnah in which he explains the discriminatory legislation encountered in the previous chapter, according to which non-Jews are treated more harshly than Jews when it comes to paying damages for the injury of a person's animal by another person's ox. Maimonides states that we should not be troubled by this legislation any more than we should be troubled by slaughtering animals because non-Jews do not have perfected human capacities and therefore do not qualify as humans—their purpose is to serve Jews. Levinger attempts to soften Maimonides' position by claiming that what Maimonides is really saying is that non-Jews do not have the Torah and therefore do not have the same opportunity to achieve intellectual perfection as Jews do. Levinger's reading, however, reads too much into this passage. The highly discriminatory nature of Maimonides' remarks has to be acknowledged here along with the ethical problems they entail.

31 Kasher, 24.

All who accept the seven [Noahide] commandments and observe them scrupulously are a "righteous gentile" and will have a portion in the world to come, provided that he accepts them because the Holy One, blessed be He, commanded them in our Torah and [it was] made known through Moses, our teacher, that his observance of them had been enjoined upon the descendants of Noah from antiquity. But if his observance of them is based on reason, he is not deemed a resident alien, nor one of the righteous gentiles, but he is one of their wise men.[32]

Here Maimonides informs us that in order for a non-Jew to achieve the status of righteous gentile and gain a share in the world to come, he must not only observe the seven Noahide laws, he also must recognize that these laws were commanded by God to Moses when the Torah was given on Mount Sinai. Scholars who insist on reading Maimonides as a universalist have made numerous attempts, some of them ingenious, to show that this passage is in line with their viewpoint. However, it is difficult to see from a plain reading of the text how this is possible. In claiming that non-Jews must recognize the truth of Jewish revelation in order to be deemed righteous and achieve immortality, and that it is insufficient for them to observe the Noahide laws because they are rational, Maimonides seems to be expressing a highly chauvinistic viewpoint.[33] A number of scholars have also denied that Maimonides believed in natural law, and this passage is often cited as a key piece of evidence in support of this assessment.[34]

Questions can also be raised about the claim made in the first reading that medieval Jewish philosophers demonstrated respect for non-Jews because the former relied heavily on Greek philosophy. What is often overlooked by scholars making this argument is that most medieval Jewish philosophers believed that Greek philosophy originated with the Jews! While there is no credible evidence

---

32 M.T. *Melakhim* 8:11.

33 Various readings of this passage are discussed in Jacob I. Dienstag, "Natural Law in Maimonidean Thought and Scholarship (On *Mishneh Torah, Kings*, VIII. 11)," *Jewish Law Annual* 6 (1988): 64–77. However, the debate has continued in scholarly literature published after Dienstag's article. See Kellner, 75–77, who attempts to read the passage as supportive of universalism. See also chapter 3, n. 160, this volume.

　　There has been much debate about an alternative reading of this passage. In some manuscripts the last clause says that a non-Jew who observes the Noahide laws on the basis of rational deduction is "*not* one of their wise men" (my emphasis). This issue is discussed by Dienstag, who concludes that this reading is a corruption of the original text (75–70). Yet, as Steven Schwarzschild notes, whichever reading is accepted, the text presents a negative view of non-Jews. See Schwarzschild, "Do Noachites Have to Believe in Revelation?" *Jewish Quarterly Review*, n.s. 52 (1962): 302.

34 See, for instance, Marvin Fox, "Maimonides and Aquinas on Natural Law," *Diné Israel* 3 (1972): v–xxxvi; José Faur, *Studies in the Mishneh Torah: Book of Knowledge* (in Hebrew) (Jerusalem: Mosad ha-Rav Kuk, 1978), 161–76.

to support this claim, medieval Jewish philosophers commonly held that the Greeks learned their wisdom from the Jews in ancient times and that eventually the source of that wisdom was forgotten. Maimonides seems to have taken a somewhat different position on this issue by claiming that the Jews and the Greeks developed similar philosophical systems in ancient times, but there was no influence of one group on the other. He held that philosophy is a rational wisdom that all human beings can discover, and therefore it is plausible that nations other than the Jews would come up with it on their own. Because of centuries of exile and persecution, the Jews eventually forgot their philosophical heritage, and therefore they had to look to Greek philosophy to discover truths that were once theirs. Yet, for our purposes, Maimonides' position differs little from that of other medieval Jewish philosophers. What he is telling us is that non-Jewish philosophy should be respected because it is, in some sense, Jewish.[35]

We can also cast doubt on the claim made in the first reading that Maimonides had a favorable view of Christianity and Islam. The passage in the *Mishneh Torah* that depicts these religions as paving the way for the messianic era can be interpreted as underscoring once again Maimonides' belief in the superiority of Judaism over other religions. Whether non-Jews will convert to Judaism in the messianic period or adopt a universal religion based on Jewish premises, Maimonides assumes the truth of Judaism and the falsehood of Christianity and Islam, and he believes that the followers of these religions will see the error of their ways. When the messiah arrives, Christians and Muslims will discover that "they inherited nothing but lies from their fathers, that their prophets and forbears led them astray."[36]

Maimonides had harsher things to say about Christianity and Islam in other places in his writings. In several passages, Maimonides identifies Christianity with idolatry.[37] Islam is vilified explicitly in his *Epistle to Yemen* and implicitly in the *Guide*. In these works Maimonides intimates that Muhammad was a false prophet, that he plagiarized from Judaism, and that he was not in control of his sexual appetites.[38] More generally, Maimonides saw all religions as plagiarisms of Judaism and believed Jews were persecuted because non-Jews were jealous that God had chosen the Jews above all other nations and had given them the Torah.[39]

35 Twerksy, 496–99.

36 M.T. *Melakhim* 11:4, censored out of most printed editions.

37 M.T. *'Avodah Zarah* 9:4, censored out of most printed editions; Eliezer Schlossberg, "The Attitude of Maimonides toward Islam" (in Hebrew), *Pe'amim* 42 (1990): 42–45.

38 Hourani, 151–53, 155–58; Schlossberg, 49–58.

39 Schlossberg, 38.

Maimonides' views on violence and war can also be interpreted in a manner different from our first reading. As we have seen, Josef Stern has offered an intriguing analysis suggesting that Maimonides interpreted the commandment to annihilate Amalek allegorically and denuded it of its violent meaning. But what about the destruction of the seven Canaanite nations? In one passage in the *Guide*, Maimonides justifies the war against the Canaanites on the basis of philosophical considerations, leaving the violence of the biblical narrative in place:

> Do you not see in the texts of the Torah, when it commanded the
> extermination of the *seven nations* and said *thou shalt save alive*
> *nothing that breatheth* (Deut. 20:16), that it immediately follows this
> by saying: *That they teach you not to do after all their abominations,*
> *which they have done unto their gods and so ye sin against the Lord your*
> *God?* (Deut. 20:18) Thus it says: do not think that this is hard-
> heartedness or desire for vengeance. It is rather an act required by
> human opinion, which considers that everyone who deviates from
> the ways of truth should be put an end to and that all obstacles
> impeding the achievement of the perfection that is the apprehension
> of Him, may He be exalted, should be interdicted.[40]

The annihilation of the Canaanites was needed because everyone who deviates from the way of truth should be killed, and in this instance the Canaanites would have led the Israelites astray. The claim is that such action was required by simple "necessity." Now certainly, as we saw in the previous chapter, Maimonides softens the biblical injunction to destroy the Canaanites with the ruling in the *Mishneh Torah* that the Israelites were required to offer terms of peace to them before attacking. However, one is hard-pressed to find similar compassion in Maimonides' position as formulated in the passage in the *Guide*. Furthermore, as noted in the previous chapter, even according to the ruling in the *Mishneh Torah*, Maimonides had no qualms about the eventual annihilation of the Canaanites because they were apparently unwilling to adopt the Noahide laws. What is also noteworthy in the passage just quoted is that once again we see a coalescence between the categories of those who are intellectually deficient and non-Jews. The Canaanites represent both these categories simultaneously.

We can also take issue here with the argument in our first reading that Maimonides' views on the messianic period represent a rejection of violence and war. Maimonides may envision the messianic period as a peaceful epoch, but he also believes that the way to get there is undoubtedly through violence.

40 *Guide* I:54, pp. 126–27.

According to Maimonides, the messianic figure is a heroic warrior who will establish his messianic credentials by waging war against the enemies of Israel and defeating them.[41]

It can be shown that other medieval Jewish philosophers also expressed negative views toward non-Jews. Gersonides provides an interesting parallel to Maimonides. This fourteenth-century philosopher believes that Jewish chosenness can be explained by a special form of providence inherited from the biblical patriarchs, and while from a theoretical standpoint it is possible that any intellectually gifted individual can pass providence on to his descendants, Gersonides focuses on the Jews as the only instance of this phenomenon.[42] Gersonides is therefore similar to Maimonides in providing a philosophical framework that theoretically makes non-Jews equal to Jews but in reality maintains the superiority of the latter over the former. Other medieval Jewish philosophers would accentuate the ascendancy of Jews over non-Jews much more strongly than Maimonides and Gersonides. This is the case particularly in the fifteenth and sixteenth centuries, when Jewish philosophy takes a conservative turn.[43]

Conclusions

Our discussion could certainly continue with rebuttals of the arguments offered in the second reading. First of all, with respect to Maimonides' harsh statements about Christianity and Islam, one could claim that Maimonides' views are understandable, especially in the case of Islam. Maimonides and his family were forced to flee Spain when he was thirteen years old in order to escape the advancing armies of the Almohads, radical Muslims who were forcing non-Muslims under their rule to convert to Islam on pain of death. Islamic persecution touched Maimonides once again after he became a renowned rabbi. He was contacted by the head of the Yemenite Jewish community for guidance because Muslim rulers were pressuring that community to accept Islam as well. Thus, it should occasion no surprise that Maimonides would speak so negatively about Islam in various writings. Nor should we be

41 M.T. *Melakhim* 11:4. See also Ravitzky, "Peace," 38, who cites a passage from Maimonides' commentary on the Mishnah that envisions a violent beginning to the messianic era.

42 Gersonides' views on Jewish chosenness are analyzed in my study *Gersonides on Providence, Covenant, and the Chosen People: A Study in Medieval Jewish Philosophy and Biblical Commentary* (Albany: State University of New York Press, 1995).

43 Isaac 'Arama and Isaac Abravanel provide good examples of this approach. For the views of 'Arama, see Sarah Heller Wilensky, *The Philosophy of Isaac 'Arama in the Framework of Philonic Philosophy* (in Hebrew) (Jerusalem: Bialik Institute; Tel Aviv: Dvir, 1956), 134–36, 171. For the views of Abravanel, see Benzion Netanyahu, *Don Isaac Abravanel: Statesman and Philosopher* (Philadelphia: Jewish Publication Society of America, 1982), 143–45.

troubled that some of his harshest views regarding Islam were expressed in his *Epistle to Yemen*, written to the Yemenite community in response to the crisis just mentioned.[44] Therefore, historical context can be invoked to explain Maimonides' hostile attitudes toward Christians and Muslims, much as it was used to explain hostile attitudes toward non-Jews in general in rabbinic Judaism.

We can also respond to the critique, offered in the second reading, of Maimonides' views of non-Jews in general. Even if Maimonides' nonessentialist viewpoint retains elements of intolerance, Maimonides still made significant moral advances over his predecessors. His way of thinking may not be sufficiently inclusive from our modern perspective, but it was significant in its time. Evidence for this assessment is the controversy that Maimonides' views generated during his lifetime and in the two centuries after his death. The Jewish community in Europe was bitterly divided over Maimonides' legacy, so much so that edicts of excommunication were issued by proponents and opponents of Maimonides against each other. And while there were many issues that gave rise to opposition against Maimonides, one was the blurring of boundaries between Jewish and non-Jewish wisdom. Maimonides' opponents were incensed by his reliance on Greek philosophy and its Islamic interpreters to interpret Judaism. Clearly, they understood that Maimonides' approach was quite radical.[45] It is certainly true that Maimonides viewed the ideas of Greek philosophy as having once been native to Judaism itself, but it is nonetheless remarkable that he would rely so heavily on non-Jewish philosophers and openly express such deep admiration for their accomplishments. In short, we can defend Maimonides by appreciating his views within the context of the development of the Jewish tradition, much as we did with rabbinic Judaism in the previous chapter. In both instances, it can be argued that Jewish thinkers and texts should be evaluated on the advances they made over previous thinkers, not on their failure to go as far as we might have hoped.

We can take this argument further by noting that the methodology of medieval Jewish philosophy gave great power to human reason, and the thinkers in this school therefore assumed the possibility that their ideas at some point could be altered or overturned. In a frequently cited passage in the *Guide*, Maimonides declares that he would have been content to reinterpret the

---

44 A number of scholars understand Maimonides' disparaging remarks about Islam as a reaction to Muslim persecution. See, for instance, Hourani, 158; Schlossberg, 47–49. An insightful discussion of Maimonides' biography is found in Herbert A. Davidson, *Moses Maimonides: The Man and His Works* (New York: Oxford University Press, 2005), chapter 1. See pp. 13–28 for a discussion of Maimonides' experience with the Almohad persecution. There has been much debate about whether Maimonides temporarily converted to Islam to avoid persecution. Davidson provides a thorough analysis of this issue.

45 I discussed this controversy briefly in the introduction to this chapter. See p. 000, this volume.

story of creation in Genesis in accordance with Aristotle's view that the world was eternal and had no beginning, had there been a compelling rational argument for that position. Maimonides could find no such argument and therefore accepted the traditional Jewish view that the world was created.[46] Maimonides implies here that there is no major dogma in Judaism that he is unwilling to reject if reason required it. Other medieval Jewish philosophers would endorse this way of thinking as well. Therefore, medieval Jewish philosophy adopted a methodology that allowed for its own critique and revision. It assumes that Judaism was a dynamic and evolving religion that could be reinterpreted in light of human reason. What this means is that the medieval Jewish philosophers would have little difficulty with our rejection of their views in favor of more contemporary perspectives.

In this sense, medieval Jewish philosophy has much in common with rabbinic Judaism. As we saw in the previous chapter, the rabbis endowed human beings with a great deal of power to interpret Jewish law. The medieval Jewish philosophers appear to have adopted the same respect for human initiative in matters of religion, but instead of using it to shape the content of Jewish law, they used it to determine the content of Jewish belief.

However, these arguments may not be enough to satisfy those who believe that a thinker's views must be evaluated by what they actually say, not by the context in which they were produced. Maimonides' negative views on other religions may reflect the historical context in which he lived, but that does not mean that they are adequate to give us moral guidance. The differences between Maimonides' historical context and ours may be too great for his views to be applicable in our era. Similarly, Maimonides' views on non-Jews in general may have been more ethically advanced within the context of the Jewish tradition as it had developed up to his time, but they are not advanced enough to satisfy modern ethical sensitivities. And even if the methodology of medieval Jewish philosophy allows for the constant rethinking of Jewish beliefs, it is the methodology that should be commended, not the views of Maimonides, which remain inadequate for guiding us in the modern period.

Our discussion has therefore led us to the same sources of ambiguity that we have seen in earlier chapters. Does one judge a text from a moral standpoint by taking into account the historical context in which it was produced, or does one judge it simply by what it says? Similarly, does one evaluate a text by taking into account how advanced it was within the context of the evolving Jewish tradition, or by its failure to have gone further? As in our previous discussions, the answers to these questions are far from clear.

46 *Guide* II:25, pp. 327–28.

5

Kabbalah

The term "Kabbalah," which means "tradition," refers to a series of schools of Jewish mysticism that evolved throughout the medieval and modern periods. Kabbalah came into being alongside philosophy, and for a number of centuries the two represented rival and contrasting interpretations of Judaism.[1]

While there has been much debate among scholars as to how one defines mysticism, it is most often understood as an attempt to have an unusually direct and intimate relationship with the divine. The division between mysticism and normal religion is not necessarily a sharp one. After all, even ordinary religious people strive to have a close relationship with the divine. It is just that mystics are much more focused on this type of experience and attempt to achieve it in an unusually intense form.

Like medieval Jewish philosophy, Kabbalah was never a monolithic phenomenon, and it encompassed a variety of schools. In recent years scholars have tended to classify these schools into two groups.[2]

[1] Gershom Scholem's *Major Trends in Jewish Mysticism* (New York: Schocken Books, 1961) was written by the founder of the modern academic field of Jewish mysticism, and though it was first published in 1941, it is still a useful introduction. Other more recent introductions include Mosheh Halamish, *An Introduction to the Kabbalah*, trans. Ruth Bar-Ilan and Ora Wiskind-Elper (Albany: State University of New York Press, 1999); Byron Sherwin, *Kabbalah: An Introduction to Jewish Mysticism* (Lanham, Md.: Rowman & Littlefield, 2006); David Ariel, *Kabbalah: The Mystic Quest in Judaism* (Lanham, Md.: Rowman & Littlefield, 2006).

[2] This classification was developed in Moshe Idel, *Kabbalah: New Perspectives* (New Haven: Yale University Press, 1988). It has also been challenged in Elliot R. Wolfson, *Through a Speculum That Shines: Vision and Imagination in Medieval Jewish Mysticism* (Princeton: Princeton University Press, 1994).

One is referred to as "ecstatic" or "prophetic" Kabbalah. This form of Kabbalah emphasizes meditation as a means to achieving a close relationship with the divine. Its founding father was Abraham Abulafia, a thirteenth-century Spanish Jew. He and his disciples devised elaborate techniques of meditation that involved special postures, controlled breathing, and, most important, mental visualizations of the letters of the Hebrew alphabet in various combinations. Some members of this school believed that the elevated spiritual state achieved by these techniques could even result in the temporary merging of one's soul with God, an experience referred to by academics as "mystical union" and often regarded as the quintessence of mysticism.

A more popular brand of Kabbalah is somewhat more intellectual in character—so intellectual, in fact, that some have questioned whether it really qualifies as mysticism. This form of Kabbalah, known in academic circles as "theosophic" Kabbalah, produced a complete and elaborate theological system focused on the ten *sefirot*, attributes of God that describe all of his characteristics and activities. While God's essence is entirely unknowable, the *sefirot* allow us to comprehend what we can know about God within the bounds of our limited human understanding. Over time, the *sefirot* were given standard names, the first four being Crown, Wisdom, Understanding, and Lovingkindness. The Kabbalists also conceived of the *sefirot* as having a standard arrangement and order, often depicted in the form of a diagram. The Kabbalists spent a great deal of energy explaining the qualities and characteristics of the *sefirot*. Each was considered a multifaceted world in its own right, reflecting some aspect of God's infinite being and activities.

What makes this form of Kabbalah such a powerful theological system is that by understanding the *sefirot*, not only does one penetrate the inner life of God, one also unlocks the secrets of the universe. Kabbalists believed that the *sefirot* were more than divine attributes; they were also metaphysical building blocks for the world below. The world was created and continues to be sustained through the *sefirot*. Kabbalists therefore expended great effort in describing how the *sefirot* and their interaction with each other could explain everything in the world. Thus, all natural phenomena were linked with the *sefirot*. For instance, each of the four basic elements in medieval science—fire, air, earth, and water—corresponded to, and had their source in, one of the *sefirot*. Human psychology could be explained in a similar fashion, since the human soul was also believed to be constructed on the paradigm of the *sefirot*. Our qualities of love, anger, and mercy were viewed as manifestations of one or another of the *sefirot*. Most important from a Jewish perspective is that the Kabbalists explained the divine commandments in light of the *sefirot*. Each of the commandments was seen as interacting in its own special way with the world of the *sefirot*. The goal was to bring harmony to the *sefirot* and thereby aid in the process of redeeming the world.

The Kabbalists generally conceived of this theological system as nothing less than a body of wisdom directly revealed by God to Moses on Mount Sinai, along with the Torah. In the medieval period, theosophic Kabbalah found its most sophisticated expression in the *Zohar*, a text that appeared in thirteenth-century Spain, and in the school of R. Isaac Luria in sixteenth-century Palestine. Eastern European Hasidism was also an outgrowth of Kabbalah. Nowadays Kabbalah has become very popular among Jewish young people in search of alternative and spiritual forms of Judaism. This interest in Kabbalah is connected with the broad phenomenon of New Age religion. Kabbalah has, therefore, found an audience among non-Jews as well, including pop stars and Hollywood actors, the most famous of whom is Madonna.

These developments would have seemed strange to medieval Kabbalists. Kabbalah was treated by its medieval interpreters as an esoteric wisdom, and attempts were made to restrict access to it even among Jews because of the fear that it could potentially be dangerous if studied by the uninitiated. This fear was heightened by the messianic movement of Shabbetai Tsevi in the seventeenth century, which drew much of its inspiration from Kabbalah.

Our discussion of Kabbalah will focus primarily on the theosophic school. We will also be mostly concerned with Kabbalistic attitudes toward non-Jews in general, since Kabbalah has much more to say about this issue than about peace and violence. Nonetheless, we will see that in some respects Kabbalistic ideas have important ramifications for the latter issues as well.

Kabbalah Promotes Violence

The negative attitude toward non-Jews in Kabbalah has already been alluded to. If Maimonides took a nonessentialist position regarding the distinction between Jews and non-Jews, the position of the Kabbalists was an essentialist one. According to most Kabbalists, the non-Jewish soul was inferior to the Jewish soul.[3] Elliot Wolfson has explored this issue in great depth. The first reading in this chapter will therefore argue that Kabbalah is intolerant toward non-Jews and that its doctrines, therefore, indirectly promote violence against them.

The view of most medieval Kabbalists is that Jewish souls originate in the realm of the *sefirot*, while non-Jewish souls come from the realm of impurity and evil known as the *sitra ahra*, or "the other side," a realm outside the *sefirot*

---

3 Kellner, chapter 1. Elliot Wolfson has provided a thorough and pioneering discussion of Kabbalistic attitudes toward non-Jews that demonstrates the depth of the Kabbalists' antipathy toward them. See Wolfson, *Venturing Beyond*, especially chapters 1 and 2. My discussion in this chapter is heavily indebted to Wolfson's analysis.

though tenuously connected with it. Non-Jews are therefore not technically human, and when the creation story in the Bible speaks of human beings having been created in the image of God, it is not referring to them.[4] Non-Jews are therefore inferior not just because of their moral or theological differences with Jews, but because of who they are. Moreover, this negative view of non-Jews seems to have been upheld not only by Kabbalists in the theosophic tradition, but by those in the ecstatic stream as well.[5]

In light of these observations, it is no surprise that Kabbalah tended to have hostile views of Christianity and Islam. Antipathy toward Christianity seems to have been especially pronounced.[6] As Wolfson has shown, only in heretical Sabbateanism does Kabbalah move toward a more inclusive attitude regarding these other religions.[7]

The Kabbalists did not generally preach violence against non-Jews. They, like most Jews in the medieval period, adopted the rabbinic position that the exile was punishment for Jewish sin and that Jews had to bear their subjugation with patience until it was time for messianic redemption. Yet, the Kabbalists also upheld the rabbinic view that vengeance would eventually be taken against the non-Jewish nations at the end of days, and here we see a violent dimension emerge in Kabbalistic thought. For instance, in Lurianic Kabbalah, the view was that Jews lived among non-Jews in exile in order to perform pious deeds that would redeem the few "sparks" of divinity that could be found among the non-Jewish nations. Eventually, the non-Jewish world would be denuded of these traces of divinity nourishing its existence, at which point it would therefore collapse and be destroyed.[8]

4 Moshe Halamish, "The Kabbalists' Attitude to the Nations of the World" (in Hebrew) *Jerusalem Studies in Jewish Thought* 14 (1998): 289–92; Wolfson, *Venturing Beyond*, chapter 1. Wolfson further argues that humanness in Kabbalah encompasses only the Jewish circumcised male. Therefore, the discrimination against non-Jews is coupled with a discrimination against women.

5 Wolfson, *Venturing Beyond*, 58–72.

6 Isaiah Tishby, *The Wisdom of the Zohar*, trans. David Goldstein (Oxford: Oxford University Press, 1989), 1:68–71; Halamish, "The Kabbalists' Attitude," 307–10; Wolfson, *Venturing Beyond*, 90–107, chapter 2. Antagonism toward Christianity is also discussed in Yehuda Liebes, *Studies in the Zohar*, trans. Arnold Schwartz, Stephanie Nakache, and Penina Peli (Albany: State University of New York Press, 1993), 149–50, 154–61. For a discussion of attitudes toward Islam in Kabbalah, see also Ronald C. Keiner, "The Image of Islam in the *Zohar*," *Jerusalem Studies in Jewish Thought* 8 (1989): 43–65 (English section).

7 Wolfson, *Venturing Beyond*, 176–85.

8 Isaiah Tishby, *The Doctrine of Evil and the "Kelippah" in Lurianic Kabbalism* (in Hebrew) (Jerusalem: Magnes Press, 1942), 138. This theory is dependent on an elaborate mythology according to which sparks of divinity fell into the world at the time of creation, and those sparks have to be redeemed in order for the messiah to come. Most of the sparks can be redeemed by Jews if they perform God's commandments. However, a small number of sparks are located in the non-Jewish world, and it is those sparks that allow the latter to exist. The teachings of Lurianic Kabbalah are summarized and discussed in Lawrence Fine, *Physician of the Soul, Healer of the Cosmos: Isaac Luria and His Kabbalistic Fellowship* (Stanford, Calif.: Stanford University Press, 2003), chapter 4.

A final criticism of Kabbalah concerns its methodology. Kabbalah presents its truths as having come from revelation. It claims that its wisdom is a secret understanding of Torah given by God to Moses on Mount Sinai and passed on among elite circles from generation to generation. Conversely, Kabbalah tends to downplay the value of philosophy because philosophy claims that its truths come from the rational human mind, which is by its nature limited in what it can comprehend. The problem here is that unlike philosophy, Kabbalah does not allow for its own critique, at least not on any conscious level. If its truths are revealed from God, no rational argument can subvert them. Thus, according to its methodological principles, Kabbalah cannot allow its views of non-Jews to be revised regardless of how morally problematic they are.

Kabbalah Promotes Peace

Our second reading will attempt to demonstrate that these judgments of Kabbalah are too harsh. With respect to Kabbalistic perspectives on non-Jews, one has to take historical context into account, as we have done in previous chapters. Kabbalah developed in medieval Europe during the centuries in which the Crusades exacted a horrific toll from Jewish communities in Western and Central Europe. And even in places in which Jews were living in relative security, this period was one in which European Jews were being increasingly marginalized in political, economic, and social life.[9] Wolfson argues that Kabbalistic portrayals of non-Jews may have been a response to Christian depictions of Jews in the twelfth and thirteenth centuries that described them as beasts and the embodiment of the Antichrist. In demonizing non-Jews, then, the Kabbalists were merely hurling back at the Christians insults similar to those directed at them. Wolfson points out that the influence of historical context on Kabbalistic views of non-Jews is evident from the fact that in this period we find the demonization of Christians in Jewish sources unconnected to Kabbalah. This observation indicates that the images of non-Jews in Kabbalah were not solely due to developments internal to Kabbalah but also larger environmental pressures.[10]

We must also point out that not all Kabbalistic sources denigrate non-Jews. In an article devoted to the treatment of non-Jews in Kabbalah, Moshe Halamish cites sources from the *Zohar* and Moses Cordovero that speak positively about righteous gentiles and envision them achieving divine rewards.[11] Halamish also

---

9 Halamish, "The Kabbalists' Attitude," 294; Wolfson, *Venturing Beyond*, 185.
10 Wolfson, *Venturing Beyond*, 45–46.
11 Halamish, "The Kabbalists' Attitude," 298.

cites a number of medieval ethical treatises written by Kabbalists that mandate the kind treatment of non-Jews.[12] What Halamish's observation may indicate is that the negative images of non-Jews in Kabbalah did not determine how Kabbalists acted in the real world. Halamish also points out that in many Kabbalistic sources, Jews are not considered inherently better than non-Jews they must earn their superior status through effort by observing the Torah's commandments.[13] In these sources, the Kabbalists therefore take a position akin to the nonessentialist viewpoint of Maimonides regarding the distinction between Jews and non-Jews.

With respect to the issue of violence, one should not be too disturbed by Kabbalistic speculations about the destruction of the non-Jewish world at the end of days. Such speculations were harmless because they were confined to the realm of mythology. The only weapons that Kabbalists felt they should use against their adversaries was the divine commandments, which were designed to bring harmony to the Godhead and redemption to the world. Certainly, Israel's enemies would be destroyed as part of this process, but Jews did not need to engage in physical combat against them for this to happen; the process was a metaphysical one. Avi Sagi makes similar observations regarding the Kabbalistic approach to Amalek. Sagi points out that in Kabbalah Amalek represents metaphysical evil, and Israel's war against Amalek is therefore metaphysical as well. The observance of the divine commandments brings redemption, and as part of this process the enemy is vanquished. Thus, according to Sagi, an attempt is made here to "disengage from the concrete, historical dimensions of the event, as well as from the literal perception of Amalek's punishment in the biblical text."[14]

We can also argue that a proper assessment of Kabbalah must also take into account its modern, popular expressions. The popularization of Kabbalah began in the 1970s when traditional Kabbalistic yeshivahs and Hasidic movements became more active, and new institutes, synagogues, and study groups were established for the study of Kabbalah and Hasidism. In the last three decades, the study and practice of Kabbalah has attracted thousands of people, many of them Jews who are neither attached to the mainstream Jewish community nor learned in traditional Jewish texts. Accompanying this trend has been the publication of hundreds of books on Kabbalah and the establishment of scores of Kabbalah-related Web pages. Most of this activity has occurred in the United States and Israel.[15]

---

12 Halamish, "The Kabbalists' Attitude," 304–5.

13 Halamish, "The Kabbalists' Attitude," 294, 297–98.

14 Sagi, "The Punishment of Amalek," 330–32. Allegorization of the battle against Amalek is also found among non-Kabbalists, including medieval Jewish philosophers. See Horowitz, *Reckless Rites*, 134–35.

15 Boaz Huss, "The New Age of Kabbalah: Contemporary Kabbalah, the New Age and Postmodern Spirituality," *Journal of Modern Jewish Studies* 6, no. 2 (2007): 109.

What is important for our concerns is that popular Kabbalah is often highly universalistic in its orientation. Many groups and institutions that study Kabbalah see it as wisdom relevant for all human beings, Jews and non-Jews alike. Some cater directly to non-Jews.[16] Furthermore, the doctrines and practices of these groups are eclectic, combining Kabbalistic beliefs and rituals with those of other religious traditions and coopting ideas from popular culture and modern science.[17] This syncretism is reflective of postmodernism, which is in turn a manifestation of the effects of globalization. The cultures of our world have becomes increasingly integrated in recent years due to a number of factors, including telecommunications, travel, and economic interdependence, and this integration has led Western culture to become open to multiple truths and thought systems, a hallmark of postmodernism. The mixture of Kabbalah with ideas and practices from other religions, popular culture, and science is thus very much a product of this new mindset.[18] In many respects, popular Kabbalah also has characteristics of New Age spirituality and religion—sometimes consciously, sometimes unconsciously. This element in popular Kabbalah has also brought its Jewish students into dialogue with non-Jews.[19]

In truth, the attempt to interpret Kabbalah as a universal wisdom has a long history. A fascinating chapter in the history of Kabbalah is the development of a Christian school of Kabbalistic learning that began in the fifteenth century when prominent Christian mystics in Renaissance Italy were drawn to this dimension of Judaism. These thinkers believed that Kabbalah reflected an original divine revelation to mankind that had been lost and had to be restored. They also held that if read properly, Kabbalah pointed to Christian truths. Christian interest in Kabbalah would eventually spread to other countries in Europe and would last until the beginning of the nineteenth century. One can make sense of this phenomenon by noting that this was not the first time Christians had coopted Jewish texts for their own purposes. After all, Christianity was based on the Hebrew Bible. Nonetheless, Christian Kabbalah was an unusual and striking instance of Jewish-Christian syncretism.[20]

The notion that Kabbalah is a universal wisdom has also been cultivated by Jewish intellectuals of the twentieth century. Martin Buber spent fifty years

---

16 Ibid.

17 Jonathan Garb, *The Chosen Will Become Herds: Studies in Twentieth Century Kabbalah* (in Hebrew) (Jerusalem: Carmel, 2005), 148–49; Boaz Huss, "All You Need is LAV: Madonna and Postmodern Kabbalah," *Jewish Quarterly Review* 95 (2005): 620.

18 Huss, "The New Age of Kabbalah," 118.

19 Huss, "The New Age of Kabbalah," 111–16.

20 Joseph Dan, ed., *The Christian Kabbalah: Jewish Mystical Books and Their Christian Interpreters: A Symposium* (Cambridge, Mass.: Harvard College Library, 1997); Philip Beitchman, *Alchemy of the Word: Cabala of the Renaissance* (Albany: State University of New York Press, 1998).

interpreting Hasidism as a religious movement with a great deal to teach all human beings, not just Jews. Louis Jacobs took a similar approach with both Kabbalah and Hasidism.[21] Since the 1990s, several books by Arthur Green have reflected the same sensibility.[22]

Thus, the universalistic orientation of popular Kabbalah in our own day and age reflects a long-standing trend in Kabbalistic speculation. What this trend indicates is that Kabbalah need not necessarily be a source of division between Jews and non-Jews but can serve as a source of inspiration for uniting them.

And yet, one has to wonder how students of popular Kabbalah today deal with the highly negative portrayals of non-Jews in the classical expressions of this school. Despite attempts both past and present to make Kabbalah a universal wisdom, this problem cannot simply be ignored. This matter is discussed by Jody Myers in a recent study on the Kabbalah Centre, the best-known of the modern institutions devoted to teaching Kabbalah and one with branches in many countries.[23] According to Myers, the leaders of the Kabbalah Centre maintain that Kabbalah is a universal revelation that was originally given to all humanity before the time of Abraham. However, human beings were reluctant to follow Kabbalah because of their attachment to material desires, and Kabbalah therefore went underground and was preserved only in elite circles. Still, Kabbalah had an influence on the formation of all the major religions, and thus these religions have elements of Kabbalah in them. The major religions, however, tended to distort the teachings of Kabbalah. Judaism is itself a corrupted version of Kabbalah, but it presents the most accurate rendering of this body of wisdom.[24] What is most important for our purpose is that, according to this account, Kabbalah in its original and pure form was not exclusivist and therefore did not denigrate non-Jews.[25] In fact, the notion of distinctions between Jews and non-Jews is inimical to the whole agenda of Kabbalah because it causes disunity in the world and interferes with the ability of human beings to connect to the divine, which is the ultimate goal of Kabbalah. The negative portrayals of non-Jews in Kabbalah, therefore, are not part of its original, authentic teaching.[26]

21 Martin Buber, *Hasidism* (New York: Philosophical Library, 1948), 159–83; Louis Jacobs, "The Relationship between Religion and Ethics in Jewish Thought," in *Contemporary Jewish Ethics*, ed. Menachem Kellner (New York: HPC Press, 1978), 55–56; Wolfson, *Venturing Beyond*, 5 n. 15.

22 Arthur Green, *Seek My Face, Speak My Name: A Contemporary Jewish Theology* (Northvale, N.J.: Jason Aronson, 1992); idem, *Ehyeh: A Kabbalah for Tomorrow* (Woodstock, Vt.: Jewish Lights, 2003).

23 Jody Myers, *Kabbalah and the Spiritual Quest: The Kabbalah Centre in America* (Westport, Conn.: Praeger, 2007), 119–127.

24 Myers, *Kabbalah and the Spiritual Quest*, 88–91.

25 Myers, *Kabbalah and the Spiritual Quest*, 121.

26 Myers, *Kabbalah and the Spiritual Quest*, 120.

Myers also cites examples of how the Kabbalah Centre comes to terms with the fact that many of its students are non-Jews. For instance, one of the leading figures in the Kabbalah Centre argues that all non-Jews who study Kabbalah fall under the rubric of "Israel," and therefore disparaging statements about non-Jews in Judaism are not directed at these people.[27] According to other representatives of the Kabbalah Centre, non-Jews who come to study Kabbalah may, in fact, have Jewish souls. Due to the many exiles, persecutions, and migrations that Jews have experienced throughout history, no one really knows nowadays who has a Jewish soul.[28]

Conclusions

These arguments in defense of Kabbalah, however, do not by any means end the discussion. On the issue of violence against non-Jews, it is certainly correct that the Kabbalists envisioned their war against the non-Jewish nations as taking place on a metaphysical plane. Still, we can argue that anger against non-Jews is palpable in Kabbalistic teaching, and we can easily imagine how this way of thinking could encourage violence. All that is needed is the belief that the war against the forces of evil on the metaphysical plane has to be helped along by war in the physical world. Kabbalah, after all, believed that the physical realm was nurtured by and functioned in parallel with the realm of the divine. The two worlds, therefore, were not detached from each other. The first individual to have made this connection was Jacob Frank, an eighteenth-century figure who was perhaps the most radical representative of heretical Kabbalah that grew out of the Sabbatean movement. Frank believed that young Jews should learn military skills in order to assemble an army and capture the Holy Land.[29] As we will see in a later chapter, a similar view was adopted by some modern religious Zionists, with dire consequences for the relationship between Israelis and Palestinians.

Regarding contemporary, popular Kabbalah, we can question whether this form of Kabbalah is really Kabbalah at all, a query that in turn casts doubt on whether this form of Kabbalah really belongs in our present discussion. Jonathan Garb argues that popular Kabbalah fundamentally distorts authentic Kabbalistic teaching because it is often focused on helping its adherents achieve spiritual experience, power, or even financial gain, and it claims to provide

---

27 Myers, *Kabbalah and the Spiritual Quest,* 119.
28 Myers, *Kabbalah and the Spiritual Quest,* 125.
29 Luz, *Wrestling with an Angel,* 27–28.

shortcuts to these goals. In classical Kabbalah, there is no notion that Kabbalistic wisdom and practice should be used to satisfy material desires. Even spiritual experience was not seen by Kabbalists as an end in itself. When Kabbalists sought mystical encounters with the divine, they saw such experiences as a means to other goals, such as prophecy or serving God's needs. Furthermore, the process of achieving mystical enlightenment was no shortcut in any sense. It was an arduous and difficult path that required one to cultivate perfect conduct and observe all the divine commandments.[30]

One can also argue that popular Kabbalah cannot insist that Kabbalah has a positive view of non-Jews without distorting its teachings. Negative portrayals of non-Jews are too much a part of the fabric of classical Kabbalah to be swept aside.[31] Furthermore, it is not clear whether popular Kabbalah has entirely shaken those portrayals. Myers points out that few people are aware of the fact that the directors and teachers of the Kabbalah Centre still believe that there is an essential distinction between Jewish and non-Jewish souls, and that Jews have a greater capacity for connecting with God than non-Jews.[32] Their essentialist position is also implied by the claim that non-Jews who study Kabbalah can do so because they may have Jewish souls. This notion assumes that Jews and non-Jews are inherently different, and that non-Jews who wish to study Kabbalah are allowed to because they may really be Jews. Finally, the notion that Judaism is the least corrupt version of Kabbalah and is therefore the closest to true divine wisdom is an example of Jewish chauvinism. While this claim does not denigrate non-Jews, it certainly makes their religions inferior to Judaism.

With regard to the sources of ambiguity that are responsible for the differences between our two readings, our discussion has touched on issues similar to those encountered in previous chapters. For instance, we have seen once again that there is ambiguity regarding the role of historical context in examining Jewish sources. It is not clear whether we should excuse Kabbalah for its negative depictions of non-Jews because of persecution that Jews experienced when Kabbalistic doctrines were being formulated, or whether these portrayals simply have to be condemned and discarded.

---

30 Jonathan Garb, "The Power and the Glory: A Critique of 'New Age' Kabbalah," trans. Stephen Hazzan Arnoff, Zeek (April 2006), http://www.zeek.net/print/604garb. I raise similar concerns about the authenticity of popular Kabbalah in my article "The Revival of Jewish Mysticism and Its Implications for the Future of Jewish Faith," in Creating the Jewish Future, ed. Michael Brown and Bernard Lightman (Walnut Creek, Calif.: Altamira Press, 1998), 39–40.

31 Wolfson, Venturing Beyond, 5 n. 15.

32 Myers, Kabbalah and the Spiritual Quest, 124.

However, our discussion has yielded a new source of ambiguity in Jewish texts that we have not yet encountered thus far in our study. In our second reading, we argued that modern popular Kabbalah provides evidence that Kabbalah is capable of having universalistic leanings. Yet, as we have just noted, some scholars believe that popular Kabbalah so distorts the teachings of classical Kabbalah that it is not really authentic Kabbalah at all, but rather a phenomenon mostly shaped by the forces of globalization and postmodernism. This debate raises the difficult question of how we judge an interpretation of Judaism, or a school within it, as legitimate. An interpretation may be regarded by some observers as an authentic reading of earlier texts, while the same interpretation may be regarded by other observers as a complete distortion of earlier texts that must therefore be discarded, and one is hard-pressed to come up with clear rules that will determine in any given instance which approach is correct. The phenomenon of popular Kabbalah is an excellent case in point. We may also note that this type of problem is especially evident in modern Judaism owing to the remarkable diversity of interpretations of Judaism that have arisen since the Enlightenment. We will encounter this issue once again in our discussion of modern Zionism, which is the subject of our next chapter.

6

Modern Zionism

In this chapter, we move to the modern period. Ideally, our discussion would deal with the full range of expressions of modern Judaism in different phases and locations. It would focus, in particular, on the major denominations as they developed in the nineteenth and twentieth centuries in Europe and later on in the United States, and it would also explore modern Zionism. However, Zionism is such a focal point of recent discussion about the issues of peace and violence in Judaism that it dwarfs all other modern manifestations of Judaism. This chapter will therefore focus exclusively on Zionism.

First, some background is in order. There is much disagreement among scholars about when the modern period actually began for Jews in Europe, but there is consensus that momentous changes occurred in the Jewish community at the end of the eighteenth century and the beginning of the nineteenth, changes that were key in the progress of the Jews toward modernization.[1] Most significant was the French Revolution, which resulted in Jews being offered citizenship in a European country for the first time and granted the basic rights and protections accompanying that status. Over the next several decades, other European countries followed suit, with similar changes for their

1 General treatments of the changes that the European Jewish community underwent in the process of modernization can be found in Michael A. Meyer, *The Origins of the Modern Jew: Jewish Identity and European Culture in Germany, 1749–1824* (Detroit: Wayne State University Press, 1967); Jacob Katz, *Out of the Ghetto: The Social Background of Jewish Emancipation, 1770–1870* (Cambridge, Mass.: Harvard University Press, 1973).

respective Jewish communities, and within a century, after a long and arduous process, Jews had become citizens in virtually every country in Europe.

The new situation pleased many Jews, but it also caused great upheaval. For centuries, Jewish life was predicated on the fact that Jews lived separately from non-Jews and that Jewish communities functioned in a semiautonomous fashion. Jews now had to deal with non-Jews as equal partners in a modern secular state. The new reality required Jews to conduct a thorough reevaluation of Jewish religion, culture, and society. The major question that Jews had to grapple with was how they could become part of the non-Jewish world while retaining their identity as Jews. Jews gave a variety of responses to this question. Some chose to leave Judaism entirely. Others attempted to reshape Judaism in a way that allowed for some accommodation to the new situation. Eventually three denominations arose, each with a different set of perspectives on this issue: Orthodox, Conservative, and Reform.

However, at the end of the nineteenth century, some Jews began to formulate an entirely different kind of response to the challenges posed by modernity. These Jews rejected the notion that they could accommodate themselves to European society, and they believed that Jews should return to the land of Israel, then called Palestine, to reestablish a Jewish state. The movement that arose in support of this new approach was Zionism.[2]

While the Zionists were certainly responding to the same problem of defining modern Jewish identity that had preoccupied Jews for the better part of a century, two major factors explain why they addressed the problem in the way that they did. The first was the growth of nationalism throughout Europe in the nineteenth century. It became fashionable in Europe to believe that human beings could flourish only when living among others in their own ethnic group, residing in their homeland, and participating in their own culture. Jews began to feel the same way about themselves and therefore began to think of reestablishing a Jewish state.

Even more important, the last two decades of the nineteenth century witnessed the sudden rise of virulent anti-Semitism throughout Europe. Anti-Semitism in Western Europe was epitomized by the Dreyfuss affair. In 1894, Alfred Dreyfuss, the only Jew on the General Staff of the French army, was convicted of treason. The evidence leading to Dreyfuss's conviction turned

    2 General treatments of Zionism include Walter Laqueur, A History of Zionism (New York: Schocken Books, 2003); Howard M. Sachar, A History of Israel: From the Rise of Zionism to Our Time, 3rd ed. (New York: Knopf, 2007). General histories of Zionist thought include Shlomo Avineri, The Making of Modern Zionism: The Intellectual Origins of the Jewish State (New York: Basic Books, 1981); Gideon Shimoni, The Zionist Ideology (Hanover, N.H.: University Press of New England, 1995); Arthur Hertzberg, The Zionist Idea: A Historical Analysis and Reader (Philadelphia: Jewish Publication Society of America, 1997).

out to be forged; yet, before he was fully exonerated in 1906, French anti-Semitism had emerged in full force. Dreyfuss certainly had his defenders among the French public. Yet, a significant faction within French society not only believed the charges against Dreyfuss, but was quite vocal about its belief that Dreyfuss was acting on behalf of a vast Jewish conspiracy bent on undermining France and its military. The hatred of Jews ignited by this group persisted in right-wing political circles in France even after Dreyfuss was proven innocent.

But the most extreme manifestation of the new anti-Semitism was a series of pogroms that jolted the Jewish community in Russia in 1881. In that year, Jewish communities in scores of cities and towns in southern Russia were attacked by violent mobs. Another major pogrom occurred in Kishinev in 1903 that was even more violent. In 1905, pogroms broke out yet again, this time in six hundred Russian cities. Not only did the Russian government not come to the assistance of the Jews, it was complicit in the violence. These events were greeted with shock by Jews throughout Europe. During the course of the nineteenth century, Jews had made significant gains in European society economically, politically, and socially as they adjusted to being citizens of European countries, and many Jews became convinced that centuries of persecution were finally behind them. The rise of modern anti-Semitism was proof that such hopes were premature. Taken together, the influence of European nationalism and the rise of anti-Semitism led some Jews to believe that there was no future for them in Europe and that they therefore had to reestablish an independent Jewish state where Jews could determine their own destiny and not be victims of non-Jewish violence.

The founder of the Zionist movement was Theodor Herzl, a Viennese journalist and playwright, whose thinking on Zionism was inspired in large part by the Dreyfuss affair. In 1897, Herzl convened the first Zionist Congress in Basel, which brought together the most prominent Zionists from all over Europe for the purpose of plotting strategies to turn the Zionist vision into a reality. By this point, Zionists had already begun emigrating to Palestine, which was controlled by the Turkish Ottoman Empire, to buy up tracts of land and settle them. As the Jewish population in Palestine gradually increased over the next decades, Zionist leaders intensified their diplomatic efforts to draw attention to their cause and to convince the international community to make Palestine a Jewish homeland. When the British took control of Palestine after the First World War, Zionist diplomacy began to focus on the new overlords. A breakthrough had already occurred in 1917 with the Balfour Declaration, which indicated a willingness on the part of the British to help establish a Jewish national home. The British, however, turned out to be inconsistent allies to the Zionists and later favored restrictions on Jewish immigration to Palestine once Palestinian nationalism began to assert itself and violence between Jews and Arabs became a serious problem. Eventually, the British decided to wash their hands of the troubled situation. In 1947 they submitted to the United Nations a partition plan for dividing Palestine into two states—one Jewish, and one Arab. The United Nations voted in favor of the resolution, giving Jews sovereignty in the land of Israel for the first time in 1,800 years. The establishment of the state of Israel could not have come at a more opportune time. Large numbers of Jewish refugees who had survived the Holocaust began flooding into the Jewish state. The celebrations were short-lived, however; war broke out between Israel and the surrounding Arab countries in 1948. Although Israel emerged victorious and now controlled more land than the partition agreement had initially grant- ed them, the Jews took heavy losses, and hundreds of thousands of Palestinians were displaced, creating a massive refugee problem.[3]

In the following decades, Israel was plagued by many more wars with the surrounding Arab countries. Israel's victory in the Six-Day War in 1967 greatly increased its size, but now, in the West Bank and Gaza, it ruled over millions of Palestinians hostile to Israel. The original Palestinian refugee problem contin- ued to fester, eventually spawning the creation of Palestinian terrorist organiza- tions that carried out attacks on Israeli civilians and created a persistent climate of fear in Israel. In recent decades, a number of attempts have been made to broker peace between Israel, on the one hand, and the Palestinians and sur- rounding Arab countries, on the other hand. There have been some successes, such as Israel's peace treaty with Egypt in 1979. However, no comprehensive settlement has yet been found that would allow Israelis to live within secure borders and to be at peace with all its Arab neighbors while giving a home to the Palestinian refugees, who now number in the millions.

The central concern of this chapter will be to examine the degree to which Judaism is responsible for the violent expressions of Zionism. Zionism was shaped by a diverse array of influences other than Judaism, such as European nationalism, which we have already mentioned. Therefore, we must explore whether Judaism was specifically responsible for fostering violent tendencies in Zionism.

There is, however, an even more basic question that must be asked here, and that is the extent to which Zionism was violent in the first place. There is a

---

3 In this chapter, the term "Palestinian" will be used for Arabs who either live in the region that before 1947 was designated as Palestine, or live elsewhere but trace their origins to that region. There is much debate over when this term becomes appropriate, because its usage depends on when Palestinians developed a national consciousness, and scholars are deeply divided on when this occurred. My choice of definition is not meant to settle the debate but merely to simplify the discussion.

great deal of dispute regarding this question. At one extreme are those who argue that at its core Zionism has been a movement that is violent, and aggressively so. From its outset, it was bent on displacing the Palestinians and taking over their land, and it was hostile to Arabs in general. Furthermore, these features of Zionism continued to guide the state of Israel after its founding. This explains why the Palestinian refugee problem has never been solved and why attempts to bring peace between Israel and the Arab world as a whole have failed. At the other extreme are those who claim that Zionism has been violent but only for defensive purposes. Certainly, there were instances in which the early Zionists, and later on the Israelis, committed acts of unprovoked violence against Palestinians and Arabs, but these were exceptional cases. Most of the violence perpetrated by Zionists and Israelis has been in response to the Palestinians and neighboring Arab countries, which have steadfastly rejected a Jewish sovereign presence in the Middle East and have waged a relentless war against it. There are also innumerable shades of opinion between these two extremes. In short, everyone is in agreement that Zionism has bred Jewish violence, but there is deep disagreement over the moral status of that violence.

We cannot analyze this question in any great detail, for it is exceedingly complex and could overwhelm our discussion here. Furthermore, an analysis of this matter is really a job for historians and is therefore beyond the scope of this study, which is focused on religion. However, we will have to engage this question to some extent in the course of our deliberations.

It should be noted that in this chapter, the two readings of violence in Zionism will not be preceded by general analyses of Zionist attitudes toward non-Jews, which is what one may have expected from the pattern of discussion in previous chapters. The change here is due to the fact that the two issues are inextricably linked. Most Zionist thinkers have reflected on the relationship between Jews and non-Jews only through the lens of Zionism. The two subjects must therefore be treated together.

Judaism and Zionism: A Critique

Our first reading will take the position that Zionism has spawned aggressive violence by Jews and that such violence is the logical outcome of ideas and imperatives in Judaism that have emerged in previous chapters. This reading will also claim that Judaism has inspired violence not just in religious Zionism, but in secular Zionism as well. Secular Zionism would have been inconceivable without Judaism, and Zionism's violent tendencies can be largely explained by its absorption of Jewish values.

We will begin with religious Zionism, since it is here that the violent ten-dencies of Zionism seem to find their most potent and dangerous expression, particularly in the wake of the Six-Day War in 1967. In the decades following that war, religious Zionists have been an enormous obstacle to peace between Israel and the Arab world by establishing settlements on territories captured by Israel and by taking a highly aggressive approach to Palestinians living in those territories and to the Arab world in general. Given the pivotal role that the Arab-Israeli conflict plays in the whole relationship between the Western world and the Muslim world, religious Zionism is a threat not just to the well-being of those directly involved in the conflict, but to world peace.[4]

One can gain a proper understanding of religious Zionism by referring to a well-known distinction made by Gershom Scholem between two major types of messianism in Judaism. The type of messianism most popular throughout the centuries has been apocalyptic messianism. According to this version, when the final redemption arrives, the world as we know it will come to a catastrophic end, and the messianic era that will follow will be miraculous and utopian and will bear little resemblance to the present world. Another, less popular version is restorative messianism. In this form of messianism, the messianic era will not bring an end to the present world, but will be characterized primarily by the restoration of Jew-ish sovereignty in the land of Israel and the rebuilding of the Temple in Jerusa-lem. The gentile nations will recognize the God of Israel, and there will be world peace. The two types of messianism do not usually appear in pure form; often one form contains elements of the other. Still, the distinction Scholem draws is help-ful in classifying approaches to Jewish messianism throughout the centuries.[5]

---

4 The emphasis in this discussion of religious Zionism will be on theology and ideology, not Halakhah, because the amount of halakhic material relevant to our analysis is much too large to be covered adequately in the present discussion. Religious Zionist thinkers in Israel and the United States have produced a large body of work debating issues involving war and violence as they pertain to the state of Israel. A focus on theology and ideology will allow us to appreciate the overall approach of religious Zionists to war and violence, and that will be sufficient for our purposes. For examples of halakhic discussions of war by Israeli authors, see, for instance, A. Bloom, ed., *Arakhim be-Mivhan ha-Milhamah* (Alon Shevut, Israel: n.d.), which focuses on the 1982 Lebanon War. See also the many issues of the Israeli journal *Tehumin*, which for years has functioned as a mouthpiece for religious Zionism and contains many articles on war and related issues. Among American thinkers, J. David Bleich has been perhaps the most prolific author in dealing with halakhic issues regarding Israel. See his many essays on this topic in J. David Bleich, *Contemporary Halakhic Problems* (New York: Ktav, 1977–89), 3 vols. Some thinkers in the Conservative movement have also written on war, though their discussions have not been as focused on Israel as Bleich's. See, for instance Dorff, *To Do the Right and the Good*, chapter 7; Artson, *Love Peace and Pursue Peace*. For a wide range of Jewish treatments of war with some references to Israel, see the essays in Daniel Landes, ed., *Jewish Reflections on Weapons of Mass Destruction*, (Northvale, N.J.: Jason Aronson, 1991); see also Kimelman, "The Ethics of National Power" idem, "Judaism, War, and Weapons of Mass Destruction."

5 Gershom Scholem, *The Messianic Idea in Judaism* (New York: Schocken Books, 1971) chapter 1. See also Lawrence Schiffman's discussion of rabbinic messianism, which is based on Scholem's distinction, in "Messia-nism and Apocalypticism in Rabbinic Texts," 1035–73.

Another distinction scholars of Jewish messianism often make that is similar to Scholem's is between passive and active messianism. In passive messianism, redemption comes primarily through divine initiative, and the influence of human beings on the messianic process is limited. In this approach, views range from the belief that the events of the redemptive process proceed according to a strictly predetermined divine plan to the belief that repentance can bring the messiah; however, even according to the latter viewpoint, messianic redemption is seen as resulting primarily from God's willful intervention in history. The talmudic source about the three oaths discussed in chapter 3, on rabbinic Judaism, is a classic expression of this approach, since it emphasizes the need for Jewish passivity and patience in waiting for the messianic process to unfold.[6] Passive messianism tends to be affiliated with apocalyptic messianism, since the latter sees the messianic period as coming about suddenly and catastrophically through divine initiative. In active messianism, the messianic era is also brought about by God's involvement in history, but here human beings are seen as playing a critical role. They must take action when they perceive that the messianic process has started in order that the process may come to fruition. The model here is the restoration of the Judean kingdom after the Babylonian exile in the sixth century BCE, which was perceived as being guided by God's hand but could not have succeeded without the determination of the Judeans to return to the land of Israel and rebuild their homeland. This approach tends to be associated with restorative messianism because the changes that take place in that form of messianism lie primarily in the political realm and must therefore be brought about by human initiative.[7]

The distinction between passive and active messianism is particularly helpful in allowing us to understand the virulent strain of religious Zionism that has come to the fore in recent decades. While religious Zionism has assumed many expressions since the beginning of the Zionist movement in late nineteenth century, the one that is of greatest interest to us here grew out of a school of thought spawned by Rabbi Abraham Isaac Kook (1865–1935), the first Ashkenazi chief rabbi of Palestine. Kook was a highly creative and charismatic religious figure, and at the center of his thinking was a form of messianism that was clearly of the activist type.

Kook's worldview was rooted in a mystical metaphysics in which all elements of creation, natural and human, were seen as gradually and inexorably

---

6 See p. 86, this volume.

7 Urbach, *The Sages*, 668–84; Jody Myers, "The Messianic Idea and Zionist Ideologies," in *Studies in Contemporary Jewry VII: Jews and Messianism in the Modern Era: Metaphor and Meaning*, ed. Jonathan Frankel (New York: Oxford University Press, 1991), 4–7.

returning to their source in God, with the endpoint of this return identified with messianic redemption.[8] This movement toward redemption is not always visible through ordinary human perception, but it can be discerned in evolutionary processes both in the natural world and in the continuous progress of human civilization. In Kook's thinking, progress in human civilization is not necessarily smooth. It sometimes requires periods of regression and destruction before progress can once again take hold and move civilization toward messianic redemption.[9] This theology was rooted both in Kabbalistic ideas and in European notions of progress that had their source in Enlightenment thought.

According to Kook, the Jewish people play a key role in the redemptive process because they are inherently closer to God than all other nations, and therefore their actions have greater impact on the cosmos. As with the redemptive process in general, the impact of the Jewish people on the cosmos is not always evident through ordinary perception, but at times it can be discerned in historical events. For Kook, the advent of Zionism was one such event, and it indicated a major turning point in the messianic process. The movement to settle the ancient land of Israel was clear evidence that the messianic process was moving forward and that its culmination was close at hand. After all, the return of the Jews to their land was one of the hallmarks of the messianic period.[10]

The major obstacle Kook had to confront was that Zionism was by and large a secular movement, and he therefore had to explain how it could serve such an important religious function. Kook solved this problem by maintaining that the secular Zionists were being motivated by the redemptive impulse guiding all of creation even though they were not at all conscious of it. Therefore, secular Zionism was, in fact, a spiritual and redemptive movement despite the fact that its adherents were entirely unaware of their role in God's plan. As we have already mentioned, in Kook's thinking, progress in the messianic process was not always smooth; destructive processes often alternated with constructive ones. Secular Zionism was an excellent example of this phenomenon

8 There is a vast literature on Kook's life and thought. Some general treatments include Tsevi Yaron, *The Teachings of Rabbi Kook* (in Hebrew) (Jerusalem: Ha-Histadrut ha-Tsiyyonit, 1983); Ezra Gellman, ed., *Essays on the Thought and Philosophy of Rabbi Kook* (Rutherford, N.J.: Fairleigh Dickinson University Press, 1991); Benjamin Ish-Shalom, *Rav Avraham Itzhak HaCohen Kook: Between Rationalism and Mysticism*, trans. Ora Wiskind-Elper (Albany: State University of New York Press, 1993); Lawrence J. Kaplan and David Shatz, eds., *Rabbi Abraham Isaac Kook and Jewish Spirituality* (New York: New York University Press, 1995). My own description and analysis of Kook's thinking is much indebted to Ravitzky, *Messianism, Zionism, and Jewish Religious Radicalism*, 101–22.

9 Abraham Isaac Kook, *Orot ha-Kodesh* (Jerusalem: Mosad ha-Rav Kuk, 1964), 1:194, 374–76; 2:544–45; *Iggerot ha-Re'iyah* (Jerusalem: Mosad ha-Rav Kuk, 1962), 1:85.

10 Abraham Isaac Kook, *Orot ha-Teshuvah*, ed. Ya'akov Filber (Jerusalem: Gal'or, 1977), 158.

in that it was both destructive in being heretical, and constructive in building up the land of Israel for the messianic period. According to Kook, this understanding of secular Zionism was also confirmed by talmudic sources claiming that the messiah would come in a time of moral decline, brazenness, and apostasy. For Kook, the secular Zionist movement seemed to fit this description precisely.[11]

Kook's teachings were further developed by his son, Rabbi Tsevi Yehudah Kook, who applied his father's ideas to the momentous events that the latter did not live to see: the Holocaust, the establishment of the state of Israel, and its struggle for survival in the face of several wars with its Arab neighbors. The younger Kook also created a loyal band of disciples who had great success in disseminating his teachings among religious Zionists. During his lifetime, the elder Kook's views did not win large numbers of adherents, but his thinking, reshaped and popularized by his son, became dominant among religious Zionists in the decades after the Six-Day War in 1967. Most important for our purposes, the younger Kook radicalized his father's teachings, and in their new form they inspired the aggressive settlement activity of religious Zionists in the territories captured by Israel in the Six-Day War and encouraged a hostile attitude toward Palestinians, Arabs, and non-Jews in general.[12]

The younger Kook followed his father's lead in believing that secular Zionism was unwittingly motivated by a divine impulse and that it was a vehicle for bringing about the messianic redemption, but he extended these ideas to the political reality of the state of Israel. Thus, the secular political state was now holy, as was its army. The wars waged by the state were also holy. Their purpose was to establish Jewish sovereignty over the geographical area that God promised to Abraham in the Bible and that marked the borders of the ancient Israelite kingdom, for according to rabbinic tradition, this land would be possessed once again by the Jewish people in the messianic period. This line of thinking

---

11 Abraham Isaac Kook, *Hazon ha-Ge'ulah* (Jerusalem: Ha-Agudah le-Hotsa'at Sifrey ha-Ra'yah, 1941), 199, 201–2; idem, *Iggerot ha-Re'iyah*, 2:186; M. *Sotah* 9:7.

12 A comprehensive analysis of the younger Kook's thought and his disciples can be found in Dov Schwartz, *Challenge and Crisis in Rabbi Kook's Circle* (in Hebrew) (Tel Aviv: Am Oved, 2001). Schwartz argues that there is a coherent theology that underlies the younger Kook's writings. Schwartz also argues that the elder Kook, the younger Kook, and their disciples formed a definable circle united by a common theology. My treatment of Tsevi Yehudah Kook is also indebted to Ravitzky, *Messianism, Zionism, and Jewish Religious Radicalism*, 80–84; Luz, *Wrestling with an Angel*, 223–24; idem, "The Jewish Religion: Restraint or Encouragement in the Use of Force? Changing Attitudes in Religious Zionism" (in Hebrew), *Peace and War in Jewish Culture*, ed. Ariel Bar-Levav (Jerusalem: Zalman Shazar Center, 2006), 255–61; Eli Holzer, "Attitudes towards the Use of Military Force in Ideological Currents of Religious Zionism," in *War and Peace in the Jewish Tradition*, ed. Lawrence Schiffman and Joel B. Wolowelsky (New York: Yeshiva University Press, 2007), 356–72; idem, *A Double-Edged Sword: Military Activism in the Thought of Religious Zionism* (in Hebrew) (Jerusalem and Tel Aviv: The Shalom Hartman Institute, Keter Publishing House, Faculty of Law at Bar-Ilan University, 2009), chapter 6.

was accompanied by a novel interpretation of the biblical commandment to settle the land of Israel. In the younger Kook's view, this imperative was fundamental to the entire Torah and was just as important as the three cardinal commandments that rabbinic tradition had declared could not be violated even on pain of death: the prohibitions against idolatry, murder, and sexual immorality. Never in Jewish law had such importance been accorded this commandment. The younger Kook was aware of the moral difficulties raised by his views, but he was untroubled by them. If Israel's wars resulted in the killing of innocent Arabs, this should not be an obstacle to the messianic process, which trumped any moral qualms about such actions. Moreover, Jewish morality was superior to gentile morality, and therefore actions that might appear to be immoral from a non-Jewish perspective were not immoral from a Jewish one. The younger Kook retained peace as an ideal, but he believed that it could be achieved only at the end of the messianic process, when the nations recognized Israel's sovereignty over the biblical land of Israel and the superiority of Judaism.

The conflict between Israel and its enemies was interpreted by the younger Kook in metaphysical terms. It was a cosmic battle between Israel, which was fighting to move the messianic process forward, and nations that were working on behalf of metaphysical evil and doing everything in their power to stop that process. In places, he identified metaphysical evil not just with Israel's Arab enemies, but with the gentile nations in general, because in his view all nations to some degree harbored hatred of Israel and wanted to hold back the messianic process. Here we have a sharply dualistic perspective that made a clear division between Israel as the manifestation of all goodness in the world, and the rest of the nations as the embodiment of all that was evil. This kind of thinking will be familiar to students of modern fundamentalism. Modern fundamentalist movements often depict their battles with their enemies in terms of a cosmic conflict between the forces of good and evil, and one is either on one side of the conflict or the other; there is no middle ground. Furthermore, such thinking tends to dehumanize the enemy as representatives of pure evil and allows its adherents to kill them with little remorse.[13]

While the basic elements of the younger Kook's thinking took shape after the 1948 War of Independence, it was further consolidated in the wake of the

---

13 Tsevi Yehudah Kook, *Li-Ntivot Yisra'el* (Jerusalem: Menorah, 1967), 1:56, 193–94; 2:157–58; idem, *Mitokh ha-Torah ha-Go'elet* (Jerusalem: Makhon Tsemah Tsevi, 1983), 1:97, 202, 218; idem, *Ba-Ma'arakhah ha-Tsiburit*, ed. Yosef Bramson (Jerusalem: Agudat Zehav ha-Arets, 1986), 112, 244–46; Ravitzky, *Messianism, Zionism, and Jewish Religious Radicalism*, 86, 122–23; Luz, *Wrestling with an Angel*, 223–24. The younger Kook's negative views of non-Jews may have roots in the thinking of his father, who believed that there was an ontological difference between Jews and non-Jews. See Wolfson, *Venturing Beyond*, 23 n. 35, 121–28; Sagi, *Judaism: Between Religion and Morality*, 173–75.

1967 war. Israelis were stunned by their seemingly miraculous victory. For the younger Kook, the victory was nothing short of a miracle in the literal sense of the term. Israel now controlled a much larger portion of the territories that were part of the land promised to Abraham, apparent proof that the messianic era was indeed unfolding. Moreover, the victory inspired the younger Kook and his followers to lobby the Israeli government for the settlement of the captured territories in order to secure Jewish sovereignty over them, block attempts on the part of the government to trade land for peace, and ensure that the messianic process continue.[14] Gush Emunim (the Bloc of the Faithful), an organization formed in 1974, became the leading force for this cause and was soon taken over by elite students of the younger Kook, who used it as a vehicle for implementing their messianic program. This organization was remarkably successful. It raised the profile of religious Zionism from a relatively marginal phenomenon in Israeli society and politics to one that had strong influence on the entire national agenda. It was extremely effective in lobbying subsequent Israeli governments to support and implement its plans. Since the founding of Gush Emunim, scores of settlements have been established throughout the territories captured in 1967, and they are populated by hundreds of thousands of Israelis.[15]

Given the inexorable nature of the redemptive process in the younger Kook's thinking, one may wonder why he felt such an aggressive settlement program was needed. Why not just watch passively as the messianic era unfolded? As Avi Ravitzky has astutely pointed out, utopian political and social movements, both secular and religious, do not preclude activism to ensure success, even if they claim to know the future. Such knowledge about the future only makes the participants in these movements more excited about bringing it about.[16]

---

14 Ehud Sprinzak, *The Ascendance of Israel's Radical Right* (New York: Oxford University Press, 1991), 43–46.

15 Sprinzak, *The Ascendance of Israel's Radical Right*, 46–45, 67–69; Ravitzky, *Messianism, Zionism, and Jewish Religious Radicalism*, 129, 131–33; Gideon Aran assumes that from the very outset the leaders of Gush Emunim were disciples of the elder and younger Kook and therefore saw the settlement of lands captured in the 1967 war as an expression of their messianic Zionism. See Aran's discussion in "From Pioneering to Torah Study: The Background to the Growth of Religious Zionism" (in Hebrew), in *Me'ah Shanot Tsiyyonut Datit: Heibetim Ra'ayoniyyim*, ed. Avi Sagi and Dov Schwartz (Ramat Gan: Bar-Ilan University Press, 2004), 3:31–72. However, Avi Sagi and Dov Schwartz reject Aran's view and contend that Gush Emunim began as an organization inspired by classical religious Zionist philosophy that was not messianic. Only later did Gush Emunim attract the followers of the two Kooks, who brought with them their messianic Zionism. Yet, even if Schwartz and Sagi are correct here, there is no question that the settlement movement eventually received much of its energy from the supporters of Kookian theology. See Avi Sagi and Dov Schwartz, "From Pioneering to Torah Study: Another Perspective" (in Hebrew), in *Me'ah Shanot Tsiyyonut Datit: Heibetim Ra'ayoniyyim*, ed. Avi Sagi and Dov Schwartz (Ramat Gan: Bar-Ilan University Press, 2004), 3:73–76.

16 Ravitzky, *Messianism, Zionism, and Jewish Religious Radicalism*, 129–33.

The leaders of Gush Emunim never produced a systematic theology. Nonetheless, they were united by a series of doctrines that could be regarded as a coherent body of thought. Much of their thinking was based on the teachings of the elder and younger Kook that we have already delineated. From the younger Kook they inherited the notion that Jews were distinct from the gentile nations and therefore needed to live in isolation from them. What is of special interest to us here is the attitude of supporters of Gush Emunim toward the Palestinians among whom they resided in their new settlement communities. The widespread view in this group was that the "Palestinian problem" did not exist. It was a vicious ploy on the part of the surrounding Arab countries to destroy Israel. Still, its adherents believed that coexistence with the Arabs was possible because the latter would eventually appreciate living under humane Jewish rule. In the meantime, the Palestinians should be presented with three choices: they could acknowledge the legitimacy of Zionism, in which case they would be granted the right to vote and serve in the Knesset and the army; they could refuse to acknowledge the legitimacy of Zionism, but if they agreed to obey the law, they would have some rights; or they could emigrate to an Arab country.[17]

Gush Emunim was further radicalized in 1978 with the signing of the Camp David Accords, which ceded the Sinai Peninsula to Egypt and promised autonomy to the Palestinians in the territories captured in the 1967 war. Not only did the accords seem to reverse the messianic process as understood in Kookian theology, but they were initiated by Menachem Begin, the hawkish prime minister who was a hero to right-wing Israelis for having served as a guerilla fighter before the founding of the state. For the adherents of Gush Emunim, Begin's concessions were a painful betrayal that elicited deep anger and a determination to resist the implementation of the accords. Fanning their anger was that violence was now becoming more common between Israeli settlers and Palestinians because the expansion of the settlements in the late 1970s brought the two groups into increasing contact. These factors inspired the followers of Gush Emunim to adopt even more negative views of Palestinians. There was now little talk of allowing Palestinians full rights in an expanded Jewish state. Some also began to speak of the Palestinians as Amalekites. The full implications of that position were developed by R. Israel Hess, who, in an article in a magazine published by Bar Ilan-University, argued that Arabs were the direct descendants of Amalek, behaved like them, and therefore had to be

---

17 Sprinzak, *The Ascendance of Israel's Radical Right*, 87–94, chapter 5; Idith Zertal and Akiva Eldar, *Lords of the Land: The War over Israel's Settlements in the Occupied Territories, 1967–2000*, trans. Vivian Eden (New York: Nations Books, 2007), 215–18.

exterminated. No rabbinic authority in Gush Emunim endorsed this view, but an important line had been crossed. It increasingly became commonplace for the supporters of Gush Emunim to equate the Palestinians with Amalekites and to embrace all that this analogy implied. That identification continues to be widespread in religious Zionist circles in the present day.[18]

Thus far, the radicalization of Gush Emunim was primarily in the realm of opinion, but it was not long before it was followed by action. In 1984, Israeli police uncovered a group that became known as the Jewish Underground. This group had come into being in reaction to the Camp David Accords. It was relatively small, consisting of a handful of leaders and several hesitant followers. Its first project was to blow up the Dome of the Rock, the mosque sitting atop the Temple Mount. The members of this group believed that the Camp David Accords were the result of God's decision to interfere with the redemptive process because he was angry that the Dome of the Rock stood on Judaism's most holy site and that Jews had let Muslims control the Temple Mount after the 1967 war. The mosque, therefore, had to be destroyed. A detailed plan was drawn up by the group but was never executed because some of them lost their nerve when rabbinic approval for the operation could not be obtained. However, other initiatives were successfully carried out, with deadly consequences. In 1980, in response to a terror attack against Jewish students in Hebron, the group placed car bombs in the cars of five Palestinian mayors, and two were seriously injured. In 1983, in response to another terror attack against Jews, the group killed three students at a Muslim college. This time, rabbinic authorization had been sought and obtained. Finally, in 1984, in response to Palestinian terror attacks on Israeli buses, a plan was made to blow up five Arab buses filled with passengers. The plot was discovered at the last minute, saving dozens of lives, and members of the group were identified and arrested.[19]

The Underground was not part of Gush Emunim. In fact, its mastermind, Yehudah Etsyon, founded the group because of his disappointment with Gush Emunim being subservient to the secular Israeli government. According to him, the younger Kook had erred in believing that a secular state had a holy essence. If the time of redemption had indeed arrived, the Jewish state had no authority if it was not governed by Jewish law, and if its actions—most notably, the signing of the Camp David Accords—impeded the redemption process. Moreover, the arrival of the redemption meant that all Jews had to work to implement the messianic kingdom immediately, which meant the conquest of

18 Sprinzak, *The Ascendance of Israel's Radical Right*, 71–73, 87–94, 121–24; Horowitz, *Reckless Rites*, 1–12, 144–47; Sagi, "The Punishment of Amalek," 332; Cromer, "Amalek as Other, Other as Amalek," 196.
19 Sprinzak, *The Ascendance of Israel's Radical Right*, 94–99.

all territories that would be included in that kingdom and the clearing of the Temple Mount of its Arab presence. Shedding blood for these purposes presented no moral problem for Etsyon because it was meant to bring the world into the messianic era.[20]

Yet, despite the fact that this was a fringe group, some of its operations were approved by rabbinical authorities in Gush Emunim. Moreover, it represented a growing tendency among religious Zionists to endorse violence against Palestinians. Other extremists took up the cause of the Underground after its demise. Rabbi Israel Ariel formed an organization called Tsefiyah that believed that all Palestinians should be evicted not just from the territories captured in 1967, but from Israel as well. He also advocated waging war to capture all the land promised by God to Abraham in the Bible. The loss of innocent Arab life presented no difficulty for Ariel because according to his reading of Jewish law, only the killing of a Jew qualified as murder.[21]

Most religious Zionists did not go as far as Ariel. However, throughout the 1980s it was clear that, on the whole, they were becoming increasingly radical in their attitudes toward the use of violence against Palestinians and Arabs. Ehud Luz points out that the change in attitude on this issue began just after the 1967 war. Prior to that war, rabbis in the religious Zionist camp were generally loath to support violence against Arab civilians, but afterward some radical rabbis began to view it as permissible or even a duty. That viewpoint became much more widespread among religious Zionists in the 1980s after the 1982 Lebanon War, and during the First Intifada in 1987–93. It was often accompanied by the claim that Jewish morality was superior to gentile, humanistic morality, and that Jews, therefore, did not need to heed condemnations from the international community, a view that, as we have seen, was supported by the younger Kook.[22] Luz attempts to explain the change by arguing that the detachment of religion from Western universalistic morality was due to a defensive reaction to modernity and secularization. In nineteenth-century Europe, when Orthodoxy began formulating a response to those forces, it often detached religion from gentile morality in order to preserve the integrity of

20 Sprinzak, *The Ascendance of Israel's Radical Right*, chapter 8, especially 251–61; Eliezer Don-Yehiya, "The Book and the Sword: The Nationalist Yeshivot and Political Radicalism in Israel" (in Hebrew), in *Me'ah Shanot Tsiyyonut Datit: Heibetim Ra'ayoniyyim*, ed. Avi Sagi and Dov Schwartz (Ramat Gan: Bar-Ilan University Press, 2004), 3:216–20. Yoni Garb argues that the Underground incorporated four different viewpoints and was not a unified phenomenon. See Jonathan Garb, "Messianism, Antinomianism, and Power in Religious Zionism: The Case of the Jewish Underground" (in Hebrew), in *Religious Zionism: An Era of Changes: Studies in Honor of Zevulun Hammer*, ed. Asher Cohen and Yisra'el Har'el (Jerusalem: Bialik Institute, 2004), 336–43.

21 Sprinzak, *The Ascendance of Israel's Radical Right*, 261–74.

22 Luz, *Wrestling with an Angel*, 228.

Judaism and Jewish identity. Luz claims that the same process has repeated itself in Israel. As secular Israelis have gradually become more secular and less Zionistic in recent decades, religious Zionists have increasingly isolated themselves in communities dictated by purely religious norms, which has led in turn to a rejection of any form of morality that smacks of Western influence and its universalistic thinking.[23]

In the 1980s, another factor entered the picture that gave more impetus to the radical wing of religious Zionism: Rabbi Meir Kahane. Kahane was an American Orthodox rabbi who founded the Jewish Defense League, a Jewish vigilante organization. In 1971, Kahane moved to Israel and immediately began preaching a brand of religious Zionism that was more radical and violent than any that had been seen up to that point. With his strong will, his gift for oratory, and his talent for finding ways to attract the attention of the media, Kahane quickly became a figure to be reckoned with. Kahane founded the organization Kach (Thus) in order to carry out his agenda.[24]

Kahane had no respect for Gush Emunim or the teachings of the two Kooks, but his thinking was similar to that of the younger Kook in a number of critical respects.[25] Kahane's views were based on an extreme bitterness toward the gentile nations, calls for revenge against them for their persecution of Jews throughout the centuries, and Jewish isolationism. According to Kahane, God did not bring about the establishment of the state of Israel because of his love for the Zionists; after all, they were secular Jews who did not deserve God's favor. Rather, he established the state because he could no longer bear the humiliation of watching the persecution of his people. That is, Israel was established not as a reward for the Jews, but as an act of revenge against the gentiles![26] Kahane also saw the gentiles as a threat because of their culture. Modern gentile culture had promised the Jews much but delivered nothing, and the only answer was for Jews to isolate themselves entirely from them. Only through

---

23 Luz, *Wrestling with an Angel*, 230–32; idem, "The Jewish Religion," 261–65.

24 Sprinzak, *The Ascendance of Israel's Radical Right*, 51–56.

25 For the presentation of Kahane's views, I am much indebted to Sprinzak, *The Ascendance of Israel's Radical Right*, chapter 7; Ravitzky, *The Roots of Kahanism*.

26 Note that here Kahane was trying to come to terms with the same problem that bothered the elder Kook, which is how the state of Israel could be established and achieve success through the actions of secular Jews. For Kook, the success of the secular Zionists was possible because God was working through secular Zionism to bring redemption. For Kahane, it was because God was working through secular Zionism to take revenge on non-Jews. Don Seeman analyzes the motif of defending God's honor in a number of modern Jewish thinkers and focuses a great deal on the radical right-wing religious rabbi, Yitshak Ginzburg, in "Violence, Ethics, and Divine Honor in Modern Jewish Thought," *Journal of the American Academy of Religion* 73, no. 4 (2005): 1015–48. Ginzburg's reflections on this issue are very similar to Kahane's, though Seeman does not mention Kahane in his analysis.

isolation could Jews develop as a holy nation, free from pernicious gentile influence.[27]

However, in Kahane's thinking, revenge was not God's sole motive for establishing the state of Israel. He also believed, as did the two Kooks, that events since the founding of the state were a clear indication that messianic redemption was just over the horizon. Yet, Jews had to repent if the redemption was to come quickly and without pain. If they did not do so, redemption would come slowly, accompanied by a great deal of suffering. The victory in the 1967 war was evidence that God was ready to bring the redemption quickly and painlessly, but the Yom Kippur War in 1973, in which Israel was far less successful, was a warning of the disasters that would befall the Jewish people if they did not repent. In short, divine anger seemed to be the key motif in Kahane's thinking: God was angry at the gentiles for anti-Semitism and therefore created the state of Israel; at the same time, his anger was ready to break forth against the Jews if they did not repent.[28]

Most important for our purposes, Kahane's views on Arabs were also extreme. According to Kahane, there was nothing wrong with taking the land of Israel from the Arabs by force. It had been promised to the Jews by God to be the place where Jews could serve him and become a holy nation free of foreign influence. Therefore Arabs could live in the Jewish state, but only if they established their loyalty, and even then they would have very few rights. Quotas on Arabs living in Israel would be maintained, with the result that even Arabs loyal to the state would have to be expelled at times in order to preserve a Jewish majority. Sexual relations between Jews and Arabs would be a capital crime. Complete separation between them would be maintained in schools, at beaches, and in other public places. Kahane also advocated counterterrorism and vigilantism against Arabs. When Jews were attacked, his followers retaliated by attacking Arabs.[29]

As an Orthodox rabbi, Kahane frequently cited Jewish sources for his views. His position on the treatment of Arabs was modeled on a midrash cited in chapter 3, on rabbinic Judaism, in which God instructs Joshua to offer three alternatives to the Canaanites: leave the land of Israel, go to war, or surrender and become resident aliens.[30] Kahane was aware of sources that seemed

27 Meir Kahane, Listen World, Listen Jew (Tucson: Institute of the Jewish Idea, 1978), 121–22, 128.

28 Meir Kahane, Israel's Eternity and Victory (in Hebrew) (Jerusalem: Institute of the Jewish Idea, 1973); Numbers 23:9 (in Hebrew) (Jerusalem: Institute of the Jewish Idea, 1974); Forty Years (Miami: Institute of the Jewish Idea, 1983), 6–7.

29 Meir Kahane, Thorns in Your Eyes (in Hebrew) (New York: Druker, 1981), 224–42.

30 What makes Kahane's interpretation here so interesting is that, as we saw in our chapter on rabbinic Judaism, this source was cited as evidence by some Jewish scholars that the rabbis were trying to soften the harshness of the biblical narrative describing Joshua's conquest. Kahane manages to use the same source for precisely the opposite purpose. This is yet one more example of how malleable Jewish sources are in the hands of interpreters when it comes to issues of peace and violence.

inconsistent with his thinking, such as the verse in the first chapter of Genesis stating that all human beings were created in the image of God, and of rabbinic sources in which the rabbis treated gentiles with great respect. However, Kahane maintained that these sources applied only to relationships with non-Jews as individuals, not to non-Jews as residents in a Jewish state. In a Jewish state, non-Jews were to be regarded as inferior to Jews.[31]

Kahane eventually entered politics and ran for the Knesset in 1977 and 1981, but he got very few votes. However, his fortunes improved when Menachem Begin stepped down as prime minister in 1983 and Yitzhak Shamir took his place. Begin's departure left a void that Kahane was happy to fill. Palestinian terrorism was also on the rise, instilling fear among Israelis. Kahane tapped into these emotions and won a seat in the Knesset in 1984. The Israeli political establishment, alarmed by Kahane's growing popularity, took action, passing a law in 1985 that prevented racist or antidemocratic parties from running for the Knesset. When elections were called in 1988, Kahane was disqualified from running. This came at the peak of Kahane's popularity. Projections were that he would have won three to five seats. Kahane died in the same violent manner in which he had lived: he was assassinated in New York in 1991.[32]

In the early 1990s, radical religious Zionism seemed to be in retreat. In 1992, Yitzhak Rabin was elected prime minister on the platform of territorial compromise with the Palestinians and Israel's Arab neighbors. The pioneering spirit of Gush Emunim appeared to be fizzling as its supporters settled into comfortable middle-class lifestyles and the quality of its leadership declined. Yet, the radical elements in religious Zionism were galvanized into action with the signing of the Oslo Accords in 1993. At first, Gush Emunim did not mount opposition to the accords because a majority of Israelis supported them. However, a wave of Palestinian terrorism soon followed, and an intense campaign was launched by Jewish right-wing groups to delegitimize Rabin as a traitor and a murderer. In February 1994, Baruch Goldstein, a disciple of Kahane and a member of Kach, murdered twenty-nine Palestinian Muslim worshipers in the Cave of the Patriarchs in Hebron before being beaten to death. Goldstein's motives stemmed from his belief that the Oslo Accords represented a major setback in the messianic process and that only radical action could stop them from being implemented.[33]

---

31 Meir Kahane, *On Faith and Redemption* (in Hebrew) (Jerusalem: Institute of the Jewish Idea, 1980), 68; idem, *Uncomfortable Questions for Comfortable Jews* (Secaucus, N.J.: Lyle Stuart, 1987), 173.

32 Sprinzak, *The Ascendance of Israel's Radical Right*, 81–87, 245–46; Yair Kotler, *Heil Kahane* (New York: Adama Books, 1986), 412–20.

33 Sprinzak, *Brother against Brother: Violence and Extremism in Israeli Politics from the Altalena to the Rabin Assassination* (New York: Free Press, 1999), chapter 7.

The mounting hostility of the right wing to the Oslo Accords culminated in another act of violence, this one unprecedented in Israel's history: the assassination of an Israeli prime minister. In 1995, Yigal Amir murdered Rabin after he spoke at a peace rally in Tel Aviv. Amir's actions have to be seen within the context of a debate that had been conducted for some time in right-wing circles of religious Zionism. Religious leaders in the settler movement had discussed whether the Oslo Accords placed Rabin in the halakhic category of a *moser* or a *rodef*. A *moser* is a Jew who informs on his fellow Jews to gentile authorities, hands Jews over to gentile authorities, or gives Jewish land away to gentiles. A *rodef* is someone who is in immediate pursuit of another individual with the intent of killing that individual. It was argued that Rabin might be a *moser* since the land of Israel was sacred property, and he was giving it away to the Palestinians via the Oslo Accords. Alternatively, he might be a *rodef* because the peace process had endangered Jewish lives by allowing the Palestinians to arm themselves. What made these allegations so serious was that according to Jewish law, one was permitted to kill a *moser* or *rodef*. The implication here was that Rabin deserved to die.

These considerations were, in part, responsible for inspiring Yigal Amir. After the assassination, Amir explained that Rabin was a *rodef* and therefore had to be killed. Amir also took his inspiration from the more amorphous concept of zealotry, which had roots in early rabbinic tradition. Under some circumstances, the rabbis permitted the killing of an individual who was engaged in an unusually heinous act, though they were reluctant to institutionalize the law. The rabbis based this notion on various biblical stories, most notably that of Phinehas, discussed in chapter 1, on the Bible.[34] Prior to his action, Amir attempted to receive approval from rabbinic authorities but failed. Ultimately, he concluded that he could act on his own because he understood the issues.[35]

The Rabin assassination led many religious Zionists to a process of reflection and soul-searching, but it is questionable whether it had any real long-term impact. In 2000, President Bill Clinton failed to forge a peace deal between Israelis and Palestinians at Camp David, which resulted in the outbreak of the Second Intifada. Religious Zionists once again began venting their anger at a left-wing Israeli government, this time led by Ehud Barak, which was prepared to make territorial concessions. That anger was further inflamed by the retreat from Gaza in 2005 initiated by Prime Minister Ariel Sharon. This event brought out bitterness among religious Zionists similar to that felt after

34 See pp. 82–3, this volume.
35 Sprinzak, *Brother against Brother*, chapter 8.

Begin signed the Camp David Accords, for here again a hawkish prime minister, a hero to the right wing, seemed to betray his supporters. Eli Holzer argues that in the wake of the retreat from Gaza, radical views are now more commonplace than ever in the mainstream of religious Zionism. Holzer also maintains that the retreat has inspired some religious Zionists to question or reject entirely, important elements of Kookian theology. Religious Zionists now doubt whether holiness resides in secular Zionism, the state, and the army, and whether they should respect these institutions.[36] Yet, there is also evidence of a tendency that is in tension with Holzer's assessment. The percentage of religious Zionists in the Israeli army has increased significantly in recent years, particularly in elite units and the officer corps, as secular Israelis have become disenchanted with militarism and have found ways to avoid army service. This trend has ominous implications for those in the peace camp as reports have surfaced of religious soldiers and commanders expressing unwillingness to evacuate West Bank settlements if ordered to do so.[37]

What should be evident by this point in our discussion is that many of the concepts that were identified in previous chapters as potentially violent in the earlier schools of Judaism have been woven together in a highly combustible combination in religious Zionism. Those concepts include the ideas that (1) the Jews are God's chosen people; (2) the land of Israel was promised to the Jews; (3) in the messianic era, Jews will regain sovereignty in their own land and their enemies will be destroyed; (4) Jews are commanded to exterminate the Amalekites; and (5) in Kabbalistic dualism, Jews represent all that is good in the world, and gentiles represent all that is evil. In the thinking of the younger Kook and his followers, all these ideas were assembled into an elaborate theology. The Jewish people were at the center of God's cosmic plan. Zionism heralded the beginning of the final stage of messianic redemption, and it would be complete only when Jews had sovereignty over the entire land promised to Abraham in the Bible. Opinions varied on the place of the Palestinians in the emerging messianic reality. According to some followers of Kookian thinking, they could have limited rights if they accepted Zionism and observed the Noahide laws. Others thought that Palestinians were Amalekites who should be expelled from the land or exterminated. In general, however, a negative attitude was expressed toward the gentile nations as a whole. All non-Jews were enemies of Israel and represented metaphysical evil. Thus, international norms of morality and human rights were of no consequence in determining how Jews should act in

36 Holzer, *A Double-Edged Sword*, pp. 287–96.

37 Much attention has been given to this problem in the popular media. See, for instance, Leslie Susser, "Holy Orders," *Jerusalem Report* (December 21, 2009), 6–9.

their relationship with Palestinians or neighboring Arab countries. The Torah's values were superior to any such norms. Meir Kahane was in general agreement with these principles, except that his thinking was not undergirded by Kabbalistic metaphysics, as was Kookian theology.

We have also encountered concepts having roots in rabbinic tradition that were used by religious Zionists to justify violence but that we have not yet seen in any of our previous discussions. The assassination of Rabin occurred against the background of a debate among religious Zionists regarding the rabbinic notions of *moser, rodef,* and zealotry. These concepts, however, were utilized to justify violence not against non-Jews, but against an Israeli prime minister.

It should also be noted that our discussion of religious Zionism points up the weakness of a central argument used earlier to support a nonviolent reading of the Bible. According to this reading, the biblical text is not as violent as it seems because when Israel wages war, God fights on behalf of Israel; war is therefore not the prerogative of human beings.[38] As Ravitzky has pointed out, Kookian theology envisions the messianic process as predetermined by God, but that does not mean that human beings should be passive. On the contrary, expectations of the coming of the messianic era have only inspired the supporters of Kookian theology to participate in its implementation eagerly, and if necessary, violently. Thus, the notion that violent actions are a divine prerogative by no means precludes human beings from executing similar actions; in fact, it may even encourage those actions.

Yet, the majority of Zionists throughout the history of the movement have been not religious, but secular in orientation. The same can be said about Jewish citizens of the state of Israel today: about 75 percent of this population is secular, and staunchly so. It is therefore important that we also take a careful look at this form of Zionism. Prior to the establishment of the state of Israel, it was in fact Zionism in its secular form that produced the movement's most violent adherents. The forefather of militaristic secular Zionism was Vladimir Ze'ev Jabotinsky (1880–1940), who headed the Revisionist party in the early Zionist congresses.[39] Jabotinsky was not really an ultranationalist. He had too much admiration for the British and too much regard for democracy and liberalism to be classified under that rubric. He was also a realist who understood that the Jewish community in Palestine was too weak to win a military struggle

---

38 See pp. 47–9, this volume.

39 General treatments of Jabotinsky include Yaacov Shavit, *Jabotinsky and the Revisionist Movement, 1925–1948* (London: F. Cass, 1988); Raphaella Bilski Ben-Hur, *Every Individual, a King: The Social and Political Thought of Ze'ev Vladimir Jabotinsky* (Washington, D.C.: B'nai Brith Books, 1993); Shmuel Katz, *Lone Wolf: A Biography of Vladimir (Ze'ev) Jabotinsky* (New York: Barricade Books, 1996); Eran Kaplan, *The Jewish Radical Right: Revisionist Zionism and Its Ideological Legacy* (Madison, Wis.: University of Wisconsin Press, 2005).

against the British. Nonetheless, Jabotinsky was a nationalist who believed in militarism as the means of forwarding the aims of Zionism and that a Jewish state should be established on both sides of the Jordan River. He also believed that a confrontation with the Palestinians was inevitable and that the question of who would rule Palestine would have to be settled by armed confrontation. Moreover, Jabotinsky's political actions did not usually convey his liberal side, and therefore his right-wing side was most influential. He created the Beitar youth movement, which fostered military values and glorified Israel's military past, as exemplified by Bar Kokhba and Masada.

Jabotinsky's thinking and the Revisionist party he created also gave rise to an ultranationalist faction within the party that was often more extreme than he was. This group included such figures as Uri Tsevi Greenberg, Abba Ahimeir, and Yehoshua Heshel Yevin, who banded together in 1931 to establish an organization known as the Berit ha-Biryonim (Covenant of the Ruffians). The group adopted the political thinking of the extreme right in Europe, which was on the rise in the interwar period. They were hostile to democracy and socialism, and they believed that Zionism should model itself on the biblical past, when the Israelites conquered their enemies and expanded their kingdom through military force. Eventually, Revisionism produced ultranationalist groups that were focused on implementing this ideology in the realm of action. The first group was an underground military organization, Etsel (National Military Organization, also known as the Irgun), which was established in 1937 and began to engage in anti-Arab terrorism. In 1940, some Revisionists established a more extreme organization, Lehi (Fighters for the Freedom of Israel), which used even more aggressive tactics against the British and the Arabs with the hope of ridding Palestine of both groups.[40]

Yet, a penchant for violence was not confined to the right wing of secular Zionism. Socialist Labor Zionism, which was the most popular form of Zionism before the establishment of the state and remained so for three decades afterward, had its own violent tendencies, albeit more subtle in form than those found among the Revisionists. Anita Shapira has written a seminal study detailing and analyzing the views of mainstream Labor Zionism on the issue of power in the pre-state years, and she shows how they gradually evolved into an aggressive ideology.[41] Initially, in the 1920s and 1930s Labor Zionism formulated a political ideology that she terms "the defensive ethos" to deal with the

---

40 Sprinzak, *The Ascendance of Israel's Radical Right*, 23–27; Shapira, *Land and Power*, 154–63, 242–48; Yosef Gorny, *Zionism and the Arabs, 1882–1948: A Study of Ideology* (Oxford: Oxford University Press, 1987), 156–73; Luz, *Wrestling with an Angel*, 177–82.

41 See the previous note.

moral question of settling Palestine and dispossessing the Arabs of their land.[42] According to this ethos, the Labor Zionists desired peace with the Palestinians but believed that the Palestinian leadership had incited hostility to Zionism among Palestinian peasants. The Labor Zionists theorized that the Palestinian leadership wanted to maintain its position of privilege vis-à-vis the peasants and feared that the Zionists would help the peasants achieve prosperity, thereby inspiring the peasants to rebel against their Palestinian leaders. The Palestinian leadership therefore convinced the peasants that the Zionists were their enemies. This understanding of the conflict was based on a classic socialist viewpoint, which understood all societal conflict as resulting from class interests. The Labor Zionists felt that eventually the Palestinian peasants would recognize the advantage of living with the Zionists and throw off the yoke of their overlords.

Yet, Shapira also shows that the early views of the Labor Zionists were often inconsistent regarding the Palestinians and that their words and actions often betrayed a hostile attitude toward them. The Labor Zionists steadfastly refused to recognize Palestinian nationalism. Thus, in effect, they granted everything to the Palestinians as human beings but nothing to them as a nation.[43] Furthermore, the Labor Zionists stated quite openly that they wanted to avoid any formal political arrangement with the Palestinians until Jewish immigration ensured a Jewish majority, so that Jews would hold the balance of power. The main question that all this raises is whether the Labor Zionists were sincere when expressing their desire for peace with the Palestinians or this was just a strategy to convince others, and perhaps even themselves, that their intentions were good. Shapira claims that there is no easy answer to this question.[44]

However, according to Shapira's analysis, there is no doubt that the defensive ethos of Labor Zionism gradually gave way to an offensive ethos that was unequivocal in its hostility to the Palestinians in the decade before the 1948 war. From 1936 to 1939, Palestinians, frustrated by the growth of the Jewish community and fearful that it would become dominant, engaged in a violent rebellion that targeted Jews. Labor Zionists could no longer pretend that Palestinian nationalism did not exist, and many of them reacted by expressing

---

42 Shapira does not provide an explanation for her terminology. Apparently, when she refers to the "defensive" ethos, she means an ethos in which violence is justified as being only for defensive purposes.

43 Shapira, *Land and Power*, 356. As Shapira notes, ironically, the views of the Labor Zionists toward Palestinians were similar to those expressed by the Count of Clermont-Tonnerre with respect to Jews after the French revolution.

44 Shapira's central arguments can be found in *Land and Power*, 116–26.

violent attitudes toward the Palestinians. Moreover, by the 1940s a new generation of Jews had come of age in Palestine that had been reared there and
viewed the land as their own. This generation was less romantic than its
socialist forebears, more honest and open about human relations, and more
direct and rude in expressing its opinions. Most important, it openly embraced
militarism and nativism, characteristics that would prepare it to emerge victorious in 1948.[45] Much research has also been done demonstrating that in the
pre-state years, many Zionists supported the notion of "transfer," the idea that
the conflict between Jews and Palestinians could be solved by resettling the
Palestinian population in Arab countries and giving the Jews sovereignty over
the entirety of Palestine. Jewish opinions varied as to whether this scheme
could be accomplished peacefully or would require the use of force. While it
comes as no surprise that many Revisionists supported this plan, scholarly
research has revealed that it also received endorsement by many in the Labor
camp, though it was spoken about in these circles in more hushed terms than
was the case with the Revisionists.[46] As for the 1948 war itself, the groundbreaking work of Benny Morris has shown that the Labor leadership, which
guided the war effort, ordered Jewish soldiers to expel many Palestinians from
their homes and villages, applauded when other Palestinians left of their own
accord, and did not allow most of them to return after the war was over.[47]

After the establishment of the state of Israel, many secular Zionists continued to support territorial maximalism. Greatly energized by Israel's victory in
the 1967 war, they formed a movement called Ha-Tnu'ah le-Ma'an Erets Yisra'el
ha-Shleimah (the Land of Israel Movement), which was devoted to ensuring
that Israel did not relinquish the territories that had been captured. Predictably,
the movement drew support from old Revisionists, who had always believed
that the entirety of the land of Israel belonged to the Jews, but what was
remarkable was that many of its members came from the Labor party, including distinguished politicians, generals, intellectuals, and artists.[48]

The secular maximalists were again galvanized by the Camp David Accords
in 1978, much as the religious Zionists were, and formed Tehiya (Renaissance),
a political party opposing Begin's territorial concessions. In addition to responding to the immediate crisis at hand, supporters of this party were devoted to

---

45 Shapira, *Land and Power*, 250–51, 343–52.

46 An extensive discussion of this issue can be found in Benny Morris, *The Birth of the Palestinian Refugee Problem Revisited* (Cambridge: Cambridge University Press, 2004), chapter 2. See also Sprinzak, *The Ascendance of Israel's Radical Right*, 27–30; Shapira, *Land and Power*, 285–86.

47 See the previous note for a full citation of Morris's central study.

48 Sprinzak, *The Ascendance of Israel's Radical Right*, 38–43.

reviving the old pioneering spirit of Zionism, which they believed was embodied in the settlement movement. What was new about Tehiya was that it attempted to unite secular and religious Zionists around the common cause of territorial maximalism. Tehiya did poorly in its first election in 1981 and subsequently joined the larger right-wing Likud party. Nonetheless, despite its small size and its lack of success at the polls, it was influential in Israeli politics.[49]

In the last couple of decades, revisionist Israeli historians have presented a reading of Labor Zionism that is more extreme than that given thus far. According to this viewpoint, Labor Zionism was devoted to territorial maximalism and was determined to rid Palestine of its Arab inhabitants well before the establishment of the state. When the 1948 war was fought, the leadership in Labor Zionism did its best to achieve these goals with a well thought out and coordinated plan. Moreover, Israel had opportunities to make peace with the Palestinians and its Arab neighbors, both before and after 1948, and to implement liberal and humane values in the new state, but it consistently passed them up in favor of nationalism and militarism. Thus, the displacement of Palestinians was the aim not just of fringe or isolated groups within Zionism, nor was it just a crime of opportunity that took place in the chaos of war. It guided the mainstream Zionist leadership, it did so from early on in its history, and it was implemented in the 1948 war with great efficiency. This reading therefore attempts to explode the myth held by the traditional Zionist reading of history that the Jews came to Palestine wanting peace with their Arab neighbors but were subject to repeated attacks and therefore had to use violence as a last resort. In addition to these charges, some have argued that Zionism was really a colonialist movement intent on taking over an underdeveloped country and exploiting its resources and its indigenous inhabitants.[50]

This understanding of Israeli history has been a key ingredient in post-Zionism, an intellectual movement that arose in the 1990s. Drawing from the work of the revisionist historians, the post-Zionists believe that the state of Israel was "born in sin." They also adopt the insights of Israeli sociologists who claim that Israel has perpetuated that sin by building a society that discriminates against Israeli Palestinians and its other non-Jewish inhabitants by insisting that Israel be a Jewish state. According to the post-Zionists, Israeli Jews have to make a choice between political liberalism and political nationalism, a choice they have hitherto avoided. Israel either has to be a Jewish state that discriminates against its non-Jewish inhabitants, or it has to be a civil state that

---

49 Sprinzak, *The Ascendance of Israel's Radical Right*, 71–80.

50 Ilan Pappé is perhaps the best-known of these historians. See his *The Ethnic Cleansing of Palestine* (Oxford: Oneworld, 2006).

does not have a specifically Jewish character and is inclusive of all groups. Post-Zionists favor the second alternative.[51]

The charges of the revisionist historians and post-Zionists, however, have been subject to intense criticism. Let us first look at the position of the revisionist historians, who insist that from the outset the leadership of mainstream Labor Zionism planned to expel the Palestinians from their land. Ehud Luz rejects this line of thinking with the argument that the revisionist historians make the mistake of assessing the intentions of the Zionists only by the practical outcome of their actions, not by anything they actually said. Thus, when the early Zionists spoke about "redeeming the land," the revisionist historians assume that they really meant expelling Arabs; when they spoke about "settlement," they really meant colonization. The revisionist historians therefore distort the intentions of the Zionists. The revisionist historians also ignore the fact that the outcome of the conflict between the Zionists and the Palestinians was shaped by both parties, not just the Zionists. If the Zionists used force against the Palestinians, one cannot assume that this was their intention in the first place. The use of force was due, at least in part, to Palestinian hostility and violence toward the Zionists. If Palestinians were driven from their homes in 1948, one cannot assume that this was due to a preconceived plan. Such expulsions have to be understood in the context of a war in which the Zionists were fighting for their lives. Moreover, Zionism was not colonialism. Palestine had no economic attraction for the Zionists because there was nothing in Palestine to exploit. They were attracted to Palestine by the opportunity to create a new Jewish homeland that would solve the problems Jews had confronted regarding their identity since the Enlightenment. Jews also felt that they had a historic right to the land based on their past and did not see themselves as foreigners. Some critics of the revisionist historians go further in claiming that their work is simply poor scholarship. The revisionists have been accused of misreading sources or entirely fabricating historical events.[52]

The arguments of the post-Zionists have also been criticized. The notion that Israelis have to choose between political liberalism and political nationalism

51 Laurence J. Silberstein, *The Postzionism Debates: Knowledge and Power in Israeli Culture* (London and New York: Routledge, 1999) Luz, *Wrestling with an Angel*, 11, 264–65; Ephraim Nimni, ed., *The Challenge of Post-Zionism: Alternatives to Israeli Fundamentalist Politics* (New York: Zed Books, 2003); Uri Ram, *The Globalization of Israel: McWorld in Tel Aviv, Jihad in Jerusalem* (London and New York: Routledge, 2008).

52 Luz, *Wrestling with an Angel*, introduction, 11, 265–68. Extensive critiques of Israeli historical revisionism and post-Zionism can be found in Efraim Karsh, *Fabricating Israeli History: The "New Historians,"* 2nd ed. (London and Portland, Ore.: Frank Cass, 2000); Anita Shapira and Derek J. Penslar, ed., *Israeli Historical Revisionism: From Left to Right* (London: Frank Cass, 2003); Shlomo Sharan, ed., *Israel and the Post-Zionists* (Brighton: Sussex Academic Press; Portland, Ore.: Ariel Center for Policy Research, 2003); Derek J. Penslar, *Israel in History: The Jewish State in Comparative Perspective* (London and New York: Routledge, 2007), chapters 1–2.

is fallacious. The world is filled with nation-states in which a majority group holds the balance of power and defines the character and culture of the state, and no one claims that such states must choose between political liberalism and political nationalism. The two can coexist so long as minority groups are given political and economic rights equal to those of the majority. Israel should be no different in this regard. Certainly, Israel has been found wanting in its treatment of its Arab citizens, but the same can be said of many other states with respect to their own minorities. Thus, the notion that Israel is a Jewish state is no less a moral problem than is the idea that France is a French state. One might retort that Israel's case is more morally problematic than it is for other nation-states because Israel was created by the flagrant conquest of an indigenous population that became a minority within it. However, there is practically no nation-state that did not come into existence under similar circumstances at some point in history. They were all formed by conquest of other peoples. It is just that for Israel, that conquest has been relatively recent. Moreover, some have claimed that nationalism can have positive moral benefits with respect to the way in which people relate to outside groups. Yael Tamir argues that the development of ethnic, national, and particularistic identity in a nation-state is a condition for developing a sense of universal justice. Social and cultural context allows individuals to achieve autonomy, make choices, and develop the faculty of criticism. Social bonds sharpen our sense of mutual responsibility, which is a prerequisite for universal justice. There is therefore no necessary contradiction between national and universal solidarity.[53]

I tend to support the critics of the revisionist historians and post-Zionists. However, we do not need to settle this debate here. The scholarship of Shapira and Morris is widely accepted, and it leaves no doubt that Zionists perpetrated acts of violence against Palestinians during the founding of the state, even if it was not as well-organized and systematic as the revisionist historians claim. It is also worth emphasizing here that, according to the definition of violence spelled out in our introductory chapter, the forceful taking of land certainly qualifies as violence. Thus, even when there was no bodily injury, the actions of Jews resulted in deprivation for Palestinians as well as serious and long-lasting psychological damage. Therefore, even when Zionists were not actually shedding blood, these actions were indeed violent, and aggressively so. Moreover, there is little doubt that Jewish violence against Palestinians has continued since the founding of the state of Israel. Most Jews in Israel acknowledge that Israeli Palestinians are discriminated against, a phenomenon that would be

53 See the sources cited in the previous note.

classified as structural violence according to the definition of violence in our introductory chapter. There is also no question that Jews have engaged in physical violence against Palestinians in the territories captured in 1967. There is much debate about the extent to which this violence has been aggressive or defensive in nature, and which side one supports in this debate will determine how one judges this violence from a moral standpoint. But this is yet another dispute that we cannot settle here, nor do we need to. There is a general consensus that, at the very least, Jews have acted violently against Palestinians and that in some instances the violence has been aggressive.[54]

But even if one can demonstrate that secular Zionism was violent toward Arabs, we have yet to determine whether that hostility emanated from Judaism. It may have been simply an expression of secular nationalism, not of religion. As we noted in the introduction to this chapter, a major factor inspiring the rise of Zionism was European nationalism, and nationalism often brings with it xenophobia and hostility toward outside groups. That nationalism is the issue here would make sense given that secular Zionism was, after all, secular, and that in many respects it had severed its ties with Judaism.

While one cannot deny that factors other than Judaism were responsible for the development of secular Zionism, the argument can be made that Judaism was highly significant in secular Zionist thinking and that it was a key element in fostering a negative attitude to Palestinians. From the beginnings of secular Zionism, most of its intellectual and political leaders formulated their ideas with the help of traditional Jewish motifs, and they relied a great deal on the Bible for their inspiration. Certainly, the overall orientation of the secular Zionists was nonreligious, even atheistic. They therefore denuded the ideas they adopted from Judaism of their metaphysical underpinnings, and they treated the Bible as a source of history and Jewish identity rather than as God's revelations. Still, secular Zionism would have been inconceivable without Judaism.[55]

A number of examples will illustrate this point, and we can begin with the very premise of Zionism. The basic right of Jews to Palestine was a fundamental

---

54 Ruth R. Wisse, *Jews and Power* (New York: Nextbook-Schocken, 2007), goes in a direction opposite that of the revisionist historians and post-Zionists, arguing that Jews and Zionists have been far too accommodating toward Palestinians and Arabs. She claims that Jews continue to hold on to views of power that were cultivated during the centuries of exile and that promote weakness. Israelis have therefore tried too hard to appease their enemies and have paid a high price for it. See especially 171–72. I am not in agreement with Wisse's analysis. My sense is that Israelis display a combination of accommodation and aggression toward Palestinians and Arabs, a confusion inspired by the complexity of their situation.

55 Two strong advocates of this position are Ehud Luz and Yosef Salmon. See Luz, *Wrestling with an Angel*, introduction; Yosef Salmon, *Do Not Provoke Providence: Orthodoxy in the Grip of Nationalism* (in Hebrew) (Jerusalem: Zalman Shazar Center, 2006), 11–15, chapters 13–15.

component of all Zionist programs in the nineteenth century, and that sentiment is clearly traceable to Judaism. Few concepts have been more central to
Judaism than the notion that the land of Israel is the homeland of the Jewish
people. As we have seen in our discussion of the Bible, at the center of God's
covenant with Abraham was the promise that his descendants would inherit
the land of Israel, and that promise defines the entire historical narrative of the
Bible. It also defines Jewish consciousness throughout the medieval period.
Jews regarded themselves as being in exile, and they longed and prayed for a
return to their homeland. It should therefore occasion no surprise that Zionists
rejected Herzl's proposal that a Jewish state be created in Uganda. One can also
add here that early Zionism attracted the support of a number of Christians
who were inspired by the biblical notion that the land belonged to the Jews.
These included powerful individuals in the U.S. Congress and Lord Balfour,
whose influence on the process leading to the establishment of the state of
Israel was enormous.[56] Christians and Jews therefore came together around
the idea of a Jewish homeland in the land of Israel because of the influence of
the Bible. Indeed, secular Zionists did not believe that the land of Israel was
God's gift to the Jewish people in any literal sense, nor did they accord it special
metaphysical status as Jewish religious thinkers had done throughout the centuries. Nonetheless, secular Zionists would have had no attachment to this territory were it not for those long-standing religious associations.

Another Jewish conception highly influential on secular Zionist thinking
and closely connected to the notion of the land of Israel as the Jewish homeland
was the idea of messianic redemption. There has been much debate about the
precise role that messianism played in early secular Zionism. Ben Zion Dinur
and Joseph Klausner, two early historians of Zionism, believed that the early
secular Zionists were in fact messianists. Their program of reestablishing Jewish sovereignty in the land of Israel was a direct continuation of the messianic
idea, which had been a central doctrine in Judaism for centuries. Jacob Katz
also believed that a principal factor inspiring secular Zionism was Jewish messianism, though he was more reserved in his conclusions than Dinur and
Klausner. According to Katz, many factors played a role in this movement, but
it was guided by an irrational element that could be explained only by an attachment to the old religious doctrine of messianism. This surmise was borne out
by the fact that Zionists were not interested merely in statehood and independence; they wanted these in the location of the ancient homeland. In addition,
there was a utopian element in secular Zionism that seemed to emanate from

56 Shapira, *Land and Power*, 41; Avalos, *Fighting Words*, 130–37.

traditional messianism. Secular Zionists believed that Zionism would solve all the Jews' problems. It would heal them of the unhealthy mental pathologies that had been fostered by the experience of exile, and it would awaken their latent powers.

More recent historians have also explored the connection between secular Zionism and traditional messianism. Yosef Salmon believes that messianism was the element of traditional Judaism that secular Zionists were most eager to preserve, and that in some respects they were more interested in messianism than religious Zionists. Ehud Luz and Anita Shapira agree that secular Zionism was indeed inspired by classical Jewish messianism in embracing the Jewish longing for redemption. However, both Luz and Shapira note that secular Zionism rebelled against messianism in believing that redemption would come through human initiative, not divine will and miracles. Stephen Sharot is even more circumspect about the connection between Zionism and traditional messianism. He claims that secular Zionism did not draw inspiration from traditional messianism at all but that it appealed to many secular Jews because it suggested a secular notion of messianism that resonated with traditional Judaism, to which many of them still had some attachment. Nonetheless, while these more recent commentators see a more muted role for traditional messianism in secular Zionism than the earlier historians did, none of them deny that it played a role in this movement.[57]

Some historians have argued that in general what motivated secular Zionism was a fervor that could be explained only by the influence of religion. According to Shapira, early Labor Zionism was energized by an all-consuming "faith" and a "love of self-sacrifice" that molded its everyday actions, the relationship between individuals, and the relationship between individuals and society. Labor Zionism therefore has to be classified as a religious movement: "its inner character was religious and it parallels the millenarian sects in Christianity and the mystical movements that had accompanied normative Judaism."[58]

---

57 Eli Lederhendler, "Messianic Rhetoric in the Russian Haskalah and Early Zionism," in *Studies in Contemporary Jewry VII: Jews and Messianism in the Modern Era: Metaphor and Meaning*, ed. Jonathan Frankel (New York: Oxford University Press, 1991), 16–17; Shapira, *Land and Power*, 254–45; Luz, *Wrestling with an Angel*, chapter 6; Salmon, chapter 13. Katz's position is conveniently summarized in his essay "Israel and the Messiah," in *Essential Papers on Messianic Movements and Personalities in Jewish History*," ed. Marc Saperstein (New York: New York University Press, 1992), 475–91. Luz claims that David Ben Gurion was motivated by messianic aspirations more than any other secular Zionist. See Luz, *Wrestling with an Angel*, 81. Luz's observation, if correct, is significant, given the enormous role that Ben Gurion played in shaping the agenda of secular Zionism both before and after the founding of the state.

58 Anita Shapira, "The Religious Motifs of the Labor Movement," in *Zionism and Religion*, ed. Shmuel Almog, Jehuda Reinharz, and Anita Shapira (Hanover, N.H.: University of New England Press, 1998), 254–55.

Luz pursues a similar line of thinking in focusing on the concept of the "wager," which he believes was key to the ethos of early Zionism. This term referred to "the resolve to ensure the survival of the Jewish people in an apparently hopeless situation." Many Jews became Zionists out of fear that there was no future for them in Europe and that Jews were in danger of dying out completely. This fear was fostered not just by anti-Semitism but also by assimilation, especially in Western Europe. It seemed that Jews had no place in Europe except by losing their Jewish identity. The only hope, therefore, was to build a Jewish homeland in Palestine. Yet, the Zionists also recognized that their chances of success were not great. Among the Zionist settlers, the sense of desperation only grew in the 1930s and 1940s, when Arab nationalism and violence had become a threat, the 1939 British White Paper had been issued restricting Jewish immigration to Palestine, and the Nazi persecution of European Jews was under way. Some Zionist thinkers spoke in almost apocalyptic terms of an impending catastrophe or of facing an abyss. Therefore, many Zionists saw Zionism as a wager, a wild shot in the dark that had to be tried because there was no other choice. Most important for our purposes is that according to Luz, this idea was rooted in traditional notions of Jewish faith that for centuries had bolstered Jewish spirits in the face of persecution.

Luz also argues that Zionist thinkers who adopted the notion of the wager tended to equate Zionism with messianic redemption, a connection we have already noted. He also demonstrates the importance of the biblical image of the "remnant of Israel" to this group of thinkers. In the biblical text, this idea originally referred to the remnant of the Jewish people that would usher in the messianic era after the widespread destruction that would result from God's judgment at the end of days. For the Zionists, this idea was used to refer to the small band of Zionists that they believed would rebuild the Jewish people in Palestine while most of the masses in the Diaspora would be lost.[59]

In another discussion, Luz analyzes how the "faith" of secular Zionist thinkers expressed itself in their use of the notion of miracles. Secular Zionists rejected miracles as they were understood by traditional Judaism; they did not believe in a God who could intervene in the natural order and in human history, and many of them did not believe in a God of any kind. Still, they spoke of "human" miracles in that they saw themselves as working against all odds to establish a Jewish state. Here too, Luz claims, their thinking reflected a connection to traditional Judaism.[60]

---

59 Luz, *Wrestling with an Angel*, chapter 4.

60 Luz, *Wrestling with an Angel*, 104–8. Apparently, Hayyim Nahman Bialik, the great Hebrew poet, also appreciated the religious element in secular Zionism. He claimed that the readiness of Zionists for self-sacrifice was on the "borderline of religiosity" (cited in Luz, *Wrestling with an Angel*, 79).

Any number of other ideas in secular Zionism can be traced to Judaism. The biblical prophets were seen by the socialist Labor Zionists as the source of the notions of social justice and universal human redemption that should guide the Zionist movement. Some of the leaders of the Labor Zionists, such as Meir Yaari and Yitzhak Tabenkin, were often compared by their followers to Hasidic rabbis. Labor Zionism also appropriated Jewish religious practices. Traditional rites of passage, such as circumcision, marriage, and burial, were coopted, though sometimes in modified form. The Sabbath was the day of rest. Jewish holidays were celebrated, though they were infused with new meaning and innovations in ritual.[61]

The Bible served as the key source of inspiration for many of the ideas and practices we have discussed. The attachment of the secular Zionists to the Bible was, in fact, as strong as that found among religious Jews. They pored over it, studied it, memorized it, and interpreted it. The Bible was therefore central to the educational system established by secular Zionists in Palestine in the 1920s and 1930s. It was used to foster love of the homeland and to justify the Jewish claim on it. It was a resource for teaching young people about its geography, flora, fauna, and physical features. It was a textbook for national history, and it was used to inculcate admiration for Jewish heroes of the past. As we have just noted, it was also a source for ethics, with the biblical prophets serving as models.[62]

As evidence of the influence of Judaism on secular Zionism, historians often cite the way in which the secular Zionists used religious language in referring to their ideas and institutions. Thus, for example, the buying of land in Palestine was referred to by the traditional phrase *ge'ulat ha-arets*, "the redemption of the land." The Jewish National Fund was called Keren Kayemet, "the everlasting principal," a play on a rabbinic source.[63]

The work of Anthony Smith strengthens the case for a connection between Zionism and Judaism by placing the foregoing observations in a wider context. Scholars of modern European nationalism have often contended that nationalism functioned as a replacement for religion. Smith argues against

---

61 Shapira, "The Religious Motifs of the Labor Movement," 258, 263–70; Shlomo Avineri, "Zionism and Jewish Religious Tradition: The Dialectics of Redemption and Secularization," in *Zionism and Religion*, ed. Shmuel Almog, Jehuda Reinharz, and Anita Shapira (Hanover, N.H.: University of New England Press, 1998), 5–6.

62 Shapira, *Land and Power*, 258–59; idem, "The Religious Motifs of the Labor Movement," 260–62; Avineri, "Zionism and Jewish Religious Tradition," 5–6.

63 M. *Pe'ah* 1:1; Shapira, "The Religious Motifs of the Labor Movement," 255–58; Avineri, "Zionism and Jewish Religious Tradition," 5–6; Ravitzky, *Messianism, Zionism, and Jewish Religious Radicalism*, 3–4; Charles S. Liebman and Eliezer Don-Yehiya, *Traditional Judaism and Political Culture in the Jewish State* (Berkeley: University of California Press, 1983), 38–40.

this approach and claims that, in fact, European nationalists often absorbed religious motifs, especially from the Bible, and used them to make the case for their cause. Thus, nationalists in various countries throughout Europe adopted biblical concepts such as chosenness, covenant, and messianic redemption to describe their mission but gave them a nationalist meaning. Smith claims that Zionism provides an excellent example of this phenomenon in its transformation of these terms for nationalist purposes.[64]

What emerges here is that secular Zionism was shaped by many of the same religious motifs that were at the core of religious Zionism. Therefore, it should not surprise us that secular Zionists would develop a hostile attitude toward Palestinians, just as their religious counterparts did. Like religious Zionism, secular Zionism was inspired by the notion that the land of Israel was the Jewish homeland and by the concept of messianic redemption, and its followers were imbued with a fervor to implement their goals that was akin to religious faith. Indeed, this form of Zionism transformed these traditional motifs in accordance with its secular orientation. Nonetheless, the emotive power of these motifs carried over into secular Zionism and became components of a framework of thinking that assumed Jews were the rightful owners of the land and that their reclaiming of it was Jewish destiny. Thus, the ideas in traditional Judaism that had violent potential were highly incendiary in secular Zionism as well. Therefore, a clash between secular Zionists and Palestine's Arab inhabitants was as inevitable as it was with religious Zionists.

Our discussion of the relationship of secular Zionism to Judaism has focused primarily on mainstream socialist Labor Zionism. It is also worth taking a brief look at right-wing secular Zionism, because here too a case can be made that the violent tendencies in secular Zionism had roots in Judaism. Micha Yosef Berdichevsky was one of the forefathers of right-wing Zionism, and at the center of his thinking was a strongly militaristic ethos inspired in part by Jewish sources. Berdichevsky had great admiration for the Bible, which he believed clearly supported such an ethos. The Bible was steeped in bloodshed, violent struggle, and slaughter, such as Joshua's brutal conquest of the

---

64 Anthony D. Smith, *Chosen Peoples* (New York: Oxford University Press, 2003), 85–94. Avineri mostly agrees with Smith's approach. He argues that in Zionism there is a dialectical relationship between religion and nationalism because nationalism always involves reinterpretation of the past and its retrieval. Since religion is often an element in a nation's past, religion frequently plays a role in nationalism. Zionism is therefore only one example of a wider phenomenon. See Avineri, "Zionism and Jewish Religious Tradition." Jacob Talmon goes even further by arguing that modern European nationalism had Jewish roots because it was influenced by the Bible, which envisioned the Israelites as an independent people living in their homeland. Therefore, when modern Zionism was created, it may have been influenced by European nationalism, but the latter was, in turn, inspired by Judaism. Therefore, nationalism appealed to Jews because nationalism had Jewish origins to begin with. See Luz, *Wrestling with an Angel*, 12–13, for a discussion of Talmon's views.

Canaanites and David's doing away with Saul's house. The Bible also consistently placed national interests above morality. For Berdichevsky, there was nothing wrong with this ethos. It described the normal and healthy functioning of a nation and should therefore serve as a model for modern Zionism. Berdichevsky vilified rabbinic Judaism, which he believed had replaced the Bible's militarism with an ethos that was weak and cowardly and that held Jews hostage for centuries. It was the rabbis who surrendered to Rome and constructed a theology of passivity and acquiescence when it came to dealing with the humiliation of the exile.[65]

Jabotinsky, however, was the one who organized the right-wing Zionists into a political party, and therefore his views on religion are key. At first Jabotinsky was hostile to religion, but he gradually grew to appreciate its value. Revisionism placed a great deal of emphasis on Jewish particularism and the uniqueness of the Jewish nation, and Jewish sources provided ample support for these ideas. Jabotinsky, therefore, came to believe in a close relationship between religion and state, and he wanted religion to have a significant role in public life in the future Jewish state.[66]

But as we have seen, Jabotinsky's views were in many respects more moderate than those of his followers, and we find much better examples of thinkers who glorified violence and made use of Jewish sources to support their viewpoint when we look at other right-wing Zionist figures in the Revisionist party. Primary in this regard was Uri Tsevi Greenberg, whom we have already mentioned. Greenberg was an influential poet supported by a small but important faction in the Revisionist party. His ideas were especially significant for Lehi, the extremist guerilla group that operated in Palestine in the decade before the establishment of the state of Israel. Greenberg's Zionism was permeated by an emphasis on the need for Jews to use violence and cultivate cruelty toward their enemies in their fight for a Jewish state. In this way, Jews would avenge the humiliation they had experienced during centuries of exile. Greenberg therefore expressed nothing but scorn for Arabs and did not believe a compromise with them was possible. Most important for our purposes is that Greenberg made use of Jewish sources, particularly the Bible, to support his views. Thus, like Berdichevsky, he invoked Joshua's conquest of the Canaanites as a model for Jewish action against Arabs. He also claimed that revenge was a legitimate Jewish response to violence perpetrated by others against Jews, as evidenced by the commandment to annihilate the Amalekites after they had attacked the

---

65 Mikha Yosef Berdichevsky, *Nemushot* (Warsaw: Tse'irim, 1899), 82; idem, *Mi-Yamin u-mi-Semol* (Breslau: Tse'irim, 1909), 27–23; Shapira, *Land and Power*, 21–23; Luz, *Wrestling with an Angel*, 54–55.

66 Liebman and Don-Yehiya, chapter 3.

Israelites and by the slaughter of the Shechemites by Simeon and Levi after the rape of Dinah. According to Greenberg, Jews who opposed violence were captive to an exilic mentality that distorted true Jewish values.[67]

Up to this point, we have looked at the attitude of secular Zionists toward religion, both on the Right and on the Left, before the establishment of the Jewish state. There is ample evidence that much of what we have said also holds true after the state comes into existence. In a well-known study, Charles Liebman and Eliezer Don-Yehiya trace the complex relationship between Zionism and religion from the period of early Zionism up to the 1980s, when their study was published. Their work is more sociological in its orientation than our analysis has been. Nonetheless, there is a good deal of overlap between the issues dealt with in their study and those we are examining. With regard to early Zionism, Liebman and Don-Yehiya confirm what we have already shown: religion was an important factor in shaping Zionism before the creation of the state. Indeed, religious ideas and practices were often transformed, used selectively, or rejected completely in this process, and Liebman and Don-Yehiya give a deft analysis of how this occurred. Nonetheless, early Zionist figures grappled with the meaning of these ideas and practices and often coopted them into their thinking. The same process continued after 1948 as Israel's political figures and leading intellectuals sought to formulate a Zionist ideology and way of life that would appeal to the citizens of the new state and galvanize their energy to build it. Views on the relationship between Zionism and religion fluctuated considerably over the next several decades, and in any given period multiple opinions were expressed on this question. Still, there was a constant need to come to terms with the role of religion in Israeli life.[68]

In light of these observations, it is perhaps no surprise that many secular Israelis since the establishment of the state have affiliated with the right wing and supported territorial maximalism. Ehud Sprinzak describes the phenomenon of "secular neofundamentalists," who in the 1980s supported Gush Emunim and such political parties as Tehiya because of a strong belief in the Jewish aspiration to return to the borders of the land of Israel as demarcated in the

---

67 Luz, *Wrestling with an Angel*, 182–84, 203; Shapira, *Land and Power*, 143–53. Another right-wing secular Zionist with similar views who is worth mentioning is Yisrael Eldad. Eldad justified violence against Palestinians and Arabs by arguing that Judaism cultivates revenge, hatred, and intolerance toward foreigners in the land of Israel. Eldad is discussed in Luz, *Wrestling with an Angel*, 184–87, 211.

68 See n. 52. The findings of Liebman and Don-Yehiya's study have been updated in Charles S. Liebman and Elihu Katz, eds., *The Jewishness of Israelis: The Guttman Report* (Albany: State University of New York Press, 1997); Shlomit Levy, Hanna Levinsohn, and Elihu Katz, "The Many Faces of Jewishness in Israel," in *Jews in Israel: Contemporary Social and Cultural Factors*, ed. Uzi Rebhun and Chaim I. Waxman (Hanover, N.H.: University of New England Press, 2004), 265–84. See also Luz, *Wrestling with an Angel*, ix; Penslar, 70–74.

Bible. This group was not small in number. In fact, Sprinzak notes that the vast majority of right-wing Israelis in the 1980s were secular.[69] It is also important to mention that the settling of the territories captured by Israel in the 1967 war could not have succeeded without the help of secular Israelis. Many of them admired Gush Emunim for continuing the spirit of the early Zionist pioneers and therefore supported their enterprise. Moreover, successive Israeli governments, both on the Right and on the Left, assisted in the building of settlements in the territories captured in 1967.[70] But what is most important for our purposes is that secular right-wing Israelis could not have formulated their views, nor would their passion for those views have been sustained, without Judaism, which attached great significance to the land of Israel as the Jewish homeland. Certainly, one should not attribute the views of secular right-wing Israelis to the influence of religion alone. Some supported the settlements, for instance, for reasons of security. Nonetheless, Jewish ideas were critical for their whole framework of thinking.[71]

Our insights about secular Zionism and its violent tendencies help provide a valuable corrective to the scholarship that has been done recently on religion and violence. Scholarship on this subject has often discussed Zionism, but the focus is almost always on religious Zionism, not secular Zionism. Thus, such scholarship often deals with R. Tsevi Yehudah Kook, Gush Emunim, Meir

---

69 Sprinzak, *The Ascendance of Israel's Radical Right*, 18. Sprinzak often refers to the secular radical right as "neo-religious." See, for instance, p. 300.

70 This whole matter is dealt with in Gershom Gorenberg, *The Accidental Empire: Israel and the Birth of the Settlements, 1967–1977* (New York: Times Books, 2006), and in Zertal and Eldar, *Lords of the Land.*

71 Don-Yehiya notes that when it comes to the issue of the Temple Mount, secular Israelis have sometimes been more radical than religious Zionists. See Don-Yehiya, "The Book and the Sword," 215. A fascinating example of a secular Israeli who supported territorial maximalism was Eliezer Livneh, who became a leading spokesman for the Land of Israel Movement in the early 1970s. The movement was united by certain principles: Israel's need for secure borders, the nonexistence of the Palestinian nation, and the insignificance of the demographic time bomb. However, initially the movement did not have a sophisticated philosophy. That was provided by Livneh, a former Knesset member in the Labor party and a journalist. In 1972 he published *Israel and the Crisis of Western Civilization* in which he argued that after the 1967 war, a whole new philosophy of Zionism was needed because it was now clear that Israel represented a new "Judeo-Israeli" civilization that was on the rise. He criticized mainstream socialist Zionism because it had been atheistic and therefore detached from the spirituality of the Jewish heritage. The new Zionism had to combine the secular and the religious. Livneh's belief was that the 1967 war had brought religious and secular Israelis together and shown that the two had overcome their differences. Livneh believed that they would now be united by a common spirituality based on the Jewish heritage. Moreover, he argued that Israel was the only hope for the future of Jews throughout the world because the West was in hopeless decline from a moral standpoint, and Diaspora Judaism therefore could not survive. The newly conquered territories also figured into Livneh's thinking. The new spiritual Zionism could thrive now that Israel ruled over more of its ancient homeland. For Livneh, the land of Israel had a mystique, and at times he cites the elder Kook in support of his thinking on this issue. Livneh's views illustrate that secular Zionism was at times quasi-religious. His opinion on the decay of the West also shares much with the views of modern religious fundamentalists throughout the world. For a discussion of Livneh's views, see Sprinzak, *The Ascendance of the Radical Right*, 56–61.

Kahane, and their followers, but not with the secular Jews in Israel. The assumption seems to be that only religious Zionists are "religious" in the normal sense of the term, and therefore only they should be examined in analyses devoted to religion and violence.[72] Yet, as we have seen, the issue is much more complicated than this. Secular Zionists, though not technically "religious," have often been violent, and their actions have been inspired in part by the same religious concepts that have motivated religious Zionists to be violent. The fact that this scholarship does not engage secular Zionism as a quasi-religious phenomenon may reflect a Western Christian bias. Western scholars tend to view religion as synonymous with beliefs and practices because these define Christianity. However, in Judaism, religion has always been inextricably tied up with ethnic and national identity, and this sets up the possibility that a Jew can identify passionately with these aspects of the Jewish experience without being devoted to Judaism's religious beliefs and practices. Secular Zionism is an excellent example of this phenomenon.

That scholars of religion and violence have missed something here is also evident from the fact that secular Zionism has some of the characteristics that are often attributed to modern religious fundamentalism. As we noted earlier, a common element uniting religious fundamentalists in various religious communities around the world is the feeling of being overwhelmed by destructive forces from without and of having no choice but to act violently against them. Such groups generally have a sharply dualistic view of the world, in which they represent all that is good, the outside world represents all that is evil, and a violent struggle between the two sides is part of a larger cosmic battle. An attitude very much akin to this way of thinking can be found among secular Zionists. For instance, Anita Shapira informs us that in the 1930s, secular Zionists saw the fight between Jews and Arabs in Palestine as a war between socialism, represented by Labor Zionism, and fascism, represented by the Palestinians, whose leaders—most notably the Grand Mufti—had allied themselves with the Nazis. As Shapira describes it, the fight, according to this way of thinking, was between the "forces of light and darkness," and between "good and evil." Thus, as in the case of religious fundamentalism, we see here a dualism in which the forces of good and evil are locked in combat, and human beings on the side of good must wage war against those allied with evil. Ehud Sprinzak provides a similar description of the mentality of the radical right in Israeli politics in the 1980s, the majority of whom were in the secular camp. He claims that the ideology of this group tended to be defined by paranoia and fear of conspiracy

---

72 See, for example, Juergensmeyer, chapter 3; Appleby, 81–85.

from any number of sources—including the Israeli Left, the Israeli media, the Arabs, and the U.S. government. There was therefore no room for political opposition because all such opposition was by definition part of the conspiracy. Sprinzak characterizes this dualistic thinking in terms strikingly similar to those used by Shapira. The radical Right, Sprinzak tells us, tended to divide the world into two groups, the "sons of light" and the "sons of darkness."[73] Of course, the juxtaposition in these instances of good and evil or light and darkness does not imply the same metaphysical underpinnings as those found in religious Zionism. The common thought pattern, however, is still striking.

The main points that emerge from our first reading of Zionism is that both religious Zionism and secular Zionism have exhibited violent tendencies throughout their history, and those tendencies can be traced to concepts and practices in Judaism that were explored in earlier chapters. The influence that Jewish sources have had on secular Zionism is more complex than in the case of religious Zionism, given that secular Zionism in many respects rebelled against Judaism. However, what is remarkable is the extent to which Jewish sources still had an impact on secular Zionists and encouraged aggression against Palestinians and Arabs.

Judaism and Zionism: A Defense

Let us now switch gears and provide a defense of Zionism. In this second reading, we will argue that Zionism has not been as violent as the first reading has claimed. Moreover, the second reading will challenge the arguments in the first that when Zionism has been violent, religion has been a central cause. The violent tendencies in Zionism have been inspired by a number of factors, and religion is by no means the most important one. Moreover, in many instances

---

73 Shapira, *Land and Power*, 231; Sprinzak, *The Ascendance of Israel's Radical Right*, 19–20. An interesting issue to explore is to what extent the ethnonational understanding of Judaism that one sees in secular Zionism is a throwback to ancient Israel and Israel in antiquity. Up to the second or third century BCE, Israelite and Jewish identity had a strong ethnonational focus, and only after that point in time do we begin to see the beginnings of Judaism as a religion separate from national and ethnic identity. (See Shaye J. D. Cohen, *The Beginnings of Jewishness: Boundaries, Varieties, Uncertainties* [Berkeley: University of California Press, 1999]). In effect, secular Zionists, particularly those on the right wing, argued for a new Jewish identity that had similarities with ethnonational Jewish identity before the second century BCE. It was in part for this reason that they revered the Bible as much as they did. It should also be pointed out that even in later rabbinic Judaism, the ethnonationalist element never disappeared. Classical Halakhah defined a Jew as one born of a Jewish mother. Thus, genealogy determined who was a Jew, not an adherence to religious beliefs and practices. Nowadays, the separation between Jewish identity and religion is much sharper and more widespread. Many Jews both in Israel and in the Diaspora regard themselves as Jews even though they are completely secular.

in which religion has, in fact, influenced Zionism, it has often promoted peaceful and benevolent behavior.

We will begin by arguing that there were factors more important than religion that inspired violent tendencies in Zionism. As has been noted on more than one occasion in this chapter, a major cause of the rise of Zionism in the late nineteenth century was European nationalism, and nationalism by its very nature is prone to develop into xenophobia and to motivate violence toward outside groups. One also has to keep in mind that the world prior to 1914 was Eurocentric. This was the age of imperialism, in which European interests took precedence over those of native populations, and therefore it should not surprise us that the first Zionists believed that their claim to Palestine was as strong as or even superior to that of the Arab population living there. In fact, Herzl was more generous than many Europeans when he formulated a plan in *The Jewish State* according to which Jews would establish a national homeland by buying land from the natives at good prices.[74] Thus, we should not put too much emphasis on religion as the source of Zionism's violent tendencies. Those tendencies are perhaps better explained by the fact that the Zionists absorbed nationalistic and imperialistic thinking from their European environment.

We must also keep in mind that the chief reason Jews gravitated to nationalism was the rise of modern European anti-Semitism. As we have already seen, anti-Semitism reared its ugly head in Western and Eastern Europe and in Russia in the last two decades of the nineteenth century. By the 1920s, the violence had claimed tens of thousands of Jewish lives. Thus, if Jewish nationalism exhibited aggressive tendencies, it is understandable; it was spawned by the outrage Jews felt over their treatment by non-Jews.

One also has to be aware that the anger Jews felt over modern anti-Semitism was due to more than the immediate violence perpetrated against them. Jews had experienced persecution for centuries in Christian Europe for having rejected Christianity and for having been held responsible for the death of Jesus. With the advent of the Enlightenment in the late eighteenth century and the gradual emancipation of Jews in the early and middle part of the nineteenth, Jews had reason to hope that anti-Jewish hatred was a thing of the past and that they would finally be accepted as Europeans. Their initial economic, political, and social success seemed to indicate that they were indeed moving in that direction. To their dismay, they discovered that this

---

74 Shapira, *Land and Power*, 16–17. Herzl did not specifically mention Arabs here because he was not certain at this point whether the Jewish homeland would be in Palestine or elsewhere.

was not the case. The outbreak of anti-Semitism in the late nineteenth century came as a rude awakening and demonstrated that Jews were still considered alien to European society and could be victims of persecution and
violence. Moreover, this anti-Semitism was not religiously motivated, at least
not in its outward form. It was a new kind of anti-Semitism based on race
and culture. Jewish outrage over the outbreak of modern anti-Semitism was
therefore compounded by a profound sense of disillusionment with European society and by dashed hopes that had been nurtured for the better part of
a century.

We must also appreciate the fact that threats to the Jewish people now had
an extensive history that went well beyond the experiences of Jews in Europe.
Jews had to deal with such threats from the biblical period onward. Much of the
history of Jews in the biblical and rabbinic periods was defined by centuries of
confrontations with a long succession of empires—the Assyrians, Babylonians,
Persians, Greeks, and Romans—bent on either dominating or destroying
them. After the destruction of the second Temple in the first century, Jews went
into exile and lived under Christian and Muslim rulers who were often hostile
to them. Thus, when modern anti-Semitism came along, it only irritated
wounds that had been festering in the collective psyche of the Jewish people for
centuries.

Of relevance here are Ehud Luz's observations regarding the notion of "the
wager", which informed the thinking of many Zionists. As explained earlier,
many Jews became Zionists out of a sense of complete desperation that Zionism was the only hope for the Jewish people. For these Jews, Zionism was not
just an attractive option among others; it was the *only* option for a dying people
that was either going to assimilate entirely into European society or be wiped
out. Moreover, the Zionists believed that their chance of successfully establishing a Jewish state was not very great and that the demise of the Jewish people
was a real possibility. Hence, the notion that Zionism was a wager, a wild shot
in the dark, with the hope that a miracle might save the Jewish people. The
concept of the wager reflects the deep sense of crisis many Jews felt as they
faced the new anti-Semitism.

What all this adds up to is that the aggressive tendencies of nationalism
and Eurocentrism were made worse in Zionism by a host of factors: the experience of anti-Semitism in Europe, the centuries-long history of persecution
that Jews had already endured, and a feeling of impending crisis about the
survival of the Jewish nation as a whole. Moreover, what was at stake here for
the Zionists was not just the establishment of a Jewish state to provide physical
security for Jews; Zionists felt the need to restore Jewish dignity and pride and
to counter hundreds of years of humiliation at the hands of their enemies.

These feelings would only exacerbate the tendencies toward violence spawned by the feelings of physical insecurity that Jews felt.[75]

Against this background, Zionists were prone to hostility toward Palestinians. They were merely transferring to their new neighbors the antipathy they felt toward non-Jews, which had already had a long history. Shapira demonstrates that Zionists of the second and third aliyah, for instance, tended to view Arab hatred toward Jews through the lens of Jewish-gentile relations in Europe.[76] Jews believed that this hatred was simply one more manifestation of the eternal hatred gentiles had always had for Jews. In Europe such hatred had been irrational and intractable, and Arab hatred was no different.[77] Conceivably, all these sentiments regarding Arabs may have not emerged in Zionism had there not been a tense relationship between the Zionist settlers and the Palestinians that worsened over time. However, friction between the two populations was inevitable given the chasm that separated them on so many levels.

The tendency of the Zionists to conflate the Arabs with their enemies in Europe became even stronger in the wake of the Palestinian rebellion that began in 1936. Labor Zionists argued that the violence was inspired by the fact that Palestinians were allied with European fascism, which had become popular in Germany, Italy, Austria, and Poland. The fight against the Palestinians was therefore part of a worldwide struggle. On the one side were fascists in Germany, Italy, and the Arab world who believed that might was right and plundered the weak, and on the other side were socialists and Jews who were fighting for the good of humanity, freedom, and equality. While this grandiose theory was fanciful in most respects, some Palestinian leaders did, in fact, forge ties with the Nazis and with Italian fascists because the latter groups opposed the imperial Western powers that had hegemony in the Middle East. Haj al-Amin al-Husseini, the Grand Mufti of Jerusalem, had a close relationship with the Nazis and in the late 1930s fled to Berlin, where he became the guest of the Nazi regime. He and his clan were instrumental in stoking hatred of Jews among Palestinians up until the 1948 war. In the 1930s, Palestinians began displaying portraits of Hitler in their shops, and swastikas were hung in the streets of their towns. The Nazi threat against the Jews of Palestine took a more concrete form when in 1941 Rommel's armies began conquering the western Egyptian desert. The Zionists feared that the Germans

---

75 Shapira, *Land and Power*, 11–14; Luz, *Wrestling with an Angel*, chapter 3.

76 The second and third aliyahs refer to waves of Jewish immigration to Palestine that occurred in 1904–14 and 1919–23 respectively. Both waves consisted primarily of Jews from Russia and Eastern Europe.

77 Shapira, *Land and Power*, 66, 68–70, 111–14, 176–77.

would overrun Palestine with the help of the Arabs and that the Jews would be annihilated.[78]

All of this brings us to the Holocaust, in which six million Jews were slaughtered. A great deal has been written on Zionist attitudes toward the Holocaust, and we cannot delve into that material here. What is important for our purposes is the general observation that the Holocaust brought a new sense of urgency to the Zionist enterprise and made the Zionists less sympathetic to the Palestinian cause.[79]

It can therefore be argued that religion is by no means the only source for the aggressive elements in Zionism, secular or religious, and perhaps not the most important one. We have to consider the influence of European nationalism and Eurocentrism on Jews along with the wounds that anti-Semitism had inflicted on them both physically and psychologically.

Our observations here should also encourage us to view Zionist hostility toward Palestinians in a sympathetic light. When one considers the centuries of persecution that Jews had endured, the rise of a new and virulent anti-Semitism in Europe despite every effort by Jews to become good Europeans, the alliance between powerful elements in the Palestinian leadership and the Nazis, and finally the Holocaust, it is not surprising that the Zionists would identify the Palestinians as representative of a hostile non-Jewish world. It is not that this identification was accurate. In fact, it was not; Palestinian anti-Zionism and European anti-Semitism were not one and the same thing, and neither of these was part of an overarching and ongoing anti-Jewish conspiracy. Yet, whether the fears of the Zionists reflected the reality is beside the point. We can certainly understand why the Zionists felt the way they did, given the traumas Jews in general had suffered at the hands of non-Jews for so many centuries. Like a child long abused by his or her superiors, Jews were lashing out at every threat around them. Nor is it being argued here that every act of the Zionists should be forgiven. As we noted earlier, most scholars today acknowledge the groundbreaking work of Benny Morris and others demonstrating that injustices were perpetrated against Palestinians. We are simply claiming that if Zionism fostered aggression against Palestinians, that aggression has an explanation that should elicit a degree of understanding often sorely missing among the critics of Zionism.

Our discussion of the role anti-Semitism played in shaping Zionism has been focused primarily on the period prior to the founding of the Jewish state.

---

78 Shapira, *Land and Power*, 230–34, 277.
79 Shapira, *Land and Power*, 319–42.

However, much of what we have said carries over into the period afterward. As several writers have noted, the establishment of the state of Israel did not solve the problem of Jewish insecurities in either the physical or the psychological realm. In fact, it may have made them worse. As early as the period of the second aliyah, during the second decade of the twentieth century, there was a realization among Zionists that they had exchanged an insecure situation in Europe for one in Palestine. That feeling would only grow over the next several decades as Zionists had to come to terms with the fact that they were surrounded by hundreds of millions of Arabs whose leaders were sworn to their destruction. While Israel emerged victorious from the 1948 war, that outcome brought little relief to the feelings of vulnerability that Israelis felt because the situation of the Jewish state remained precarious. The same goes for subsequent wars. The elation brought about by Israel's stunning victory in 1967 was tempered a few short years later by the Yom Kippur War in 1973, when Israel achieved at best a partial victory. Ehud Luz notes that Israelis still feel like survivors in their own country.[80]

At the time of this writing, Israel continues to feel its vulnerability. Its northern border is threatened by Hezbollah, which is bent on its destruction. The president of Iran, Mahmoud Ahmadinejad, has stated publicly that Israel "should be wiped off the map" as Iran develops nuclear weapons that could strike Israel. Hamas, a militant Palestinian organization devoted to Israel's destruction, is in control of Gaza and has made significant inroads in Palestinian communities in the West Bank.

What makes it difficult for non-Jews to relate to Israel's sense of vulnerability is how strong the Jewish state appears. It has a modern army that is one of the largest, best trained, and best equipped in the world. Its citizens enjoy a standard of living that rivals that of European countries. Moreover, it receives support from the United States and from highly successful Jewish communities throughout the world. The U.S. Jewish community has been particularly influential in shaping the policies of the United States toward Israel, and it has been aided by the powerful Christian evangelical community. It is, therefore, hard to conceive of Israelis and Jews in general as victims. Yet, they are. Beneath the façade of strength, Jews both in Israel and in the Diaspora communities still carry with them, consciously or unconsciously, the collective memory of hundreds of years

---

80 Shapira, *Land and Power,* 79, 369–70; Luz, *Wrestling with an Angel,* 88–90. Yet, elsewhere Luz criticizes religious Zionist rabbis in Israel who express fear of non-Jews because, according to Luz, this way of thinking is reminiscent of the attitude of Eastern European Jews before the establishment of the state of Israel. These rabbis fail to see that Jews now have power and are not dependent on non-Jews. See Luz, "The Jewish Religion," 264–65.

of persecution, and most recently the Holocaust. Therefore, Jews feel anything but secure.

These observations provide yet one more argument against the judgments of Israeli revisionist historians and post-Zionists. These thinkers virtually ignore historical context in judging the actions of the Zionists. They show little or no sympathy with the fact that Jews who settled Palestine were running away from virulent European anti-Semitism, which allowed no real place for them in European society, and that they were therefore desperate in their quest to build a homeland that would provide a safe haven for them.

Let us now delve more deeply into the issues raised here by looking more carefully at religious and secular Zionism in turn. In our first reading, we assumed that the aggressive tendencies of religious Zionism came from Judaism, but a closer look at this form of Zionism will reveal that its aggression may have also been inspired by forces outside Judaism, and those forces, in many instances, seem to have distorted Jewish teachings. In their recent work on religious Zionism, both Dov Schwartz and Avi Sagi have argued that religious Zionism is largely the product of modernity. Chief among the modern forces shaping religious Zionism in its early years was nationalism, which, we have already noted, was a basic element in all forms of modern Zionism. Religious Zionists also coopted into their thinking the modern notion that human initiative and activism shaped history. Thus, in Kookian Zionism, messianic redemption would come only if Jews actively sought to establish a Jewish state. These observations partly explain why religious Zionists had difficulty getting the support of the Orthodox community when the Zionist movement began to take shape. The wedding of religion and nationalism was considered revolutionary by Orthodox Jews. The same goes for the notion that messianic redemption depended largely on human action.[81] While messianism was a central principle of faith in Judaism, it was much harder to justify the notion of a return to the land of Israel as a central tenet of Judaism in its own right before the advent of the messiah.[82]

Some of the key ideas of the younger Kook also provide excellent examples of how nationalism distorted traditional Jewish teaching. Take, for instance, his

---

81 Dov Schwartz, *Religious Zionism between Logic and Messianism* (in Hebrew) (Tel Aviv: Am Oved, 1999), chapter 1; idem, *Faith at the Crossroads: A Theological Profile of Religious Zionism*, trans. Batya Stein (Leiden: E. J. Brill, 2002), 137–40; Avi Sagi, "From the Torah State to the Land of Israel—From a Broken Dream to Another Dream: A Study in the Crisis of Religious Zionism" (in Hebrew), in *Me'ah Shanot Tsiyyonut Datit: Heibetim Ra'ayoniyyim*, ed. Avi Sagi and Dov Schwartz (Ramat Gan: Bar-Ilan University Press, 2004), 3:457–73. Not all religious Zionists were as focused on redemption as followers of Kook were, most notably R. Reines. Schwartz argues, however, that when read carefully, even Reines's writings were focused a great deal on messianic redemption. See Schwartz, *Religious Zionism*, chapter 3.

82 Luz, "The Jewish Religion," 255–56; Schwartz, *Faith at the Crossroads*, 139–40.

notion that the settlement of the land of Israel was as fundamental to Judaism as the three cardinal commandments, which Jews must not violate even on pain of death. Kook was rendering a decision on an extremely weighty issue in Jewish law with little authority or precedent to support him.[83] The younger Kook's use of Kabbalistic metaphysics to justify the use of military force to bring the messianic redemption can also be judged as tendentious. According to medieval Kabbalah, Jews fought against evil and brought the world closer to redemption by observing the divine commandments, which in turn strengthened God, who was empowered to defeat the forces of evil in the world. The younger Kook and his followers took a crucial step beyond this thinking when they declared that Jews must help the messianic process along by fighting evil physically in the mundane realm. It was for this reason that the younger Kook glorified Israel's army and saw the military as playing a crucial role in the messianic enterprise in expanding Israel's borders to include all the land promised by God to Abraham. There was no real precedent for using Kabbalistic thinking in this way.[84]

Some scholars have argued that the philosophy of Gush Emunim is also much more nationalistic than it is religious.[85] Religious Zionists, however, have been consistent in their unwillingness to admit their modernism, and they maintain that self-deception by justifying their thinking on the basis of ideas and texts drawn from the tradition, as if their values have always been those of Judaism.[86]

Questions can also be raised about the legitimacy of Meir Kahane's thinking as an authentic reading of Judaism. During his lifetime not a single halakhic authority publicly supported Kahane's views. As Sprinzak has noted, Kahane was a one-man show who never saw the need to argue for his positions and who rejected the views of his opponents by simply pushing them away

83 Another instance in which Tsevi Yehudah's position had no precedent in Jewish sources was his view that Diaspora Judaism had little value. See Luz, *Wrestling with an Angel*, 256–57.

84 Ravitzky, *Messianism, Zionism, and Jewish Religious Radicalism*, 81–82.

85 Janet Aviad, "The Messianism of Gush Emunim," in *Studies in Contemporary Jewry VII: Jews and Messianism in the Modern Era: Metaphor and Meaning*, ed. Jonathan Frankel (New York: Oxford University Press, 1991), 197–213; Garb, "Messianism, Antinomianism, and Power."

86 Sagi, "From the Torah State." As another example of the unwillingness of religious Zionists to admit change, Sagi argues that before 1967, religious Zionists were involved in secular Israeli society and culture and strove to shape them, but afterward their emphasis shifted to settling the territories captured in the 1967 war. This change occurred because religious Zionists lost hope in transforming Israeli secular culture into a religious culture, and their efforts were therefore directed to a new enterprise. Yet, religious Zionists have steadfastly claimed that they had not changed and that their settlement activity was the focus of their thinking all along. See also Avi Sagi, "Religious Zionism: Between Introversion and Openness" (in Hebrew), in *Judaism: A Dialogue Between Cultures*, ed. Avi Sagi, Dudi Schwartz, and Yedidia Z. Stern (Jerusalem: Magnes Press, 2000), 124–68. This is a slightly earlier article that argues similar points.

with venomous attacks and threats.[87] Kahane's views were supported by some after his death, but this group is relatively small in number.[88]

A discussion of outside influences on religious Zionism must also take into account one more factor. The most pernicious elements of religious Zionism began to assert themselves in the 1970s, the same period in which we witness the rise of radical religious fundamentalism worldwide, and some believe that this is no coincidence. Studies conducted by such analysts as Mark Juergensmeyer and Jessica Stern have shown that there is a striking similarity in the worldviews of fundamentalist groups across the globe. These commonalities have already been alluded to earlier in our discussion. Fundamentalists tend to have a worldview that is sharply dualistic. They believe that there is a battle on a cosmic scale between the forces of good and evil, that the true believers represent the good, and that the forces of evil are constantly threatening to overwhelm them. The forces of evil are often identified with secularism, which globalization has brought to everyone's doorstep, and that is an evil so pernicious that the only way to deal with it is with violence. Fundamentalist groups therefore regard such violence as self-defense. They see themselves not as terrorists, but as militants merely protecting themselves from a lethal threat. According to Juergensmeyer and Stern, religious Zionism from the 1970s onward has had many of the features of this fundamentalist worldview and is therefore an expression of the rise of fundamentalism elsewhere.[89]

This understanding of religious Zionism has to be qualified somewhat. Kookian Zionism did not view secularism in wholly negative terms. As we have seen, the two Kooks believed that secular Zionism had a hidden holy essence and that it fulfilled a divine mission, albeit unconsciously. However, the followers of Kookian Zionism never respected secular Zionism as an end in itself, and they have grown increasingly critical of secular Israelis for not recognizing the messianic import of the Jewish state. Moreover, Meir Kahane and his followers openly vilified secularism and therefore exemplify religious fundamentalism as described in the analyses of Juergensmeyer and Stern. Yet, what is

---

87 Sprinzak, *The Ascendance of Israel's Radical Right*, 239, 244–45. One can also question whether Jewish sources allow the imperative to wipe out Amalek to be used as justification for violence against Palestinians. See Norman Lamm, "Amalek and the Seven Nations: A Case of Law vs. Morality," in *War and Peace in the Jewish Tradition*, ed. Lawrence Schiffman and Joel B. Wolowelsky (New York: Yeshiva University Press, 2007), 201–38; Carmy, "The Origin of Nations and the Shadow of Violence," 163–200. Both Carmy and Lamm reject the idea that the command to slaughter Amalek is applicable in our time.

88 See, for instance, Mikha'el ben Horin, ed., *Barukh ha-Gever: Sefer Zikaron la-Kadosh Dr. Barukh Goldshtain h.y.d.* (Jerusalem: "Shalom 'al Yisrael," 1995), in which a number of extreme right-wing Zionists eulogize Baruch Goldstein, the perpetrator of the 1994 massacre of Palestinian Muslim worshipers in Hebron.

89 Juergensmeyer, *Terror in the Mind of God*; Stern, *Terror in the Name of God*.

most important for our purposes is that we have identified one more environmental factor that shaped the radical elements in religious Zionism. Religious Zionism has to be understood as part of the broad phenomenon of the rise of religious fundamentalism throughout the world since the 1970s, which has been inspired by a reaction against secularism. This insight further strengthens our argument that the violent tendencies of religious Zionism are traceable not to Judaism alone, but to outside forces as well.

We must also ask whether the Jewish dimension of religious Zionism consistently promoted violence. In fact, that is far from the case. What is often forgotten by the critics of religious Zionism is that throughout a large portion of its history, religious Zionism did not have overtly violent tendencies. The roots of religious Zionism can be traced back to the middle of the nineteenth century, and yet it was only from the 1970s onward that a violent element began to emerge within it on a grand scale.[90] Moreover, even after religious Zionism took a radical turn, a peaceful wing of religious Zionism has always existed, and this wing regards its version of Zionism as more authentically Jewish than that of the radicals.

The forerunners of religious Zionism were R. Tsevi Hirsch Kalischer (Prussia, d. 1874) and R. Judah Alkalai (Serbia, d. 1878). These rabbis were contemporaries but did not know each other. They espoused a naturalistic and activist messianism much as R. Abraham Kook did years later, and they therefore called on Jews to begin the process of emigration to Palestine and the formation of agricultural settlements in preparation for the messianic era. At the same time, they insisted that the redemptive process be conducted without violence. According to Alkalai, this was the meaning of the oath in the well-known talmudic passage in which the Jewish people promise "not to ascend the wall." What this meant for Alkalai was that the Jews had to bring about redemption gradually, not by a sudden thrust. According to both Alkalai and Kalischer, a second oath in the same talmudic passage, in which the Jewish people pledge not to "rebel against the nations," meant that Jews should go to Palestine only with the consent of the gentile nations.[91]

Alkalai and Kalischer, however, lived before the formal beginnings of the Zionist movement. The first major figure in organized religious Zionism was R. Isaac Jacob Reines (1839–1915), who founded the Mizrahi movement in

90 Schwartz, *Faith at the Crossroads*, 160–68.

91 Judah Alkalai, *Kitvey ha-Rav Yehudah Alkala'i*, ed. Yitshak Verfel (Jerusalem: Mosad ha-Rav Kuk, 1944), 201, 202, 240, 288, 302, 529; Hirsch Tsevi Kalischer, *Ha-Ketavim ha-Tsiyyoniyyim shel ha-Rav Tsevi Kalisher*, ed. Israel Klausner (Jerusalem: Mosad ha-Rav Kuk, 1947), 97, 244, 258; Ravitzky, *Messianism, Zionism, and Jewish Religious Radicalism*, 26–32.

1902. He believed that the purpose of Zionism was to save the Jews of Europe from persecution and assimilation, not to bring messianic redemption. A Jewish state would be a safe haven for Jews both physically and spiritually. Most important for our purposes, Reines's Zionism was nonviolent. The purpose of Judaism, according to him, was to cultivate the culture of "the Book," a culture that was moral and spiritual, and to oppose the culture of "the Sword," the culture of violence in the non-Jewish world. The centuries of Jewish exile served the purpose of enabling the Jewish people to achieve moral and spiritual perfection by isolating them from political life and preventing them from waging war, and Jews should carry those values with them in the construction of a Jewish state. Reines was thus opposed to military activism as a means of achieving the goals of Zionism. He too interpreted the talmudic passage about the three oaths in light of his outlook. In his opinion, the passage taught that Jews should not engage in the use of military force before the coming of the messianic period.[92]

A number of important leaders in religious Zionism took positions on military force similar to Reines's. For instance, the elder R. Kook and R. Avigdor Amiel, the chief rabbi of Tel Aviv in the 1930s, followed Reines in drawing a contrast between the culture of the sword among the nations and the culture of the book among the Jews, and they believed that the Diaspora had prepared the Jews to return to the land of Israel to establish a peaceful society in preparation for the messianic period. The same rabbis also believed that only religious Zionism could restrain the potential for aggression and chauvinism in secular Zionism. Some religious Zionists, such as R. Amiel, expressed their distaste for extreme Jewish nationalism by equating it with idol worship.[93]

After an Arab rebellion began in 1936, there was a realization among all Zionists that Zionism would not succeed without the use of military force. Many religious Zionists both inside and outside the Mizrahi movement therefore permitted the use of such force. However, they insisted that force be used only in the cause of self-defense and that Jews continue cultivating ethical sensitivity to bloodshed.[94] Thus, for instance, R. Meir Berlin (1880–1949), a leading figure in the Mizrahi party, rejected the position adopted by many right-wing

---

92 Isaac Jacob Reines, *Sha'arey Orah ve-Simhah* (Vilna: Rom Press, 1899), 42; Ravitzky, *Messianism, Zionism, and Jewish Religious Radicalism*, 32–35; Holzer, "Attitudes towards the Use of Military Force," 372–80; idem, "The Use of Military Force in the Religious-Zionist Ideology of Rabbi Jacob Reines and his Successors," in *Studies in Contemporary Jewry XVIII: Jews and Violence: Images, Ideologies, Realities*, ed. Peter Y. Medding (New York: Oxford University Press, 2002), 74–94; idem, *A Double-Edged Sword*, chapter 1.

93 Luz, "The Jewish Religion," 247–55; Holzer, "Attitudes towards the Use of Military Force," 391–93, 394–95, 398–99, 401–4; idem, *A Double-Edged Sword*, chapters 4–5.

94 Holzer, *A Double-Edged Sword*, pp. 167–77.

Zionists that the Arab community was collectively responsible for Arab terror against Jews and that it was therefore permissible to retaliate against Arabs who were not involved in the violence. He supported clemency for Arab rioters sentenced to death by the British on condition that Arab leaders promote peaceful relations with Jews. He also opposed a proposal supporting the transfer of Palestinians to Arab countries.[95] R. Amiel and R. Isaac Herzog Halevi, the Ashkenazi chief rabbi, also condemned retaliation against Arab terror that would cause the loss of innocent life.[96] This does not mean that these religious Zionists were political moderates. On the whole, they were adamant about the Jewish right to Palestine. Still, when it came to the issue of overt violence, moral considerations were at the forefront of their thinking.[97] This restrained approach toward violence was also favored by important religious Zionist rabbis after the founding of the state in 1948. Only after the 1967 war did the views of religious Zionists undergo a substantial change on this issue as the younger Kook's thinking began to become influential.[98]

What comes out of this portion of our analysis is that religious Zionism was mostly peaceful for a substantial portion of its history. The violent elements that emerged in it took the better part of a century to come to the fore. Furthermore, the Jewish element in religious Zionism often encouraged peaceful behavior.

We can strengthen our argument by taking a closer look at the thought of R. Abraham Isaac Kook, whose theology inspired the creation of the radical wing of religious Zionism. In fact, Kook's Zionism was decidedly nonviolent, as we have already mentioned, and it was only by distorting his views that his followers were able to use them to justify violence. Kook believed that in the emerging messianic age, Jews would exert influence on the world through the holy life they would lead in the land of Israel, a life synonymous with the observance of God's commandments, and he explicitly ruled out the use of force of any kind in accomplishing this goal. Jews had fought wars in the biblical period only because it was a violent era, and they had to do so in order to survive, but that age had forever passed, and wars were no longer needed. Moreover, as we

95 Gorny, 242, 275.

96 Luz, *Wrestling with an Angel*, 205–7. Luz notes that these rabbis justified their position by using the phrase *musar ha-yahadut* or *musar yehudi*, "Jewish morality." This phrase referred to a meta-halakhic principle deriving from scripture, tradition, and Jewish experience that dictated the proper ethical treatment of human beings, including non-Jews. Invented in the nineteenth century by European Jewish thinkers who believed that Judaism was the most humanitarian religion, it was later adopted by a number of religious Zionist rabbis; Ahad Ha-Am, a secularist, made use of it as well.

97 Gorny, 242.

98 Luz, "The Jewish Religion," 253–55; Holzer, *A Double-Edged Sword*, chapter 4.

have just noted, Kook believed that the Jewish exile had a beneficial effect in preparing Jews for political life by inculcating in them moral sensitivity and antipathy toward the use of force. Kook's nonviolence was evident in his understanding of the talmudic passage regarding the three oaths. Kook believed that these oaths applied to the messianic age, not just to the period of the exile. Therefore, even in the messianic era, Jews were not allowed to "ascend the wall"—that is, to use force to reoccupy the land of Israel. Kook's thinking on violence was also greatly affected by the First World War. He believed that the war was caused by a corrupt culture of secularism that glorified the use of force. However, the war had eradicated this culture, and the culture of Judaism would now rise in Palestine in the emerging messianic era to teach religious principles that would inculcate peaceful values. The world was ripe for having the Jews reenter political life and create a new kind of state, free of evil and barbarism. Kook was well aware of the dangers of modern nationalism, which could lead to the glorification of might and violence, but he also believed that the Jewish people's essence would protect them from falling into this trap.[99]

That Kook saw Zionism as benefiting humanity should come as no surprise. We saw in chapter 1, on the Bible, that there is much ambiguity regarding the relationship between God's chosen people and the gentile nations, but according to one reading, the line of Abraham was meant to bring blessings to the rest of the world and help the nations achieve redemption. Kook therefore chose an understanding of Jewish chosenness that was grounded in the Bible but was far more benevolent toward the non-Jewish world than the rival reading adopted by his son.

Even after the 1967 war, when religious Zionism began to take an aggressive turn due to the growing influence of the younger Kook and his disciples,

99 Abraham Isaac Kook, *Orot* (Jerusalem: Mosad ha-Rav Kuk, 1963), 13–15, 104; idem, *'Olat ha-Re'iyah* (Jerusalem: Mosad ha-Rav Kuk, 1985), 1:233; Ravitzky, *Messianism, Zionism, and Jewish Religious Radicalism*, 135; Holzer, "Attitudes towards the Use of Military Force," 346–56; idem, *A Double-Edged Sword*, pp. 98–105. In our first reading, we cited sources in Kook's writings that indicated that there was an ontological difference between Jews and non-Jews. However, one finds other sources in his writings that express a highly positive attitude toward non-Jews (see n. 13). See Halamish, "The Kabbalists' Attitude to the Nations of the World," 306. Mention can also be made of R. Aharon Shmuel Tameret (d. 1931), a pacifist Orthodox Russian rabbi who expressed great concern about the potential for violence in Zionism. Like Reines, Amiel, and the elder Kook, Tameret believed that the Jewish exile was divinely ordained so that Jews could perfect themselves as a spiritual and moral people devoted to God without being corrupted by the trappings of power. Tameret therefore censured political Zionism, which he believed had placed too much emphasis on nationalism. Tameret was similar to Amiel and Leibowitz in believing that when nationalism was treated as an end in itself, it became a form of idolatry, because it glorified the state, the land, and violence and devalued the worth of the individual. Nonetheless, Zionism could be redeemed if it built a political state that gave primacy to Jewish spirituality and ethics and avoided militarism and violence. Tameret, however, never attracted a following. See Luz, *Wrestling with an Angel*, 122–29; Holzer, "Attitudes towards the Use of Military Force," 385–404; idem, *A Double-Edged Sword*, chapter 3.

not all religious Zionists approved of the new direction. A vocal minority strongly criticized the younger Kook and his camp because of the ethical difficulties raised by their ideas and actions. This group believed in the right of Jews to self-defense, but they also held that religious and ethical principles placed strict limits on the use of violence. They therefore opposed the new militaristic brand of religious Zionism. In the 1970s and 1980s, several organizations were formed to promote this viewpoint, most notably 'Oz ve-Shalom/Netivot Shalom and Meimad.[100]

A prominent and influential opponent of the younger Kook within the Orthodox camp was Yeshayahu Leibowitz. Leibowitz's early writings in the 1940s and early 1950s reflected an interest in bringing together Zionism and Orthodoxy in a manner similar to that of many of his religious Zionist compatriots. However, by the mid-1950s Leibowitz's thinking underwent a significant change. He began to voice strong opposition to Jewish nationalism because, in his thinking, it had become an end in itself, an absolute. For Leibowitz, making the state into an ultimate value was idolatry, a position similar to that of R. Amiel, mentioned earlier. There was only one absolute in Judaism, and that was God, whom the Jew was commanded to worship through the observance of his commandments. Moreover, because Jewish nationalism had become an absolute, it had also become immoral, as evidenced by the brutality of Jews in their treatment of Arabs. Judaism, with its strong opposition to idolatry, was supposed to serve as a check on such behavior. Leibowitz's criticisms of Jewish nationalism were initially directed at secular Zionism. However, they were eventually applied to religious Zionism as represented by the younger Kook and his supporters. Here, too, according to Leibowitz, nationalism had become idolatrous and immoral in that the Jewish state and the land itself had become objects of idolatrous veneration and had inspired a desire to dispossess Palestinians of their rights. It should be noted that Leibowitz did not deny the need of the Jewish state to use violence for the purpose of self-defense. What was critical for Leibowitz was the motivation for such violence. The state should use violence only for the purpose of preserving itself as a necessary instrument for the fulfillment of basic human needs, not as an absolute value in its own right.[101]

It is also important to point out that even within the sector of the religious Zionist camp that supported the younger Kook and his program, there were

---

100 Mordechai Bar-On, *In Pursuit of Peace: A History of the Israeli Peace Movement* (Washington, D.C.: United States Institute of Peace, 1996), 170–72.

101 Much of Leibowitz's thinking on Jewish nationalism can be found in *Judaism, Human Values, and the Jewish State*, ed. Eliezer Goldman, trans. Yoram Navon, Zvi Jacobson, Gershon Levy, and Raphael Levy (Cambridge, Mass.: Harvard University Press, 1995). See also Holzer, *A Double-Edged Sword*, pp. 259–75.

divisions about the extent to which force could be used for messianic ends. The discovery of the Jewish Underground in 1984 caused shock among the supporters of Gush Emunim, most of whom did not believe that Jews were capable of terrorism and did not approve of it. They were also furious at the Underground for acting without the approval of a respected rabbinic authority. In fact, after the members of the Underground were arrested, major rabbinic authorities in Gush Emunim disseminated halakhic rulings condemning their actions. There was a similar reaction from these rabbis when the Oslo Accords were signed and some supporters of Gush Emunim threatened violence against the Israeli government. Most major rabbis in Gush Emunim and the nationalist yeshivas denounced these threats. The Hebron massacre and the Rabin assassination brought yet another round of condemnations from these same rabbis, who expressed consternation that their followers could perpetrate such actions.[102] Once again, we see that the Jewish element in Zionism, far from encouraging violence, has often acted as a restraint on it.

In the first decade of the twenty-first century, the nationalist yeshivas have increasingly retreated from political activism, claiming that they must focus on cultivating religious leadership that can bring about religious and political changes in Israeli society. Yet, Eliezer Don-Yehiya claims that in truth this move also reflects a desire to separate from secular Israeli society altogether, much as ultra-Orthodox Jews have done. Don-Yehiya concludes from this development that Jewish religious fundamentalism need not give birth to political radicalism and violence. The same forces that encouraged Gush Emunim and its supporters to become violent have also encouraged them to retreat from political involvement. With these insights, Don-Yehiya therefore shows that the Jewish element in religious Zionism is not necessarily violent.[103]

One of the most important considerations here concerns the actual size of the group of religious Zionists that at present advocates violence. It is frequently pointed out that in terms of absolute numbers, this group is actually quite small. There are over 200,000 settlers living in the West Bank—less than 5 percent of the population of Israeli Jews. Moreover, a substantial percentage of Jews living in the West Bank are not affiliated at all with religious Zionism, but bought homes there because of cheap housing. Thus, only a relatively small number of Israeli Jews living in the West Bank are a threat to peace.

---

102 Sprinzak, *The Ascendance of Israel's Radical Right*, 251–61; idem, *Brother against Brother*, 294–95; Don-Yehiya, "The Book and the Sword," 210–25; Garb, "Messianism, Antinomianism, and Power," 337–40.

103 Don-Yehiya, "The Book and the Sword," 226–28.

When we speak about religious Zionism, we also need to look at a group of thinkers who are not normally classified under that rubric, such as Martin Buber and Hillel Zeitlin. These intellectuals are not referred to as religious Zionists because, for most academic scholars, "religious" here is generally synonymous with "Orthodox." Yet, this use of the term "religious" is misleading. Buber and Zeitlin were deeply religious individuals, and their thinking on Zionism reflected that religiosity; it is just that their religiosity was not that of Orthodox Judaism. A fair assessment of whether the Jewish element in religious Zionism promotes violence must therefore deal with these figures as well.

Buber and Zeitlin provide some of the strongest evidence that religion need not be an inspiration for violence in religious Zionism and that it can foster peaceful behavior. Let us look briefly at Buber, since he was by far the most famous representative of non-Orthodox religious Zionism. In Buber's thinking, Zionism had to be guided by the Jewish tradition, which he believed was synonymous with religious humanism. For Buber, this religious humanism was in turn identical with his I-Thou philosophy, which taught that human beings live their lives to the fullest by seeking to create deep and meaningful relationships with each other based on reciprocity and mutual respect. Nationalism was acceptable only if it took this philosophy into account. It was permissible for nationalism to be concerned with the national interest, but it also had to recognize the rights of those who did not belong to the national group. Nationalism was not acceptable if it was driven by violence and ambition for power and trampled outsiders underfoot. For this reason, Buber was entirely opposed to Jews having sole sovereignty because of fears that the exercise of Jewish power would lead to the second brand of nationalism and violence against the Palestinians. He therefore advocated a binational state in which Jews and Palestinians would share power and live as equals. Buber participated in an organization known as Ihud (Unity), founded in 1942, which worked to implement this idea, and it included a number of other famous like-minded intellectuals. Buber was no pacifist; he believed in the use of violence for self-defense, a position for which he argued passionately in a famous letter to Mahatma Gandhi. Nonetheless, Buber's thinking can be classified as broadly nonviolent.[104] Most important, he believed that his nonviolent stance represented the most authentic reading of the Jewish tradition. Thus, once again,

---

104 Luz, *Wrestling with an Angel*, 168–74. I disagree with Luz, who says that Buber adopted a mode of thinking somewhere between secular Zionism and traditional discourse. In fact, his Zionism was thoroughly religious in the sense that it was interpreted through the lens of his I-Thou philosophy, which gave a central place to the individual's encounter with God, or the "I-eternal Thou" relationship, in Buber's terminology.

the Jewish component of religious Zionism did not necessarily foster aggressive violence against Palestinians and Arabs. In fact, in Buber's thinking, true religious Zionism had to reject such violence.[105]

Let us round out this portion of our discussion by looking at religious Jews who reject not only militant religious Zionism, but Zionism altogether. A substantial number of ultra-Orthodox Jews fall into this category. They believe that redemption must come solely through God's initiative and that Jews can hasten the redemption only by observing God's commandments and having faith in him. The establishment of the state of Israel is therefore blasphemous because it established Jewish sovereignty in the Holy Land through human initiative and is secular in character. This criticism applies not just to secular Zionists, but to religious Zionists as well. The latter also lack the necessary faith in God, as evidenced by their attempt to force the redemption. In recent years, the ultra-Orthodox community in Israel has witnessed the growth of a more favorable viewpoint on the Jewish state within its ranks. The position of these Jews is somewhere between those of religious Zionism and of ultra-Orthodox anti-Zionism. They do not see the state of Israel as the beginning of the messianic redemption, but they nevertheless view it in a positive light.[106] Still, a good portion of ultra-Orthodox Jews remain opposed to the very existence of the Jewish state.

What is key for our concerns is that ultra-Orthodox anti-Zionists are nonviolent when it comes to Palestinians and Arabs. In fact, many of them believe that the biblical land of Israel should be governed by Palestinians, who are the rightful owners of the land, until the messiah comes.[107] Secular and religious

---

105 The basis of Buber's thought is his classic *I and Thou*, trans. Walter Kaufmann (New York: Scribner, 1970). Buber's writings on the relationship between Jews and Arabs in Israel-Palestine are collected in *A Land of Two Peoples*, ed. Paul R. Mendes-Flohr (Chicago: University of Chicago Press, 2005). Another figure who was an excellent representative of this approach was Hillel Zeitlin (?–1942), who is discussed in Luz, *Wrestling with an Angel*, 123–25. A more contemporary example of this way of thinking is provided by Moshe Greenberg, a Bible scholar whose work was cited in chapter 2, on biblical Judaism. See the works cited in that chapter, especially his article "A Problematic Heritage," 23–24. In addition to these works, see his article "On the Political Use of the Bible in Modern Israel: An Engaged Critique," in *Pomegranates and Golden Bells: Studies in Biblical, Jewish, and Near Eastern Ritual, Law, and Literature in Honor of Jacob Milgrom*, ed. David P. Wright, David Noel Freedman, and Avi Hurvitz (Winona Lake, Ind.: Eisenbrauns, 1995), 461–71. Here Greenberg argues that biblical and rabbinic Judaism support humane and ethical behavior toward non-Jews and that there are objective criteria for this assessment. He therefore claims that the debate between right-wing and left-wing religious Zionists regarding the treatment of Palestinians cannot be attributed to the way in which each camp reads traditional sources in a subjective manner. In fact, the debate can be settled decisively and objectively in favor of the left-wing viewpoint. Our study casts doubt on Greenberg's assessment. However, Greenberg's essay is nonetheless insightful and thoughtful.

106 This group is known as *haredi le'umi* or by the short-form *hardal*. This viewpoint is examined by Ya'ir Sheleg, *Recent Developments among Religious Jews in Israel* (in Hebrew) (Jerusalem: Keter, 2000), 249–63.

107 Ravitzky, *Messianism, Zionism, and Jewish Religious Radicalism*, 13–26, chapters 2, 4, 5.

Zionists often vilify ultra-Orthodox anti-Zionists for their views and brand them as extremists, and yet in many respects this group represents a viewpoint that is well grounded in Jewish tradition. That certainly seems to be the case with respect to their views on violence. In our chapter on the Bible, we argued in our second reading that the biblical narratives involving war could be interpreted in a nonviolent manner because they assumed that God initiated war, not human beings. In our discussion of rabbinic Judaism, we saw a similar emphasis. When the rabbis described the vanquishing of Israel's enemies in the messianic period, God waged war, not human beings. Thus, ultra-Orthodox anti-Zionists are on firm Jewish ground when they claim that it is God who can use violence to reestablish Jewish sovereignty in the land of Israel but human beings must not. Ultra-Orthodox anti-Zionists also give a plausible reading of the talmudic passage involving the three oaths when they interpret it to mean that Jews must not establish a sovereign Jewish state in the land of Israel before the coming of the messiah.[108] Therefore, however eccentric this group of ultra-Orthodox Jews may appear to most other Jews, their commitment to nonviolence vis-à-vis Palestinians and Arabs is very much within the parameters of the Jewish tradition.[109]

We must also take note of religious Jews who opposed Zionism but were not Orthodox. Both Hermann Cohen (1842–1919) and Franz Rosenzweig (1886–1929), two of the leading Jewish philosophers in the modern period, opposed Zionism because of their discomfort with Jewish nationalism and the violence it could foster. For Cohen, humanity was moving gradually but inexorably toward a morally perfect world, and Jews had a special role to play in guiding this process because Judaism had the best understanding of what true morality was. Moreover, Jews had given up statehood and worldly happiness to devote themselves to this spiritual mission. This sacrifice was the secret of Jewish survival, as symbolized by the suffering servant in the book of Isaiah. Cohen therefore downplayed any political element in Judaism and rejected Zionism. Rosenzweig was at best ambivalent toward Zionism. He believed that war and violence had always defined the historical process and that, as a result, European civilization was on the verge of collapse. Rosenzweig's views were formed while serving as a soldier in the First World War, an experience that led him to detest nationalism and imperialism. According to Rosenzweig, Judaism could help save European civilization because Jews lived above history in a timeless messianic realm that represented redemption for mankind, and they therefore

---

108 Ravitzky, *Messianism, Zionism, and Jewish Religious Radicalism*, 22–23.
109 Boyarin, *A Radical Jew*, 256.

provided a model for the goal toward which all human beings should strive. For this reason, Rosenzweig was uncomfortable with the idea of Jewish nationalism because it meant the normalization of Jewish existence within the realm of history and therefore went against the very mission of Judaism. These ideas also led Rosenzweig to conclude that Jews could not wage war. For gentile nations, war was acceptable because they lived in history. However, Jews lived in a realm separate from history, and, therefore they could not engage in war. Rosenzweig was well aware of the narratives in the Bible describing Israel's wars, but for him they belonged to a mythical Jewish past that was no longer relevant.[110] Thus, we have here two leading Jewish philosophers who were religious and rejected Zionism in part because of their antipathy to nationalism and its potential for violence.

To sum up our observations on religious Zionism, we have shown in this second reading that despite the label "religious," this brand of Zionism was shaped by a host of outside forces, and these forces may best explain its violent tendencies. The influence of these forces was sometimes positive in that religious Zionism absorbed them into its thinking, albeit without acknowledging their influence. Nationalism was the most important influence of this kind. In other instances, the influence of outside forces was negative in that the thinking of religious Zionism was fashioned as a reaction against them. Thus, in addition to reacting against anti-Semitism, as all forms of Zionism did, the direction of religious Zionism, especially from the 1970s onward, was also determined by its antipathy to secularism, and in this respect it shares a good deal with fundamentalist communities in other religions. What emerges here, therefore, is that the relationship between the violent tendencies in religious Zionism and its use of Jewish teachings is complex. The outside influences that shaped religious Zionism have often caused it to distort Jewish teachings for the purpose of justifying violence. However, we also saw instances in which Jewish teachings were used by prominent religious Zionists to encourage peaceful behavior. Therefore, there is no simple correlation between the Jewish dimension of religious Zionism and violence.

Let us now move on to secular Zionism. In our first reading, we described secular Zionism as having aggressive violent tendencies much as religious Zionism had, and we argued that this was true for left-wing Labor Zionism, not just right-wing Revisionist Zionism. However, at least one major scholar disagrees with this assessment. Ehud Luz argues that from the outset Labor Zionism did not support violence. Labor Zionists believed in a pragmatic,

110 Luz, *Wrestling with an Angel*, 129–38.

evolutionary approach to Zionism, and they therefore rejected extreme revolutionary activity and the unrestrained use of force. Their moderation followed from an emphasis on individualism. Zionism was a means for the individual to achieve self-realization and self-fulfillment through labor and creativity, and they therefore believed that the individual should not sacrifice everything for the collective. There was value in Zionism for the individual even if the dream of a Jewish state could not be realized immediately. As a result, Labor Zionism did not turn militarism and sovereignty into absolute values. This approach stood in marked contrast to that of Jabotinsky's Revisionists, who believed that all values in Zionism should be subordinated to sacrifice on the battlefield. Thus, when it came to the question of Arabs, Labor Zionists used a flexible ethics. They recognized that in some instances military force was needed, while in other cases dialogue was preferable. There were certainly some Labor Zionists who favored a militaristic approach. However, moderation tended to win out in the party as a whole.[111]

Luz goes on to argue that the Labor party continued on the path of moderation even after the founding of the state. This moderation was encapsulated in the slogan *ein bereirah* (there is no choice), which meant that Jews had to fight wars for their own survival and that violence had been foisted upon them by Palestinians and Arabs who refused to accept Zionism. This slogan was born in the late 1930s and continued to be central in mainstream Israeli thinking up to the 1982 invasion of Lebanon. It inspired Jews to maintain a sense of their own morality, and it was meant to dampen hatred of the enemy. A related idea on which Luz focuses to illustrate the moderation of mainstream Labor Zionism both before and after the founding of the state was the notion of *tohar ha-neshek* (purity of arms). This idea applied to the Israeli army and dictated that lethal force against enemies be used with restraint and only for defensive purposes.[112]

We should also mention groups that were to the left of mainstream Labor Zionism and emphasized peaceful coexistence with Palestinians. The most prominent of these in early Zionism was Berit Shalom (Covenant of Peace), which was established in 1925. Its leadership was made up of leading Jewish intellectuals in Palestine, including Samuel Hugo Bergman, Ernst Simon, and

---

111 Luz, *Wrestling with an Angel*, 51–52, 188–97. Luz contrasts his understanding of the Labor Party's position with that of Shapira. According to Luz, Shapira believes that the Labor Party exercised restraint when it came to violence against Palestinians only for pragmatic reasons; they knew that an immediate, comprehensive solution to the Palestinian problem was not possible. This is not an accurate characterization of Shapira's position, which is far more nuanced. See, pp. 161-3, this volume. Still, Luz is correct in noting that in his understanding, the Labor party was more accommodating of Palestinians than Shapira believes it was. Gorny is closer to Luz in his views on this matter. See Gorny, 178, 312–13.

112 Shapira, *Land and Power*, 223; Luz, *Wrestling with an Angel*, 87–88, 204–8.

Gershom Scholem. They believed that Jewish settlement in Palestine had to proceed without the use of force. Some were pacifists, but most were not, because they believed that violence could be used for self-defense. Central to their platform was the belief that Jews and Arabs in Palestine should join together to form a binational state in which the two groups would have equal rights regardless of which was in the majority. Berit Shalom suggested a constitutional arrangement guaranteeing that power was shared equally by the two groups. Berit Shalom eventually disbanded, but many of its members later founded Ihud, the platform of which was similar to that of Berit Shalom.[113] Neither Berit Shalom nor Ihud won much popular support, but they were nonetheless influential because of the prominence of their leaders. Moreover, their legacy has been carried on in some respects by the many peace groups that have arisen in Israel, especially since the 1967 war. These groups have achieved much greater popularity than Berit Shalom and Ihud, and they have been supported by substantial sectors of the Israeli population.[114]

We must certainly concede that there were at least some elements in secular Zionism that had violent tendencies. There is no question that right-wing secular Zionism from its early beginnings was militaristic and displayed a deep hostility toward Palestinians and Arabs, and some Labor Zionists were sympathetic to that viewpoint. But even if we make this concession, the question that must be asked is whether the violent tendencies in secular Zionism were traceable to Judaism. One can argue that, as with religious Zionism, secular Zionism was the product not just of Judaism, but of nationalism as well, and the latter could just as easily be blamed for any violent tendencies in secular Zionism. Moreover, the influence of nationalism on secular Zionism often resulted in the distortion of Jewish ideas, as was the case in religious Zionism. In fact, this tendency was far stronger in secular Zionism because secular Zionists were less beholden to traditional Judaism in the first place. As we noted in our first reading, when secular Zionism adopted religious motifs, they often denuded them of their religious meaning because secular Zionists, on the whole, could not accept the traditional notion of a God who was personal and active in human affairs. Thus, even when secular Zionists used religious terms to describe their enterprise, those terms were employed in a manner very distant from their original meaning. Moreover, many secular Zionists openly opposed traditional Judaism and saw Zionism as a new and fresh beginning for the Jewish people, which no longer needed religion for their survival.

---

113 Shapira, *Land and Power*, 163–70; Gorny, 118–28.
114 Bar-On, *In Pursuit of Peace*.

An excellent illustration of how secular Zionism adopted Jewish motifs but stripped them of their religious meaning is provided by looking more closely at the relationship between secular Zionism and messianism. Several scholars have noted that even though secular Zionists often used traditional messianic ideas to describe their enterprise, their understanding of those ideas was anything but traditional. In traditional Jewish messianism, the Jewish exile was seen as divine punishment, and the future reestablishment of Jewish sovereignty in the Holy Land was viewed as divine reward. In secular Zionism, both were explained by human causes. The Jewish exile was attributed to political conditions, and the redemption of the Jewish people would come about by political means. God was nowhere in the picture here. Thus, it could be argued that when secular Zionists used messianic language, it was not really an expression of genuine messianic longings or beliefs.[115]

We also find many instances in which secular Zionists entirely rejected Jewish ideas. Some secular Zionists were adamant about maintaining a strict separation between messianism and Zionism. Others openly rejected the notion of Jewish chosenness as a burden they did not want to carry. It was common for secular Zionists to speak about the desire for "normalcy" for the Jewish people, to be a nation like all other nations. This, in fact, was Herzl's sentiment.[116]

One can also question the degree to which secular Zionism was dependent on Judaism as a religion by taking note of the Jewish texts from which they drew inspiration. On the whole, secular Zionists revered the Bible but rejected rabbinic Judaism. This tendency was particularly strong among right-wing secular Zionists. Thinkers in this group, such as Berdichevsky and Brenner, looked to the Bible to provide models for militarism, heroism, and bravery whom modern Zionists should emulate. They were highly critical of rabbinic Judaism, which they blamed for introducing an ethos of weakness and submissiveness into Judaism. They created what Ehud Luz has referred to as a counterhistory by glorifying the militarism of the Maccabees, the Zealots, Bar Kokhba, and

---

115 Myers, "The Messianic Idea," 7–8; Lederhendler, "Messianic Rhetoric"; Yaacov Shavit, "Realism and Messianism in Zionism and the Yishuv," in *Studies in Contemporary Jewry VII: Jews and Messianism in the Modern Era: Metaphor and Meaning*, ed. Jonathan Frankel (New York: Oxford University Press, 1991), 100–127. Lederhendler, 17, quotes Gershom Scholem, who maintained that messianism shorn of the miraculous element was no longer messianism, and therefore secular Zionism was, in effect, antimessianic. Liebman and Don-Yehiya argue throughout their study that the reinterpretation of Judaism described here permeated the politics and society of the early Zionists before the founding of the state and of Israelis after its founding. Early Zionists and Israelis attempted to create a "civil religion" in which the focus was no longer on divine will but human initiative. Liebman and Don-Yehiya conclude that this civil religion was very different from traditional religion.

116 Ravitzky, *Messianism, Zionism, and Jewish Religious Radicalism*, 35; Shapira, *Land and Power*, 25–28; Luz, *Wrestling with an Angel*, 218.

those who died at Masada, and by vilifying R. Yohanan b. Zakkai, who led the Jews to surrender to Rome in the first century. As we saw in chapter 3, on rabbinic Judaism, the rabbis lionized R. Yohanan for his actions, played down the militarism of the Maccabees, and were critical of the Zealots and Bar Kokhba. As for Masada, rabbinic literature made no mention of it, probably because the rabbis did not look favorably on suicide even in the cause of freedom.[117] The counterhistory created by secular Zionists was connected to another motif in their thinking: the "negation of the exile," which is examined in a study by Yael Zerubavel. At the center of secular Zionist thought was a tendency to deny any value to Jewish life during the centuries of Jewish exile, from the destruction of the Jewish commonwealth in the first century up to the creation of the Jewish state in 1948.[118] All of this raises questions about the Jewish character of secular Zionism. Classical Judaism is not the Bible; it is the Bible interpreted through the lens of rabbinic Judaism. One can therefore argue that the ties that these secular Zionists had with Judaism were tenuous, given that they cut themselves off from Judaism's core dimension.

We can also point to some instances in which secular Zionists openly embraced Judaism but used it to produce ideologies emphasizing peace. As we discovered with religious Zionism, religion was at times a source of inspiration for humanistic ideals, not chauvinism or violence, and one finds similar examples of this approach among secular Zionist intellectuals. For a number of them, Zionism was bound up with the redemption of humankind. The belief was that a state governed by true Jewish values could serve as a model of moral excellence for the non-Jewish world.[119] Not surprisingly, one finds this approach among secular Zionists on the left of the political spectrum. These include A. D. Gordon, Moses Hess, Ahad Ha-Am, Hayim Weitzmann, and Ben-Gurion.

Ahad Ha-Am was by far the best-known and most influential representative of this way of thinking. He believed that the distinctiveness of the Jewish people lay in their ethics. Thus, the true meaning of Jewish chosenness was that Jews would serve as models of ethical behavior for the rest of the world. In the Bible, the best representatives of Judaism's ethics were the classical prophets, who harangued the Israelites about their ethical failures. Also serving as models of ethical conduct were the rabbis, who chose peace over war in their struggle with Rome. It was, in fact, the ethical dimension of Judaism that

---

117 Shapira, *Land and Power*, 310–19; Luz, *Wrestling with an Angel*, 42–44, 54–55.

118 Yael Zerubavel, *Recovered Roots: Collective Memory and the Making of Israeli National Tradition* (Chicago: University of Chicago Press, 1995).

119 Luz, *Wrestling with an Angel*, 218–19.

was responsible for Jewish survival because strength comes from spiritual power, not physical might. In his vision of the Jewish state, Ahad Ha-Am therefore rejected the concept of normalcy espoused by Herzl. Jews had a special mission; they were not a nation like all others. More central to our concerns, Ahad Ha-Am also spoke out passionately on several occasions against Jews mistreating Palestinians or perpetrating acts of violence against them.[120] Like most of the Zionists we have explored, Ahad Ha-Am was not a pacifist in that he believed in violence for self-defense, but he condemned unprovoked violence or violence used for the sake of revenge.[121]

One has to concede that Ahad Ha-Am was a secularist despite the religious tone of his ideas. His understanding of Judaism was therefore quite different from that of traditional Judaism. Still, he openly acknowledged rabbinic Judaism as a source of his thinking, and this put him at odds with right-wing secular Zionists, who saw no value in this form of Judaism. He also parted company with the latter group by appreciating the value of Jewish communities in the Diaspora, not just in the past, but in the present as well. For Ahad Ha-Am, the goal of Zionism was not the "negation" of the Jewish Diaspora, but the creation of a Jewish state that would serve as a cultural center for Jews throughout the world. In sum, Ahad Ha-Am's Zionism was informed by an ethics of peace that, in part, drew its strength from an admiration for rabbinic diasporic Judaism.[122]

Therefore, it can be argued that much of mainstream secular Zionism did not have violent tendencies, and when it did display such tendencies, often Judaism was not the culprit. The influences of nationalism and anti-Semitism were more significant. Moreover, in some instances, it is not even clear that

---

120 Ahad Ha-Am, *Ten Essays on Zionism and Judaism*, trans. Leon Simon (New York: Arno Press, 1973), 45–47; idem, *Kol Kitvey Ahad Ha-'Am* (Tel Aviv: Dvir, 1961), 1:20, 3:230–31; Shapira, *Land and Power*, 18–21; Gorny, 26–33, 99–104; Luz, *Wrestling with an Angel*, 52–53, 199.

121 Luz, *Wrestling with an Angel*, 199.

122 Similar views were developed by Simon Rawidowicz (1897–1957), an academic scholar whose thinking on Zionism has been brought to light in a recent study by David N. Myers, *Between Arab and Jew: The Lost Voice of Simon Rawidowicz* (Waltham, Mass.: Brandeis University Press, 2008). Daniel Boyarin uses rabbinic and diasporic Judaism to reject the notion of a Jewish state. Boyarin pleads for one state in Israel-Palestine, which will have neither a Jewish nor Palestinian identity. Boyarin bases his thinking on the belief that diasporic Jewish identity is a more moral form of Jewish identity than that which Jews have adopted in the state of Israel because Jews in the diaspora have never strived to dominate other groups as Israelis have in their relationship with Palestinians. Jews in the diaspora have lived as minorities among non-Jews, a situation that has allowed them to adopt the best elements of non-Jewish culture around them. Jews in Israel-Palestine should adopt this diasporic way of living by sharing power with Palestinians in the Holy Land. In this way, Jews will cease to dominate Palestinians. What Boyarin has done is to effectively reverse the counterhistory of right-wing secular Zionists. While the latter group denied the value of rabbinic Judaism and the diaspora in their construction of a new Jewish identity in the land of Israel, Boyarin argues that rabbinic and diasporic Judaism is precisely what is needed for Jews living there. See Boyarin's final chapter in *A Radical Jew*.

Judaism was a factor at all in encouraging the violent tendencies of secular Zionism, because many secular Zionists radically reinterpreted Jewish teachings in light of nationalism or entirely rejected them. We also saw instances in which secular Zionists openly embraced Jewish tradition and used its teachings to develop ideologies that were benevolent and peaceful. Thus, the conclusions in this portion of our second reading are similar to those regarding religious Zionism. The relationship between Judaism and the violent elements in secular Zionism is complex, and it is much too simplistic to assume a direct correlation between the two.

Conclusions

Our two readings have provided very different understandings of Zionism. According to the first, Zionism has strong violent tendencies, and those tendencies are best explained by the influence of Judaism. Certainly other factors contributed to the violent dimension of Zionism, but at its core Zionism is a Jewish phenomenon, and therefore its propensity for violence is traceable to Judaism as well. This assessment applies not just to religious Zionism, but also to secular Zionism. Even though secular Zionism in many respects reshaped or rejected elements of the Jewish tradition, it preserved key components of Judaism that were bound to foment violence, most notably the belief that Jews had a fundamental right to their ancient homeland. According to our second reading, Zionism has violent tendencies, but they are not nearly as prominent as the first reading suggests. Moreover, the violent elements of Zionism are best explained by forces outside Judaism. Zionism absorbed European nationalism and Eurocentrism, and it arose as a reaction to modern anti-Semitism. Religious Zionism in recent decades has been shaped by the encroachments of secularism, a factor responsible for the rise of fundamentalism worldwide. It is these outside forces that have been primarily responsible for the violent tendencies in Zionism. There is therefore no necessary correlation between the violent elements of Zionism and Judaism. The outside forces that shaped Zionism often caused it to distort the Jewish teachings it absorbed, or, as in the case of secular Zionism, to leave Judaism by the wayside altogether. Furthermore, when Judaism influenced Zionism, it often acted to restrain violence and to encourage peaceful behavior.

As in previous chapters, the discussion does not have to end here. Those who support the first reading can raise questions about the second. For instance, if in the second reading the claim was made that the aggressive tendencies of Zionism were largely the product of outside forces such as nationalism, the same conclusion could be drawn with regard to the Zionism of those who rejected violence. One could argue that the latter were influenced by universal-istic thinking, which was common in Europe among humanists and socialists. This was the case not only with such liberal thinkers as Buber and Ahad Ha-Am, but also with Orthodox Zionists, such as Reines and the elder Kook. Therefore, one can question whether the benevolent and peaceful elements of Zionism were any more Jewish than the aggressive elements.

In the second reading, we argued that the aggressive tendencies in Zion-ism were understandable given the desperation that Jews felt about their bleak situation in Europe. Yet, not all Jews or Zionists used this situation as a justifi-cation for dispossessing the Palestinians of their land. Some important Zionist thinkers, including Ahad Ha-Am and the members of Berit Shalom, under-stood full well the problem of settling in a country that was already occupied by another people.[123] In the pre-state years, some Jews also pondered whether Zionism would, in fact, *endanger* Jewish survival. Rosenzweig expressed con-cern that if Jews became attached to a specific piece of land, they could be wiped out.[124] His fears have proven almost prophetic given the vulnerability of the state of Israel since its founding.

The second reading attempted to minimize the problem of violent reli-gious Zionism by noting that adherents to this way of thinking constitute a minuscule portion of the Israeli population. This argument can be countered by noting once again that this group could not have succeeded in establishing settlements in the West Bank without the help of several secular Israeli govern-ments and support from the Israeli public in general. Moreover, even though the numbers of violent religious Zionists are small, they wield tremendous influence as obstacles to a peace agreement between Israelis and Palestinians.

One can also question whether the secular Zionists who were identified in the second reading as wanting peace with the Palestinians really saw them as equals. As a number of commentators have noted, Zionists in this camp, such as Ahad Ha-Am, often viewed the Palestinians through a paternalistic lens. They hoped for a majority of Jews in Palestine so that the Palestinians could be absorbed into the Jewish state and benefit from its culture and wealth. This way of thinking was benevolent, but only in a limited sense. While this approach was most com-mon among early Zionists, it has also been taken up by Israelis in more recent times. As we noted in our first reading, a paternalistic attitude toward Palestin-ians was also expressed by supporters of Gush Emunim in its early years.[125]

123 Shapira, *Land and Power*, 42–43, 163–72.

124 Luz, *Wrestling with an Angel*, 82–84

125 Luz, *Wrestling with an Angel*, 195–97. Even Ahad Ha-Am was guilty at times of this type of paternalism. See Gorny, 99–104.

Some of the reasons for the differences between the two readings are similar to those encountered in earlier chapters. Once again, an implicit question was whether historical context should be a factor in judging the violent attitudes and actions of Jews. The first reading functioned with the premise that it should not; if Zionism was violent, it should be judged negatively. The second reading claimed that historical context was of central importance. The relentless persecution of Jews throughout the centuries and their dashed hopes regarding the improvement of their condition in Europe should significantly soften any criticism of Zionism.

Another point of disagreement was determining whether, when a thinker or school of thinkers in Judaism had strayed sufficiently from its basic teachings, it had distorted them. In the first reading, it was assumed that the violent tendencies in Zionism were very much an expression of Judaism. In the second reading, those tendencies were seen as the product of outside influences, and the latter had so radically reshaped Jewish ideas that the connection of those ideas to authentic Judaism was tenuous at best.

In general, our discussion of Zionism has been the most complex of all the subjects we have dealt with in our study, and no wonder. Zionism has absorbed all the conflicting tendencies of Judaism regarding the relationship between Jews and non-Jews that have evolved over the centuries. Furthermore, it has been shaped by a host of outside forces that further complicate Jewish thinking on this issue. Thus, whichever of the two readings one favors, all must agree that modern Jews face an exceedingly daunting challenge in grappling with the religious meaning of a sovereign Jewish state in their ancient homeland and how it affects their relationship with the outside world.

7

Conclusions

Two very different readings of Judaism have emerged from our study. According to one reading, Judaism promotes peace. In the Bible, all human beings are created in God's image, and when God selects the Israelites as his chosen people, his intent is that the blessings experienced by the Israelites will be shared with other nations. This notion is fully realized in the messianic era when there will be peace among the nations. Certainly, there is violence in the Bible—most notably, the wars that Israel wages against the Canaanites and Amalekites—but several interpretations were given to explain why these wars are not as troubling as they may seem. Moreover, in rabbinic Judaism, the emphasis on peace is even more pronounced than it is in the Bible. Through a bold reinterpretation of the biblical text, the rabbis soften the violent elements in the biblical text and construct a Judaism that focuses primarily on passivity and piety as Jews await the coming of the messiah during the period of the exile. Medieval Jewish philosophy implicitly develops the peaceful emphasis even further by accentuating a universalism predicated on the notion that intellectual perfection is the ultimate goal for all human beings. Moreover, Maimonides, the leading figure in this school, further mitigates the violence of earlier sources by insisting that the Canaanites and Amalekites had to be offered terms of peace before Israel waged war on them, a condition absent from the biblical text. Maimonides also adopts the notion that the messianic period will be one in which there will be peace among the nations. Medieval Kabbalah certainly has a negative view of non-Jews, but it never advocated physical violence against them. Moreover, the negative portrayals of non-Jews in Kabbalah have not stopped modern students from constructing a universalistic reading of Kabbalah that is implicitly peaceful. With modern Zionism and the creation of the state of Israel, Jews have regained political and military power and have once again engaged in collective violence against their enemies. However, one must recognize that much of this violence has been inspired by factors having little to do with Judaism, such as secular nationalism, Jewish fears of Arabs engendered by centuries of persecution from the non-Jewish world in general, and the desperation of European Jews, especially those in Eastern Europe, who believed that Zionism represented the only chance for Jews to survive as a people. Furthermore, much of the violence by Israelis has been meant to ward off the aggression of Palestinians and Arabs against Jews. What is remarkable is how the benevolent elements of Judaism have restrained Jewish violence from being even more extreme.

According to a second reading, Judaism promotes violence. In the Bible, the focus of the historical narrative is mostly on the Israelites, who are elevated above other nations through the doctrine of chosenness. That doctrine in turn provides justification for the genocidal wars against the Canaanites and Amalekites, wars that are the worst examples of religious violence in the history of Judaism. The Bible's vision of the messianic period is another example of the moral difficulties with the doctrine of chosenness. At its worst, the Bible depicts this period as one in which God's enemies will be destroyed, and at its best it presents a chauvinistic description of that era as one in which the Israelites will be ascendant over other nations, with all of them worshipping the God of Israel. In rabbinic Judaism, the rabbis certainly oppose violence against their non-Jewish enemies, but they do so because it is impractical, not because they oppose violence in principle. They approve of the wars that were fought in the distant past against the Canaanites and Amalekites, and they envision the future messianic era as one in which war will be waged once again to defeat their enemies. In early and medieval rabbinic Judaism, the Amalekites also become a flexible symbol for all enemies that the Jews encounter. The embers of anger against non-Jews and the potential for that anger to foment violence are therefore allowed to smolder. Medieval Jewish philosophy is less universalistic than is often assumed. Maimonides has negative things to say about Christianity and Islam, and he vilifies all people—Jews and non-Jews—who do not seek a life of intellectual perfection. Furthermore, Maimonides still endorses violence against the Canaanites and Amalekites, despite his creative understanding of the commandments to annihilate them, and while the culmination of the messianic era is characterized by peace in his thinking, it is a

peace that comes about through war. Kabbalah does not openly endorse violence against non-Jews, but it expresses the most negative views of non-Jews in
Judaism by associating them with the realm of pure evil, and it envisions the
messianic era as a period in which the non-Jewish world will be destroyed.
Modern Zionism represents the active revival of the violent tendencies in Judaism, which have emerged in the open once again because Jews have regained
political and military power. In religious Zionism, the endorsement of violence
is predicated on many of the incendiary beliefs just described: the belief that
Jews are superior to other nations, that God promised the land of Israel to
them, that the world is on the cusp of the messianic period, during which the
Jews will return to the land, and that non-Jews are the enemy "other," as taught
by Kabbalah. Secular Zionism does not subscribe to these premises in their
literal meaning, but it has translated many of them into nationalist ideals that
have inspired violence as well. Mainstream Zionism was at best insensitive and
paternalistic toward Palestinians and at worst physically violent toward them,
and when the opportunities arose to dispossess them of their land, it did. Zionism, therefore, has been not only violent, but aggressively so.

That these two viewpoints have successfully engaged every major school in
Judaism is in itself noteworthy. It should lay to rest commonly held misconceptions that some schools in Judaism clearly endorse one of the two perspectives.
Most notable in this respect is what we have discovered regarding rabbinic
Judaism. Jewish scholars and ethicists commonly see rabbinic Judaism as a
school that rejected much of the violence in the Bible and in its stead favored a
more peaceful understanding of Judaism. That indeed is one possible interpretation of rabbinic Judaism. However, we have shown that another reading of
rabbinic Judaism is possible, according to which the rabbis preserved the violence of the Bible. Another instance in which commonly held perceptions were
overturned was in our discussion of medieval Jewish philosophy. Scholars of
this field generally read this school of Judaism—Maimonides, in particular—as
supporting a universalistic and benevolent Judaism. We have shown, however,
that here too another reading is possible.

As I noted in my introductory chapter, some may think that the two viewpoints I have presented are too polarized and artificial—that when it comes to
complex issues of the kind analyzed in this study, the truth lies somewhere
between the extremes. I will reiterate my initial reaction to this challenge: I
adopted the format of presenting the two viewpoints because I believed that it
would provide clarity regarding the moral dilemmas inherent in Judaism on
the issues of peace and violence. Moreover, I believe that my study has demonstrated that the two viewpoints are in no sense contrived. Each presents a plausible interpretation of Judaism based on a cogent reading of the sources.

Furthermore, each viewpoint relied on the insights of previous academic scholars. Both, therefore, deserved to be heard as independent understandings of Judaism.

Throughout this study, I also probed why it was that Jewish texts were ambiguous on the issues of peace and violence. Perhaps the most obvious reason, and one that cropped up again and again, was that there was a myriad of sources that expressed different views on these matters, even within a single school or time period. Two readings of Judaism were therefore possible because each was selective regarding the sources it cited and those it chose to emphasize.

That the two viewpoints were selective in their readings of sources also meant that they became more polarized as our study progressed because the format and character of Jewish texts changed from one period to the next. The Bible invited two readings, but because of its history of redaction, the isolation and characterization of texts supporting each of the readings were not always an easy task. In many instances, redactors had combined traditions from different sources into one text and attempted to smooth over the differences in their conflicting perspectives, with the result that those perspectives could be detected only with careful analysis. When we came to rabbinic Judaism, we also dealt with different opinions that had been redacted together in the same texts, but here we had multiple texts redacted by different individuals or schools. We also encountered discrete views expressed by or attributed to specific rabbis. Opposing perspectives were therefore more extreme in rabbinic texts than in biblical ones because the pressure applied by redactors to create unified works was diminished. Individual rabbinic opinions were openly displayed in all their variety and mutual inconsistency. Once we reached the medieval period, there were no redactors at all. We encountered separate works produced by different authors presenting positions worked out in great detail. The perspectives here were therefore even wider apart than those in the rabbinic literature.

The gradual polarization in Jewish texts can be illustrated by looking at the general perspectives of the two viewpoints on non-Jews. In the Bible, we saw texts expressing positive and negative views toward non-Jews, sometimes within the same text. Thus, for example, in the book of Isaiah, universalistic passages were redacted together with passages that were particularistic. In rabbinic Judaism, opposing views regarding non-Jews became more radical. We saw rabbis who depicted non-Jews as animals alongside others who saw them as equivalent to high priests, a range of opinion that was greater than anything found in the biblical text. In medieval texts, the polarity of views on non-Jews became even more pronounced, with Kabbalistic sources presenting the view that non-Jews represented the realm of pure evil and medieval Jewish philosophers arguing that non-Jews who had achieved intellectual perfection were closer to God than Jews who had not.

In addition to encountering different texts with contrasting perspectives, we also saw a good many instances in which the same text or group of texts could be interpreted in different ways because of the texts' inherent ambiguity. Thus, for instance, in our treatment of the Bible, the opening verses in Genesis 12, in which Abraham is first summoned by God, invited two very different readings regarding the relationship between Abraham's descendants and the gentile nations. In our discussion of rabbinic Judaism, we analyzed a striking aggadic passage regarding God's command to Saul to annihilate the Amalekites, which could be read in two ways as well.

Another common source of ambiguity in our study had to do with the role of historical context in the moral evaluation of Jewish texts and ideas. The viewpoint that interpreted Judaism as nonviolent frequently invoked historical context to explain positive depictions of violence in Jewish sources. Those depictions were understood as reactions to the violence Jews themselves experienced at the hands of non-Jews, and therefore the claim was made that such depictions were not representative of Jewish ethics and were, in some sense, forced on Jews by their historical circumstances. They were more the product of fear in the face of dire situations than expressions of true Judaism. What was remarkable was the number of instances in which this argument could be made. Jews experienced subjugation and persecution from other nations in every period in Jewish history. Even in ancient Israel, when Jews had political and military power, they spent a good deal of time battling nations and empires out to destroy them or having to make peace with the fact that they were living under foreign rule. During the entire six-hundred-year period of the second Temple, Jews had sovereignty for less than a century when the Hasmonean dynasty was in power. As we saw in our chapter on the Bible, historical context was used to explain the narratives describing the Canaanite conquest. These narratives were fictional accounts composed in the seventh century BCE that were designed to strengthen the Judahites' identity in the face of the threat of the Assyrian Empire, which was poised to destroy them.

We can also add here that despite Jewish suffering, there was always a strand in Judaism that viewed non-Jews in positive terms and did not preach violence against them. Thus, when Jews were given the chance to join European society in the early eighteenth century, that positive strand came to the fore as large numbers of Jews welcomed the opportunity to become part of a culture that had persecuted them for centuries. Even today, in a post-Holocaust era, the same way of thinking can be found among Jews who feel that past Jewish suffering not only does not give them a license to persecute their enemies, it creates an obligation for compassion toward them. Ehud Luz has demonstrated that there has been a consistent strain in Israeli thought and literature that subscribes to this way of thinking and argues that the past travails of Jews should make them more sympathetic to the plight of their Arab enemies, not less so. Thus, the use of historical context functions as a powerful tool for the viewpoint that insists on a benevolent understanding of Judaism, not just because it mitigates the harshness of the violent sources in Judaism, but also because it highlights the virtue of Jews who have been willing to rise above their suffering and have been determined to forge a positive relationship with the non-Jewish world.[1]

However, the opposing viewpoint that saw Judaism as promoting violence was not receptive to the use of historical context to explain Jewish violence. This viewpoint insisted on looking at the texts themselves for the lessons they had to teach, and historical context was not a good enough excuse for ignoring the moral problems they raised, especially those texts that depicted extreme violence in a positive way. If the biblical text espoused genocide against the Canaanites, it did not help to point out that the texts describing those imperatives were composed at a time when the Israelites were attempting to shore up their identity in the face of the Assyrian threat. As Gerd Lüdemann argues, genocide is *always* wrong, whether in the modern period or in the ancient world. The biblical narratives about the Canaanites therefore could not be salvaged by looking at them within their historical context.[2] And while Luz's observations are interesting for their descriptions of how some Jews have used past suffering for positive purposes, one has to note that Luz also describes an opposing viewpoint, well represented in Israeli culture, that argues that the tribulations Jews have experienced in their history should encourage them to treat their enemies without any sympathy whatsoever.[3]

---

1 Luz, *Wrestling with an Angel*, chapter 12.

2 Lüdemann, *The Unholy in Holy Scripture*, 54.

3 Luz, *Wrestling with an Angel*, chapter 12. My observations here raise questions about Louis Newman's position on the problem of historicism in Jewish ethics (*Past Imperatives*, chapter 7). That problem is, if all sources on Jewish ethics are a product of their historical environments as academic analysis often attempts to demonstrate, then how do we avoid extreme ethical relativism? Newman solves the problem by arguing for what is, in effect, a Jewish process theology. Judaism is the product of encounters that each generation of Jews has with the mysterious divine presence. We must therefore accept a certain degree of historical relativism as Jews in each period reformulate their understanding of the divine presence and its meaning for their lives. However, Newman expresses confidence that this will not lead to complete moral chaos because moral decisions will be made collectively and with the help of classical Jewish texts. Newman's theology may work for many issues in Jewish ethics, but it is hard to imagine how it would help with the type of issues we are dealing with in our study. Can one really say that the biblical sources describing the Canaanite conquest were legitimate interpretations of Israel's encounter with the divine presence? And if so, what makes Meir Kahane's reading of Judaism any less legitimate than Buber's? Lüdemann's statement points up the difficulty here. If genocide is always wrong, then one cannot easily salvage the biblical narratives describing the Canaanite conquest as an expression of revelation.

There are other difficulties with the use of historical context to explain the violence in Jewish texts, difficulties that have not yet been raised in this study but that deserve mention nonetheless. While Jewish ethicists often use historical context to explain away unpleasant Jewish texts, they generally do not apply the same thinking to Jewish texts that are more to their liking. In fact, I cannot recall a single instance of an interpretation of this kind. What justifies this selectiveness? If one is willing to invoke historical context with morally problematic texts, one should be willing to do the same with benevolent ones as well. Why not analyze in the same fashion the notion that human beings are created in the image of God, or the imperative to love one's neighbor as oneself? One could say that these concepts also emerge from within a defined historical context very different from our own and are therefore not relevant in our day and age. If one is going to adopt a historicist perspective that relegates ancient texts celebrating violence to a distant past and renders them impotent for guiding us in the modern period, we should do so with all Jewish texts, even those we like. Yet, Jewish ethicists are reluctant to do this—and for obvious reasons: Jewish texts could no longer function as sources that impart lessons of timeless import. Still, Jewish ethicists must at least acknowledge that they are being inconsistent in their use of historical context, or else they should find some standard that allows them to decide that some texts are bound to their historical context and are therefore no longer relevant, while other texts transcend that context. But the main point that emerges from this discussion of historical context is that it is a complex issue that once again invites ambiguity in a moral evaluation of Jewish texts.

Yet another source of ambiguity in our study also had to do with context but involved the place of Jewish texts within the context of the evolving Jewish tradition. The viewpoint that believed that Judaism promoted nonviolence often argued that Jewish sources frequently softened the violence of earlier sources through interpretation. This approach implicitly celebrated Judaism's capacity for interpretation in general, and the early rabbis were lionized as trailblazers on this issue because their literature was filled with creative and innovative readings of the Bible, and their method of interpretation was highly influential on all later forms of Judaism. The viewpoint that read Judaism benevolently also seemed to connect this view of interpretation with the notion that Jewish revelation is progressive in nature. That is, interpretation was not only celebrated, it was a tool by which Judaism gradually weeded out whatever violence was present in earlier sources. It was also assumed that we as moderns are interpreters who belong in the chain of this interpretive tradition as well, and we therefore have the authority to rid the Jewish tradition of whatever remnants of violence remain within it by our own interpretation of the sources.

This entire way of thinking, I should emphasize, is quite common among Jewish ethicists, even when its premises are not explicitly acknowledged.

The viewpoint that believed that Judaism promoted violence was skeptical about this approach. The argument here, once again, was that Jewish sources had to be evaluated only by what they said, and if they espoused violence, focusing on how those sources engaged in interpretation of earlier traditions could not save them. While Jewish sources often mitigated the harshness of earlier texts, those later sources did not get rid of the violence altogether.

The division between the two viewpoints on this issue was therefore centered on the question of whether one judges a source positively, because it reflects moral progress over its predecessors, or negatively, because it leaves much to be desired in light of our contemporary moral standards. Put another way, the viewpoints were divided over whether one evaluates a source by looking at how far it has come from a moral standpoint or by looking at how far it has yet to go.

No example better illustrates the dilemma here than the midrashic source that retells the story of the Canaanite conquest and informs us that Joshua had to offer terms of peace to the Canaanites. According to this source, the Canaanites either had to leave the land of Israel, go to war, or surrender and become resident aliens. This source was later canonized into law in Maimonides' legal code. The viewpoint that insisted on a benevolent reading of Judaism cited scholars who saw the midrashic source and its use by Maimonides as remarkable instances of interpretation in which violent biblical sources were boldly and creatively reread by later interpreters because of moral considerations. In the biblical text, the Canaanites were not given the choices spelled out by the midrash and Maimonides, and these later interpretations were therefore rereading the text because of objections to the notion that the Canaanites would be killed without first being given the option to flee or surrender.[4] However, we also saw in our chapter on Zionism that the very same sources were invoked by Meir Kahane for his own purposes. According to Kahane, the Palestinians should be offered the same terms specified in those texts: either leave the land, go to war, or become resident aliens.[5] Thus, Kahane had no interest in the moral "progress" that these sources represented within the context of the Jewish tradition. They had to be read as they were. They specified what Jews should do, and their instructions had to be followed to the letter. Kahane's use of these sources therefore highlights the limitations of the approach taken by those who

---

4 See pp. 94–5, this volume.
5 See pp. 156–7, this volume.

express confidence that later Jewish sources correct the moral difficulties of earlier sources. While the sources under discussion may represent moral progress over the biblical text, they still espouse violence of both a physical and a structural nature in that the enemies of the Jews must either abandon their claim on the land, be killed, or be subjugated to Jewish rule. Maimonides' understanding of these imperatives is even more problematic from a moral standpoint in that, according to his reading, the third option includes the provisions that the Canaanites must adopt the Noahide code, that they are to be employed as servants to the Jews, and that they are to live in a lowly and humiliating condition. Moreover, the author of the midrashic source and Maimonides must acknowledge that after the Canaanites refused the offer made by Joshua according to their reading, they were systematically slaughtered—men, women, and children.

However, this does not mean that Kahane was right. The key question here, which is difficult to resolve, is whether we should focus on the moral progress that the midrash and Maimonides represent in comparison to the Bible or highlight the moral deficiencies of these sources in comparison with our own modern ethical standards. There is no easy answer to this question.

One other difficulty with the notion that violent Jewish sources can be defanged through interpretation is that if one celebrates interpretation in the Jewish tradition, one has to be prepared for the possibility that in our period interpretation might yield views that are *more* violent than their predecessors. The readings of Judaism espoused by Meir Kahane and Tsevi Yehudah Kook are a case in point. Their understanding of Judaism was at times worse, from a moral standpoint, than that of their medieval predecessors. Put another way, the notion assumed by the benevolent viewpoint that revelation is progressive and that later interpreters always offer more peaceful readings of Judaism than earlier ones is not necessarily correct. The reverse may occur in that later thinkers may present interpretations of Jewish texts that are, in fact, less peaceful than earlier ones.

One final source of ambiguity that emerged in our study had to do with the limits of interpretation in Judaism. Each of the two viewpoints rejected interpretations adduced by the opposing perspective on the premise that they were distortions of Judaism. For instance, the viewpoint that believed that Judaism promoted peace questioned whether the violent religious Zionism developed by Tsevi Yehudah Kook and his followers was a legitimate reading of Judaism. Among the arguments presented to make this point was the claim that this brand of religious Zionism was perhaps more a product of modernity than it was an authentic understanding of Judaism, and that its emphasis on messianism was not properly grounded in Jewish sources. Similar questions were raised about secular Zionism, which also made use of Jewish ideas but stripped them of their original metaphysical underpinnings. Here too the question was raised of whether interpretation had, in fact, severed Zionism's connection with authentic Judaism. Conversely, the viewpoint that believed that Judaism promoted violence cast doubt on the notion that New Age Kabbalah could be viewed as an expression of a universalistic and benevolent Judaism, because it was not clear whether it qualified as true Kabbalah. New Age Kabbalah so radically reinterprets key ideas in medieval Kabbalah that one has to question whether there is any real relationship between the two. Yet, such judgments about what is and is not authentic Judaism are difficult to assess. Most Jewish thinkers agree that interpretation is central in Judaism, that Judaism has evolved over time because of it, and that Judaism will remain a vital and vibrant religion only if Jews continue to engage in interpretation. However, it is not at all clear what the limits of interpretation should be, and it is difficult to come up with hard-and-fast rules to determine when an interpretation has crossed the line and created a way of thinking that is no longer genuinely Jewish.

The main body of this study began with God's promise to Abraham in the first verses of Genesis 12 that he and his descendants would be a chosen people and that they would inherit the land of Canaan. As part of this covenantal agreement, God also informed Abraham about the relationship between him and his descendants, on the one hand, and the rest of the nations, on the other. Yet, it was unclear what the precise nature of that relationship was. According to one reading, the nations would receive God's blessings through Abraham. According to another, they would aspire to be blessed like Abraham, but they would not necessarily be the beneficiaries of his blessing.

In some sense, our entire study has been an extended discussion of these few verses. God's promise that Abraham's descendants would inherit the land of Israel has led us to the central theme of this study. According to the biblical account, the Israelites used violence to take possession of the land. When they were dispossessed of the land in the first century, their identity was shaped by the hope of gaining possession of it once again. In our day and age, that hope has become a reality. Yet, the repossession of the land has brought with it great challenges as Jews have had to grapple with the moral question of using violence to achieve their goals. As we have shown, Jews are sharply divided on this issue, with some embracing violence, others opposing it, and still others taking a position in between the two options.

The ambiguity of the biblical text regarding Abraham's relationship to the nations of the world led us to another central theme in our study, one that served as critical background to the exploration of Jewish views on violence. We have seen that in every period in Jewish history, Jews have been divided over their understanding of the relationship they should have with the non-Jewish world, a division going back to God's summons to Abraham. For some, that relationship should be guided by the spirit of the first reading of Abraham's link to the nations. Jewish chosenness implies a close bond with the non-Jewish world, one that requires Jews to focus on their commonality with non-Jews and help them experience God's blessings. For others, Jews should follow the second reading: Jewish chosenness means that Jews are distinct from and superior to the gentile nations, and until the time of the messianic era, Jews need to remain separate from them, all the while cultivating their relationship with God in order to bring redemption to the world.

The ambiguities this study has explored therefore have their roots in a passage that, according to traditional Judaism, contains the first reference to Jewish peoplehood. From the very beginning, it would seem, Jews were conflicted about their place in the world and how they should behave toward other nations, and the history of Judaism has been rife with ambiguities regarding these issues ever since. It is also likely that as Judaism looks to the future, the same ambiguities will persist for some time to come.

Yet, the ambiguities discussed here do not belong to Judaism alone. All of the world's major religions are plagued with ambiguities regarding peace and violence, and this is especially the case with the other two Abrahamic faiths that drew their inspiration from Judaism. Christianity and Islam have both inherited the question of what role Abraham's heirs should play in relation to the nations of the world because he is, after all, their forefather as well. These religions have also struggled throughout their respective histories to define the meaning of chosenness, and their definitions of this concept betray as much variety as we find in Judaism.

I will therefore close out the main body of this study by reiterating a plea I made in my introduction. It is my hope that my analysis will serve as inspiration for scholars of other religions to examine their own traditions and engage in the same kind of reflection I have provided here regarding Judaism. My plea is directed particularly at scholars in the Abrahamic communities. The violence that the Abrahamic religions have brought to the world in recent years is perhaps the greatest threat to the well-being of humanity in our day and age, but the most effective antidote to that violence may lie in the peaceful dimension of those very same religions. Gaining a proper understanding of this duality may therefore be crucial for ensuring that it is peace that will prevail, not violence.

Epilogue

Personal Reflections on Where We Go from Here

While the main goals of this study have been accomplished, my reader at this point is likely to be troubled by its practical ramifications. If Judaism is indeed ambiguous when it comes to the issues of peace and violence, does it mean that Judaism provides no sure guidance on these matters? Are we left with nothing more than confusion?

I would be remiss if I did not address these questions, seeing as they are of some urgency. One encounters ambiguities in practically every sphere of Jewish ethics, and therefore it is not unusual for Jewish ethicists to express a wide range of views on any given moral issue. Moreover, Jewish ethicists have tended increasingly to deal with this multiplicity of viewpoints by resisting the temptation to choose one opinion over another and by leaving it up to the conscience of the individual to decide what the best course of action should be on specific moral questions. The reasoning behind this approach is that in the modern period the Jewish community has become remarkably diverse and, therefore, no one position on any given moral matter will win the assent of all Jews. Thus, we must respect multiple viewpoints so long as they are informed by a knowledge of Jewish sources and are well thought out. This approach is distinctly postmodern in its rejection of the notion that there are universal systems of thought and practice applicable in all places and times, and in its support of the idea that truth is at best partial and fragmentary.[1]

Yet, when it comes to issues of peace and violence, the ramifications of ambiguity are far greater than in any other sphere of Jewish ethics, and these issues therefore do not lend themselves easily to a postmodern approach. The two viewpoints in this study parallel right-wing and left-wing political positions in the Jewish community regarding the state of Israel and its relationship to Palestinians, the Arab countries, and the Muslim world as a whole. Jews who uphold the viewpoint claiming that Judaism promotes peace tend to belong to the left-wing camp, while those who uphold the viewpoint maintaining that Judaism promotes violence tend to belong to the right-wing camp. The correspondence I am suggesting is not perfect; in our study, the viewpoint that equated Judaism with violence did so as a critique of Judaism, while the Jews who belong to the right wing generally view violence in a positive light. Still, the overlap between these positions is significant. I am also aware of the fact that my categorization of Jews into left-wing and right-wing camps is simplistic. Each camp itself can be further subdivided into multiple groups. Still, for the purposes of this discussion, this crude categorization will suffice.

It is therefore highly problematic to declare in postmodern fashion that both readings of Judaism in our study are legitimate and we should leave the decision about which view is correct to the individual conscience. First of all, from a pragmatic standpoint, a clear Jewish position is more urgently needed here than in any other area of Jewish ethics, because when it comes to the Israeli-Palestinian conflict, the state of Israel has to act as a collective.[2] Secondly, the issues dealt with in our study are simply too serious for us to accept all viewpoints. The survival of Israel may very well depend on whether it adopts a right- or left-wing orientation. Israel is home to almost half the population of Jews in the world and has become central to the identity of Jews everywhere. Thus, once again, it is imperative that Jews take a stand on which of the viewpoints in our study they support. Moreover, the well-being of the entire world

---

1 See Newman, *Past Imperatives*, chapter 7. Newman proposes a postmodern process theology for Judaism. According to this theology, Judaism evolves as Jews in each generation respond to the mystery of the divine by gleaning insights from Jewish texts and by responding to the historical context in which they find themselves. Newman therefore insists that Jewish communities nowadays have to solve moral questions on the basis of these two factors. The postmodern emphasis here is also found in other places in Newman's works. He frequently attempts to understand divergent positions in Jewish ethics without determining which one is correct. S. Daniel Breslauer develops a postmodern approach to Jewish ethics similar to Newman's in *Toward a Jewish (M)orality: Speaking of a Postmodern Jewish Ethics* (Westport, Conn.: Greenwood Press, 1998).

2 Though, in point of fact, Israel often tries to please constituencies on both sides of the political spectrum, and this approach frequently results in such problems.

may be at stake here. As we noted at the beginning of this study, the issue of religious violence is the most pressing one of our time, and Jews are at the center of this issue because the Israeli-Palestinian conflict represents the fault line between the Muslim and Western worlds. No other ethical matter in Judaism has ramifications outside the Jewish sphere to the extent that this one does. Thus, once again, the acceptance of all viewpoints will not do here.

What I am arguing seems to be tacitly recognized by Jewish ethicists across the political spectrum. Jewish ethicists on both the right and the left are reluctant to give recognition to the opposing viewpoint when it comes to the issues of peace and violence, in general, and the Israeli-Palestinian conflict, in particular. These issues are too highly charged for either side to allow for diversity. That this is the case with right-wing thinkers should come as no surprise. The thinking of right-wing Jewish thinkers has always been marked by a muscular approach toward disagreement, one that leaves little room for opposition. However, what is noteworthy is that an unwillingness to consider the opposing viewpoint is found among liberal Jewish thinkers as well. I have yet to encounter a liberal Jewish ethicist who has been willing to declare that all Jewish viewpoints on peace and violence, or the Israeli-Palestinian conflict, are legitimate expressions of Judaism that need to be accorded respect—including those of the right wing. No liberal Jewish thinker will say that the violent views of Meir Kahane, Tsevi Yehudah Kook, or the settlers on the West Bank have the same standing as those espousing peace, and that Jews are free to adopt whichever viewpoint speaks to their conscience. Thus, when liberal Jewish ethicists support a postmodern pluralism regarding ethical issues, this approach does not seem to include the issues dealt with in this study. Once again, there appears to be a recognition that these matters are too serious to be left to the whims of individual conscience.[3]

---

3 The strong feelings that liberal Jewish ethicists have on these issues may also have roots in the nineteenth century, when liberal Jews were striving for acceptance among Europeans. In this period, Jews argued that the essence of Judaism was ethical monotheism, which included a universal ethics seeking to bring peace and harmony to the world. Their view was that Judaism had taken on many forms throughout the centuries, but it had always preserved this essence. What inspired this way of thinking was a desire to show that at the core of Judaism was an ethics that could be shared with Christians and that Judaism therefore had a place in European society, even though its outward form remained foreign. Newman astutely argues that this background explains why modern Jewish scholars, most of whom had liberal sensibilities, did not develop an academic field in ethics until recently. They were unable to think of the essence of Judaism as something subject to academic analysis, because they would have had to acknowledge the contradictory strains within Jewish ethics, and this would have threatened the ethical "essence" of Judaism of which they were so enamored. (See Newman, *Past Imperatives*, 1–10). These views have gradually waned in the last half century, paving the way for the development of an academic field in Jewish ethics. However, the fact that liberal Jewish ethicists are still unwilling to acknowledge right-wing views on peace and violence as legitimate expressions of Judaism may indicate that these ethicists still hold fast to the notion that Judaism is, in its essence, a religion meant to bring peace to the world.

I would therefore like to close this study by sharing some observations about which of the two viewpoints explored in the preceding chapters should be favored. I must emphasize a number of points before I begin. First, the observations I am offering here are tentative. They began to develop as I worked through the issues in this study, and I hope to develop them further in a later study. Secondly, the emphasis in this discussion will be more on constructive ethics than has been the case up to this point. This is due to the nature of the questions being asked here. I will be focusing on the future rather than on the past, and this emphasis therefore invites creative speculation more than strict academic analysis. Finally, the present discussion will be far more personal than the discussion has been thus far in that I will be speaking a good deal about my own experiences as a participant in interfaith dialogue and an activist in peacemaking.[4]

I will begin by noting what I hope is understood at this point: in order to determine which viewpoint in this study is preferable, we cannot be guided solely by an analysis of Jewish texts. Our study has shown that ambiguity in the Jewish textual tradition regarding peace and violence is both broad and deep. We will therefore not attempt to argue that one of the viewpoints is to be favored on the basis of textual evidence alone.

It would seem, therefore, that our only alternative is to go outside the texts and engage the real world. We must focus on the realm of the empirical. More specifically, we must ask which viewpoint makes more sense on the basis of pragmatic and practical concerns. This approach may seem irreligious, but I would like to leave that concern aside for the moment. The more immediate problem is that pragmatism is far too ill-defined a category to be of much use unless we give it more precise definition. What is considered pragmatic will vary considerably from person to person, depending on what goals are valued and how one achieves those goals most efficiently.

Yet, I believe there is one major pragmatic concern that all Jews can agree upon and that can frame our discussion. Almost all committed Jews, regardless of which viewpoint in our study they support, and regardless of whether they are on the Right or the Left, are committed to the survival and well-being of Judaism and the Jewish people. Of course, almost every human community has survival instincts. However, for Jews these instincts seem to have been especially strong. One of the most basic and distinctive elements in Judaism is the great emphasis it places on the value of life in this world, and that emphasis concerns not just the individual but the collective as

---

4 See my preface for some autobiographical details on this aspect of my career.

well.[5] Jews, as a people, see themselves as critical in God's plan for history up to and including the messianic period, and therefore Jewish theologians have never entertained the possibility that Jews and Judaism may disappear before the arrival of that era. The concern with survival is therefore not just a matter of pragmatism, but a religious imperative as well. Thus, while in one sense we have gone outside the realm of Jewish texts, in another sense we remain within their purview.

Before I explain why the these observations are significant for our discussion, I would like to expand on Jewish attitudes to survival in order to demonstrate just how important they are in Jewish thinking. It is rabbinic Judaism in particular that seems to have elevated the imperative of survival to a central principle in Jewish thinking. Its entire program was predicated on survival in the wake of the destruction of the second Temple. The rabbis reshaped Judaism in order to ensure its longevity and vitality despite this catastrophe, and they did so with great boldness and creativity. Their program was centered on the development of biblical law and the belief that, in the period of exile, Jews could continue to have a relationship with God through the observance of that law. Certainly, not all of God's commandments could be obeyed in a post-Temple era, most notably those involving the sacrifices. But the rabbis insisted that Jews continue to obey the laws they could still observe, and that this was good enough to maintain a relationship with God. Moreover, they found innovative ways to preserve the rituals of the Temple in symbolic form, most significantly by replacing sacrifice with prayer. The rabbis also displayed pragmatic wisdom and foresight in the realm of ethics. They encouraged their followers to give up their political independence, eschew violence against their enemies, and accommodate themselves to gentile rule. They valued the preservation of the Jewish community over independence. Of course, in our chapter on rabbinic Judaism, we debated whether the rabbis chose this course of action because of idealistic ethical reasons or because they recognized that there was no viable alternative. But for our present concerns, it is immaterial which interpretation is correct. All can agree that, at the very least, the rabbis were focused on the preservation of Judaism and the Jewish people and that this concern was central to their thinking.

5 Artson, 33–50; Reuven Kimelman, "The Rabbinic Theology of the Physical," 4:946–76. The argument has recently been put forward by Eliezer Diamond that rabbinic Judaism was more positively disposed to asceticism than scholars have been willing to acknowledge, and that its asceticism had an influence on later forms of Judaism. See Diamond, *Holy Men and Hunger Artists: Fasting and Asceticism in Rabbinic Culture* (Oxford: Oxford University Press, 2004). If true, the thesis that Judaism gives ultimate value to life in this world may have to be modified. However, my sense is that the this-worldly ethic of Judaism is preponderant in Judaism.

This pragmatic way of thinking, in fact, permeated all levels of rabbinic law. Take, for example, the institution of *takkanot*. These were laws legislated by the rabbis for one of two purposes: to create prescriptions that did not exist in the Torah but were needed owing to changes in economic and social realities, or to amend laws that did exist in the Torah but had to be rethought for the same reasons.[6] Here we see rabbinic pragmatism at its best. A well-known example of this type of legislation is the *prozbul*, a legal maneuver that allowed debts to be collected after the sabbatical year, even though according to the Torah all debts were canceled in that year. The *prozbul* was essential for the economic well-being of the Jewish community during the early rabbinic period because Palestine had shifted to a money-based economy that could not have functioned if the original legislation of the Torah had been upheld. The Torah's prescriptions therefore had to be circumvented.[7] Another example is that, out of concern for social order and the public good, the rabbis in a number of instances imposed punishments on criminals that were far stricter than those dictated by the Torah.[8] Here too the laws of the Torah were circumvented for the sake of the well-being of Jewish society. The rabbis also created legislation to make it easier for a woman to be released from her marriage when her husband was dead but there was insufficient proof from a strictly halakhic standpoint to establish that he was deceased. This legislation was particularly important in the early rabbinic period, when the Jews were at war with the Romans and Jewish men who were involved in the war could not be located and were presumed dead. Here again, concern for the well-being of Jewish society trumped biblical law.[9]

Another legal concept that is often used in conjunction with *takkanot* and also reflects rabbinic pragmatism is *hora'at sha'ah*. This phrase refers to legislation enacted by the rabbis that was temporary in nature and in open violation of biblical law. Its purpose was to deal with public emergencies that involved threats to the well-being of Judaism or the Jewish people.[10] A frequently cited

---

6 For a general discussion of these issues, see Menachem Elon, "*Takkanot*," in *The Principles of Jewish Law*, ed. Menachem Elon (Jerusalem: Keter, n.d.), 73–91.

7 Deut. 15:1–6; M. *Shevi'it* 10:3–4; B.T. *Gittin* 36b.

8 B.T. *Sanhedrin* 46a; Maimonides, M.T. *Hilkhot Rotse'ah* 2:4.

9 M. *Yevamot* 15:1, 16:6–7; *'Eduyot* 1:12. When it comes to *takkanot*, one cannot always separate religious and moral motivations from pragmatic ones. The last instance is a case in point. The rabbis may have been motivated by moral reasons to enact their legislation. After all, there were humanitarian reasons for not wanting a situation in which a woman could not remarry because the whereabouts of her husband could not be determined. In this instance, therefore, pragmatic social policy and humanitarian ethics overlapped.

10 B.T. *Yoma* 69b; *Ketubot* 15a, *Sahnhedrin* 78b, 80b; Haim H. Cohn, "Extraordinary Remedies," in *The Principles of Jewish Law*, ed. Menachem Elon (Jerusalem: Keter, n.d.), 550–54; *Intsiklopidiyah Talmudit*, ed. Shelomoh Yosef Zevin (Jerusalem: Mosad ha-Rav Kuk, 1947–2009), 8:512–27.

justification for legislation of this kind is the biblical story in which Elijah confronts the prophets of Baal on Mount Carmel and challenges them to a contest
to see whose deity is the true God. Both Elijah and the prophets of Baal prepare
sacrifices, and they pray to their respective deities to see which sacrifice will be
consumed. Elijah emerges the victor when a fire descends from heaven and
devours his offering.[11] Rabbinic law prohibits sacrifices outside the precincts of
the Temple in Jerusalem, and therefore the rabbis had to explain Elijah's
actions. They did so by invoking the notion of *hora'at sha'ah*; the laws of the
Torah had to be temporarily suspended in this instance because the people of
Israel had strayed in great numbers after foreign gods, and they had to be
brought back to the true faith. Elijah's dramatic actions were therefore needed
to convince them of God's sovereignty.[12]

The rabbis often justified legislation that violated biblical law with a radical
interpretation of Psalm 119:126, which reads: "It is time to act for the Lord; they
have violated your Torah." This verse seems to dictate that when the Torah has
been violated, one must act on God's behalf to counter such transgressions.
However, the rabbis, playing on an ambiguity in the Hebrew, reversed its meaning entirely. According to their reading, we violate the Torah *in order* to act on
God's behalf! As one rabbi put it, in some instances "it is better that one letter
of the Torah be uprooted than the entire Torah be forgotten in Israel."[13] Another
source tells us that "there are times when the disregard of the Torah may be its
foundation."[14] In other words, sometimes the laws of the Torah have to be broken in order to ensure the long-term well-being of Judaism and the Jewish
people.

The rabbis' boldness is predicated on their belief that they had great power
to interpret God's word, an issue we touched upon in our chapter on rabbinic
Judaism.[15] The rabbis held that God had given the Torah to them to determine its
meaning and that he had empowered them to apply its commandments in the
mundane world. It was therefore their right, even their duty, to implement the
type of bold legislation we have been describing here. Hanina Ben-Menahem
has shed light on rabbinic thinking about such matters by demonstrating that
authority in rabbinic law resided more in the person of the rabbi than in the
system of law he upheld, an approach to law quite different from that found in
the modern Western world, where the system of law is more important than the

---

11 I Kings 18:19–46.
12 B.T. *Yevamot* 90b.
13 M. *Berakhot* 9:5; B.T. *Temurah* 14b, *Yoma* 69b.
14 B.T. *Menahot* 99a–b.
15 See chapter 3, p. 96.

individual who implements it. The rabbi had authority not only because he was expert in the law, but because of his virtues, which were expressed in his personality and conduct. He was therefore expected to rule in accordance with the virtues he embodied, not simply in accordance with predetermined legal formulae. Consequently, it was not unusual for the rabbis to deviate from legal precedent when they felt the situation warranted it.[16]

We should not exaggerate the creative dimension of rabbinic Judaism. Modern Jewish theologians looking for a modern message in rabbinic sources often make it seem as if there were no restrictions whatsoever on rabbinic legal innovation. This is not the case. The rabbis exercised great caution when it came to the employment of *takkanot* and *hora'at sha'ah*, and they did not deviate from precedent whenever they pleased. They were well aware of the dangers inherent in this type of legislation. Moreover, there is evidence that some rabbis were quite conservative and therefore minimized or rejected innovative interpretation and legislation in Jewish law.[17] Nonetheless, the pragmatic dimension of rabbinic Judaism is one of its most salient features. The majority of rabbis seem to have understood that when interpreting and legislating in matters of law, one must always keep in mind the preservation of Judaism and the Jewish people, and that may mean violating laws in the short term for the sake of long-term goals.[18] This feature of rabbinic Judaism may also help explain why it eventually became the dominant form of Judaism in the wake of the destruction of the second Temple. Several groups with their own versions of Judaism competed with the rabbis in the first centuries of the common era, all claiming that they represented the true Judaism, but rabbinic Judaism became ascendant while almost all the others disappeared.[19]

---

16 Hanina Ben-Menahem, *Judicial Deviation in Rabbinic Law: Governed by Men, Not Rules* (Chur and New York: Harwood Academic, 1991); idem, "Talmudic Law: A Jurisprudential Perspective," in *The Cambridge History of Judaism: The Late Roman–Rabbinic Period*, ed. Steven T. Katz (Cambridge: Cambridge University Press, 2006), 877–98, especially 893.

17 On this last point, see Menachem Fisch, *Rational Rabbis: Science and Talmudic Culture* (Bloomington: Indiana University Press, 1997). Fisch argues there were two strains in early rabbinic jurisprudence: a traditionalist strain that was highly conservative and eschewed innovation in Jewish law, and a dynamic antitraditionalist strain that embraced innovation. Fisch claims that it was the latter strain that ultimately shaped the redaction of the Babylonian Talmud. Louis Newman proposes a similar duality in Judaism but applies it more broadly to the whole notion of covenant. Newman claims that in modern Jewish ethics there are two models for the covenantal relationship between God and the Jewish people: the contract model and the dynamic model. The contract model tends to be more conservative in assuming that the content of the covenantal agreement between God and the Jews is fixed, while the dynamic model assumes a more fluid agreement. See Newman, *Past Imperatives*, chapters 2–3; idem, *An Introduction to Jewish Ethics*, 113–17, 139–41.

18 I would speculate that this quality of rabbinic Judaism helps explain why Judaism has been so successful a religion, despite the hardships Jews have experienced throughout the centuries.

19 The most notable exception is, of course, Christianity, but the Samaritans are another group that has survived until the present today, though in very small numbers.

I must reiterate that for rabbinic Judaism the type of pragmatism we are describing here is not irreligious as we had earlier feared. Rabbinic Judaism is often misunderstood on this point. In being pragmatic, in saying openly that the Torah needed to be violated in some circumstances, the rabbis were not attempting to circumvent God's will. The rabbis believed that it was, in fact, God's will that they take practical considerations into account when probing the divine word. Again, the rabbis saw themselves as partners with God in shaping Judaism. Pragmatism, far from being sacrilegious, was in fact a divine mandate.

I would like to take our discussion of rabbinic pragmatism one step further by analyzing it in light of contemporary discussions in philosophical ethics. The pragmatism of the rabbis corresponds to an approach in philosophical ethics known as consequentialism. According to this approach, the moral worth of actions is judged on the basis of their consequences. The best-known school of consequentialism is utilitarianism. This takes several forms, but its classic formulation dictates that we should always act so as to bring about the greatest happiness of the greatest number of people. Rabbinic Judaism is not strictly utilitarian in its thinking, at least not according to this formulation, but it has utilitarian elements in it and is broadly consequentialist in that it puts a great deal of emphasis on the practical outcome of its interpretations and legislation.[20]

A consequentialist school that may provide a good model for understanding rabbinic Judaism is American pragmatism. Here "pragmatism" refers to a distinctive approach toward philosophy developed at the beginning of the twentieth century by a group of American philosophers that included C. S. Pierce, William James, and John Dewey. Pierce, who founded this school, argued that the meaning of propositions is determined solely by their practical application—by being "tested" in the real world, so to speak. Thus, to cite a simple example, an adjective such as "hardness" has no meaning in the abstract. It means something only when an object displays certain qualities when interacting with other objects in the physical world, when its hardness brings about certain tangible effects. James extended Pierce's pragmatic principle by using it as a means to determine whether a statement was actually true. That is, James was interested not just in what statements meant, which was

---

20 There is a vast literature on consequentialism. For brief but good introductions, see Harry J. Gensler, *Ethics: A Contemporary Introduction* (London and New York: Routledge, 1998), chapter 8; David O. Brink, "Some Forms and Limits of Consequentialism," in *The Oxford Handbook of Ethical Theory*, ed. David Copp (New York: Oxford University Press, 2006), 380–423; Julia Driver, *Ethics: The Fundamentals* (Malden, Mass.: Blackwell, 2007), chapters 3–4.

Pierce's concern, but in whether those statements actually corresponded to reality. Thus, according to James, all statements could be verified by testing them in the world. Even the validity of metaphysical beliefs could be determined by this method. This led to one of James's most famous and controversial assertions: religious beliefs were true if they inspired well-being and happiness in an individual, because in doing so they "worked" in the real world by bringing that person concrete benefits. John Dewey expanded the pragmatic principle even further by applying James's approach to ethics. Thus, the morality of an action could also be determined by the concrete benefits it brought about in the real world. He also applied the same principle to social groups, not just individuals, as James had. Thus, according to Dewey, actions that brought benefits to society as a whole were better than those that benefitted the individual alone. This explains Dewey's great interest in education, democracy, and the overall reform of society.[21]

American pragmatism therefore developed a consequentialist approach to ethics that in some respects parallels that found in rabbinic Judaism. Just as Dewey believed that the validity of ethical prescriptions had to be determined by the benefits they brought to a society, so too the rabbis often formulated legislation for the sake of enhancing social order and the public good. Moreover, if in American pragmatism the pragmatic principle was used both as a standard for right action and as a standard for metaphysical truth, in rabbinic ethics moral decision-making straddled both concerns simultaneously. The moral prescriptions of the rabbis that were based on a concern for social order and the public good not only dictated proper behavior, they were also statements about truth in attempting to implement what they believed was God's will.

Some modern Jewish thinkers have been influenced by American pragmatism, most notably Mordecai Kaplan and, more recently, Peter Ochs and Robert Gibbs. Kaplan was impressed by James early in his career, but his thinking ultimately had more in common with that of Dewey. Kaplan believed in applying the pragmatic principle to both theology and social ethics.[22] Ochs has reflected on Pierce's pragmatism as a means to reading the Bible, and Gibbs has shown an interest in James's pragmatism for the purpose of exploring

21 There are a number of excellent surveys of American pragmatism. See, for instance, Horace S. Thayer, *Meaning and Action: A Critical History of Pragmatism*, 2nd ed. (Indianapolis: Hacket, 1981); Cornelis De Waal, *On Pragmatism* (Belmont, Calif.: Wadsworth, 2005).

22 Richard Libowitz, *Mordecai M. Kaplan and the Development of Reconstructionism* (New York: Edwin Mellen Press, 1983), 23–41; Allan Lazaroff, "Kaplan and John Dewey," in *The American Judaism of Mordecai M. Kaplan*, ed. Emanuel S. Goldsmith, Mel Scult, and Robert M. Seltzer (New York: New York University Press, 1990), 173–96. Lazaroff argues that there are also significant differences between Kaplan and Dewey on a number of issues.

theoretical ethics.[23] However, the influence of pragmatism on Jewish ethics has been relatively meager. Moreover, the reflections of these thinkers on pragmatism have not been brought to bear on the sphere of applied ethics, in general, nor the issues of peace and violence, in particular.

Perhaps it is no surprise that Jewish ethicists have not shown more interest in pragmatism nor in consequentialism in general. Consequentialism brings with it many difficulties. For instance, the utilitarian principle, which deems an action moral if it brings about the greatest happiness of the greatest number, could be used as an instrument for tyranny over the minority that does not benefit from that action. It is also exceedingly difficult to determine standards for what "happiness" is. American pragmatism brings with it similar problems in that there is great difficulty in determining the standards for deciding whether and to what extent an action is beneficial to the individual or society. However, I am not suggesting that consequentialism be the only standard for Jewish ethics. All I am arguing is that consequentialism has a role to play in Jewish ethics and that it has not been sufficiently appreciated.

It is also clear that consequentialism was by no means the only standard used by the rabbis in moral decision-making. In fact, rabbinic ethics is governed by a complex mixture of approaches that correspond to a number of schools in contemporary ethics in addition to consequentialism, schools that place more emphasis on immovable norms of behavior. These include divine command ethics (the belief that the morality of actions is determined by God's will), deontological ethics (the belief that some actions are intrinsically good regardless of their consequences), and virtue ethics (the belief that morality is achieved when actions are inspired by good character traits). The decision as to which of these various approaches comes to the fore in rabbinic thinking is governed in part by the specifics of a given situation, and much of rabbinic ethics is therefore contextual and situational as well. This eclecticism in rabbinic ethics and its contextual emphasis provide another instance of resonance between rabbinic ethics and contemporary ethical thinking. Some modern philosophers argue that the best approach to ethics is to combine two or more methodologies, because no single one is adequate for moral decision-making. This way of thinking is often allied with a contextual and situational approach to ethics in which the mixture of methodologies may change in light of the circumstances.[24]

---

23 Peter Ochs, *Pierce, Pragmatism, and the Logic of Scripture* (Cambridge: Cambridge University Press, 1998); Robert Gibbs, *Why Ethics? Signs of Responsibilities* (Princeton: Princeton University Press, 2000).

24 Mark Lance and Margaret Little, "Particularism and Antitheory," in *The Oxford Handbook of Ethical Theory*, 567–94. Feminist ethicists have also argued for an eclectic and contextual approach to ethical questions. See Driver, chapter 9; Virginia Held, "The Ethics of Care," in *The Oxford Handbook of Ethical Theory*, 537–66.

What we have established thus far is that the principle of survival is a value that the vast majority of committed Jews uphold, that it has religious meaning because rabbinic Judaism had a strongly pragmatic orientation in which the concern for survival figured prominently, and that it has philosophical meaning in being connected to a legitimate approach in contemporary philosophical ethics. But let us now get back to the main concerns of our study. What do rabbinic pragmatism and the issue of survival have to do with Jewish views on peace and violence, and how does all this help us cope with the problem of ambiguity?

The point I have been leading up to is that rabbinic pragmatism may, in fact, provide a solution to this problem. As we noted at the beginning of this chapter, the state of Israel contains half of world Jewry and is central to the identity of Jews worldwide, and therefore the survival of Israel will determine the long-term health and well-being not only of Jews in Israel, but of the Jewish people as a whole. We also noted that the survival of Israel may very well depend on whether it adopts a right- or left-wing orientation, and the two viewpoints we have analyzed in this study correspond to these perspectives. The question we must therefore ask is which viewpoint in our study has the greater chance of ensuring Israel's survival. It is clearly that viewpoint that has greater merit because it is the position that will best address the rabbinic concern for the longevity of Judaism and the Jewish people. In other words, what I am suggesting here is that because pragmatism and its attendant focus on Jewish survival are such basic principles in rabbinic Judaism and in Jewish culture in general, we should use these principles as criteria for deciding whether Jews should support a peaceful or violent reading of Judaism, with the state of Israel as our focus.[25]

I could easily conclude my discussion at this point. After all, a good deal has been accomplished in that I have given the debate between right-wing and left-wing viewpoints a focus and a direction. What has emerged from our deliberations is that religiously committed Jews, regardless of whether they support one wing or the other, should not focus solely on religious concepts or texts in their debates about Israel's course of action. Just as important, if not more so, is the pragmatic question of which course of action stands the best chance of ensuring Jewish survival. Moreover, I have shown that the focus on pragmatism does not take us out of the realm of religion; in Judaism, pragmatism is,

---

25 My approach raises questions about whether different areas of Jewish ethics require different methodologies. My claim here is that consequentialism and contextualism are key to dealing with the ethics of peace and violence, but that may not be the case with other types of questions in Jewish ethics. This issue is touched on briefly in Newman, *An Introduction to Jewish Ethics*, 175.

in fact, a religious principle in its own right. To take our discussion any further would remove us from the realm of religion and place us in the realm of politics as we delve into the question of which position provides better prospects for Israel's survival, and perhaps that discussion is best left to those who are more expert in the politics of the Middle East than I.

Yet, I believe I should say something about the political issues. First, my academic training and my involvement in interfaith dialogue have given me some insight into these matters, insight that I believe is worth sharing. This is in part because politics and religion, while conceptually separate, are so intertwined in the Middle East that they are not easily separated. Secondly, I began this epilogue with the observation that my readers are likely to be curious about the practical ramifications of my study and that we must examine those ramifications because too much is stake for us not to. I will therefore wade into political waters, if only briefly, in order to complete my discussion.

So which viewpoint do I support as the one best able to ensure Jewish survival? Is it the right-wing or the left-wing one? I will begin with the observation that the issue of survival has traditionally been seized upon by right-wing Jews, both religious and secular, as the best justification for their way of thinking. While the right wing encompasses a broad range of views, Jews in this camp typically argue that the best way for Israel to ensure that it will not be destroyed by its enemies is to maintain a strong army and deal with these enemies with military force. They also tend to believe in holding on to the territories captured by Israel in the 1967 war and granting Palestinians at most limited autonomy. Most in this camp also maintain that the left wing, which takes a conciliatory view toward Israel's enemies and believes in the creation of a Palestinian state, is engaged in naive and wishful thinking, and that their strategy will only weaken Israel and ensure its downfall. If this reasoning is correct, then, in light of the considerations of our discussion thus far, Jews should endorse the viewpoint in our study that sees Judaism as supportive of violence—and not as a critique of Judaism, but rather as the best interpretation of Judaism in light of current circumstances.

There was a time in my life when I had sympathy with this perspective. However, in recent years I have come to see its limitations. Israel has a right to use force against its enemies in order to ensure its survival. It still faces numerous threats today, and it needs a strong military to confront them. But, to my mind, one of the greatest dangers for Israel at the present time is in believing that physical force is the best means to deal with these threats. Militarism alone cannot solve Israel's problems, and it may make them worse.

This argument could have been made at any point since the founding of the state, but its validity nowadays is greater than ever. The Arab and Muslim nations in the Middle East are developing and acquiring weapons that are more and more powerful. Several of Israel's neighbors have missiles that can now strike deep into Israeli territory. Iran is developing nuclear weapons, and it is only a matter of time before other Muslim countries do. Israel's enemies have also found effective ways to fight Israel militarily. The 2006 Lebanon War is a case in point. Israel is therefore having great difficulty maintaining its military edge over its enemies.[26] Furthermore, no nation can keep up its military guard indefinitely in the way that Jews on the Right envision. It has often been said that Israel cannot afford to lose a single war. Yet, if the viewpoint of the Right prevails, more wars will inevitably follow, and eventually Israel will lose one of them—if not in the near future, then fifty years from now, or a hundred, or two hundred. It is only a matter of time.

Factors internal to Israeli society also raise serious questions about the viewpoint of the right wing. The cohesion of Israel's society is critical for maintaining a tough military stance, but that society is becoming increasingly fragmented as it becomes more diverse, and that fragmentation is likely to increase in the coming years. The Jewish identity of Israel has also been weakened. Secular Zionism, which was dominant in Israeli society in the early years of the state, was unable to pass on a compelling vision to the next generation. Secular Israelis, who now make up three-quarters of the Israeli population, are therefore lacking ideological fervor and have grown increasingly weary of living in a country under constant threat. There is also the demographic time bomb. At current birth rates, it will not be long before the Palestinian population surpasses the Jewish population in the combined geographical area of Israel and the territories captured in 1967. Thus far, the right wing has offered little guidance to cope with these problems.

I therefore take a position that is on the left of the political spectrum—though not as far left as some. I endorse some form of accommodation with Palestinians, the Arab nations, and the Muslim world as a whole. The central issue, of course, is the Palestinian problem, and here I support the establishment of an independent Palestinian state. What precise form this state should take would have to be determined by politicians on both sides of the conflict. I personally favor a two-state solution of the kind that has been talked about for decades. I am *not* in favor of a one-state solution, which has been suggested in recent years in far-left Jewish circles. According to this scheme, Jews and Arabs would share power in a state that stretches from the Mediterranean to the Jordan

---

26 These concerns are explained in an op-ed by Benny Morris, "Why Israel Feels Threatened," *New York Times*, December 29, 2008.

River, and such a state would neither be Arab nor Jewish. The problem is that the history between these groups is too long and bitter and their cultures too different for them to be able to live comfortably together under one government. Arab and Jewish identities are also unlikely to disappear, as supporters of this approach envision. Moreover, the vast majority of Jews would find such an arrangement unacceptable. Too many Jews have too much of an emotional investment in the notion of an independent Jewish state to give it up.

In general, Israel has the best chance of surviving if it adopts a strategy that involves shrewd diplomacy designed to separate radical Palestinians, Arabs, and Muslims from moderates by offering incentives to them to live in peace with Israel while at the same time isolating the radicals. Creating a Palestinian state would be part of that strategy because it would pull the rug out from under the radical elements in the Arab world, who have used the Palestinian issue to drum up support for their cause.

Jews on the Right with whom I have shared these views have often argued against accommodation with the Palestinians because it was tried during the Oslo process and failed. They claim that the Oslo Accords did not stop Palestinian terrorism against Israelis, and in fact they led to the Second Intifada. A full response to this assessment is beyond the scope of the present discussion. However, I will say, first, that the experiment in accommodation was rather short-lived. The Oslo process lasted a mere seven years, not nearly enough time to solve a conflict that had gone on for over a hundred years and was so highly charged. Getting Israelis and Palestinians to live together in peace will require far more patience than either side displayed here. Secondly, the Oslo process did not include strong enough mechanisms for educating Israelis and Palestinians about each other's history and the depth of their respective suffering. The old hatreds therefore remained and easily erupted into the open when provoked.

In many respects, Jews are in a situation very similar to the one the rabbis confronted under Roman rule in the first centuries of the Common Era. At that time, the Jewish people were threatened by a powerful enemy, and its society and leadership were internally divided. Today, Israel contains almost half the world's Jewish population, it is again being threatened by its enemies, and its society is fragmented as well. This analogy may not seem apt, given that Israel is an independent state with its own army, whereas the Jews under Roman rule had neither sovereignty nor a strong military. In fact, for many Jews the state of Israel was founded so that Jews would *not* face the situation that they did under Roman rule. But when one takes into account the growing threats to Israel both externally and internally, the analogy is appropriate. Israel is far more vulnerable than those on the right wing admit. Jews would therefore be wise to adopt a strategy similar to that of the rabbis, a strategy in which they recognize the strength of their enemies (which grows daily), the dangers involved in using force to defeat them, and the need to find ways to live in peace with them. Such a strategy would involve giving up some things in the short term for the sake of long-term goals, much as the rabbis did.

I must emphasize that this way of thinking is as authentically Jewish as that of the religious Zionists who support a messianic agenda. In fact, pragmatism was far more basic to rabbinic Judaism than messianism ever was. As we have shown, pragmatism permeated the halakhic system. Messianism, by contrast, merited relatively little discussion in rabbinic literature. In fact, rabbinic pragmatism caused many rabbis to deliberately deemphasize messianism, as we have already noted. The Mishnah, the first major rabbinic legal compilation, hardly mentions it. The preponderance of rabbinic opinion has always been against dwelling on messianic speculations. The rabbis consistently urged Jews to worry about matters of this world, not the next, and focus on observing God's commandments.[27]

Jews on the Right may accuse me of suggesting a strategy based on weakness, not strength, and that, if implemented, would ensure the demise of the Jewish state. I would like to preempt such criticism first by pointing out again that my approach does not deny that Israel should have a strong army and that it should use force in some circumstances. Self-defense is a sacrosanct principle in Judaism, and I will uphold it as well. But the real question here is how one defines strength and weakness. Many on the Right function under the assumption that strength is equated with military might. I argue that this is not the case, especially for Israel in its current situation. An exclusive dependence on military power makes Israel weak and may bring about its destruction. To my mind, Israel will be strong if, in addition to maintaining its army, it has a realistic understanding of the dangers it faces and combines clever diplomacy and territorial concessions to neutralize them.

I do not have any illusions here that my strategy will solve all problems. Giving Palestinians a state will not automatically make them love Jews or accept Israel's existence. Nor will it have that effect on the Arab nations or the Muslim world as a whole. I also admit that the strategy I am suggesting is a gamble. It may not work. It may expose Israelis to more violence. However, I believe that it stands more of a chance of success than the strategy of the right wing, which I believe will, in the long run, fail.

Yet, while liberal Jews may applaud my endorsement of the benevolent reading of Judaism, they may be troubled by a number of questions about the arguments I have presented. First, the viewpoint in our study that gives Judaism a peaceful reading brings with it more than just a series of prescriptions for moral action. It includes an entire worldview, a universalistic theology predicated on such concepts as the notion that non-Jews are created in God's image. If pragmatism is the focus here, then what is the status of these concepts? Can pragmatism dictate how one should believe in addition to prescribing a course of action? William James answered this question in the affirmative. He was willing to declare religious beliefs true just because they resulted in desirable effects on the lives of believers. (However, James's critics have cast doubt on this line of thinking because it is a stretch to declare that religious beliefs are true just because they are practically beneficial.) A second question is whether the approach I have taken is too self-centered, too focused exclusively on Jewish concerns to be effective in the Middle East conflict. Do Jews not also have a mandate to have compassion for the Palestinians as human beings who have suffered? Is compassion not also an important dimension of Jewish ethics? Is it not also key to solving the Israeli-Palestinian conflict? A third question is whether my overall approach is too cold and intellectual to provide a compelling vision for Jews themselves to adopt. While every individual and group wants to survive, does survival offer enough motivation for Jews to act in the manner I have suggested? In sum, what all these questions touch on is the inner life of belief and emotion as it affects the self and its relation to others, factors that have been absent from my discussion thus far.

I would therefore like to supplement the arguments I have presented up to this point with another series of considerations. I will begin by focusing on the issue of Jewish attitudes toward non-Jews, which underlies the first two questions. By dealing with this issue, I hope to address the third question as well.

I believe that the universalistic theology encompassed by the benevolent reading of Judaism should be upheld by Jews, and that, by the same token, it should compel compassion toward non-Jews, in particular Palestinians. However, I will not argue for these positions on the basis of a Jamesian pragmatism; rather, I will dwell on my own personal experience. Therefore, even though pragmatism will not be the focus here, my arguments will remain in the realm of the empirical, an emphasis I have tried to maintain throughout this discussion.

I find the universalist theology allied with the benevolent reading convincing simply because some of the most magnificent people I have met in my life have been non-Jews. I have met them at every stage of my life and in every sphere. They include acquaintances, family friends, students, and colleagues. I therefore cannot accept rabbinic sources that equate non-Jews with animals, nor the Kabbalistic notion that non-Jews are inherently evil. My experience tells me that these characterizations are simply not true. Conversely, the same experience teaches me that non-Jews are created in God's image. I have seen non-Jews display love, generosity, and kindness toward me and others that is every bit as deep and sincere as that offered by my fellow Jews. A number of these non-Jews have become role models for me. If this does not make them creatures in God's image, I do not know what does.

American Jews may regard what I am saying as obvious. Today most Jews in the United States function comfortably in the non-Jewish world, and therefore it is assumed that non-Jews and Jews are equal in God's eyes. However, I may be departing from the views of some of my fellow Jews in saying that my attitude also extends to Palestinians, Arabs, and Muslims. I have met many individuals from these groups in the academic world and in the world of peace work, in which I have been involved for a number of years, and they have displayed the same wonderful qualities that American non-Jews have. They have accorded me respect, they have expressed deep regard for Judaism, and they have shown remarkable sensitivity to the predicament of Jews in the Middle East. Some of them have spent their lives working for the improvement of understanding between Jews and their respective communities. Many of them have done so at great risk to their own lives.

Of course, the argument I am making is somewhat weaker than my previous arguments. When I justified the peaceful reading of Judaism on the basis of rabbinic pragmatism and its concern for survival, I was dealing with Jewish positions to which most Jews would assent. But the present argument is dependent primarily on my own empirical experience. In fact, right-wing Jews with whom I have spoken have often claimed that they have had very different experiences with non-Jews—in particular Palestinians, Arabs, and Muslims—and they therefore reject my assessment. Right-wing Israelis, in particular, have pressed the issue even further, claiming that they have far better acquaintance with Arabs than I do, seeing that they have had to live with them side by side and interact with them on a regular basis, whereas I, as an American Jew, have not. However, what I have discovered—and here again I rely on personal experience—is that, on the whole, the experience of these right-wing Jews is often limited. American right-wing Jews have had relatively little interaction with Palestinians, Arabs, and Muslims. I have frequently asked such Jews whether they have any friends from these groups, and the vast majority have never had a conversation with these people, let alone made any attempt to befriend them. Israeli right-wing Jews do interact with Palestinians with regularity, but these interactions are often defined by an imbalance of power to which many Israelis are oblivious. An Israeli who has gotten to know Palestinians by employing them to build his home or deliver his groceries has not really gotten to know them in any genuine sense. It is a relationship between unequal parties so long as Israelis remain in the superior position from a political, economic, and military standpoint. It is unequal so long as Palestinians know that they are of value to Israelis as a source of low-priced labor.

I also find my fellow Jews, many of whom are highly educated, lacking in acquaintance not just with individuals from the other side of the conflict, but with their history. They know very little about the Israeli-Palestinian conflict and the history of the Arab and Muslim worlds in general. They may have read a great deal of history about the founding of the state of Israel, but they are unfamiliar with basic studies that are now widely accepted among Jewish and non-Jewish academics documenting the suffering and victimization of Palestinians when the state of Israel was created. They also have little sense of the degree to which the West has humiliated the Arab and Muslim world in the past two centuries, and how Arabs and Muslims perceive the establishment of the state of Israel as part of the problem. They are also surprisingly lacking in knowledge about Islam as a religion. Thus, while the observations I am sharing here are based on my own personal experience, my sense is that I, and other Jews who have engaged in peacemaking, are better informed than many of those on the Right with whom I have spoken.

One challenge I have often heard from my fellow Jews is that the Palestinians, Arabs, and Muslims I have met are not truly representative of their respective communities. Certainly, I am told, there may be good people among them, but they are few and far between. My response to this charge is that if one does not get to know people from these communities, it is hard to make such judgments.

But in fairness to Jews on the Right, I must concede that prejudice and hatred against Jews in general and Israelis in particular runs very deep among Palestinians, Arabs, and Muslims. I am certainly not blind to this problem, and I have sometimes been shocked at how strong and irrational the antipathy is. I have often been struck by the wild misconceptions that Muslims have of Jews and Judaism. I have had conversations with Muslims who believe that all Jews throughout the world are violent, right-wing messianists who are determined to bring down the Muslim world. It is also well-known that the press in the Arab and Muslim world often depicts Jews in terms and images borrowed directly from the worst anti-Jewish literature of the medieval period or from the more recent anti-Semitic propaganda of the Nazis.[28]

And if Jews are ignorant of the history of Palestinians, Arabs, and Muslims, the same is true in reverse. I have found that people from these groups

---

28 Matthias Kuntzel, *Jihad and Jew-Hatred: Islamism, Nazism, and the Roots of 9/11*, trans. Colin Meade (New York: Telos Press, 2007).

have little knowledge about Judaism.[29] They are unaware of the long history of persecution that Jews have experienced. They may have familiarity with the Holocaust, but they have no concept of how much Jews suffered in the centuries prior to it. Muslims also commonly believe that Jews living under Islamic rule in the medieval period were treated well, but historians have shown that the reality was not nearly as rosy as Muslims claim.[30] Palestinians, Arabs, and Muslims therefore fail to comprehend that, in light of the centuries of Jewish persecution, the establishment of the state of Israel was an act of desperation by Jews who did not believe that they had any future without an independent state. Moreover, they have little understanding of just how vulnerable Jews still feel. Many of them have no idea that the number of Jews in the world is tiny—only fourteen million—and that half their population lives in Israel. In addition, they often have wildly inflated views of the strength of the Jewish community. I have listened to Arabs and Muslims claim that American Jews control the U.S. media, the U.S. financial system, and the U.S. Congress. No doubt this assessment is based in part on the fact that the Israeli army is one of the strongest armies in the world. They also judge Jewish strength on the basis of how successful Jews have been, politically, economically, and socially, in the West, particularly in the United States. What they do not see is the fear that permeates the Jewish conscience, and that underneath the army uniforms and the fine business suits are a people very much worried about their longevity. (And if Jews do, in fact, control the U.S. financial system, I would like to know how I could join the conspiracy so as to secure for myself a larger house and a nicer car.)

All of this raises the question of whether Palestinians, Arabs, and Muslims are any more ready to make peace than Jews are. They may not be. But this only stiffens my resolve to urge Palestinians, Arabs, and Muslims to get to know Jews and Judaism in the same way that Jews must get to know them. I am unwilling to give up hope for peace just yet.

---

29 To cite a personal story, I once sat with an Iranian ayatollah at an interfaith conference in Italy who asked me whether it was true that all Jews believed that their messianic kingdom would stretch from the Nile to the Euphrates. His concern was that the state of Israel had designs on conquering and controlling this entire territory. I wasn't sure how to respond to such a question. Certain Jewish texts do envision a messianic kingdom governing the geographical area described by the cleric, but Israel is mostly a secular state that has no interest in messianism, and it certainly has no interest in ruling over more Arabs in Jordan, Egypt, and Iraq. It already has its hands full with the Arabs over which it presently rules! Moreover, even religious Jews do not think in these terms. In the many conversations I have had with right-wing religious Zionists, I have not heard one of them ever mention the need for Israel to conquer territory up to the messianic borders referred to by the cleric.

30 Mark R. Cohen, *Under Crescent and Cross: The Jews in the Middle Ages* (Princeton: Princeton University Press, 2008). Cohen shows that Jews were treated better under medieval Islamic rule than under medieval Christendom but that living under Muslims still brought with it serious disadvantages for Jews.

I am not suggesting that mutual understanding will solve all problems. The radical elements on either side of the divide are not likely to change their way of thinking no matter how well acquainted they become with the other side. The Meir Kahanes and Osama bin Ladens will remain the way they are to the bitter end. Nor is the formation of personal relationships between moderates guaranteed to succeed; after all, sometimes people from the two sides meet and do not come to like each other. I know of plenty of instances in which dialogue groups involving Jews and Arabs have started up and then broken down, often because of a crisis in the Israeli-Palestinian conflict that polarized the discussion. There is also the logistical problem of getting the two sides together in sufficient numbers to make any significant difference. There are eighty-five Muslims for every Jew in the world, and the imbalance in numbers makes it difficult for every Muslim to even meet a Jew, let alone become friends with one. Most Jews and Muslims are also separated by great distances geographically, and there are political, cultural, and linguistic barriers dividing them that are not easily overcome. Still, I believe that there is a broad population on both sides that can be persuaded to think differently. Moreover, just because the process will not be easy does not mean we should not try. The question is, what alternatives do we have? I do not believe we have many.

I also have the sense that when dialogue fails, it is often because of the absence of skilled facilitators and mediators who know how to draw out the deeper issues that separate the two sides but are hard to face and articulate. Laypeople who attempt to put together dialogue groups often have an unrealistic sense of their capacity for dealing with such problems. Even when professional mediators are involved, dialogue is not always successful. I have participated in dialogues that have been guided by such mediators, and even in these instances the discussion often does not get to the underlying issues that separate the two sides.

But in the end, we must brave these obstacles and be guided by a positive vision. Despite all the difficulties involved, despite all the problems that need to be overcome, the best chance for peace between the two sides is through mutual understanding, and that has not yet happened.

I will therefore conclude with a plea to both sides. I will plead with my fellow Jews to get to know Palestinians, Arabs, and Muslims. Learn about their history; educate yourselves in their religion; sensitize yourselves to the suffering of the Palestinians and to the humiliation and indignities that Arabs and Muslims in general have endured at the hands of the West for two centuries; try to understand why the establishment of the state of Israel has been so difficult for them to accept. I will also plead with Palestinians, Arabs, and Muslims to get to know Jews. Get to know Jewish history, religion, and culture; make yourselves aware of the long history of persecution that Jews have had to endure and why they still feel very insecure, despite all their successes; do your best to comprehend why the establishment of Israel is a lifeline, both physically and spiritually, for Jews throughout the world.

In general, we must all move past the distortions and half-truths that have caused so much bloodshed and work to form meaningful relationships through an open and honest attempt to experience each other's worlds. We must all move away from the dark myths about the other side that have captivated our thinking and toward an enlightenment founded on an empirical understanding of the reality lived by the other side. If we can do this, if we can truly make an effort to get into each other's minds and hearts, maybe, just maybe, we will someday live in peace.

Bibliography

Abou El Fadl, Khaled. *The Great Theft: Wrestling Islam from the Extremists.* New York: HarperSanFrancisco, 2005.

Abravanel, Don Isaac. *Perush 'al ha-Torah.* Standard edition.

Ahad Ha-Am. *Kol Kitvey Ahad Ha-'Am.* Tel Aviv: Dvir, 1961.

———. *Ten Essays on Zionism and Judaism.* Translated by Leon Simon. New York: Arno Press, 1973

Albright, William Foxwell. *From the Stone Age to Christianity: Monotheism and the Historical Process.* New York: Doubleday, 1957.

Alkalai, Judah. *Kitvey ha-Rav Yehudah Alkala'i.* Edited by Yitshak Verfel. Jerusalem: Mosad ha-Rav Kuk, 1944.

Anatoli, Jacob. *Malmad ha-Talmidim.* Lyck: M'kize Nirdamim, 1866.

Appleby, R. Scott. *The Ambivalence of the Sacred: Religion, Violence, and Reconciliation.* Lanham, Md.: Rowman & Littlefield, 2000.

Aran, Gideon. "From Pioneering to Torah Study: The Background to the Growth of Religious Zionism" (in Hebrew). In *Me'ah Shanot Tsiyyonut Datit: Heibetim Ra'ayoniyyim,* ed. Avi Sagi and Dov Schwartz, 3:31–72. Ramat Gan: Bar-Ilan University Press, 2004.

Ariel, David. *Kabbalah: The Mystic Quest in Judaism.* Lanham, Md.: Rowman & Littlefield, 2006.

Artson, Bradley Shavit. *Love Peace and Pursue Peace: A Jewish Response to War and Nuclear Annihilation.* New York: United Synagogue of America, 1988.

Ashmore, Richard D., Lee Jussim, and David Wilder, eds. *Social Identity, Intergroup Conflict, and Conflict Reduction.* Oxford: Oxford University Press, 2001.

Avalos, Hector. *Fighting Words: The Origins of Religious Violence.* Amherst, N.Y.: Prometheus Books, 2005.

Aviad, Janet. "The Messianism of Gush Emunim." In *Studies in Contemporary Jewry VII: Jews and Messianism in the Modern Era: Metaphor and Meaning*, ed. Jonathan Frankel, 197–213. New York: Oxford University Press, 1991.

Avineri, Shlomo. *The Making of Modern Zionism: The Intellectual Origins of the Jewish State*. New York: Basic Books, 1981.

———. "Zionism and Jewish Religious Tradition: The Dialectics of Redemption and Secularization." In *Zionism and Religion*, ed. Shmuel Almog, Jehuda Reinharz, and Anita Shapira, 1–9. Hanover, N.H.: University of New England Press, 1998.

Avot de-Rabi Natan. Edited by Solomon Schechter. D. Nutt and J. Kauffmann: London and Frankfurt, 1887.

Babad, Joseph. *Minhat Hinukh*. New York: Pardes, n.d.

Babylonian Talmud. Standard edition.

Bainton, Roland. *Christian Attitudes towards War and Peace: A Historical Survey and Critical Re-evaluation*. Nashville: Abingdon Press, 1960.

bar Hiyya, Abraham. *Hegyon ha-Nefesh ha-'Atsuvah*. Edited by Geoffrey Wigoder. Jerusalem: Mosad Bialik, 1971.

Bar-On, Mordechai. *In Pursuit of Peace: A History of the Israeli Peace Movement*. Washington, D.C.: United States Institute of Peace, 1996.

Barr, James. *Biblical Faith and Natural Theology*. Oxford: Clarendon Press, 1993.

Barrett, Lois. *The Way God Fights: War and Peace in the Old Testament*. Scottsdale, Pa.: Herald Press, 1987.

Barton, John. "Understanding Old Testament Ethics." *Journal for the Study of the Old Testament* 9 (1978): 44–64.

———. "The Basis of Ethics in the Hebrew Bible." *Semeia* 66 (1994): 11–22.

———. *Ethics and the Old Testament*. Harrisburg, Pa.: Trinity Press International, 1998.

———. "Imitation of God in the Old Testament." In *The God of Israel*, ed. Robert P. Gordon, 35–46. Cambridge: Cambridge University Press, 2007.

Beitchman, Philip. *Alchemy of the Word: Cabala of the Renaissance*. Albany: State University of New York Press, 1998.

Ben-Horin, Mikha'el, ed. *Barukh ha-Gever: Sefer Zikaron la-Kadosh Dr. Barukh Goldshtain h.y.d.* Jerusalem: "Shalom 'al Yisrael," 1995.

Ben-Hur, Raphaella Bilski. *Every Individual, a King: The Social and Political Thought of Ze'ev Vladimir Jabotinsky*. Washington, D.C.: B'nai Brith Books, 1993.

Ben-Menahem, Hanina. *Judicial Deviation in Rabbinic Law: Governed by Men, Not Rules*. Chur and New York: Harwood Academic, 1991.

———. "Talmudic Law: A Jurisprudential Perspective." In *The Cambridge History of Judaism*, vol. 4, *The Late Roman–Rabbinic Period*, ed. Steven T. Katz, 877–98. Cambridge: Cambridge University Press, 2006.

Ben-Sasson, H. H. "The Uniqueness of the Jews According to Twelfth-Century Figures" (in Hebrew). *Perakim* 2 (1971): 145–218.

Berdichevsky, Mikha Yosef. *Nemushot*. Warsaw: Tse'irim, 1899.

———. *Mi-Yamin u-mi-Semol*. Breslau: Tse'irim, 1909.

Berger, David. "Jews, Gentiles, and the Modern Egalitarian Ethos: Some Tentative Thoughts." In *Formulating Responses in an Egalitarian Age*, ed. Marc D. Stern, 93–101. Lanham, Md.: Rowman & Littlefield, 2005.

Berger, Michael S. "Taming the Beast: Rabbinic Pacification of Second-Century Jewish Nationalism." In *Belief and Bloodshed: Religion and Violence across Time and Tradition*, ed. James K. Wellman Jr., 47–62. Lanham, Md.: Rowman & Littlefield, 2007.

Berkovits, Eliezer. *Not in Heaven: The Nature and Function of Halakha*. New York: Ktav, 1983.

Biale, David. *Power and Powerlessness in Jewish History*. New York: Schocken Books, 1986.

Birch, Bruce C. *Let Justice Roll Down: The Old Testament, Ethics, and the Christian Life*. Louisville: Westminster/John Knox, 1991.

———. "Moral Agency, Community, and the Character of God in the Hebrew Bible." *Semeia* 66 (1994): 23–37.

Blau, Yitzchak. "Biblical Narratives and the Status of Enemy Civilians in Wartime." *Tradition* 39, no. 4 (2006): 8–28.

Bleich, J. David. *Contemporary Halakhic Problems*. 3 vols. New York: Ktav, 1977–89.

Blidstein, Gerald J. "Menahem Meiri's Attitude toward Gentiles: Apologetics or Worldview?" In *Binah: Jewish Intellectual History in the Middle Ages*, ed. Joseph Dan, 3:119–33. Westport, Conn.: Praeger, 1994.

———. *Political Concepts in Maimonidean Halakhah* (in Hebrew). 2nd rev. ed. Ramat Gan: Bar-Ilan University Press, 2001.

Bloom, A., ed. *Arakhim be-Mivhan ha-Milhamah*. Alon Shevut, Israel: n.d.

Boyarin, Daniel. *Unheroic Conduct: The Rise of Heterosexuality and the Invention of the Jewish Man*. Berkeley: University of California Press, 1997.

———. *A Radical Jew: Paul and the Politics of Identity*. Berkeley: University of California Press, 1994.

Breslauer, S. Daniel. *Toward a Jewish (M)orality: Speaking of a Postmodern Jewish Ethics*. Westport, Conn.: Greenwood Press, 1998.

Brett, Mark G. "Nationalism and the Hebrew Bible." In *The Bible in Ethics*, ed. John W. Rogerson, Margaret Davies, and M. Daniel Caroll R., 136–63. Sheffield: Sheffield Academic Press, 1995.

Brink, David O. "Some Forms and Limits of Consequentialism." In *The Oxford Handbook of Ethical Theory*, ed. David Copp, 380–423. New York: Oxford University Press, 2006.

Buber, Martin. *Hasidism*. New York: Philosophical Library, 1948.

———. *I and Thou*. Translated by Walter Kaufmann. New York: Scribner, 1970.

———. "Imitation of God." In *Israel and the World: Essays in a Time of Crisis*, 66–77. Syracuse: Syracuse University Press, 1997.

———. *A Land of Two Peoples*. Edited by Paul R. Mendes-Flohr. Chicago: University of Chicago Press, 2005.

Carmy, Shalom. "The Origin of Nations and the Shadow of Violence: Theological Perspectives on Canaan and Amalek." In *War and Peace in the Jewish Tradition*, ed. Lawrence Schiffman and Joel B. Wolowelsky, 163–99. New York: Yeshiva University Press, 2007.

Castelli, Elizabeth A. "Feminists Responding to Violence: Theories, Vocabularies, and Strategies." In *Interventions: Activists and Academics Respond to Violence*, ed. Elizabeth A. Castelli and Janet R. Jacobsen, 1–12. New York: Palgrave Macmillan, 2004.

Cherry, Conrad. *God's New Israel: Interpretations of American Destiny.* Englewood Cliffs, N.J.: Prentice Hall, 1971.

Clements, Ronald E. "Monotheism and the God of Many Names." In *The God of Israel,* ed. Robert P. Gordon, 47–59. Cambridge: Cambridge University Press, 2007.

Cohen, Gerson D. "Esau as Symbol in Early Medieval Thought." In *Studies in the Variety of Rabbinic Cultures,* 243–69. Philadelphia: Jewish Publication Society of America, 1991.

Cohen, Mark R. *Under Crescent and Cross: The Jews in the Middle Ages.* Princeton: Princeton University Press, 2008.

Cohen, Shaye J. D. *The Beginnings of Jewishness: Boundaries, Varieties, Uncertainties.* Berkeley: University of California Press, 1999.

———. *From the Maccabees to the Mishnah.* 2nd ed. Louisville: Westminster/John Knox Press, 2006.

Cohn, Haim H. "Extraordinary Remedies." In *The Principles of Jewish Law,* ed. Menachem Elon, 550–54. Jerusalem: Keter, n.d.

Cohn, Robert L. "Before Israel: The Canaanite as Other in Biblical Tradition." In *The Other in Jewish Thought and History: Constructions of Jewish Culture and Identity,* ed. Laurence J. Silberstein and Robert L. Cohn, 74–90. New York: New York University Press, 1994.

Collins, John J. "The Zeal of Phinehas: The Bible and the Legitimation of Violence." *Journal of Biblical Literature* 122, no. 1 (2000): 3–21.

Cott, Jeremy. "The Biblical Problem of Election." *Journal of Ecumenical Studies* 21, no. 2 (Spring 1984): 199–228.

Cromer, Gerald. "Amalek as Other, Other as Amalek: Interpreting a Violent Biblical Narrative." *Qualitative Sociology* 24, no. 2 (2001): 191–202.

Cross, Frank Moore. *Canaanite Myth and Hebrew Epic.* Cambridge, Mass.: Harvard University Press, 1973.

Crüsemann, Frank. "Human Solidarity and Ethnic Identity: Israel's Self-Definition in the Genealogical System of Genesis." In *Ethnicity and the Bible,* ed. Mark G. Brett, 58–76. Leiden: E. J. Brill, 1996.

Curtis, Edward M. *The Image of God: Genesis 1:26–28 in a Century of Old Testament Research.* Stockholm: Almqvist and Wiksell, 1988.

Dan, Joseph, ed. *The Christian Kabbalah: Jewish Mystical Books and Their Christian Interpreters: A Symposium.* Cambridge, Mass.: Harvard College Library, 1997.

Davidson, Herbert A. *Moses Maimonides: The Man and His Works.* New York: Oxford University Press, 2005.

Davies, Eryl W. "Walking in God's Ways: The Concept of *Imitatio Dei* in the Old Testament." In *True Wisdom,* ed. Edward Ball, 99–115. Sheffield: Sheffield Academic Press, 1999.

Davies, W. D. *The Territorial Dimension of Judaism: Jewish Constructs in Late Antiquity.* Berkeley: University of California Press, 1982.

De Waal, Cornelis. *On Pragmatism.* Belmont, Calif.: Wadsworth, 2005.

Deuteronomy Rabbah. In *Midrash Rabbah.* Standard edition.

Diamond, Eliezer. *Holy Men and Hunger Artists: Fasting and Asceticism in Rabbinic Culture.* Oxford: Oxford University Press, 2004.

Dienstag, Jacob I. "Natural Law in Maimonidean Thought and Scholarship (On *Mishneh Torah, Kings*, VIII.11)." *Jewish Law Annual* 6 (1988): 64–77.

Dobbs-Weinstein, Idit. "The Maimonidean Controversy." In *A History of Jewish Philosophy*, ed. Daniel H. Frank and Oliver Leaman, 331–49. London and New York: Routledge, 1997.

Don-Yehiya, Eliezer. "The Book and the Sword: The Nationalist Yeshivot and Political Radicalism in Israel" (in Hebrew). In *Me'ah Shanot Tsiyyonut Datit: Heibetim Ra'ayoniyyim*, ed. Avi Sagi and Dov Schwartz, 3:187–228. Ramat Gan: Bar-Ilan University Press, 2004.

Dorff, Elliot N. *To Do the Right and the Good: A Jewish Approach to Modern Social Ethics.* Philadelphia: Jewish Publication Society of America, 2002.

———. *The Unfolding Tradition: Jewish Law after Sinai.* New York: Aviv Press, 2005.

Driver, Julia. *Ethics: The Fundamentals.* Malden, Mass.: Blackwell, 2007.

Eisen, Robert. *Gersonides on Providence, Covenant, and the Chosen People: A Study in Medieval Jewish Philosophy and Biblical Commentary.* Albany: State University of New York Press, 1995.

———. "The Revival of Jewish Mysticism and Its Implications for the Future of Jewish Faith." In *Creating the Jewish Future*, ed. Michael Brown and Bernard Lightman, 27–44. Walnut Creek, Calif.: Altamira Press, 1998.

———. "Human Security in Jewish Philosophy and Ethics." In *Globalization and Environmental Challenges: Reconceptualizing Security in the 21st Century*, ed. Hans Günter Brauch, Úrsula Oswald Spring, Czeslaw Mesjasz, John Grin, Paul Dunay, Navnita Chadha Behera, Béchir Chourou, Patricia Kameri-Mbote, and P. H. Liotta, 3:253–62. Berlin: Springer-Verlag, 2008.

Elon, Menachem. "Takkanot." In *The Principles of Jewish Law*, ed. Menachem Elon, 73–91. Jerusalem: Keter, n.d.

Esther Rabbah. In *Midrash Rabbah.* Standard edition.

Exodus Rabbah. In *Midrash Rabbah.* Standard edition.

Faur, José. *Studies in the Mishneh Torah: Book of Knowledge* (in Hebrew). Jerusalem: Mosad ha-Rav Kuk, 1978.

Fine, Lawrence. *Physician of the Soul, Healer of the Cosmos: Isaac Luria and His Kabbalistic Fellowship.* Stanford, Calif.: Stanford University Press, 2003.

Fisch, Menachem. *Rational Rabbis: Science and Talmudic Culture.* Bloomington: Indiana University Press, 1997.

Fonrobert, Charlotte Elisheva, and Martin S. Jaffee, eds. *The Cambridge Companion to the Talmud and Rabbinic Literature.* Cambridge: Cambridge University Press, 2007.

Fox, Everett. "Stalking the Younger Brother: Some Models for Understanding a Biblical Motif." *Journal for the Study of the Old Testament* 18 (1993): 45–68.

Fox, Marvin. "Maimonides and Aquinas on Natural Law." *Diné Israel* 3 (1972): v–xxxvi.

———. *Interpreting Maimonides.* Chicago: University of Chicago Press, 1990.

Fraade, Steven D. "Navigating the Anomalous: Non-Jews at the Intersection of Early Rabbinic Law and Narrative." In *The Other in Jewish Thought and History*, ed. Laurence J. Silberstein and Robert L. Cohn, 145–65. New York: New York University Press, 1994.

Frank, Daniel H., and Oliver Leaman, eds. *A History of Jewish Philosophy*. London and
New York: Routledge, 1997.

Frank, Daniel H., and Oliver Leaman, eds. *The Cambridge Companion to Medieval
Jewish Philosophy*. Cambridge: Cambridge University Press, 2003.

Friedman, Richard Elliot. *Commentary on the Torah*. San Francisco: HarperSanFrancisco, 2001.

Gafni, Isaiah M. *Land, Center and Diaspora*. Sheffield: Sheffield Academic Press, 1997.

Galtung, Johan. "Cultural Violence." *Journal of Peace Research* 27, no. 3 (1990): 291–305.

Garb, Jonathan. "Messianism, Antinomianism, and Power in Religious Zionism: The
Case of the Jewish Underground" (in Hebrew). *Religious Zionism: An Era of
Changes: Studies in Honor of Zevulun Hammer*, ed. Asher Cohen and Yisra'el
Har'el, 323–63. Jerusalem: Bialik Institute, 2004.

———. *The Chosen Will Become Herds: Studies in Twentieth Century Kabbalah* (in
Hebrew). Jerusalem: Carmel, 2005.

———. "The Power and the Glory: A Critique of 'New Age' Kabbalah," trans.
Stephen Hazzan Arnoff. *Zeek* (April 2006): http://www.zeek.net/print/604garb.

Gellman, Ezra, ed. *Essays on the Thought and Philosophy of Rabbi Kook*. Rutherford, N.J.:
Fairleigh Dickinson University Press, 1991.

Gendler, Everett E. "War and the Jewish Tradition." In *Contemporary Jewish Ethics*, ed.
Menachem Kellner, 197–200. New York: HPC Press, 1988.

Genesis Rabbah. Edited with notes by J. Theodor and Ch. Albeck. 3 vols. Jerusalem:
Wahrmann Books, 1965.

Gensler, Harry J. *Ethics: A Contemporary Introduction*. London and New York: Routledge, 1998.

Gibbs, Robert. *Why Ethics? Signs of Responsibilities*. Princeton: Princeton University
Press, 2000.

Glatzer, Nahum N. "The Attitude toward Rome in Third-Century Judaism." In *Essays in
Jewish Thought*, 1–15. University, Ala.: University of Alabama Press, 1978.

———. "The Concept of Peace in Classical Judaism." In *Essays in Jewish Thought*,
36–47. University, Ala.: University of Alabama Press, 1978.

Goldenberg, Robert. *The Nations That Knew Thee Not: Ancient Jewish Attitudes toward
Other Religions*. New York: New York University Press, 1998.

———. "The Destruction of the Temple: Its Meaning and Consequences." In *The
Cambridge History of Judaism, vol. 4, The Late Roman–Rabbinic Period*, ed. Steven T.
Katz, 191–205. Cambridge: Cambridge University Press, 2006.

Gopin, Marc. *Between Eden and Armageddon: The Future of World Religions, Violence and
Peacemaking*. New York: Oxford University Press, 2000.

———. *Holy War, Holy Peace: How Religion Can Bring Peace to the Middle East*. New
York: Oxford University Press, 2002.

Gordon, Martin L. "The Philosophical Rationalism of Jacob Anatoli." Ph.D. diss.,
Yeshiva University, 1974.

Gordon, Robert P. "Introducing the God of Israel." In *The God of Israel*, ed. Robert P.
Gordon, 3–19. Cambridge: Cambridge University Press, 2007.

Gorenberg, Gershom. *The Accidental Empire: Israel and the Birth of the Settlements,
1967–1977*. New York: Times Books, 2006.

Gorny, Yosef. *Zionism and the Arabs, 1882–1948: A Study of Ideology.* Oxford: Oxford University Press, 1987.

Green, Arthur. *Seek My Face, Speak My Name: A Contemporary Jewish Theology.* Northvale, N.J.: Jason Aronson, 1992.

———. *Ehyeh: A Kabbalah for Tomorrow.* Woodstock, Vt.: Jewish Lights, 2003.

Green, William Scott. "Otherness Within: Toward a Theory of Difference in Rabbinic Judaism." In *To See Ourselves as Others See Us: Christians, Jews, and "Others" in Late Antiquity,* ed. Jacob Neusner and Ernst S. Frerichs, 49–69. Chico, Calif.: Scholars Press, 1985.

Greenberg, Moshe. *Election and Power* (in Hebrew). Haifa: Ha-Kibbutz Ha-Me'uhad, 1985.

———. "Mankind, Israel, and the Nations in the Hebraic Heritage." In *Studies in the Bible and Jewish Thought,* 369–93. Philadelphia: Jewish Publication Society of America, 1995.

———. "On the Political Use of the Bible in Modern Israel: An Engaged Critique." In *Pomegranates and Golden Bells: Studies in Biblical, Jewish, and Near Eastern Ritual, Law, and Literature in Honor of Jacob Milgrom,* ed. David P. Wright, David Noel Freedman, and Avi Hurvitz, 461–71. Winona Lake, Ind.: Eisenbrauns, 1995.

———. "A Problematic Heritage: The Attitude toward the Gentile in Jewish Tradition—An Israeli Perspective." *Conservative Judaism* 48, no. 2 (1996): 25–35.

Greenspahn, Frederick E. *When Brothers Dwell Together: The Preeminence of Younger Siblings in the Hebrew Bible.* New York: Oxford University Press, 1994.

Grosby, Steven. *Biblical Ideas of Nationality Ancient and Modern.* Winona Lake, Ind.: Eisenbrauns, 2002.

Grüneberg, Keith Nigel. *Abraham, Blessing, and the Nations: A Philological and Exegetical Study of Genesis 12:3 in Its Narrative Context.* New York: Walter de Gruyter, 2003.

Guttmann, Julius. *Philosophies of Judaism.* Translated by David Silverman. New York: Schocken Books, 1973.

Hadas-Lebel, Mireille. *Jerusalem against Rome.* Translated by Robyn Fréchet. Leuven: Peeters, 2006.

Halamish, Mosheh. "The Kabbalists' Attitude to the Nations of the World" (in Hebrew). *Jerusalem Studies in Jewish Thought* 14 (1998): 289–311.

———. *An Introduction to the Kabbalah.* Translated by Ruth Bar-Ilan and Ora Wiskind-Elper. Albany: State University of New York Press, 1999.

Halbertal, Moshe. *Between Torah and Wisdom: Rabbi Menachem ha-Meiri and the Maimonidean Halakhists in Provence* (in Hebrew). Jerusalem: Magnes Press, 2000.

Halivni, David Weiss, "Can a Religious Law Be Immoral?" In *Perspectives on Jews and Judaism: Essays in Honor of Wolfe Kelman,* ed. Arthur A. Chiel, 165–70. New York: Rabbinic Assembly, 1978.

Halkin, Hillel. Review of Elliot Horowitz, *Reckless Rites. Commentary* 121, no. 6 (2006): 65–69.

Hanson, Paul D. "War and Peace in the Hebrew Bible." *Interpretation* 38 (1984): 341–62.

———. *The People Called God: The Growth of Community in the Bible.* San Francisco: Harper & Row, 1986.

Harris, Sam. *The End of Faith: Religion, Terror, and the Future of Reason.* New York: W.W. Norton, 2004.

———. *Letter to a Christian Nation.* New York: Knopf, 2006.

Hartman, Donniel. "The Morality of War." *S'vara* 2, no. 1 (1990): 20–24.

Held, Virginia. "The Ethics of Care." In *The Oxford Handbook of Ethical Theory,* ed. David Copp, 537–66. New York: Oxford University Press, 2006.

Hertzberg, Arthur. *The Zionist Idea: A Historical Analysis and Reader.* Philadelphia: Jewish Publication Society of America, 1997.

Hirshman, Marc. *Torah for All the World's Peoples* (in Hebrew). Tel Aviv: Ha-Kibbutz ha-Me'uhad, 1999.

———. "Rabbinic Universalism in the Second and Third Centuries." *Harvard Theological Review* 93, no. 2 (2000): 101–15.

Hitchens, Christopher. *God Is Not Great: How Religion Poisons Everything.* New York: Twelve Hachette Book Group, 2007.

Holzer, Eli. "The Use of Military Force in the Religious-Zionist Ideology of Rabbi Jacob Reines and his Successors." In *Studies in Contemporary Jewry XVIII: Jews and Violence: Images, Ideologies, Realities,* ed. Peter Y. Medding, 74–94. New York: Oxford University Press, 2002.

———. "Attitudes towards the Use of Military Force in Ideological Currents of Religious Zionism." In *War and Peace in the Jewish Tradition,* ed. Lawrence Schiffman and Joel B. Wolowelsky, 356–72. New York: Yeshiva University Press, 2007.

———. *A Double-Edged Sword: Military Activism in the Thought of Religious Zionism* (in Hebrew). Jerusalem and Tel Aviv: The Shalom Hartman Institute, Keter Publishing House, Faculty of Law at Bar-Ilan University, 2009.

Horowitz, Elliot. "From the Generation of Moses to the Generation of the Messiah: The Jews Confront 'Amalek' and His Incarnations" (in Hebrew). *Zion* 65 (1999): 425–54.

———. *Reckless Rites: Purim and the Legacy of Jewish Violence.* Princeton: Princeton University Press, 2006.

Hourani, George. "Maimonides and Islam." In *Studies in Islamic and Judaic Traditions,* ed. William M. Brinner and Stephen D. Ricks, 153–65. Atlanta: Scholars Press, 1986.

Husik, Isaac. *A History of Medieval Jewish Philosophy.* Philadelphia: Jewish Publication Society of America, 1958.

Huss, Boaz. "All You Need is LAV: Madonna and Postmodern Kabbalah." *Jewish Quarterly Review* 95 (2005): 611–24.

———. "The New Age of Kabbalah: Contemporary Kabbalah, the New Age and Postmodern Spirituality." *Journal of Modern Jewish Studies* 6, no. 2 (2007): 107–25.

ibn Tibbon, Moshe. *Persush 'al Shir ha-Shirim.* Lyck: M'kize Nirdamim, 1874.

Idel, Moshe. *Kabbalah: New Perspectives.* New Haven: Yale University Press, 1988.

Intsiklopidiyah Talmudit. Edited by Shelomoh Yosef Zevin. Jerusalem: Mosad ha-Rav Kuk, 1947–2009.

Ish-Shalom, Benjamin. *Rav Avraham Itzhak HaCohen Kook: Between Rationalism and Mysticism.* Translated by Ora Wiskind-Elper. Albany: State University of New York Press, 1993.

Ivry, Alfred. "Islamic and Greek Influences on Maimonides' Philosophy." In *Maimonides and Philosophy*, ed. Shlomo Pines and Yirmiyahu Yovel, 139–56. Dordrecht: Martinus Nijhoff, 1986.

Jacobs, Louis. "The Relationship between Religion and Ethics in Jewish Thought." In *Contemporary Jewish Ethics*, ed. Menachem Kellner, 41–57. New York: HPC Press, 1978.

———. *A Tree of Life: Diversity, Flexibility, and Creativity in Jewish Law*. New York: Oxford University Press, 1984.

Jaffee, Martin S. *Early Judaism: Religious Worlds of the First Judaic Millennium*. 2nd ed. Bethesda, Md.: University Press of Maryland, 2006.

Jerusalem Talmud. Standard edition.

Juergensmeyer, Mark. *Terror in the Mind of God: The Global Rise of Religious Violence*. Berkeley: University of California Press, 2000.

Kahane, Meir. *Israel's Eternity and Victory* (in Hebrew). Jerusalem: Institute of the Jewish Idea, 1973.

———. *Numbers 23:9* (in Hebrew). Jerusalem: Institute of the Jewish Idea, 1974.

———. *Listen World, Listen Jew*. Tucson: Institute of the Jewish Idea, 1978.

———. *On Faith and Redemption* (in Hebrew). Jerusalem: Institute of the Jewish Idea, 1980.

———. *Thorns in Your Eyes* (in Hebrew). New York: Druker, 1981.

———. *Forty Years*. Miami: Institute of the Jewish Idea, 1983.

———. *Uncomfortable Questions for Comfortable Jews*. Secaucus, N.J.: Lyle Stuart, 1987.

Kaiser, Walter C., Jr. *Toward Old Testament Ethics*. Grand Rapids, Mich.: Academie Books, Zondervan, 1983.

Kalischer, Hirsch Tsevi. *Ha-Ketavim ha-Tsiyyoniyyim shel ha-Rav Tsevi Kalisher*. Edited by Israel Klausner. Jerusalem: Mosad ha-Rav Kuk, 1947.

Kaminsky, Joel S. "The Concept of Election and Second Isaiah: Recent Literature." *Biblical Theology Bulletin* 31 (2001): 135–44.

———. *Yet I Loved Jacob: Reclaiming the Biblical Concept of Election*. Nashville: Abingdon Press, 2007.

Kaplan, Eran. *The Jewish Radical Right: Revisionist Zionism and Its Ideological Legacy*. Madison, Wis.: University of Wisconsin Press, 2005.

Kaplan, Lawrence J. "Maimonides on the Singularity of the Jewish People." *Da'at* 15 (1985): 5–27 (English section).

Kaplan, Lawrence J., and David Shatz, eds. *Rabbi Abraham Isaac Kook and Jewish Spirituality*. New York: New York University Press, 1995.

Karsh, Efraim. *Fabricating Israeli History: The "New Historians."* 2nd ed. London and Portland, Ore.: Frank Cass, 2000.

Kasher, Hannah. "'Beloved Is Man Who Is Created in the Image [of God];' Conditional Humanism (According to Maimonides) vs. Unintentional Humanism (According to Leibowitz)" (in Hebrew). *Da'at* 41 (1998): 19–29.

Katz, Jacob. *Exclusiveness and Tolerance: Studies in Jewish-Gentile Relations in Medieval and Modern Times*. New York: Behrman House, 1961.

———. *Tradition and Crisis: Jewish Society at the End of the Middle Ages*. New York: Schocken Books, 1971.

———. *Out of the Ghetto: The Social Background of Jewish Emancipation, 1770–1870.* Cambridge, Mass.: Harvard University Press, 1973.

———. "Israel and the Messiah." In *Essential Papers on Messianic Movements and Personalities in Jewish History,*" ed. Marc Saperstein, 475–91. New York: New York University Press, 1992.

Katz, Shmuel. *Lone Wolf: A Biography of Vladimir (Ze'ev) Jabotinsky.* New York: Barricade Books, 1996.

Katz, Steven T., ed. *The Cambridge History of Judaism. Vol. 4, The Late Roman–Rabbinic Period.* Cambridge: Cambridge University Press, 2006.

Keiner, Ronald C. "The Image of Islam in the *Zohar.*" *Jerusalem Studies in Jewish Thought* 8 (1989): 43–65 (English section).

Kellner, Menachem. *Maimonides on Judaism and the Jewish People.* Albany: State University of New York Press, 1991.

Kimelman, Reuven. "Non-Violence in the Talmud." *Judaism* 17 (1968): 316–34.

———. "The Ethics of National Power: Government and War from the Sources of Judaism." In *Authority, Power, and Leadership in the Jewish Polity,* ed. Daniel Elazar, 247–94. Lanham, Md.: University Press of America, 1991.

———. "Judaism, War, and Weapons of Mass Destruction." In *Ethics and Weapons of Mass Destruction,* ed. Sohail Hashmi, 363–84. West Nyack, N.Y.: Cambridge University Press, 2004.

———. "The Rabbinic Theology of the Physical: Blessings, Body and Soul, Resurrection, Covenant and Election." In *The Cambridge History of Judaism,* vol. 4, *The Late Roman–Rabbinic Period,* ed. Steven T. Katz, 946–76. Cambridge: Cambridge University Press, 2006.

Knight, Douglas A. "Introduction: Ethics, Ancient Israel, and the Hebrew Bible." *Semeia* 66 (1994): 1–8.

Kook, Abraham Isaac. *Hazon ha-Ge'ulah.* Jerusalem: Ha-Agudah le-Hotsa'at Sifrey ha-Ra'yah, 1941.

———. *Iggerot ha-Re'iyah.* Jerusalem: Mosad ha-Rav Kuk, 1962.

———. *Orot.* Jerusalem: Mosad ha-Rav Kuk, 1963.

———. *Orot ha-Kodesh.* Jerusalem: Mosad ha-Rav Kuk, 1964.

———. *Orot ha-Teshuvah.* Edited by Ya'akov Filber. Jerusalem: Gal'or, 1977.

———. *Olat ha-Re'iyah.* Jerusalem: Mosad ha-Rav Kuk, 1985.

Kook, Tsevi Yehudah. *Li-Ntivot Yisra'el.* Jerusalem: Menorah, 1967.

———. *Mitokh ha-Torah ha-Go'elet.* Jerusalem: Makhon Tsemah Tsevi, 1983.

———. *Ba-Ma'arakhah ha-Tsiburit.* Edited by Yosef Bramson. Jerusalem: Agudat Zehav ha-Arets, 1986.

Korn, Eugene. "Moralization in Jewish Law: Genocide, Divine Commands, and Rabbinic Reasoning." *Edah Journal* 5, no. 2 (2006): 2–11.

Kotler, Yair. *Heil Kahane.* New York: Adama Books, 1986.

Kraemer, David. *Responses to Suffering in Classical Rabbinic Literature.* New York: Oxford University Press, 1995.

Kreisel, Howard. *Maimonides' Political Thought: Studies in Ethics, Law, and the Human Ideal.* Albany: State University of New York Press, 1999.

Krug, Etienne G., Linda L. Dahlberg, James A. Mercy, Anthony B. Zwi, and Rafael Lozano, eds. *World Report on Violence and Health*. Geneva: World Health Organization, 2002.

Kuntzel, Matthias. *Jihad and Jew-Hatred: Islamism, Nazism, and the Roots of 9/11*. Translated by Colin Meade. New York: Telos Press, 2007.

Lamentations Rabbah. In *Midrash Rabbah*. Standard edition.

Lamm, Maurice. "After the War: Another Look at Pacifism and Selective Conscientious Objection." In *Contemporary Jewish Ethics*, ed. Menachem Kellner, 221–38. New York: HPC Press, 1988.

Lamm, Norman. "Amalek and the Seven Nations: A Case of Law vs. Morality." In *War and Peace in the Jewish Tradition*, ed. Lawrence Schiffman and Joel B. Wolowelsky, 201–38. New York: Yeshiva University Press, 2007.

Lance, Mark, and Margaret Little. "Particularism and Antitheory." In *The Oxford Handbook of Ethical Theory*, ed. David Copp, 567–94. New York: Oxford University Press, 2006.

Landes, Daniel, ed. *Jewish Reflections on Weapons of Mass Destruction*. Northvale, N.J.: Jason Aronson, 1991.

Laqueur, Walter. *A History of Zionism*. New York: Schocken Books, 2003.

Lazaroff, Allan. "Kaplan and John Dewey." In *The American Judaism of Mordecai M. Kaplan*, ed. Emanuel S. Goldsmith, Mel Scult, and Robert M. Seltzer, 173–96. New York: New York University Press, 1990.

Lederhendler, Eli. "Messianic Rhetoric in the Russian Haskalah and Early Zionism." In *Studies in Contemporary Jewry VII: Jews and Messianism in the Modern Era: Metaphor and Meaning*, ed. Jonathan Frankel, 14–33. New York: Oxford University Press, 1991.

Leibowitz, Yeshayahu. *Judaism, Human Values, and the Jewish State*. Edited by Eliezer Goldman. Translated by Yoram Navon, Zvi Jacobson, Gershon Levy, and Raphael Levy. Cambridge, Mass.: Harvard University Press, 1995.

Levenson, Jon D. *The Hebrew Bible, the Old Testament, and Historical Criticism: Jews and Christians in Biblical Studies*. Louisville: Westminster/John Knox Press, 1993.

———. *The Death and Resurrection of the Beloved Son: The Transformation of Child Sacrifice in Judaism and Christianity*. New Haven: Yale University Press, 1993.

———. "The Universal Horizon of Biblical Particularism." In *Ethnicity and the Bible*, ed. Mark G. Brett, 143–69. Leiden: E. J. Brill, 1996.

———. "The Exodus in Biblical Theology: A Rejoinder to John J. Collins." In *Jews, Christians, and the Theology of the Hebrew Scriptures*, ed. Alice Ogden Beilis and Joel S. Kaminsky, 263–75. Atlanta: Society of Biblical Literature, 2000.

Levine, Baruch. *The JPS Commentary on the Torah: Leviticus*. Philadelphia: Jewish Publication Society of America, 1989.

Levinger, Ya'akov. "Human Perfection among the Gentiles According to Maimonides" (in Hebrew). In *Hagut 2: Bein Yisra'el La-'Amim*, 27–35. Jerusalem: Ministry of Education and Culture, 1978.

Levy, Shlomit, Hanna Levinsohn, and Elihu Katz. "The Many Faces of Jewishness in Israel." In *Jews in Israel: Contemporary Social and Cultural Factors*, ed. Uzi Rebhun and Chaim I. Waxman, 265–84. Hanover, N.H.: University of New England Press, 2004.

Libowitz, Richard. *Mordecai M. Kaplan and the Development of Reconstructionism.* New York: Edwin Mellen Press, 1983.

Lichtenstein, Aaron. *The Seven Laws of Noah.* New York: Rabbi Jacob Joseph School Press, 1981.

Liebes, Yehuda. *Studies in the Zohar.* Translated by Arnold Schwartz, Stephanie Nakache, and Penina Peli. Albany: State University of New York Press, 1993.

Liebman, Charles S., and Eliezer Don-Yehiya. *Traditional Judaism and Political Culture in the Jewish State.* Berkeley: University of California Press, 1983.

Liebman, Charles S., and Elihu Katz, eds. *The Jewishness of Israelis: The Guttman Report.* Albany: State University of New York Press, 1997.

Lind, Millard C. *Yahweh Is a Warrior: The Theology of Warfare in Ancient Israel.* Scottsdale, Pa.: Herald Press, 1980.

Lipton, Diana. "Remembering Amalek: A Positive Biblical Model for Dealing with Negative Scriptural Types." In *Reading Texts, Seeking Wisdom: Scripture and Theology,* ed. David F. Ford and Graham Stanton, 139–53. Grand Rapids, Mich.: William B. Eerdmans, 2004.

Loewe, Raphael. "Potentialities and Limitations of Universalism in the Halakhah." In *Studies in Rationalism, Judaism and Universalism: In Memory of Leon Roth,* ed. Raphael Loewe, 115–50. London: Routledge and K. Paul, 1966.

Lüdemann, Gerd. *The Unholy in Holy Scripture.* Translated by John Bowden. Louisville: Westminster/John Knox Press, 1997.

Luz, Ehud. *Wrestling with an Angel: Power, Morality, and Jewish Identity.* Translated by Michael Swirsky. New Haven: Yale University Press, 2003.

———. "The Jewish Religion: Restraint or Encouragement in the Use of Force? Changing Attitudes in Religious Zionism" (in Hebrew). In *Peace and War in Jewish Culture,* ed. Ariel Bar-Levav, 247–76. Jerusalem: Zalman Shazar Center, 2006.

Machinist, Peter. "The Biblical View of Emergent Israel and Its Contexts." In *The Other in Jewish Thought and History,* ed. Laurence J. Silberstein and Robert L. Cohn, 35–60. New York: New York University Press, 1994.

Maimonides. *The Guide of the Perplexed.* Translated by Shlomo Pines. Chicago: University of Chicago Press, 1963.

———. *Iggerot ha-Rambam.* Edited and translated into Hebrew by Ya'akov Shilat. 3 vols. Jerusalem: Ma'aliyot Press, 1995.

———. *Mishneh Torah.* Standard edition.

Marks, Richard G. *The Image of Bar Kokhba in Traditional Jewish Literature: False Messiah and National Hero.* University Park, Pa.: Pennsylvania State University Press, 1994.

McDonald, Patricia M. *God and Violence: Biblical Resources for Living in a Small World.* Scottsdale, Pa.: Herald Press, 2004.

McTernan, Oliver. *Violence in God's Name: Religion in an Age of Conflict.* Maryknoll, N.Y.: Orbis Books, 2003.

Mekhilta de-R. Ishmael. Edited by H. S. Horowitz and I. A. Rabin. Frankfurt: J. Kauffmann, 1931.

Meyer, Michael A. *The Origins of the Modern Jew: Jewish Identity and European Culture in Germany, 1749–1824.* Detroit: Wayne State University Press, 1967.

Midrash Tehillim. Edited by Solomon Buber. Vilna: Rom Press, 1891.

Mirsky, Yehudah. "The Political Morality of Pacifism and Nonviolence: One Jewish View." In *War and Its Discontents: Pacifism and Quietism in the Abrahamic Traditions*, ed. J. Patout Burns, 47–66. Washington, D.C.: Georgetown University Press, 1996.

Moberly, R. W. L. *The Bible, Theology, and Faith: A Study of Abraham and Jesus*. Cambridge: Cambridge University Press, 2000.

———. "Is Monotheism Bad for You? Some Reflections on God, the Bible, and Life in the Light of Regina Schwartz's *The Curse of Cain*." In *The God of Israel*, ed. Robert P. Gordon, 106–11. Cambridge: Cambridge University Press, 2007.

Morris, Benny. *The Birth of the Palestinian Refugee Problem Revisited*. Cambridge: Cambridge University Press, 2004.

———. "Why Israel Feels Threatened." *New York Times*. December 29, 2008.

Moses of Coucy. *Sefer Mitsvot Gadol*. Venice, 1522.

Mullen E. Theodore, Jr. *Narrative History and Ethnic Boundaries: The Deuteronomic Historian and the Creation of Israelite National Identity*. Atlanta: Scholars Press, 1993.

Musto, Ronald G. *The Catholic Peace Tradition*. Maryknoll, N.Y.: Orbis Books, 1986.

Myers, David N. *Between Arab and Jew: The Lost Voice of Simon Rawidowicz*. Waltham, Mass.: Brandeis University Press, 2008.

Myers, Jody. "The Messianic Idea and Zionist Ideologies." In *Studies in Contemporary Jewry VII: Jews and Messianism in the Modern Era: Metaphor and Meaning*, ed. Jonathan Frankel, 3–13. New York: Oxford University Press, 1991.

———. *Kabbalah and the Spiritual Quest: The Kabbalah Centre in America*. Westport, Conn.: Praeger, 2007.

Nahmanides. *Perushey ha-Torah*. Edited by C. Chavel. 2 vols. Jerusalem: Mosad ha-Rav Kuk, 1975.

Netanyahu, Benzion. *Don Isaac Abravanel: Statesman and Philosopher*. Philadelphia: Jewish Publication Society of America, 1982.

Neusner, Jacob. *Messiah in Context: Israel's History and Destiny in Formative Judaism*. Philadelphia: Fortress Press, 1984.

Newman, Louis E. *Past Imperatives: Studies in the History and Theory of Jewish Ethics*. Albany: State University of New York Press, 1998.

———. *An Introduction to Jewish Ethics*. Upper Saddle River, N.J.: Pearson/Prentice-Hall, 2005.

Niditch, Susan. *Underdogs and Tricksters: A Prelude to Folklore*. San Francisco: Harper & Row, 1987.

———. *War in the Hebrew Bible: A Study in the Ethics of Violence*. New York: Oxford University Press, 1993.

Nimni, Ephraim, ed. *The Challenge of Post-Zionism: Alternatives to Israeli Fundamentalist Politics*. New York: Zed Books, 2003.

Novak, David. *The Image of the Non-Jew in Judaism*. Lewiston: Edwin Mellen Press, 1983.

———. *The Election of Israel: The Idea of the Chosen People*. Cambridge: Cambridge University Press, 1995.

————. *Natural Law in Judaism*. Cambridge: Cambridge University Press, 1998.

————. *Covenantal Rights: A Study in Jewish Political Theory*. Princeton: Princeton University Press, 2000.

————. "Gentiles in Rabbinic Thought." In *The Cambridge History of Judaism*, vol. 4, *The Late Roman–Rabbinic Period*, ed. Steven T. Katz, 647–62. Cambridge: Cambridge University Press, 2006.

Numbers Rabbah. In *Midrash Rabbah*. Standard edition.

Ochs, Peter. *Pierce, Pragmatism, and the Logic of Scripture*. Cambridge: Cambridge University Press, 1998.

Ollenburger, Ben C. "Introduction." In *Holy War in Ancient Israel*. Translated and edited by Marva J. Dawn, 1–34. Grand Rapids, Mich.: William B. Eerdmans, 1991.

Orlinsky, Harry M. "Nationalism-Universalism and Internationalism in Ancient Israel." In *Essays in Biblical Culture and Biblical Translation*, 78–116. New York: Ktav, 1974.

————. "The Situational Ethics of Violence in the Biblical Period." In *Violence and Defense in the Jewish Experience*, ed. Salo W. Baron and George S. Wise, 38–62. Philadelphia: Jewish Publication Society of America, 1977.

Pappé, Ilan. *The Ethnic Cleansing of Palestine*. Oxford: Oneworld, 2006.

Penslar, Derek J. *Israel in History: The Jewish State in Comparative Perspective*. London and New York: Routledge, 2007.

Pines, Shlomo. "Translator's Introduction." In Maimonides, *The Guide of the Perplexed*, translated by Shlomo Pines, lvii–cxxxiii. Chicago: University of Chicago Press, 1963.

Porton, Gary G. *Goyim: Gentiles and Israelites in Mishnah-Tosefta*. Atlanta: Scholars Press, 1988.

Pruitt, Dean G., and Sung Hee Kim. *Social Conflict: Escalation, Stalemate, and Settlement*. 3rd ed. New York: McGraw-Hill, 2004.

Rackman, Emanuel. "Violence and the Value of Life: The Halakhic View." In *Violence and Defense in the Jewish Experience*, ed. Salo W. Baron and George S. Wise, 113–41. Philadelphia: Jewish Publication Society of America, 1977.

Rakover, Nahum. *Law and the Noahide: Law as a Universal Value*. Jerusalem: Library of Jewish Law, 1998.

Ram, Uri. *The Globalization of Israel: McWorld in Tel Aviv, Jihad in Jerusalem*. London and New York: Routledge, 2008.

Ramsbotham, Oliver, Tom Woodhouse, and Hugh Miall, eds. *Contemporary Conflict Resolution: The Prevention, Management, and Transformation of Deadly Conflicts*. 2nd ed. Cambridge: Polity Press, 2006.

Ravitzky, Aviezer. *The Roots of Kahanism: Consciousness and Political Reality*. Translated by Moshe Auman. Jerusalem: Shazar Library, 1986.

————. *Messianism, Zionism, and Jewish Religious Radicalism*. Translated by Michael Swirsky and Jonathan Chipman. Chicago: University of Chicago Press, 1996.

————. "Peace: Historical versus Utopian Models in Jewish Thought." In *History and Faith: Studies in Jewish Philosophy*, 22–45. Amsterdam: J. C. Gieben, 1996.

————. "Prohibited War in Jewish Tradition." In *The Ethics of War and Peace: Religious and Secular Perspectives*, ed. Terry Nardin, 115–27. Princeton: Princeton University Press, 1996.

Reines, Isaac Jacob. *Sha'arey Orah ve-Simhah*. Vilna: Rom Press, 1899.

Rodd, Cyril S. *Glimpses of a Strange Land: Studies in Old Testament Ethics*. Edinburgh: T & T Clark, 2001.

Rogerson, John W. "Discourse Ethics and Biblical Ethics." In *The Bible in Ethics*, ed. John W. Rogerson, Margaret Davies, and M. Daniel Caroll R., 17–26. Sheffield: Sheffield Academic Press, 1995.

Römer, Thomas. *Dieu obscur: Le sexe, le cruauté et la violence dans l'Ancien Testament*. Geneva: Labor et Fides, 1996.

Roth, Joel. *The Halakhic Process: A Systematic Analysis*. New York: Jewish Theological Seminary of America, 1986.

Rothbart, Daniel, and Karina V. Korostelina, eds. *Identity, Morality, and Threat: Studies in Violent Conflict*. Lanham, Md.: Lexington Books, 2006.

Rowlett, Lori. *Joshua and the Rhetoric of Violence: A New Historicist Analysis*. Sheffield: Sheffield Academic Press, 1996.

Rowley, Harold H. *The Biblical Doctrine of Election*. London: Lutterworth, 1950.

Rubenstein, Jeffrey L. *The Culture of the Babylonian Talmud*. Baltimore: Johns Hopkins Press, 2005.

Sachar, Howard M. *A History of Israel: From the Rise of Zionism to Our Time*. 3rd ed. New York: Knopf, 2007.

Sacks, Jonathan. *The Dignity of Difference: How to Avoid a Clash of Civilizations*. 2nd ed. London: Continuum, 2003.

Safrai, Shmuel, ed. *The Literature of the Sages*. Philadelphia: Fortress Press, 1987.

Sagi, Avi. "The Punishment of Amalek in Jewish Tradition: Coping with the Moral Problem." *Harvard Theological Review* 87, no. 3 (1994): 323–46.

———. *Judaism: Between Religion and Morality* (in Hebrew). Tel Aviv: Hakibbutz Hameuchad, 1998.

———. "Religious Zionism: Between Introversion and Openness" (in Hebrew). In *Judaism: A Dialogue Between Cultures*, ed. Avi Sagi, Dudi Schwartz, and Yedidia Z. Stern, 124–68. Jerusalem: Magnes Press, 2000.

———. "From the Torah State to the Land of Israel—From a Broken Dream to Another Dream: A Study in the Crisis of Religious Zionism" (in Hebrew). In *Me'ah Shanot Tsiyyonut Datit: Heibetim Ra'ayoniyyim*, ed. Avi Sagi and Dov Schwartz, 3: 457–73. Ramat Gan: Bar-Ilan University Press, 2004.

Sagi, Avi, and Daniel Statman. "Divine Command Morality and the Jewish Tradition." *Journal of Religious Ethics* 23 (1995): 49–68.

Sagi, Avi, and Dov Schwartz. "From Pioneering to Torah Study: Another Perspective" (in Hebrew). In *Me'ah Shanot Tsiyyonut Datit: Heibetim Ra'ayoniyyim*, ed. Avi Sagi and Dov Schwartz, 3: 73–76. Ramat Gan: Bar-Ilan University Press, 2004.

Said, Edward. "Michael Walzer's *Exodus and Revolution*: A Canaanite Reading." *Grand Street* 5 (Winter 1986): 86–106.

Saldarini, Anthony J., and Joseph Kanofsky. "Religious Dimensions of the Human Condition in Judaism." In *The Human Condition: A Volume in the Comparative Religious Ideas Project*, ed. Robert C. Neville, 101–32. Albany: State University of New York Press, 2001.

Salmon, Yosef. *Do Not Provoke Providence: Orthodoxy in the Grip of Nationalism* (in Hebrew). Jerusalem: Zalman Shazar Center, 2006.

Sarachek, Joseph. *Faith and Reason: The Conflict over the Rationalism of Maimonides.* Williamsport: Bayard Press, 1935.

Sarna, Nahum M. *Exploring Exodus: The Heritage of Biblical Israel.* New York: Schocken Books, 1987.

———. *The JPS Commentary on the Torah: Genesis.* Philadelphia: Jewish Publication Society of America, 1989.

———. *The JPS Commentary on the Torah: Exodus.* Philadelphia: Jewish Publication Society of America, 1991.

Schiffman, Lawrence H. *From Text to Tradition: A History of Second Temple and Rabbinic Judaism.* Hoboken, N.J.: Ktav, 1991.

———. "Messianism and Apocalypticism in Rabbinic Texts." In *The Cambridge History of Judaism,* vol. 4, *The Late Roman–Rabbinic Period,* ed. Steven T. Katz, 1053–72. Cambridge: Cambridge University Press, 2006.

Schlossberg, Eliezer. "The Attitude of Maimonides toward Islam" (in Hebrew). *Pe'amim* 42 (1990): 38–60.

Scholem, Gershom. *Major Trends in Jewish Mysticism.* New York: Schocken Books, 1961.

———. *The Messianic Idea in Judaism.* New York: Schocken Books, 1971.

Schwally, Friedrich. *Der heilige Krieg im alten Israel.* Leipzig: Deiterich, 1901.

Schwartz, Baruch J. "Commentary on Leviticus." In *The Jewish Study Bible,* ed. Adele Berlin and Marc Zvi Brettler, 203–280. New York: Oxford University Press, 1999.

Schwartz, Dov. *Religious Zionism between Logic and Messianism* (in Hebrew). Tel Aviv: Am Oved, 1999.

———. *Challenge and Crisis in Rabbi Kook's Circle* (in Hebrew). Tel Aviv: Am Oved, 2001.

———. *Faith at the Crossroads: A Theological Profile of Religious Zionism.* Translated by Batya Stein. Leiden: E. J. Brill, 2002.

Schwartz, Regina. *The Curse of Cain: The Violent Legacy of Monotheism.* Chicago: University of Chicago Press, 1997.

Schwarzschild, Steven S. "Do Noachites Have to Believe in Revelation?" *Jewish Quarterly Review,* n.s. 52 (1962): 297–309; 53 (1962): 30–65.

Schweid, Eliezer. "The Annihilation of Amalek and Eradication of the Amorite" (in Hebrew). *Moznayim* 33 (1971): 201–9.

Seeman, Don. "Violence, Ethics, and Divine Honor in Modern Jewish Thought." *Journal of the American Academy of Religion* 73, no. 4 (2005): 1015–48.

Selengut, Charles. *Sacred Fury: Understanding Religious Violence.* Walnut Creek, Calif.: Altamira Press, 2003.

Septimus, Bernard. *Hispano-Jewish Culture in Transition: The Career and Controversies of Ramah.* Cambridge, Mass.: Harvard University Press, 1982.

Sermoneta, Giuseppe. "Prophecy in the Writings of R. Yehudah Romano." In *Studies in Medieval Jewish History and Literature,* vol. 2, ed. Isadore Twersky, 337–74. Cambridge, Mass.: Harvard University Press, 1984.

Shapira, Anita. *Land and Power: The Zionist Resort to Force, 1881–1948.* Translated by William Templer. New York: Oxford University Press, 1992.

————. "The Religious Motifs of the Labor Movement." In *Zionism and Religion*, ed. Shmuel Almog, Jehuda Reinharz, and Anita Shapira, 251–72. Hanover, N.H.: University of New England Press, 1998.

Shapira, Anita, and Derek J. Penslar, eds. *Israeli Historical Revisionism: From Left to Right*. London: Frank Cass, 2003.

Shapiro, David S. "The Jewish Attitude towards Peace and War." In *Studies in Jewish Thought*, 1:316–63. New York: Yeshiva University Press, 1975.

————. "The Doctrine of the Image of God and *Imitatio Dei*." In *Contemporary Jewish Ethics*, ed. Menachem Kellner, 127–51. New York: HPC Press, 1978.

Sharan, Shlomo, ed. *Israel and the Post-Zionists*. Brighton: Sussex Academic Press; Portland, Ore.: Ariel Center for Policy Research, 2003.

Shavit, Yaacov. *Jabotinsky and the Revisionist Movement, 1925–1948*. London: Frank Cass, 1988.

————. "Realism and Messianism in Zionism and the Yishuv." In *Studies in Contemporary Jewry VII: Jews and Messianism in the Modern Era: Metaphor and Meaning*, ed. Jonathan Frankel, 100–127. New York: Oxford University Press, 1991.

Sheleg, Ya'ir. *Recent Developments among Religious Jews in Israel* (in Hebrew). Jerusalem: Keter, 2000.

Sherwin, Byron. *Kabbalah: An Introduction to Jewish Mysticism*. Lanham, Md.: Rowman & Littlefield, 2006.

Shimoni, Gideon. *The Zionist Ideology*. Hanover, N.H.: University Press of New England, 1995.

Shremer, Adiel. "Midrash and History: The Power of God and the Hope of Redemption in the World of the Tannaim in the Shadow of the Roman Empire" (in Hebrew). *Zion* 72 (2007): 5–36.

Sifra. Edited by Louis Finkelstein. 5 vols. New York: Jewish Theological Seminary, 1991.

Sifre Deuteronomy. Edited by Louis Finkelstein. New York: Jewish Theological Seminary, 1969.

Sifre Numbers. Edited by H. S. Horovitz. Jerusalem: Shalem Books, 1992.

Silberstein, Laurence J. *The Postzionism Debates: Knowledge and Power in Israeli Culture*. London and New York: Routledge, 1999.

Silver, Daniel J. *Maimonidean Criticism and Maimonidean Controversy, 1180–1240*. Leiden: E. J. Brill, 1965.

Simon, Uriel. *Seek Peace and Pursue It: The Bible in Light of Topical Issues, Topical Issues in Light of the Bible* (in Hebrew). Tel Aviv: Yediot Ahronot, 2002.

Sirat, Colette. *A History of Jewish Philosophy in the Middle Ages*. Cambridge: Cambridge University Press, 1986.

Smith, Anthony D. *Chosen Peoples*. New York: Oxford University Press, 2003.

Smith-Christopher, Daniel L. "Between Ezra and Isaiah: Exclusion, Transformation, and Inclusion of the 'Foreigner' in Post-Exilic Biblical Theology." In *Ethnicity and the Bible*, ed. Mark G. Brett, 117–42. Leiden: E. J. Brill, 1996.

Song of Songs Rabbah. In *Midrash Rabbah*. Standard edition.

Sparks, Kenton L. *Ethnicity and Identity in Ancient Israel: Prolegomena to the Study of Ethnic Sentiments and Their Expression in the Hebrew Bible*. Winona Lake, Ind.: Eisenbrauns, 1998.

Sprinzak, Ehud. *The Ascendance of Israel's Radical Right*. New York: Oxford University Press, 1991.

———. *Brother against Brother: Violence and Extremism in Israeli Politics from the Altalena to the Rabin Assassination*. New York: Free Press, 1999.

Stern, Jessica. *Terror in the Name of God: Why Religious Militants Kill*. New York: Ecco, 2004.

Stern, Josef. "Maimonides on Amalek, Self-Corrective Mechanisms, and the War against Idolatry." In *Judaism and Modernity: The Religious Philosophy of David Hartman*, ed. Jonathan W. Malino, 359–92. Hampshire: Ashgate, 2006.

Stern, Philip D. *The Biblical Herem: A Window on Israel's Religious Experience*. Atlanta: Scholars Press, 1991.

Stern, Sacha. *Jewish Identity in Early Rabbinic Writings*. Leiden: E. J. Brill, 1994.

Stone, Suzanne Last. "Sinaitic and Noahide Law: Legal Pluralism in Jewish Law." *Cardozo Law Review* 12 (1990–91): 1157–1214.

Strack, H. L., and G. Stemberger. *Introduction to Talmud and Midrash*. Translated by Markus Bockmuehl. Edinburgh: T & T Clark, 1991.

Strauss, Leo. "The Literary Character of the *Guide of the Perplexed*." In *Persecution and the Art of Writing*, 38–94. Glencoe, Ill.: Free Press, 1952.

———. *Philosophy and Law*. Translated by Fred Baumann. Philadelphia: Jewish Publication Society of America, 1987.

Strong, John T. "Israel as a Testimony to YHWH's Power: The Priests' Definition of Israel." In *Constituting the Community: Studies on the Polity of Ancient Israel in Honor of S. Dean McBride Jr.*, ed. John T. Strong and Steven S. Tuell, 89–106. Winona Lake, Ind.: Eisenbrauns, 2005.

Stroumsa, Sarah. "Saadya and the Jewish *kalam*." In *The Cambridge Companion to Medieval Jewish Philosophy*, ed. Daniel H. Frank and Oliver Leaman, 71–90. Cambridge: Cambridge University Press, 2003.

Stulman, Louis. "Encroachment in Deuteronomy: An Analysis of the Social World of the D Code." *Journal of Biblical Literature* 109 (1990): 613–32.

Susser, Leslie. "Holy Orders." *Jerusalem Report* (December 21, 2009), 6–9.

Tajfel, Henri, and John C. Turner. "The Social Identity Theory of Intergroup Behavior." In *The Psychology of Intergroup Relations*, ed. Stephen Worchel and William G. Austin, 7–24. Chicago: Nelson Hall, 1986.

Tanhuma. Edited by S. Buber. 2 vols. New York: Sefer, 1946.

Thayer, Horace S. *Meaning and Action: A Critical History of Pragmatism*. 2nd ed. Indianapolis: Hacket, 1981.

Tigay, Jeffrey H. *The JPS Commentary on the Torah: Deuteronomy*. Philadelphia: Jewish Publication Society of America, 1996.

———. "Commentary on Deuteronomy." In *The Jewish Study Bible*, ed. Adele Berlin and Marc Zvi Brettler, 356–450. New York: Oxford University Press, 1999.

Tishby, Isaiah. *The Doctrine of Evil and the "Kelippah" in Lurianic Kabbalism* (in Hebrew). Jerusalem: Magnes Press, 1942.

———. *The Wisdom of the Zohar*. Translated by David Goldstein. 3 vols. Oxford: Oxford University Press, 1989.

Tosefta. Edited by M. S. Zuckermandel. Jerusalem: Wahrmann Books, 1970.

Turshen, Meredith. "Definitions and Injuries of Violence." In *Interventions: Activists and Academics Respond to Violence*, ed. Elizabeth A. Castelli and Janet R. Jacobsen, 29–36. New York: Palgrave Macmillan, 2004.

Twersky, Isadore. *Introduction to the Code of Maimonides* (Mishneh Torah). New Haven: Yale University Press, 1980.

Urbach, Ephraim E. *The Sages: Their Concepts and Beliefs.* Translated by Israel Abrahams. Cambridge, Mass.: Harvard University Press, 1987.

Van Houten, Christiana. *The Alien in Israelite Law.* Sheffield: Sheffield Academic Press, 1991.

Volkan, Vamik D. *The Need to Have Enemies and Allies: From Clinical Practice to International Relationships.* Northvale, N.J.: Jason Aronson, 1988.

———. *Bloodlines: From Ethnic Pride to Ethnic Terrorism.* Boulder, Colo.: Westview Press, 1997.

von Rad, Gerhard. *Holy War in Ancient Israel.* Translated and edited by Marva J. Dawn. Grand Rapids, Mich.: William B. Eerdmans, 1991.

Warrior, Robert Allen. "Canaanites, Cowboys, and Indians: Deliverance, Conquest, and Liberation Theology Today." *Christianity and Crisis* 49 (1989): 261–66.

Weigert, Kathleen Mass. "Structural Violence." In *Encyclopedia of Violence, Peace, and Conflict*, ed. Lester Kurtz, 3:431–36. San Diego: Academic Press, 1999.

Weippert, Manfred. "'Heiliger Krieg' in Israel und Assyrien: Kritische Anmerkungen zu Gerhard von Rads Konzept des 'Heiligen Krieges im alten Israel.'" *Zeitschrift für die alttestamentliche Wissenschaft* 84 (1972): 460–93.

Wells, Jo Bailey. *God's Holy People: A Theme in Biblical Theology.* Sheffield: Sheffield Academic Press, 2000.

Wilensky, Sarah Heller. *The Philosophy of Isaac 'Arama in the Framework of Philonic Philosophy* (in Hebrew). Jerusalem: Bialik Institute; Tel Aviv: Dvir, 1956.

Williamson, Paul R. *Abraham, Israel and the Nations.* Sheffield: Sheffield Academic Press, 2000.

Wilson, Robert R. "Sources and Methods in the Study of Ancient Israelite Ethics." *Semeia* 66 (1994): 55–63.

Wisse, Ruth R. *Jews and Power.* New York: Nextbook-Schocken, 2007.

Wolfson, Elliot R. *Through a Speculum That Shines: Vision and Imagination in Medieval Jewish Mysticism.* Princeton: Princeton University Press, 1994.

———. *Venturing Beyond: Law and Morality in Kabbalistic Mysticism.* New York: Oxford University Press, 2006.

Wright, G. E., and R. H. Fuller, eds. *The Book of Acts of God: Christian Scholarship Interprets the Bible.* London: Duckworth, 1960.

Yaron, Tsevi. *The Teachings of Rabbi Kook* (in Hebrew). Jerusalem: Ha-Histadrut ha-Tsiyyonit, 1983.

Yuval, Israel J. "Vengeance and Damnation: From Jewish Martyrdom to Blood Accusations" (in Hebrew). *Zion* 58 (1993): 25–89.

Zertal, Idith, and Akiva Eldar. *Lords of the Land: The War over Israel's Settlements in the Occupied Territories, 1967–2000.* Translated by Vivian Eden. New York: Nations Books, 2007.

Zerubavel, Yael. *Recovered Roots: Collective Memory and the Making of Israeli National Tradition.* Chicago: University of Chicago Press, 1995.

Index

Abou El Fadl, Khaled, 10n.3
Abraham, 18, 35, 36, 90, 149,
    151, 154, 159, 168, 184, 209,
    214–15
  blessing of, in Genesis 12:3,
    19–20, 36, 37n.81, 62, 64, 189,
    209, 214–15
Abravanel, 91–2, 106, 120
Adam and Eve, 18, 121
Ahad Ha-Am, 70, 188n.96, 199,
    199–200, 202
Albalag, Isaac, 120
Albright, William Foxwell, 26
Al-Husseini, Haj al-Amin, 176, 180
Alkalai, Judah, 186
Amalekites
  commandment to annihilate, 23,
    27, 28–9, 55–6, 91–2, 93–4,
    94–5, 104–6, 107, 110, 117, 120,
    134, 159, 173, 205, 206, 208
  identified with Christians, 105,
    107, 117
  identified with Nazis, 105
  identified with Palestinians, 105,
    152–3, 185n.87
  identified with Rome, 82n.73, 105
  King Saul and, 56, 91, 105, 110
'Amey ha-arets, 79
Amiel, Avigdor, 187, 190

Amir, Yigal, 158
Amos, book of, 40–1, 54
Anatoli, Jacob, 119
Anti-Semitism. *See* Jews:
    persecution of; Muslims,
    anti-Semitism of; Zionism:
    anti-Semitism and
Appleby, R. Scott, 3, 4
Arabs. *See* Israel, state of: conflict
    with Arabs
Aran, Gideon, 151
Ariel, Israel, 154
Aristotelian philosophy, 112, 114–115,
    116
Artson, Bradley Shavit, 49n.128,
    69n.6, 94n.136, 104n.176
Avalos, Hector, 21–2, 22n.31,
    61n.162

Bar Hiyya, Abraham, 120
Bar Kokhba revolt, 65, 79, 81, 103,
    161, 198, 199
Barak, Ehud, 158
Barr, James, 24–5, 26, 27
Barton, John, 16, 59n.160
Begin, Menachem, 152, 157, 159
Ben-Gurion, David, 199
Ben-Menahem, Hanina, 223–4
Ben-Sasson, H. H., 102

Berdichevsky, Micha Joseph, 70, 172, 198
Berit ha-Biryonim, 161
Berit Shalom, 196–7, 202
Berlin, Meir, 187
Bible, 15–64, 205, 206, 208
    Christian violence and, 27–28, 56–7
    methodology of studying ethics of,
        15–17
    See also Zionism: Bible and
Bin Laden, Osama, 237
Bleich, J. David, 146n.4
Boyarin, Daniel, 89n.106, 105n.179,
    200n.122
Brenner, Yosef Hayyim, 70, 198
Brett, Mark, 52
Buber, Martin, 135–6, 192–3, 202

Cain, 21, 35, 87
Camp David Accords (1979), 144, 152,
    153, 159, 163
Canaanites, 54
    child sacrifice and, 24, 26
    commandment to annihilate, 23–8,
        47–55, 61–2, 63, 90–1, 93, 94–5,
        99–100, 107, 109, 125, 156, 172, 173,
        205, 206, 209, 210, 212
Childs, Brevard, 16n.6
Chosen people. See Jews: as the chosen
    people
Christian scholars
    on methodology in biblical ethics, 15–17
    on rabbinic Judaism, 66n.2
    on right-wing Zionism, 4–5
Christianity, 70n.9, 77, 101, 102, 107,
    116–7, 119, 124, 126–7, 132, 176,
    206, 215
    See also Bible: Christian violence and;
        Christians; Christian scholars;
        Kabbalah: Christian interest in;
        Zionism, Christian support for
Christians, 10, 27–28, 56–7, 101, 102, 107
    persecution of Jews, 80–1, 133–4
    tolerance toward Jews, 113
    See also Christian scholars;
        Christianity; Fundamentalism,
        Christian; Kabbalah: Christian
        interest in; Zionism: Christian
        support for
Chronicles, book of, 54
Cohen, Gerson, 84n.78

Cohen, Hermann, 194–5
Cohen, Mark C., 236n.30
Collins, John J., 33
Consequentialism, 225, 227
Converts, to Judaism, 98, 103
Cott, Jeremy, 20, 23, 50
Cromer, Gerald, 92n.126
Crusades, 57, 133

David (King of Israel), 89, 93, 173
Deuteronomic History, 23–4, 27, 53, 54,
    56, 63
Dewey, John, 225–6
Dialogue, Jewish-Muslim. See Jewish-
    Muslim dialogue
Diamond, Eliezer, 221
Dinah, rape of, 174
Dinur, Ben Zion, 168
Divine election. See Jews: as the chosen
    people
Dome of the Rock, 153
Don-Yehiya, Eliezer, 174, 191, 198n.115

Edom, identified with Rome, 82, 84n.78
Egypt, peace treaty with Israel. See Camp
    David Accords (1979)
Ein bereirah (slogan), 196
Esau, 38, 55, 82
Ethics, Jewish. See Jewish Ethics
Ethnicity, 12n.5, 13, 42, 45, 46, 47, 52, 53,
    60, 80, 166
    See also Jews: ethnic identity of
Etsel, 161
Etsyon, Yehudah, 153–4
Ezra and Nehemiah, 31, 44–5

Fascism, 176, 180–1
Fisch, Menahem, 224n.17
Foreigner, in the Bible, 43–44
Fraade, Steven, 76
Frank, Jacob, 137
Fundamentalism, 150, 176–7, 185–6
    Christian, 17
    Jewish, 150

Garb, Jonathan, 137
Garden of Eden, 18, 59n.159, 121
Gaza, 144, 158–9
Genesis, book of, 54, 55, 62
    sibling rivalries in, 20–21, 22, 37–8, 54

Gersonides, 126
Gibbs, Robert, 226–7
Glatzer, Nahum, 88n.100
God
  as warrior, 32, 48, 61
  mercy and compassion of, 58
  war, as prerogative of, 47–8, 58, 85,
    160, 194
  See also Jews: God's love for; Jews:
    God's punishment of; Image of
    God, man created in; Imitation of
    God
Goldenberg, Robert, 80, 83n.75
Goldstein, Baruch, 157, 185n.88
Gopin, Marc, 3, 4
Greek philosophy, 112–3, 123–4, 127
  See also Aristotelian philosophy
Greenberg, Moshe, 35n.76, 37, 49n.130,
    193n.105
Greenberg, Uri Tsevi, 173–4
Greenfield, Liah, 52
Gush Emumin, 151–4, 155, 157, 174, 175,
    184, 191, 202

Hadas-Lebel, Mireille, 83n.75, 84n.78
Halamish, Moshe, 133–4
Halevi, Isaac Herzog, 188
Halevi, Judah, 115–6, 122
Halkin, Hillel, 102
Hamas, 182
Harris, Sam, 10, 17
Herem, 24–5
Herzl, Theodor, 143, 168, 198, 200
Hezbollah, 182
Hillul ha-shem, 76
Hirshman, Marc, 98
Historical context, as a source of
    interpretation, 42–3, 64, 78–80, 110,
    126–7, 128, 138, 203, 209–11
Hitchens, Christopher, 10, 17
Holocaust, 149, 181, 183
Holzer, Eli, 159
Hora'at sha'ah, 223
Horowitz, Elliot, 102, 105, 107
Human rights, 73
Human security, 13n.8

Ibn Ezra, Abraham, 102, 119
Ibn Kaspi, Joseph, 120
Ibn Tibbon, Samuel, 120

Idolatry, 24, 27, 33, 38, 44, 50, 56, 72, 74,
    75, 76n.48, 77, 83n.75, 99–100
Ihud, 192
Image of God, man created in, 18, 34, 63,
    132, 157, 205, 211, 233, 234
Imitation of God, 31–3, 57–6, 89
  in Christianity, 59, 60n.161
Intifada, 154, 158, 231
Isaac, 19, 38, 55
Isaiah, book of, 31–2, 39–40, 41, 42,
    208
Ishmael, 38, 55
Islam, 10n.3, 116–7, 124, 132, 206, 215,
    235
  extremism and, 17, 126
  See also Muslims; Islamic philosophy
Islamic philosophy, 112, 113, 116
Israel, land of. See Land of Israel
Israel, state of
  conflict with Arab states, 144, 145, 146,
    149, 164, 165, 176, 182, 182–3, 210,
    218, 229–30
  creation of, 144
  religion and, 173, 174
  vulnerability of, 230–2
  See also Israeli-Palestinian conflict;
    Post-Zionism; Revisionist Israeli
    historians; War of Independence,
    Israeli; Zionism
Israeli-Palestinian conflict, 6, 7, 137, 152,
    164–6, 166–7, 172, 177, 180, 181,
    196, 202, 205, 207, 218–19, 229,
    230–1, 233, 235
  two-state solution of, 230–1
  See also, Palestinians
Israelites, insecurity of, 50–3

Jabotinsky, Vladimir Ze'ev, 160–2,
    173–4
Jacob, 19, 38, 54, 82n.75
James, William, 225–6, 233
Jeremiah, 83, 103
Jewish ethics
  methodology of, 217–8
  postmodern, 217, 218, 219
  See also Rabbinic Judaism: philosophy
    of ethics and; Rabbinic Judaism:
    pragmatism and
Jewish-Muslim dialogue, 237
Jewish Underground, 153–4, 191

Jews
    American, 234, 236
    as the chosen people, 19f., 34–43,
        126, 159, 189, 205, 206, 207,
        214–15
    Diaspora, 170, 175n.70, 177n.73, 182,
        184n.73, 187, 200
    ethnic identity of, 4, 44, 176, 177n.73
    exile of, 189, 198, 199, 200n.122,
        205
    God's love for, 19–20, 21, 38, 45–6, 74
    God's punishment of, 38, 83
    in the Islamic world, 236
    persecution of, 80, 110, 126, 127n.44,
        138, 143, 155, 170, 178–9, 181–3, 187,
        203, 205, 209–10, 236
    survival of, 220–1, 228–32
Joshua, 49, 70, 89, 90, 156, 212–13
Joshua, book of, 24, 26, 48–49, 53n.140,
        63
Juergensmeyer, Mark, 185

Kabbalah, 129–140, 159, 205–6
    Abraham Isaac Kook and, 148
    Christian interest in, 135
    methodology of, 133
    popular, 134–7, 139, 214
    Tsevi Yehudah Kook and, 184
    See also Non-Jews: Kabbalah on
Kahane, Meir, 155–7, 160, 175–6, 184–5,
        212–3, 219, 237
Kaiser, Walter, 16n.6, 39n.90
Kalischer, Tsevi Hirsch, 186
Kaminsky, Joel S., 17n.9, 28, 34n.70, 37,
        38, 42n.101, 44n.109, 46, 61
Kaplan, Lawrence J., 115n.5
Kaplan, Mordecai, 226
Kasher, Hannah, 122
Katz, Jacob 77, 101, 168
Kellner, Menachem, 114, 115, 122n.30
Kimelman, Reuven, 67, 69
Klausner, Joseph, 168
Knight, Douglas A., 17n.8
Kook, Abraham Issac, 147–9, 152, 185–6,
        188–9, 155n.26, 159, 160, 183, 186,
        187, 202
Kook, Tsevi Yehudah, 149–51, 152, 153,
        159, 175, 183–4, 188, 189, 190, 213,
        219
Korn, Eugene, 95

Lamentations, book of, 83
Land of Israel, 23, 24, 148, 149, 150, 151,
        154, 159, 168, 172
Land of Israel Movement, 163, 175n.71
Lebanon War, first (1982), 154, 196
Lebanon War, second (2006), 230
Lehi, 161
Leibowtiz, Yeshayahu, 190
Levenson, Jon D., 16, 26n.43, 34,
        39n.90, 46
Levinger, Jacob, 115n.5, 122n.30
Liebman, Charles, 174, 198n.115
Likud Party, 164
Lind, Millard, 47–8, 51
Lipton, Diana, 55–6
Livneh, Eliezer, 175n.71
Lüdemann, Gerd, 31, 210
Luz, Ehud, 69, 154, 165, 169, 170, 179,
        182, 188n.96, 195–6, 198–9, 210

Maccabees, 199
Machinist, Peter, 52
Maimonidean controversy, 112–3, 127
Maimonides, 112–3
    on Christianity and Islam, 116–7, 124,
        126–7
    on the messianic period, 116–7, 118,
        120–1, 124, 125–6
    on the Noahide laws, 123, 125, 213
    on war, 93, 94–5, 100–101, 107–8, 109,
        117–8, 125–6, 205, 206, 207, 212–13
    See also Maimonides controversy;
        Non-Jews: Maimonides on
Marks, Richard, 81
Masada, 161, 199
McDonald, Patricia, 48–9, 54–5
Medieval Jewish philosophy, 111–128, 205
    methodology of, 128
    radical branch of, 120
    See also Messianic Period: medieval
        Jewish philosophy on; Non-Jews:
        medieval Jewish philosophy on; War:
        medieval Jewish philosophy on
Meimad, 190
Meiri, R. Menahem, 77, 80–1, 101
Messianic period, 146–7, 154, 215, 221
    Bible on, 30–1, 39–40, 205, 206
    Kabbalah on, 132, 207
    medieval Jewish philosophy on, 116–7,
        118, 120–1, 124, 125–6

rabbinic Judaism on, 83, 84–6, 101–2,
  102–3
Zionism on, 159, 160, 187, 189
See also Maimonides: on the messianic
  period; Messianism; Temple (in
  Jerusalem): in messianic period
Messianism
  Abraham Isaac Kook and, 148–9
  active vs. passive, 147
  apocalyptic vs. restorative, 146
  Meir Kahane and, 156
  nationalism and, 172
  Tsevi Yehudah Kook and, 149–50, 150–1
  ultra-Orthodox Judaism and, 193
  Zionism and, 146–7, 168–9, 170, 183,
    184, 186, 198, 232
  See also Messianic period; Maimonides:
    on the messianic period; Temple (in
    Jerusalem): in messianic period
Mipney darkey shalom, 74, 100–101
Mipney hata'einu, 82, 84, 103
Moberley, R. W. L., 53n.140
Monotheism, 21
Morris, Benny, 163, 166, 181
Moser, 158, 160
Moses, 90
Muslims, 10
  anti-Semitism of, 235
  See also Islam; Jewish-Muslim
    dialogue; Maimonides: on
    Christianity and Islam
Myers, Jody, 136–7, 138
Nahmanides, 92, 95, 106
Narboni, Moses, 120
Nationalism, 21, 176
  ancient Israelite, 47, 52, 177n.73
  Palestinian, 162, 164
  religion and, 171–2
  See also Zionism: nationalism and
Natural law, 35–6, 72–3
Nazis, 176, 180–1
Newman, Louis, 210n.3, 218n.1, 219n.3
Niditch, Susan, 25, 26n.43, 29, 42n.102,
  50–1, 54, 61, 62
Noah, 18, 34, 71
Noahide laws, 71–3, 74–5, 98–100, 198,
  110, 123, 159
  as natural law, 72–3, 123
  See also Maimonides: on the Noahide
    laws

Non-Israelites, 19–20, 24n.34, 30, 34–47,
  208
  See also Amalekites; Canaanites;
    Non-Jews
Non-Jews, 209–10, 215, 233–4
  Kabbalah on, 131–2, 133–4, 135–7, 138,
    159, 205–6, 207, 208, 233
  Maimonides on, 113, 114–7, 121–4, 126,
    206
  medieval Jewish philosophy on, 113,
    114–7, 118–120, 121–124, 126, 208
  Meir Kahane on, 155–6, 156–7
  rabbinic Judaism on, 71–81, 97–101,
    208, 233
  Tsevi Yehudah Kook on, 150
  See also Non-Israelites
Novak, David, 35–6, 67, 69, 72–3, 80n.67

Ochs, Peter, 226
Orlinsky, Harry M., 26n.42
Oslo Accords, 157, 191, 231
'Oz ve-Shalom/Netivot Shalom, 190

Pacifism, 13, 96, 192, 197
Palestinians, 144, 145, 146, 149, 152, 154,
  156, 158, 159, 161, 162–3, 166–7, 172,
  180–1, 190, 192, 200, 212–13, 230,
  231, 233, 234–5
  terrorism and, 144, 157, 188
  transfer of, 163, 188
  See also Amalekites: identified with
    Palestinians; Israeli-Palestinian
    conflict; Nationalism: Palestinian
Particularism. *See* universalism and
  particularism
Peace, definition of, 13
Peace movements, 57, 190
Pedersen, Johannes, 42n.101
Persians, rabbinic attitudes of, 80n.67
Phinehas, 32–3, 58, 158
Pierce, C. S., 225
Porton, Gary, 74n.31
Post-Zionism, 164–6, 183
Pragmatism, philosophical school of,
  225–8, 233
  See also Rabbinic Judaism:
    pragmatism of
Prophets, biblical, 171, 199
Prophets, books of the, 30–1, 39–43
Puritans, 27, 57

Rabbinic Judaism, 65–110, 205, 207, 208
    asceticism and, 22n.5
    biblical interpretation in, 96, 109, 223
    liturgy of, 88, 90
    manhood in, 89, 103–4
    methodology of studying ethics of,
        67–69
    pacifism and, 96
    philosophy of ethics and, 227
    pragmatism of, 221–5, 227, 228–9, 232
    relationship of to the Roman empire,
        82–7, 101–3, 81–2, 84, 86, 103, 199,
        200, 231
    Zionists thinkers on, 70
    See also Christian scholars: on
        rabbinic Judaism; Messianic period:
        rabbinic Judaism on; Non-Jews:
        rabbinic Judaism on; War: rabbinic
        Judaism on
Rabin, Yitzhak, 157–8, 191
Ravitzky, Avi, 151, 160
Rawidowicz, Simon, 200n.122
Reines, Isaac Jacob, 186–7, 202
Religion, violence and, 3–5, 21–23, 175–6
Remnant of Israel, 170
Revisionist Israeli historians, 164, 183
Rodd, Cyril, 16, 29–30, 42n.102, 59, 62,
    63
Rodef, 158, 160
Roman empire. See Edom, identified
    with Rome; Rabbinic Judaism:
    relationship of to the Roman empire
Romano, Judah, 119
Römer, Thomas, 51n.135
Rosenzweig, Franz, 194–5, 202
Rowley, H. H., 26, 39n.90
Rubenstein, Jeffery, 103–4

Saadiah Gaon, 118–9
Sagi, Avi, 67, 69, 91–2, 95, 105n.180,
    106, 134, 151n.15, 183, 184n.86
Salmon, Yosef, 169
Sanhedrin, 93, 107
Sarna, Nahum, 36–7
Scholem, Gershom, 146–7, 197, 198n.115
Schwartz, Dov, 149n.12, 151n.15, 183
Schwartz, Regina, 12n.5, 21, 22n.30
Schweid, Eliezer, 38
Seeman, Don, 155n.26
Self-defense. See Violence: defensive

Sennacherib, 93
Settlements, Israeli, 146, 149, 151, 164,
    175
    See also Settlers, Israeli
Settlers, Israeli, 153, 164, 191, 202, 219
    terrorism and, 153–5, 157, 158
    See also Settlements, Israeli
Shalom, 42n.102
Shapira, Anita, 161–3, 166, 169, 176, 180
Sharon, Ariel, 158–9
Shechemites, 82n.73, 174
Sibling rivalries, in Genesis. See Genesis:
    sibling rivalries
Sihon, 90–1
Six-Day War, 144, 146, 149, 151, 153, 154,
    156, 163, 175, 182, 188, 189, 197, 229
Smith, Anthony, 172
Smith-Christopher, Daniel L., 42–3
Social identity theory, 45–6, 53, 80
Sprinzak, Ehud, 174–5, 176–7, 184–5
Stern, Jessica, 185
Stern, Josef, 117, 125
Stern, Sacha, 74, 75, 76n.48, 77n.58, 78,
    80n.67, 97–98
Strong, John, 19n.15

Tajfel, Henri, 45n.114
Takkanot, 222, 224
Tameret, Aharon Shmuel, 189n.99
Tamir, Yael, 166
Tehiya Party, 163–4, 174
Temple (in Jerusalem), 30
    destruction of first, 83–4
    destruction of second, 65, 70, 82,
        84, 103
    messianic period and, 40–1, 42, 43,
        66, 146
Terrorism. See Kahane, Meir;
    Palestinians: terrorism and; Settlers,
    Jewish: terrorism and
Theosebeis, 98
Three oaths, 86, 147, 186, 187, 189, 194
Tigay, Jeffrey, 56n.151
Tohar ha-neshek, 196

Ultra-Orthodox Judaism. See Messianism:
    ultra-Orthodox Judaism on;
    Zionism: ultra-Orthodox Judaism
    and,
Underground. See Jewish Underground

Universalism and particularism, 31, 34,
   39, 40, 46, 61, 73
Urim ve-tumim, 93
Utilitarianism, 225

Van Houten, Christiana, 43n.107
Violence,
   ancient Near East, 49
   defensive, 12–13, 96, 232
   definition of, 11–12
   structural, 12, 14, 166–7
Volkan, Vamik, 45n.114

War, 13
   in self-defense, 93
   in the ancient Near East, 49
   medieval Jewish philosophy on, 117–18,
      120–1, 125–6
   obligatory and discretionary, 93–4, 107,
      108
   rabbinic Judaism on, 87–8, 92–6,
      104–9
   See also God: war as a prerogative of;
      Maimonides: on war
War of Independence, Israeli, 144, 150,
   163, 164
Weber, Max, 46
West Bank, 144, 159, 191, 202
Williamson, Paul, 37
Wilson, Robert, 16n.6
Wisdom literature, 45
Wisse, Ruth R., 167n.54
Wolfson, Elliot R., 131, 132, 133
Wright, George Ernst, 26, 27–8

Yohanan ben Zakkai, 74, 81–2, 86, 199
Yom Kippur War, 156, 182

Zechariah, 59n.159
Zeitlin, Hillel, 192
Zerubavel, Yael, 199
Zionism, 6–7, 141–203, 206, 207
   anti-Semitism and, 142–3, 144, 170,
      178–81, 202
   attitudes to Arabs in, 180
   Bible and, 167, 171, 173, 198–9
   Christian support for, 168, 182
   Halakhah and, 146n.4
   history of, 142–4
   insecurity of, 182–3
   Labor, 161–3, 164–66, 169, 171, 176,
      196–7
   miracles and, 170
   nationalism and, 142, 144, 164, 165–6,
      167, 178, 183, 184, 189, 190, 192,
      194, 195, 197, 201–2, 205
   opponents of, among Jews, 193–5
   rabbinic Judaism and, 70, 173,
      198–9
   religious, 146–60, 169, 172, 175, 177,
      183–192, 202, 207
   Revisionist, 163, 172–4, 197
   secular, 4–5, 148, 155, 159, 160–77, 185,
      195–201, 207, 214, 230
   secular, influence of religion on,
      167–72, 174–77, 197–201, 206
   ultra-Orthodox Judaism and, 193–4
   See also Christian scholars: on
      right-wing Zionism; Israel, state
      of: conflict with Arabs; Israeli-
      Palestinian conflict; Messianic
      period: Zionism on; Messianism,
      Zionism and; Post-Zionism;
      Rabbinic Judaism: Zionist
      thinkers on